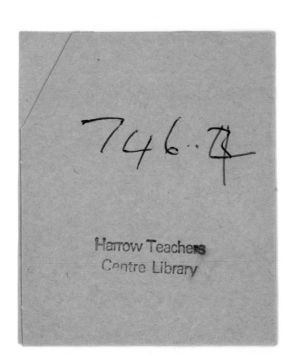

A WORLD OF
EMBROIDERY

A WORLD OF EMBROIDERY

Mary Gostelow

Line drawings by the author and Janet Watson

Mills & Boon London

First published in Great Britain 1975 by
Mills & Boon Limited, 17–19 Foley Street, London W1A 1DR

© Mary Gostelow 1975

ISBN 0 263 05655 4

Made and printed in Great Britain by
Butler & Tanner Limited
Frome and London

Contents

Introduction and acknowledgements

This is of necessity a personal work. With a field as vast, and hitherto as relatively unexplored, as that of embroidery, past and present, no record can be complete. I have had the temerity, however, to attempt to whet the appetite of the reader for a greater repast and an understanding of the embroidered arts through the medium of this anthology—formed by one traveller, collector and perpetual student.

A heritage of many centuries of involvement with the needle and subsequent decoration is today enjoying a long overdue revival of participation and appreciation in many countries. There is greater awareness of embroidery and what it has to offer than at any time before. Embroidery is both old and new. It is found in most cultures, in all parts of the world, worked by men and women of all ages.

As I have travelled I have collected typical pieces from many continents and tried, while learning and cataloguing, to correlate the works of different people, from different periods of history. It has become increasingly clear that many styles and schools of art have been international—in some cases universal. Many of the supposedly 'creative stitcheries' being produced today do in fact owe an allegiance, not always immediately apparent, to traditional works of another era.

How, then, has embroidery attempted to relate to contemporary movements in other fields of the applied arts? What social, religious, political or other factors have been influential? For what items should the discerning collector bid when embroidery comes up, as it does with increasing frequency, in the sale rooms? What embroidered souvenirs are likely to be found on the traveller's route or on the holiday-maker's cruise? How does the enthusiast look after his pieces: how can he best display, refurbish and conserve?

These are a few of the questions concerning everyone who cares for embroidery as an art. The illustrations in this work have been chosen with variety, interest and unfamiliarity in mind: they are not all unique treasures and many are, indeed, embroideries generally accessible to the enthusiast. It is hoped that both collector and practising embroiderer will, through design ideas and diverse information, glean inspiration from many parts of the world.

The book therefore falls into two sections. The first is factual, with relevant embroidery history defined by the political boundaries of today. This matter of classification poses an almost insoluble problem since, as in all fields of art, in many cases embroidery movements have straddled geographic and national frontiers, and political boundaries have, themselves, been subjected to continual change. National questions have been here decided in a frequently arbitrary, though it is hoped not illogical, fashion. Material in this first part of the book offers an insight into embroidery and the role it has played and is playing today. Only when a type of embroidery, or a stitch used therein, is unique to one country is a description of the practical aspect of that work included in this section.

The latter part of the book, 'Stitchery', contains practical information, listing and describing all common—and many uncommon—forms of embroidery and how to do them. The comprehensive list of embroidery stitches included in this primer is, possibly, the most complete in existence today. There is a detailed index to the whole book, with cross-referencing to facilitate oscillation from one section to another, and to afford maximum reference value, unique in the art today.

I make no excuse for omissions and should, indeed, welcome information concerning them. I entertain the hope that even so brief an introduction will illuminate exciting openings to the enormous world of embroidery.

While researching and writing, I have been continuously encouraged and helped by experts and other interested arts lovers around the world.

I should here especially like to thank my husband, Martin Gostelow, without whom my now insatiable wanderlust might have remained forever dormant. He has taken most of the colour and many of the black and white photographs in the book and has advised my progress throughout.

I have been given invaluable help and advice by Santina Levey of the Victoria and Albert Museum and by Joan Bryant and Janet Watson of Mills & Boon. I should also like to thank, for their assistance in so many different ways:

The Aide-de-Camp to Her Majesty the Queen of the Netherlands; the Aktiebolaget Nordiska Kompaniet, Stockholm; the Alexander Turnbull Library, Wellington, and Mrs. June Starke; the American Museum in Britain and Mrs. E. M. Gonin; the Reverend John Armson; the Most Reverend His Grace the Archbishop of Canterbury; the Archdeacon of Southern Melanesia; the Arts Council of

Great Britain; the Association of New Zealand Embroiderers' Guilds and Miss M. L. Austin; the Auckland Institute and Museum and Judy Smith;

Dr S. M. Bard; Alison Barrell; Mrs. Robert Barton; Mrs. J. Beckford; Miss Alice Beer; Mrs. Beverley Bennett; Mrs. Nancy Bennett; Mr. Hubert Birdwood; the British Museum and Miss Shelagh Weir; Miss Anabel Boome; Richard Box; Mr. V. C. Buckley; Mrs. Dale Bumpers; Jo Bucher; Anne Butler; the Butterick Fashion Marketing Company UK Ltd.;

The Canadian Craftsmen's Association and Sheila R. Stiven; the Canadian Eskimo Arts Council, the Canadian Guild of Crafts and Mr. Paul Bennett; Stina Carlstedt-Duke; City of Liverpool Museums and Dr. Dorothy Downes; City of Norwich Museums and Miss Pamela Clabburn; Joy Clucas; Messrs. J. & P. Coats Ltd.; Mr. J. M. Cobban; the College of Fashion and Clothing Technology, Mrs. Wade and Mrs. Nicholson; Colonial Williamsburg Foundation and Sandra C. Shaffer; the Commonwealth Institute and Mr. Nigel Wagstaff; Miss Sylvia Compton-Miller; *The Connoisseur* and Susan Livingstone-Learmouth; Mr. Christopher Cooke; the Cooper-Hewitt Museum of Decorative Arts and Mr. Milton Sonday; the Counted Thread Society and Mrs. John C. Stears; *Country Life*; the Courtauld Institute and Stella Mary Newton; the Crafts Council of Australia and Miss Jenny Battersby;

Mrs. E. M. de la Rosa; the Denver Art Museum and Miss Imelda G. DeGraw; the Department of National Education, Pretoria, Mrs. P. M. Wilby and Miss Ida Blignaut; Dollfus-Mieg & Cie and Mme Serieyx; Jane Dorner; Ione Dorrington; Miss K. R. Drummond;

Eastgate House Museum, Rochester and Mr. M. Moad; Ursula, Countess of Eglinton and Winton; the Earl of Elgin and Kincardine; the Embassy of the Cameroon Republic and Mme. Sao; the Embassy of the Republic of Chile and Mrs. Sylvia Celis; the Embroiderers' Guild, Miss Alexandra N. Beale, Miss Lynette de Denne and Mr. Gardner; the Embroiderers' Guild of America Inc., Miss Beverly Grossaint, Miss Linda Ormesson and Mrs. Jack D. Raulston; the Embroiderers' Guild of New South Wales and Mrs. Gwen Noble; the Embroiderers' Guild of South Africa and Mrs. M. Friggens; Mrs. L. J. Epperson;

Mrs. Marion Felix; Mrs. Barry Fell; Mrs. Karen Finch; Mr. Jack Franses; Mrs. Hermyone Fremlin-Key; Mr. and Mrs. Alfred Friendly;

Mr. and Mrs. Anthony Gaddum; Gawthorpe Hall, Lancashire, and Gail Kemp; Mrs. Cora Ginsburg; the Girl Guides Association, Miss E. J. Allen-Williams and Miss E. G. Mitchell; Mr. Thomas Goff; Mrs. R. H. Gottschalk;

The Earl of Haddington; Hope Hanley; Mr. David Heathcote; the Henry Francis du Pont Winterthur Museum, Delaware, and Mrs. L. Delmar Swan; the Henry Morrison Flagler Museum, Palm Beach, and Cathryn J. McElroy; Mr. Colin Hoare; Hoechst UK Ltd.; Mrs. David Housego; Mrs Sheldon J. Howe; the Hudson's Bay Company and Helen Burgess; Carla Hunt; Mrs. Cyril Hunt; the ICA Förlaget AB, Stockholm, and Birgitta O'Nils;

Mrs. Peter James; Messrs. JEM Patchwork Templates; Miss Ivy Johnson;

Mrs. E. J. Kalf; the Kenya Museum Society and Mrs. James Michaelsen; Nancy Kimmins;

Cdr. and Mrs. John Lang; Loftleidir Icelandic and Mr. J. H. Chilvers; the Lord Chamberlain's Office and Miss Jane Hood; Mrs. Murray Lowry;

Ann Mactaggart; Mrs Irving Mann; the Massada Press Ltd., Jerusalem; Lisa Melen; the Metropolitan Museum of Art, Miss Jean Mailey and Barbara Teague; Moyra McNeill; Mrs. Naomi Micklam; Mr. John Morley; Musées Royaux d'Art et d'Histoire, Brussels, and Mme. Risselin Steenbrugen; Museum Bellerive, Zürich, and Dr. Erika Billeter; the Museum of Art of Rhode Island School of Design and Eleanor Fayerweather; the Museum of Contemporary Crafts, New York, and Mr. Paul J. Smith; the Museum of Fine Arts, Boston, Mrs. Markell and Mr. Larry Salmon; the Museum of Fine Arts, Montreal, and Miss Ruth A. Jackson; the Museum of Navaho Ceremonial Art, Santa Fé; Muzeum Górnóslaskie, Bytom, and Dr. Barbara Bazielich;

The National Library, Ottawa; the National Museum, Wellington, and Dr. R. K. Dell; the National Museum of Iceland and Miss Elsa E. Gudjónsson; the National Organisation of Hellenic Handicrafts and Mr. Gristos Iliopoulos; the National Trust for Places of Historic Interest or Natural Beauty, Mr. Robin Fedden and Mrs. G. F. Pettit; the Nationalmuseet, Copenhagen, and Mr. Fritze Lindah; the Needle and Bobbin Club and Mrs. Norris W. Harkness; Mary Stephens Nelson; the Newark Museum, New Jersey, and Helen G. Olsson; the North Western Museum and Art Gallery Service and Miss Jean Glover; Old Sturbridge Village and Mrs. Jane C. Nylander;

Tania Diakin O'Neill;

Norma Papish; Mrs. Lorna Parkin; Parham Park, Sussex, and Miss Rosemary Courcier; Mrs. Olive Pass; Mr. John Pedler; the Philadelphia Museum of Art and Mrs. James P. McGarvey; the Phoebus Publishing Company; Mrs. Raymond Prudhoe; Herta Puls; the Polish Institute and Sikorski Museum, London, and Capt. R. S. Dembinski;

Mrs. M. J. Rademeyer; the Lady Ramsay-Fairfax-Lucy; Joanne

Reed; Lois M. Rieger; Riksantikvarieämbetet, Stockholm, and Mrs. Inger Estham; Judith Rodker; Mr Cornelius Van S. Roosevelt; the Royal Anthropological Institute Library, London; the Royal Ontario Museum, Mrs. K. B. Brett and Dorothy Burnham; the Royal Scottish Museum and Mr. R. Oddy; Mrs. Charles Runge; Pat Russell;

Mrs. A. C. Sampietro; Schenectady Museum, New York, and Mrs. William R. Foote; Margaret B. Schiffer; Joan Schwarz; the Schweiz Landesmuseum, Zürich, and Dr. Jenny Schneider; the Schweizer Heimatwerk and Dr. Elisabeth Stähli; Miss Elspeth H. Scott; Selskabet til Haandarbejdets Fremme, Copenhagen, and Mr. John Hansen; Eirian Short; Mrs. Robert Smith; the Smithsonian Institution and Miss Doris Bowman; Cynthia Sparks; Stellenbosch Museum, Cape Province, and Mr. Marius le Roux; Mrs. A. H. Steyn; the Reverend and Mrs. Charles Stires; Mrs. Irving M. Strauch; Margaret Swain;

Claudie Tardits; the Textile Museum, Washington DC; the Hon. Mrs. T. W. M. Tirikatene-Sullivan; Louise Todd; Sarah Tomlin; Yanis Travassaros;

Universitetet i Trondheim Museet and Mr. Oddmunn Farbregd;

The Valentine Museum, Richmond, Virginia, and Mrs. Mildred J. Davis; Mrs. Lyda van Rensburg; Mrs. Minnie van Rensburg; Mr. and Mrs. Richard van Wagenen; Mrs. Hetsie van Wyk; the Victoria and Albert Museum and Joan Edwards, Mr. John Irwin, Pauline Johnstone, Mr. Donald King, Veronica Murphy and Linda Parry;

Audrey Walker; Mrs. Mary Walker; the Washington Cathedral Needlepoint Committee and Mrs. Philip Rollings; the Wellington Cathedral Linen Guild and Mrs. Dorothy Zohrab; the Welsh Folk Museum and Dr. Ilid Anthony; the Earl of Wemyss and March; Lady Victoria Wemyss; Mr. Peter Wentworth; the Whitworth Art Gallery, Manchester, and Mrs. Joan Allgrove; the Reverend G. K. Welch; Mr. Don Willcox; Mrs. Nigel Williams; Erica Wilson; Mrs. George Wilson; Mrs. Harry Powell Wilson Jr.; Woodrow Wilson House;

Mrs. A. H. Younger; the Lady Rachel Younger.

Milton Abbas, Dorset   Mary Gostelow

Publisher's note

The diagrams in this book have all been specially drawn and are to that extent original. However, anyone who attempts to portray the working of stitches must lean to a greater or less extent on *Mary Thomas's Dictionary of Embroidery Stitches*, published by Hodder & Stoughton. We gladly acknowledge the help we have received from

11

this indispensable book. We are also indebted to Coats Sewing Group for permission to make use of their *100 Embroidery Stitches*.

For a small number of diagrams, our artist has been helped by referring to books by Thérèse de Dillmont, Winsome Douglass, Jacqueline Enthoven, Pauline Johnstone, Moyra McNeill, Erica Wilson; and to *Embroidery* magazine. Details of these publications are given in the reference list at the end of this book.

PART I
The Nations

Afghanistan

Afghanistan's mosaic of peoples reflects a history of interaction with her neighbours. The Afghan Tajiks, for instance, are an Iranian people, and western artistic influence has also come through the Baluchis in the south-west of the country. In the north, the Uzbeks and Turkmen have brought in influences of their own former countries. Apart from the minority groups of the Hazaras and the Kizilbashes, however, all factions of Afghans today are Sunni Moslem and, according to the decree of that branch of Islam, no human or animal representation is to be found in the arts.

AFGHANISTAN—*18th-century asymmetrical border.*
(Cooper-Hewitt Museum of Decorative Arts and Design. Erskine Hewitt Collection)

Traditionally much of Afghan embroidery has been closely allied, and possibly played a subservient role, to the working of knotted carpets and *kilims* (woven carpets). Many of the motif and colour combinations found in embroidery are similar to those of the other textile arts. As with carpet production, too, embroidery has often been a sporadic affair. The complicated 18th-century border, with diamond motifs covering the entire 'field' (carpet terminology for main 'ground', or base fabric), now in the Cooper-Hewitt Museum of Decorative Arts in New York, shows the same degree of asymmetry found in many floor coverings. It also features an *abrash*, a fluctuation of colour. Artists were often hampered by their inability to dye enough thread at one time and, with the natural vegetable and animal dyes they used, a slightly different shade was obtained with each dye lot.

Today, alas, fine embroidery production is not significant. With a seemingly insatiable demand from the West for thick sheepskin coats roughly decorated with vivid satin-stitch embroidery, the country's artists have tried to cater for this appetite and concentrated their talents on a mass market.

Africa—General

The diverse stitcheries of Africa run the gamut from Masai beadwork to the sophisticated abstract designs of the Hausa. Some of the continent's countries as they stand today, with political frontiers rarely corresponding to tribal boundaries so that, in many cases, tribal art straddles more than one nation, do not offer enough unique embroidery traits to enable equal coverage to be given to all.

Not unnaturally the embroidery of South Africa (p. 235) requires a separate chapter all its own, being utterly self-sufficient and with no relativity to any other African art. Other countries, too, have dissimilar attributes and these are, therefore, entered under their own headings:

Arab Republic of Egypt (p. 61)
Dahomey (p. 55)
Ethiopia (p. 95)
Kenya (p. 174)
Morocco (p. 181)
Niger and Nigeria (p. 191)
Sierra Leone (p. 232)
Zaire (p. 315).

An overall introductory picture of the embroidery of the continent, however, would bisect Africa with a sweeping curve, starting north from South Africa and running up through Zaire before swinging west through the Sahara. Africa's embroidery is therefore divided into regions of the west coast, the east coast, the southern peninsula and the north coast.

Throughout the west coast appliqué is dominant, especially in Dahomey, Togo and Zaire. Originally the wearing of applied work was restricted to those with power, either civil or military.

In some areas there is a textile tradition that is not directly related to the embroidered arts. In Ghana the *kente*, the traditional woven blanket with striking geometric patterning, bears designs that could easily have been adapted to an embroidery needle, although in only one known case has embroidery specifically descended from the *kente*. A ceremonial belt from Zoko in the Upper Region, item no. 64.264 now in the Museum of the Department of Archaeology at the University of Ghana in Legon, is about 29 in. (74 cm) long, of red, white and black felt with fine yellow, red and white silk stitching throughout, and was bought from an Ashanti by Kurontihene, Kwame Osei, in 1929. Design and colour are typically *kente*.

And in some west-coast countries there is no embroidered art at all: national museums have as yet no embroideries on show (the Musée des Arts et Traditions du Gabon, for example, features decorated furniture and wickerwork amongst its exhibits—but not one item is stitched).

In eastern Africa a wide selection of stitcheries is to be found, ranging from the *shamma* of Ethiopia to the white embroidered caps of Zanzibar. The whole of Tanzania, in fact, has a tradition of head-wear embroidery, possibly resulting from Moslem penetration of the region. Examples are to be seen in the National Museum at Dar es Salaam. There is also bead or cowrie-shell embroidery on a leather ground.

In the Sudan the slim, dark-eyed women often have machine-embroidered floral motifs on their delicately coloured cotton robes. There can be few more attractive sights than that of a young girl in Omdurman, walking serenely and slowly in the intense heat, with her head held high, wearing a full-length swathed robe of pale rose with embroidery in an overall design of silk satin-stitch sprays.

To the west of the Sudan, there is some affinity between embroidery design and that found in the Hausa regions of northern Nigeria. Once again the design for festive attire draws inspiration from Arab architecture and art, with patterns related in an arbitrary fashion to local tradition.

In southern Africa, apart from the plethora of embroidery in South Africa and the Portuguese-inspired work of Mozambique, there is very little embroidery (the Luderitz Museum in South West Africa states categorically there is 'no embroidery or stitchery'). In Botswana, for example, Mr. A. C. Campbell, Curator of the National Museum and Art Gallery, says 'there are only two stitches used . . . in the production of skin mats when two skins are sewn together— these are ordinary hemming and blanket stitches'. Malawi has stitched basketwork, as can be seen in the markets in Blantyre and around the country (and there are examples in the Commonwealth Institute, London), but there is no further heritage of stitchery.

Across the massive wastes of the Sahara there is also little embroidery tradition. To the north, separated by such impenetrable distance from their continental brothers of the rest of Africa, the arts bear little relation to 'African work' in general.

Egyptian embroidery is allied closely to that of other Moslem countries and is, therefore, Middle Eastern in affinity, as to a lesser degree is the work of Libya. Morocco has similar Arab connexions,

18

but her embroidery is independent enough to warrant a separate section.

Algeria and Tunisia echo the arts of Morocco, although Tunisia does have a unique form of stitchery known as 'Tunisian crochet', a bigamous marriage of knotting with both crochet and knitting, which further adorns the textiles of that country.

Albania

Although her arts are sometimes associated with those of her neighbour, Yugoslavia, Albania has in fact long maintained the independence of all facets of her cultural life. The country was, indeed, almost autonomous during Turkish domination of the Balkans until the 19th century. She was fully independent, under the rule of King Zog, for a while between the two World Wars and, in 1945, eventual independence from Italian supremacy was regained.

There has, since then, been something of a void in information from Albania. What is known of embroidery of this largely agricultural country is, therefore, predominantly pre-1945.

As in the south of Yugoslavia, association with Turkish arts continued long after any Turkish presence had departed. There was a tendency for townswomen to wear sumptuous robes with much elaborate embroidery. Most of the embroidery threads were of silk: there was some metal thread work, of gold, silver or brass.

In the University of Aberdeen, Marischal College, Anthropological Museum, there is an exquisite example of delicate silver embroidery on a white ground. Such collections of embroideries from Albania—and from other places on their route—were often fruits of the labours of travellers returning from their 'Grand tours' at the end of the 19th or beginning of the 20th centuries, and items in these collections are often late 19th-century work. As an earlier example, in November 1809 Byron wrote to his mother that the Albanian dresses were 'the most magnificent in the world', the gold work particularly appealing to him. One that he brought back is now in the Museum of Costume, Assembly Rooms, Bath. (*In My Hot Youth*, ed. Leslie A. Marchand, published by John Murray.)

Another intrepid traveller was Miss Edith Durham. She was an energetic and enthusiastic British lady who first went to Montenegro in 1900, 'for her health'. She subsequently went to Albania and Yugoslavia many times, her sketchbook always to hand and with her eyes open for interesting ethnographic data. At the personal request of King Nikola of Montenegro she was Commissioner of the 1907 Balkan States Exhibition in Earls Court, and she was variously correspondent for *The Times* and the *Manchester Guardian* during the Balkan War of 1912. Her personal collection of embroideries both of Albania and Yugoslavia constitutes the Durham Collection at the Bankfield Museum, Halifax, Yorkshire, the catalogue to which contains sketches with revealing annotation by Miss Durham herself.

Australia

Australia is a Federal Commonwealth. The vast distances between her major cities have historically hindered any inter-action between the six states and there is resultant individuality amongst the various arts.

There is no traditional Aboriginal stitchery. Surprisingly, too, there has been little noticeable foreign influence brought with settlers of the last hundred years. German and Norwegian immigrant groups have, it is true, introduced their own stitcheries and patterns, but, in the main, production has not spread outside the original ethnic groupings of newly settled Australians. 'Danish cross stitch patterns' are popular, but more as an international art form than as an accompaniment to settlers from Denmark.

Embroidery, there a truly feminine art, has had to plot its own relatively self-educated path. Australian creative embroiderers have used their own initiative and skills to execute works that are purely of their country.

Where Australian embroiderers stand out is in their sensitivity to environmental atmosphere and feeling. In stitcheries with specific three-dimensional intent they impart some of the characteristic impact of the countryside around them. With increasing confidence, Australian artists are designing and executing exciting and note-worthy embroideries.

The annual Summer School of Creative Embroidery held at the University of New England, Armidale, New South Wales, some 400 miles north of Sydney, has been gathering impetus with each session. Every year a different theme is brought into focus. The 1974 theme, 'The world around us', had three main lecturers, two of them, Cynthia Sparks (who came specially from England for that year's course) and Pat Langford (who exhibits frequently in Sydney), the innovators of the School in 1969. The third tutor, Heather Joynes, now in charge of organising the programme, exhibited at the Toronto World Craft Fair in 1974.

The Armidale Summer School attracts a regular nucleus of keen and skilled artists, some of whom have never before embroidered. The enthusiasm and confidence of the group, however, has already released unique talent that is worthy of attention. The works from the 1973 School, on the theme 'The Australian scene', included creative representations of bark, mulga country scenes and mining views, all imbued with an expression peculiarly Australian.

The first New South Wales Embroiderers' Guild was formed in the 1950's by Margaret Oppen, a graduate of the Royal School of Needle-work and sometime pupil of Erica Wilson. It is a self-sufficient and lively group, with a magazine, *The Record*. It is an independent guild. Other such institutions around the country (in Victoria, in Canberra and Hyde Park, South Australia, for instance) are branches of the London-based Embroiderers' Guild.

The guilds do much to promote a universal understanding of em-broidery. Because of the area of each territory involved, they have their own dependent groups. Most central guilds have embroidery collections and libraries. A particularly outstanding comprehensive embroidery exhibition was that mounted by the New South Wales Guild for the Opera House Festival to celebrate the opening of Sydney Opera House in October 1973. The theme of the exhibition was 'Australia'.

The Crafts Council of Australia is promoting embroidery. The Country Women's Association of Victoria is another keen body: they published an authoritative manual in 1968 detailing many types of embroidery and they do much to stimulate embroidery interest.

General embroidery supplies are readily available in most big cities. There is a growing availability of Japanese supplies on the market.

Austria

Embroidery of Austria has during the centuries been interrelated to that of her neighbours. Particularly during the apogee of the Austro-Hungarian Empire in the 18th century, the finesse and workmanship of the embroiderers of Vienna was known from Paris to Moscow.

A fine example of the noticeable pomp and splendour of much early Austrian embroidery is the Gösser Cope, 1230–60, now in the Österreichisches Museum für Angewandte Kunst in Vienna. The embroidery, with polychrome silk on a white linen ground, is alas today somewhat the worse for its many years of wear. The detailed square panel surround, with 54 complete—and many more fragmented—motifs in separate compartments bordered by fine bands of crossed embroidery, is nevertheless indicative of the elaborate patterning of the time. The central back panel of the embroidery consists of a main roundel depicting a saint surrounded by four smaller roundels of animals and religious symbols.

As a corollary to the religious embroideries, secular works, particularly those of peasant dress, have been equally outstanding and, also, instrumental in encouraging regional costume in neighbouring parts of Europe.

In Innsbruck and Bavaria (West Germany), for example, one today still sees women of all ages wearing traditional *dirndls*, short dresses with full skirts and a tight bodice, with a delicate blouse underneath. Both dress and blouse are often elaborately embroidered, as is the crisp white apron that completes the outfit. *Loden* (jackets of the menfolk) are not generally embroidered, though this strong wool fabric is sometimes utilised as embroidery ground.

Throughout their period of eminence the Hapsburgs were faithful patrons of the arts. Embroidery in Austria reached a peak during the time of the Empress Maria Theresa in the late 18th century. It is known that she commissioned many items both of lace and embroidery.

By the early 19th century Austria had established a firm niche in fashionable artistic outlook. The 1814 Congress of Vienna, at which many of the rulers of Europe assembled, had the effect of promoting Viennese high fashion generally and, as an accompaniment thereto, the fine textile arts of Viennese specialists.

Machine embroidery came to Austria a few years later than in some other European countries. The first hand-operated embroidery machine was installed in Lustenau, in the province of Vorarlberg, in 1868, and the first motor-driven machine, a Schiffli product, was imported from Saxony in 1898. Vorarlberg rapidly became a thriving embroidery centre. By the outbreak of the First World War, indeed, 1,339 shuttle embroidery machines were registered in the province.

Twentieth-century embroidery has understandably declined. During both wars Austria suffered considerably. It was not until 1955 that she eventually regained her independence.

Vorarlberg does, however, continue to be a leading embroidery centre. There are still over 1,000 registered embroidery machines, nearly all power-driven, and much of the industry is continued by outworkers in their homes.

Current Austrian embroidered art is perhaps generally best known for its machine-stitched embroidered clothing. Delicate whitework patterning, and polychrome embroidery on blouses, skirts and other garments, are exported to many parts of the world.

Embroidery in Austrian collections today is similarly cosmopolitan. Outstanding treasures to be seen in Vienna include the 'Golden Fleece vestments' (p. 98), since 1953 housed in the Treasury of the Hofburg Palace, the sumptuous 'Coronation mantle' from the 12th-century Sicilian workshops of Palermo, to be seen in the Kunsthistorisches Museum, and the English 'Melk chasuble', an outstanding example of Opus Anglicanum, now in the Museum für Kunst und Industrie.

Belgium

Belgian textiles are generally associated with the various laces of the country. Brussels, Antwerp, Valenciennes are but three of the centres that have given their name to a particular kind of lace. Interest in the hand-worked textile field has therefore been dominated by that industry.

Embroidery in Belgium has been historically influenced by her neighbours. She was part of the 'Low Countries', variously under Germanic, Spanish, French or Dutch rule until 1830. There is Dutch association in the embroideries of the Antwerp area. The Flemish-speaking parts of the country show significant German heritage. The Walloon section features, in embroidery terms, a French connexion.

In such a predominantly Catholic country, ecclesiastical embroidery has played a major part in the art. *Or nué* was popular in the 14th century. In the Musées Royaux d'Art et d'Histoire, or Musée du Cinquantenaire, in Parc du Cinquantenaire in Brussels, there is a particularly beautiful *antependium* from St. Martin's Church in Liège. Dating from the middle of the 14th century, the work shows St. Sévérin of Cologne being visited by a heavenly host. The saint himself has rather too well nourished a face for the traditional poverty associated with the canonised. But otherwise the lines, proportions and perspectives of this piece are remarkably photographic.

The same museum has another *antependium* from the Abbey of Grimbergen, an example of *broderie brabançonne* from the Province of Brabant (most famous for its *dentelle brabançonne*—Brabant lace). Worked in the first half of the 16th century, the central panel shows the Last Supper and, once again, the deep folds and flowing lines of garments lend a natural, if somewhat sculptured, air to the work. The Supper takes place under elaborate arches with acanthus columns to either side. The minutiae of a bowl of exotic fruits in one corner, detail of the gargoyle handle on a water jug, wreaths and garlands hanging overhead, are notable. So, too, is the fact that the only hungry being present is an emaciated dog eagerly devouring scraps under the table.

An unusual form of embroidery was manifested in Belgium after the First World War. To show their appreciation to President Wilson and the Belgian Food Relief committee for the flour sent to them during the war, groups of Belgians embroidered the empty sacks and sent them back to America. They embroidered the actual printed lettering on the sacking and added wording and motifs as necessary. The sacks, three of which are in Woodrow Wilson House today, were delivered in an embroidered box inscribed, in satin-stitched letters 2 in. (5 cm) high, 'Donated by Belgian Food Relief Committee, Chicago, U.S.A.' Similar sacks can be seen at the Smithsonian Institution, also in Washington, D.C.

There is some elaborate domestic embroidery still found today in Belgium. In the main, however, any item that could be has been decorated with lace. Embroidery is not immediately evident.

BELGIUM—*early 16th-century mitre, an example of the splendid ecclesiastical embroideries from Flanders in the Renaissance. Gold and silver thread and silk are worked in split stitch and laid and couched embroidery. To the left is the Virgin and Child and to the right St. Augustine of Hippo. The reverse shows St. Leonard and St. Mary Magdalene, the lappets show St. Peter and St. Paul. The tall shape of the mitre is indicative of its date (earlier mitres were more squat and of simpler design). The coat of arms shows that the mitre was commissioned for Willem van der Molen, who was, in 1518, the first abbot of Heylissem to receive the right to use the mitre. (The Victoria and Albert Museum, Crown Copyright)*

27

Museums have good collections of foreign works, such as the 9th-century English 'Chasuble of St. Harlindis and St. Relindis' at Maaseik. Belgium's own embroidery has not, in the past, been prolific and the situation remains the same today.

Bolivia

A long-isolated country which now has no seaport, Bolivia has been noticeably deprived of outside influence in her arts since the end of the Spanish colonial era in 1824. There has admittedly been some German immigration. And there has been regular movement, too,

BOLIVIA—*detail of* 'Los Corredores' *('The Bean Runners') by Nancy Hemenway,* c. *1971. Bayetage, appliqué and stitchery on handwoven wool.*
(The artist)

of prosperous 'international' Bolivians to and from Europe. But neither activity has resulted in sizeable embroidery inspiration.

There is today some Indian embroidery, particularly on the borders of necks and cuffs of blouses. Unlike Central American versions of the *pollera* (full-length regional dress with layers of flounces to the skirt), the similarly voluminous outfits of Bolivia are not embroidered. In the main, home-produced embroidery has been confined to the less affluent—mostly Andean Indian—sections of

BOLIVIA—*detail of 'Cardenales' ('Cardinal Birds') by Nancy Hemenway. Twentieth-century bayetage, appliqué and stitchery on handwoven wool to a pre-Colombian theme. (The artist)*

30

the population. What work is done is carried out by male artists: their women prefer to knit.

One costume that does feature embroidery is the dress of the *diablada*, the 'devil' dance held during the annual carnival 40 days before Easter. The dance originated at Oruro and is today a strange blend of old heretical pagan beliefs and Christian symbolism. The central actor has a heavy and elaborate feather and appliqué costume with some satin-stitch motifs and stones applied with stay stitching.

Bolivian culture of yesterday and materials of today have inspired an American artist, Nancy Hemenway, in her *bayetage* work, peculiarly a combination of appliqué and stitchery on a ground of hand-woven Bolivian wool. Her themes are taken from the Tiahuanaco and other pre-Columbian Bolivian and Peruvian cultures. She incorporates such traditional motifs as 'Los corredores' ('The bean runners') with contemporary cultural themes like 'Harvesting from Lake Titicaca' and a delightful picture of trout.

Bulgaria

Embroidery of Bulgaria has much in common with that of neighbouring Eastern European and Balkan countries. Some of the designs and motifs used are similar to those found in Yugoslavia and Romania. Much of the whitework and cording relates to that found in Turkey, under whose control Bulgaria fell for some centuries prior to 1908.

Admittedly today driving along the main autoroutes through Sofia to the Turkish border, roads which are used by international truckers and travellers, one does not see much of the traditionally embroidered costume being worn. In Sofia, the capital, the overall neutrality of the city's colour schemes is enlivened with scarlet by way of banners and posters—but these are printed and not embroidered.

A deep brick-red, however, is one of the three main embroidery colours throughout the country, the other two colours being dark blue and dark green.

Border embroidery dominates Bulgarian work. There are various categories of bordering:

Narrow borders (often with floral motifs in stroke or square stitch, in one or two colours)

Cross-stitch borders (sometimes with added stroke stitch, sometimes with added slanting Slav stitch)

Broad borders (with big geometrical or floral motifs filled in with slanting Slav stitch or cross stitch and often outlined in black).

Throughout all Bulgarian embroideries the most usual stitches are back stitch, cross stitch, flat stitch, slanting Slav stitch and stroke stitch. Often the work is two-sided. There is frequently black back-stitch outlining and tendrils around a design, of which each block is worked in one solid colour.

Rossitza Tchoukanova (*Broderie Nationale Bulgare*, p. 5) divides the country into 24 different embroidery regions, 11 in the west and 13 in the east, each of which has its own distinctive style.

Embroidery in the main, however, is worked in silk or cotton thread on a heavy white or black linen ground. There is some gold filling work.

From Kula to Lovech there is particularly fine overall work on women's jackets. In Ikhtiman there are panels around skirt hems

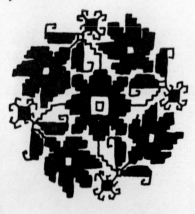

BULGARIA—*typical motif from Lovech.*

△ *AFGHANISTAN – detail of modern silk on cotton embroidery, bought in Kabul in 1971.*
(Author's collection.)

▽ *AUSTRALIA – "The Terrace", machine embroidery and super-imposed hand knotting, representation*
of a back street view of an area of Sydney. Shirley Barton, 1973.
(The artist)

△ *AUSTRALIA* – "*Mulga Country*" *by Dora Dreyfus, 1973, 42 × 30 in. (107 × 76 cm).
(The artist)*

▽ *BELGIUM – embroidered flour sacks sent to
USA after World War I. (Woodrow Wilson House,
Washington D.C. Photo: Nancy Papish)*

▽ *CAMEROON – a modern appliqué by Claudie
Tardits taken from the story of the four sons of
Aymon. (The artist)*

and around neck openings. In Samokov and Graovo there are also finely embroidered neck openings.

Sofia has panel work on short jackets, ordinary whitework and, also, some of the most original embroidery in the country. Corded embroidery on men's jackets and coats is done with white straight lines (either on the black or white ground) in long flat stitch, with curving lines branching off forming spirals or wavy lines. Sometimes this work is so complicated, with a combination of geometry and flora in design, that it gives the appearance of lace work.

Two typical Bulgarian embroideries that can be found in the country are *oshivtsi* and *rukavtsi*. *Oshivtsi* are applied pieces of fabric, usually with predominantly red or orange ground, found along the front openings of women's dresses. Patterns are generally geometric or floral. *Rukavtsi* are strips of black homespun about 18 in. long, tapering from 3 to 4 in. wide at the bottom to 1 in. at the top of each strip, where it is attached to a sleeveless overdress (*sukman*).* The wider lower half of the *rukavtsi* is richly embroidered in white cotton to look like cording and there should be a rosette centrally placed at the top of each strip. Examples of both these items, with other local embroideries, are displayed at the Ethnographic Museum in Sofia.

* About 45, 10 and 2·5 cm.

Cameroun

A combination of French and Islamic influence with typical indigenous design is apparent throughout this West African country. Primary colours are used in the main. Recognisable motifs (particularly around Foumban) are the two-headed snake, spider or locust, and crescent, with outlining and filling. Foumban stitches, chain and satin, are worked on a heavy linen or cotton ground. Most of the embroidery decorates clothing or table linen.

To the north of the country, in Maroua, there is more noticeably an imported feeling of design. Linens and clothing from here are more regular in pattern. Colour schemes are more controlled and, possibly, less pleasing as a result. Cornely stitching (similar to that found throughout western Africa and in the Middle East) produces a machined tambouring for all-over patterns on domestic items.

Until 1960 or so whitework (*Jour* embroidery) was popular. Young girls were required to embroider their trousseaux in Hardanger embroidery with needleweaving and cutwork, using heavy cotton thread. This traditional handworked 'exercise' has now generally lapsed in favour of machine-made, bought pieces for a girl's wedding chest.

Modern foreign influence has been particularly felt in the capital, Yaoundé. In 1965 Claudie Tardits, a Belgian artist who had been living in the country for some years, was encouraged to adapt Cameroun masks and motifs to the concept of wall hangings. Starting with imported fabrics found in Yaoundé stores, she had her first exhibition in the city in 1969. Claudie Tardits' original inspiration came from the shapes and symbolism in the country's native art. She found that these transposed well to stitched collage. Tardit hangings are a revealing personal interpretation of the anthropology of Cameroun.

Canada

The oldest embroidery in the country is that of the Indians. The Wood Cree and the Assiniboine, for example, were particularly fine bead workers and many examples of their arts are to be found today.

The stitching of porcupine quills, known as 'quill work' or, erroneously, 'Canadian embroidery', is found on items such as boxes, trays and other souvenirs fashioned out of local bark. After the quills were chewed to make them pliable, they were fashioned into a long thread and dyed or left in their various natural hues. The thread was worked to a pre-designed pattern: the bark was studded with holes of various sizes through which embroidery was executed. 'Quill work' was also used on leather, in which case stitching did not go right through the ground fabric.

Moose hair was similarly worked (a moosehair embroidery is to be seen today at Blair Atholl, Scotland), as was appliqué of moosehide.

'Quill work' was a speciality too of French-Canadian nuns. According to one source, as late as 1880 the good ladies were still themselves chewing quills. And one birch-bark box has attached to it a note dated 1883 inscribed 'Made by Nuns of the Ursuline Convent at Quebec, dyed moose hair on birch bark. Known to be 100 years old now'.

From the 16th century came the influence of foreign explorers and, following them, early French settlers who would have brought their linen, their clothing and their embroidery skills. French influence is still apparent throughout Quebec.

The British colonial influx accelerated after 1763 with the end of French rule and, again, in the 1780's when Loyalists moved north from the newly independent United States. They introduced British ideas and design into Canadian embroidery. The Royal Ontario Museum has an early 18th-century quilted linen English spread, a polychrome work in chain stitch with floral design in a central lozenge and in the corners. This would possibly have inspired similar creations. But, as has always happened with local variants to an imported theme, indigenous motifs (floral or animal) are incorporated in the basic design.

'Jacobean' embroidery, such as the holly set with gently twisting bough, leaf and berry design now in the same Museum, inspired bed-

35

CANADA—*1799 show towel,*
41 × 14 in. (104 × 36 cm),
inscribed 'In dem Leben
war ich dein, in dem Tod
vergesnet mein' *('In life I*
was yours, in death remember
me'). Probably worked as a
sampler. From Waterloo
County, Ontario.
(Doon Pioneer Village,
Kitchener, Ontario. Photo:
Royal Ontario Museum)

hangings. Typical canvas-work designs were adapted and utilised for the Canadian home.

There is some German influence in embroidery in Ontario. Germans fighting with the British army in America until as late as 1783 had to flee north and they settled in English-speaking areas. German immigration has in fact continued to the present day.

At Doon Pioneer Village in Kitchener, Ontario, show towels from Waterloo County illustrate German influence in local embroidery. Show towels, often highly embroidered pieces of fabric, were designed to be displayed or carried over ordinary towels as a decorative cover. Often such pieces were worked as samplers.

A show towel worked by Ania Shoemaker in 1832 illustrates the fact that from about this date they became much more elaborate, with complicated stitching and designs. Many show towels feature a branched heart design with the letters O E H B D D E. This stands for 'O edel Herz bedenk dein End' ('Oh noble heart, consider thine end').

Elisabeth Bauman's 1840 piece, also from Waterloo County, in cotton and linen on a cotton ground, includes the complicated eight-pointed German star motif.

After the 1745 Scottish rising, and following various Highland clearance programmes, there was a massive removal from Scotland. Whitework in Canada gleaned particular inspiration from the Ayrshire flowering movement of the late 18th and early 19th centuries.

In the 19th century, too, Berlin wool work was particularly popular. Whether the designs came direct from Berlin from 1804 on or whether they came via England or France is not certain. Probably both channels were used, with certain addenda and variations accompanying those designs brought to Canada by the longer routes. Both with and without added beading, Berlin wool work dominated the Canadian embroidery field for many decades of the century.

Most Canadian quilts are woven. The art of stitched quilting has, however, been extensively promoted by such organisations today as that of the Upper Canada Village in Morrisburg, Ontario, and people like Mrs. Luella Weaver, who convenes a regular group in Kitchener. Traditional North American quilted patterns are combined with some modern interpretations.

Canadian ecclesiastical embroidery has long been a speciality of the Quebec region. The 1967 exhibition at the National Gallery, Ottawa, 'Three Hundred Years of Canadian Art' featured some of the most beautiful pieces. An early 18th-century altar frontal with Holy Ghost design, worked by Jeanne le Ber (1662–1724), now in the Notre Dame Church Museum, was particularly outstanding.

Among the most exciting modern embroidered art works being

produced in Canada are the hangings (*neevingatah*) from Baker Lake in the Central Arctic.

With only one annual import of supplies, when the snows melt in late August and a ship comes to the Lake up the Chesterfield Inlet from Hudson Bay itself, Baker Lake is a self-sufficient community. There has long been a tradition of appliqué. For centuries the women have used a form of inlaid appliqué to decorate their caribou-skin garments, using shapes cut from the soft underside of the animal for the applied motifs. Now the main stitcheries of the area are the Baker Lake wall hangings.

In 1966 Mrs. Elizabeth Whitton managed the first Baker Lake sewing project. Jack and Sheila Butler took over in 1969 as official advisers to the co-operative and, initially utilising fabric left over from Mrs. Whitton's project, started the appliqué wall hangings. Using melton or duffle cloth as backing and motif fabric, the embroiderers often completed their works in sections which were, finally, then sewn together.

They are large hangings. And they are primitive. But they are delightfully honest, with a style that is original and obviously that of the artist alone.

It is a woman's work. After the main backing is cut into sections (of $\frac{1}{4}$ or $\frac{1}{8}$ yd.—about 25 or 12 cm) at the co-operative shop, she takes her materials home and works there. Apparently many of the embroiderers sit on their beds to work, a pose reminiscent of a past when they would have done their caribou sewing squatting on sleeping platforms cut from snow in their igloos.

Rita Ahveeleeayok is one well-known Baker Lake artist. She worked a hanging, 20 × 12 ft. (6 × 3·6 m), a saga of community life showing adults, children, dogs and igloos. She cut her patterns and did her sewing in the family's tiny three-roomed house with an incessant stream of relatives and friends coming in to talk and admire and help. She never saw her work unfolded until it was finally unveiled at the gymnasium of the Kamanitauk Public School, in which it now hangs.

Possibly the most famous of the artists, however, is Jessie Ooonark, who has already held several one-man shows, most recently at the Innuit Gallery of Eskimo Art in Toronto. Much of her design is symbolic. There are many circular shapes, representing the drum of the Eskimo drum dance, a ritual of a hunting religion. She also features the Eskimo knife, a triangular motif with one side rounded. And she brings in the present mechanical age with her portrayal of snowmobiles.

Jessie Ooonark has produced an artistic family: her daughters Marealik, Mummukshoarluk and Jouseapik are all names for which

CANADA—*show towel worked by Elisabeth Bauman in 1840, cotton and linen on a linen ground, showing German influence in the eight-pointed star motif. From Waterloo County, Ontario. (Doon Pioneer Village, Kitchener, Ontario. Photo: Royal Ontario Museum)*

37

it is worth looking out. Canadian Arctic Producers Limited are giving much publicity to the Baker Lake wall hangings and they will undoubtedly become even more sought after in the near future.

There is, overall, from ancient to modern, a sincere understanding throughout Canada of the art of embroidery. One complete survey was that held at the Maltwood Memorial Museum of Historic Art in Victoria, British Columbia, in March 1973.

CANADA—*bed coverlet worked by Mme. Fortin, c. 1873, from St. Urbain, Charlevoix County, Quebec. 61¾ × 79 in. (1·57 × 2·01 m), wool on homespun ground. (The Montreal Museum of Fine Arts. Gift of Mrs. F. Cleveland Morgan, 1958)*

Chile

Chile was under Spanish rule from the 16th century until 1810 and, today, there is typically colonial Spanish influence in design throughout her arts.

The most outstanding modern embroidery is that of Isla Negra ('Black Island'), off the central coast.

Inspired by a doctor's wife, Señora Lenore Sobrino de Vera, and under the sponsorship of the Sociedad de Arte Contemporaneo, the women of this fishing community have transposed their stylised impressions of life around them to bright and colourful embroidered 'tapestries'.

The islanders seem imbued with an emotional imagination. Pablo Neruda, the Nobel Prize-winning Chilean poet, writing of the island's embroideries in 1972, said:

> Every house that I have known for the last thirty years took up and hung out a flower-like tapestry. At first dark and silent, these houses suddenly filled with coloured threads, of the palest blue, of deep violet, of bright scarlet. These women who work them come from true stock and chose to work with the colour of the heart. They have names like Mercedes (the wife of José Luis), or they are called Eufemia, or Edulia, Pura, Adela or Adelaida. They are called as they have always been called; as they ought to be called. They have names like flowers would have, if flowers could choose their names. And they embroider with their names, and with the pure colours of earth and sun and sea—with spring itself.
>
> There is nothing more lovely than these tapestries which, in their prime simplicity, give out a joyousness that has had to overcome much suffering.
>
> (Reproduced by kind permission of the Institute of Contemporary Arts, London)

The Isla Negra embroiderer works in bright-coloured thick wool yarn, depicting domestic motifs and scenes of the agricultural life of her island environment as she works. Lack of perspective gives a Cézanne-like simplicity to the representation.

A comprehensive exhibition of Isla Negra embroideries was held at the Institute of Contemporary Arts, London, in 1972. The 20 exhibits sported titles such as 'My orchard' and 'House with sun flowers': all were a remarkable insight into the honesty of the artists.

39

China

China today has perhaps a greater degree of unity and central control of her patchwork of races, languages and religions than ever before. Her peoples are mainly Han, with important admixtures of Mongols, Tibetans, Manchus and other minority groupings. The influences of religious movements, some originating within her borders, have been incalculable. Although officially discouraged today, Confucianism, Taoism, Buddhism, Islam and Christianity have left indelible marks upon the arts of the country.

It is thought that sericulture, silkworm farming, was in fact developed by the Chinese as early as 2000 BC. It is recorded also that Huang Ti, the so-called 'Yellow Emperor', had threaded decoration to his Imperial Crown. What is certain, however, is that the silk industry and embroidery as such have played an interrelated and important role for a very long time.

Dating can sometimes be facilitated by calendar-associated representation featuring the particular Chinese Year (in rotating order, that of the Rat, the Ox, the Tiger, the Hare, the Dragon, the Snake, the Horse, the Sheep, the Monkey, the Cock, the Dog and the Boar). Colouring, too, denotes age. Work of the Sung Dynasty (AD 960–1127) favoured brown, that of the Ming Dynasty (1368–1644) green, and that of the Ch'ing Dynasty (1644–1911) yellow.

Stitches found throughout Chinese embroidery are generally satin stitch, tent stitch, cross stitch, French knots, Peking (or Chinese) knots, Pekinese stitch, back stitch, laid and couched work and pattern darning.

Voiding is typically oriental. In many Chinese embroideries different blocks of colour are rigidly separated, with no subtle colour 'bleeding' or 'blending' between each motif.

Metal thread embroidery is sometimes skilfully employed in unusual association. A modern needlepainting of 'The aqueduct', for instance, worked in Peking in the early 1960's, has gold thread work, laid and couched in white and red thread in square or diamond blocks, decorating what can only be the concrete of the bridge portrayed. The representation of a modern utilitarian construction by an ancient mineral is, surprisingly, remarkably appropriate.

Calligraphic motifs have been omnipresent throughout the history of Chinese embroidery. Some frequently used symbols are shown here. The 'FU' character, typical of the ambiguity of Chinese script, stands also for 'bat'. Sometimes, therefore, that animal is similarly portrayed to symbolise both prosperity and happiness (which are taken to be synonymous).

The numerical representation of eight seems to bear import. The 'eight genii of Taoism' (sometimes called the 'eight immortals') represent poverty, wealth, aristocracy, plebeianism, age, youth, masculinity and femininity. The 'eight colts of Mu Wang' represent animals who are reputed each to have performed incredible tricks for their imperial master in the 10th century BC.

Clothing embroidery has, in the main, been reserved for ceremonial robes for those with power and authority. The Empress was the only woman accorded her own status symbol (a phoenix).

Exclusively imperial robes were highly regimented in design and colouring. Both Emperor and Empress were allowed to wear dark midnight blue silk with dragon and sun embroidered motifs. In early times, the Imperial Dragon was unique in having five claws (his more public counterpart only had three). Peculiar to imperial robes, too, was an ancient design series known as 'The twelve ornaments', symbolic of authority and power, divided into representation on the upper and lower of the Emperor's two robes. The series consisted of:

(on the upper robes): the sun
the moon
the stars
mountains
the Imperial Dragon
pheasant
(on the lower robe): two goblets
a spray of pondweed
fiery flames
rice grains
an axe
'ya' character.

The Ming Dynasty (1368–1644) was a time of continual strife, with constant pressure from Mongols and Manchus to the north of the country and serious internal rebellions. Towards the end of the dynasty it was apparently felt necessary to sustain a certain *joie de vivre* of members of the court, held virtually captive by court eunuchs, then at the height of their power. This was, therefore, a period of enforced celebration of calendar festivals. Special badges were fashioned with motifs such as the 'gourd of great good fortune', representative of the New Year festival.

CHINA—*calligraphic elements often found on embroideries. From left to right: 'double HSI' for 'double happiness'; 'SHOU' for longevity, held high in Chinese esteem; 'FU' for prosperity;*

'CH'U MEN P'ING-AN' (*'may you meet with all comfort and happiness on going out of doors'), found on some handbags. (Reproduced by kind permission of the Embroiderers' Guild, London, from* Embroidery *magazine, September 1935, p. 71)*

41

CHINA—*circular medallion from the robe of a Ming Emperor, late 16th or early 17th century. A powerful winged dragon (ying) pursues its sacred pearl. Foreground embroidery of satin stitch against a background of horizontal stripes worked in vertical satin stitch. (University Museum, University of Pennsylvania)*

42

CHINA—*detail of dragon robe in the imperial yellow silk, dated as Ming Dynasty by cloud scroll design. The five-clawed Lung dragon was worn only by the Emperor's family, and the robe was embroidered by two court embroiderers sitting either side of a vertical frame. Using one needle between them, they worked identical patterns on either side.*
(The National Trust. The Kay-Shuttleworth Collection at Gawthorpe Hall)

In the Letcher Collection of the University Museum of the University of Pennsylvania there is an exquisite example of a 16th-century satin-stitch panel, identifiable by a pair of Chinese phoenix to an empress. The background is of cherry blossom and the seasonal gourds.

Much Ming embroidery, in fact, features this fine workmanship,

CHINA—p'u-tzu ('Mandarin square') 1644–52 (early Ch'ing Dynasty).
*Such squares, worked in two parts and worn either side of the lower
front neck of his robe, indicated an official's rank. This one of a pair
of egrets belonged to a sixth-rank (civil) official. Blue-black satin ground
with jewels in the sea, embroidery in satin stitch, Bokhara couching,
couched gold work.*
(University Museum, University of Pennsylvania)

44

with minute stitching and general perfection of execution. Contemporary woven arts were similarly superb (*k'o-ssu*, or slit tapestry, was often designed with close connexion to embroidery).

Complexity of symbolism throughout the embroidered arts of China is particularly apparent in *p'u-tzu*, 'mandarin squares', first instituted under the dynastic laws of 1391 and continued throughout until 1911. These coat-badges, worn divided on either side of the front, and in one piece on the back, of an official's robe, were indicative of professional rank.

There were in all nine classes of official, both civil and military, and permissible representation of each was strictly controlled. Motifs varied slightly with each dynasty, but in general civil officials wore bird symbols and military officers wore animal symbols. Motifs for civil officials of the Ch'ing Dynasty (1644–1911), for instance, were:

1st rank.   Choice of white crane (symbol of longevity) or golden Manchurian pheasant (symbol of duty).
2nd rank.   Golden Manchurian pheasant.
3rd rank.   Peacock with one eye (symbol of splendour) or a wild 'cloud' goose (symbol of loyalty).
4th rank.   Wild 'cloud' goose.
5th rank   Silver pheasant with five scalloped plumes.
6th rank.   Choice of egret or mandarin duck (a wedding symbol).
7th rank.   Mandarin duck.
8th rank.   Choice of quail or paradise flycatcher.
9th (and subsequent unclassed) ranks.   Paradise flycatcher.

After 1911, many examples of *p'u-tzu* of all ranks, military and civil, reached the West. Some squares were subsequently re-utilised for other clothing decoration or furnishing.

There was a wide degree of individualism to embroidered mandarin squares. A great variety of intricate stitches was employed, sometimes with metal purl embellishment. In the latter part of the 17th century there was a general shortage of raw silk and, therefore, early Ch'ing Dynasty *p'u-tzu* can be distinguished by the more economical method of surface stitching (rather than the two-sided stitching more usually worked). The size of the work gradually diminished as well, to attain minimum proportions in the Yung-cheng Period of 1723–35.

Possibly the most elegant of all *p'u-tzu* are those from the middle of the 18th century, refined products indicative of that elegant period. They were small in overall size, but the embroidery was magnificent. At the beginning of the 19th century, landscaped backgrounds found in earlier works gave way to a more formalised patterning, typically with the representative animal or bird for the official's rank perched on the middle of three rocks projecting from a tumbling and turbulent sea.

In 1791 Chinese needlepaintings, with delicate usage of fine one-stranded silk on a silk ground, were included amongst the fitments presented to Prince William V of Orange for a 'Chinese Room' at the Royal Palace of Huis ten Bosch in The Hague. The intricate panels are still there today, representative of the painstaking skill that contributed to the finished result of such needlepainting (see also p. 185).

CHINA—*detail of sampler, silk and silk gauze, 18th or 19th century. (Cooper-Hewitt Museum of Decorative Arts, New York. J. Pierpont Morgan Collection)*

Oriental floss silk embroidery was a model for the increasingly popular use of silk in embroidery in England and America in the late 19th century. During that time in China, however, embroidery suffered a general decline of craftsmanship. European traders demanded an endless supply of work for their own markets (European enthusiasts proved to have an insatiable appetite for anything even vaguely 'oriental'), and there was coincidental competition of the machine and industrial age with the increasingly fierce political and other pressing demands of what were to prove to be the last few decades of the Empire.

It was not until 1911, indeed, with the Wuchang proclamation of the Republic, that embroidery in general began to regain an upward curve. Although the full extent of embroidery production in China generally today is not known, the fine 22 ft. wide (6·7 m) embroidered mural shown at the 1970 Canton Trade Fair must surely be indicative of a continuation of high standards.

Chinese needlepaintings are being increasingly sought after by collectors. The Royal Academy's 1935 Exhibition, and recent exhibitions in London, New York and Washington DC, have presented retrospective collections from the Ming Dynasty to the present day. One such exhibition, in Harrods in June 1973, for example, included spot-motif needlepainting from Kwangtung Province, typical voiding from Peking and representative examples of contemporary embroidery from the centres of Soochow and Hunan.

Both men and women execute needlepaintings. Several artists work at one embroidery, for the long and short stitching and flat satin stitching is frequently so minute and intricate that each embroiderer has to rest his eyes after a couple of hours' work. Designs today are both traditional, with portrayal of such motifs as chrysanthemums and sunflowers, and modern, an outstanding example of which is a powerful and emotional 'Female construction worker' (1958), with a bold lady, her face strong and beautiful, striding confidently towards the future.

There is an enormous range of embroideries yet to be revealed to the western world. In the central areas of China there is little noticeable regionalisation, although work from the south tends to be more brilliantly coloured, and less subtle in tone combination, than that from the north. Indeed, some of the most delicately shaded work comes from north of the Yang-tse river, generally from the more isolated communities.

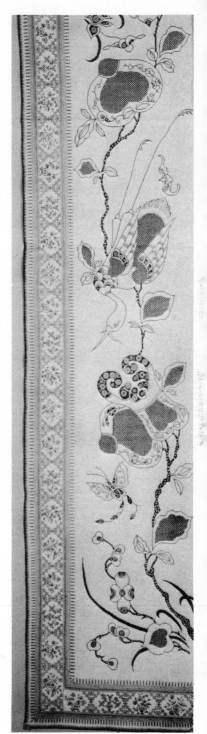

CHINA—*19th-century valance.*
(Cooper-Hewitt Museum of Decorative Arts and Design)

In the western provinces of Shensi, Szechuan and Yunnan, there is a wide heritage of cross-stitch embroidery, in blue cotton on a locally woven cotton ground. Within the provinces themselves, embroidery design has been peculiarly local. A sampler bought in Tungchuan in Yunnan in 1932, for example, has 47 design groupings, many of them thought to be unique to that town.

Some of the finest examples of embroidery from these provinces are found on *wo tan* (bed valances), sometimes with intricate cross-stitch roundels that show a certain relationship to similar designs from Sassanid Persia.

It is thought that much contemporary Chinese everyday embroidery may still relate to dynastic derivation. Much of Chinese art has always been urban and, today, communal life carries on such cooperation.

To the extreme south-west of the country is Tibet. From 1911 to 1950 it was virtually independent, though its status was never clearly defined. In 1950, however, Chinese Communist forces invaded and, after continual sporadic fighting, Tibet was finally in 1965 set up in its present state as an autonomous region of China.

Traditionally Tibetan needlework featured much appliqué, as decoration to clothing, saddle blankets and for tents and awnings that were sometimes used in lamasery courtyards. Particularly from the Gyangtse area of central Tibet, silk appliqué and embroidery *gos sku* ('fabric images'), wall hangings, have achieved a high degree of splendour and skill. All such embroidery is done by men.

If the hanging depicts a central motif of deity or saint it is technically a *tanka* (a name covering also a painted hanging). The religious figure so shown is usually surrounded by lower beings, with a border to either side. Small *tankas* are rare—most examples are on a rather grand scale. They were traditionally hung in lamaseries and in Bhutan temples: today it is believed they are exported throughout China and Mongolia.

Until 1965, in the region's capital, Lhasa, the annual spring 'Daylight of the brilliant treasures' was one eye-opening festival during which two hangings, reputedly each 70 x 80 ft. (21 x 24 m), of Buddha were displayed on the wall of the Dalai Lama's palace.

What has influenced the design of *tankas* is unclear. It has been suggested that the high quality of workmanship points to Chinese heritage, but the original skill could possibly have come from India via Bhutan.

There is an outstanding collection of Tibetan appliqué and embroidery in Newark Museum, New Jersey, originally gathered by Dr. Albert L. Shelton, a medical missionary at the beginning of the 20th century.

48

CHINA (Tibet)—*detail of appliqué tent used for summer outings. This
section of the roof has cotton and woollen motifs on a heavy white cotton
ground, machine-stitched and held with coloured cotton tape. The roof
was held in place by corner ropes of yak hair covered with blue cotton
cloth and decorated with yak-hair pompoms dyed red. Overall tent size:
15 × 10 × 10 ft. (height) (4·5 × 3 × 3 m), c. 1930.
(Courtesy of the Newark Museum, N.J. Thomas L. Raymond Bequest)*

CHINA (Tibet)—*appliqué
tanka (hanging). 'Four-armed
Avalokitesvara', satin, damask
and silk. The Bodhisattva of
Mercy (believed to be
reincarnated in each Dalai
Lama) has two hands in
devotion and two holding a
rosary of glass beads and
a lotus blossom. All applied
forms are outlined with
embroidery and there is some
gold couched work. 4 ft. 6½ in.
× 2 ft. 9½ in. (137 × 85 cm),
17th century.
(Courtesy of the Newark
Museum, NJ)*

50

Cyprus

CYPRUS—*detail of Levkara whitework cloth, probably late 1930's.*
(From Greek Island Embroidery *by Pauline Johnstone, Tiranti)*

Under the Cyprus Act of 1960 the island is an independent sovereign republic, but her arts, as many other facets of life, still bear direct relationship to those of mainland Greece and Turkey. The origins of her embroidery, therefore, can accordingly be attributed to the work of those two countries.

Although Nicosia was at one time a centre for silk production, found particularly in the Ayios Kassianos and Ayios Antonios quarters of the city, embroidery in Cyprus was nearly always on a cotton ground. Until commercial threads were available, monochrome embroidery in red on a white ground was generally worked.

As well as Greek and Turkish, there is also noticeable Italian affinity. Venice ruled the island in the 15th and early 16th centuries, and her influence is apparent particularly in Cypriot whitework, of which especially fine examples are found on festive garments such as the *bolia*, a bridal veil of cobweb-fine ground, traditionally worn only thrice (on the day of the wedding itself, on the following Sunday, when the bride visited her parents, and on the Sunday after that, when her parents returned the visit).

Levkara, a small village south of Nicosia, has long been a centre of fine whitework embroidery, called *tagiadhes* from the Italian *punto tagliato*. Although they never achieved the same degree of finesse as their Italian masters, the artists of Levkara and the surrounding district combined Venetian cutwork with whitework and satin stitching. 'Levkara work' is often referred to simply as 'Cyprus embroidery'. One particularly beautiful example of historical Levkara work is a *bolia*, 8 × 6 in. (20 × 15 cm), in the Museum of Greek Popular Art in Athens.

Levkara work has enjoyed a certain 20th-century revival as a home-based 'cottage industry'.

Czechoslovakia

A comprehensive assessment of the arts of Czechoslovakia today would necessarily fall into the areas of Bohemia, to the west of the country, the central region of Moravia, and Slovakia.

Until 1918, all three regions were part of the Austro-Hungarian empire. Bohemian embroidery, in particular, owes some allegiance to the arts of northern Austria. Centring on Prague, the national capital, the main costume points are scattered equally around Bohemia. Embroidery and costume are, as is often the case, closely related: in some Bohemian villages, apparently, a girl had to embroider a minimum of eight complete outfits for her future wedding chest.

Bohemian handwork fell prey to the universal onslaught of the industrial machines of the 19th century. Embroidery, therefore, reached its peak prior to the middle of that century. Over their full *dirndl* skirts, Bohemian women often wore delicate whitework aprons, adorned with fine cutwork similar to *broderie anglaise*. Whitework neckerchiefs were equally exquisite, often with small floral motifs and a scalloped edge.

CZECHOSLOVAKIA—*floral border motif, satin stitch.*

Many young Bohemian girls wore neat close-fitting caps, of a shape immortalised by Mary Tudor in 16th-century England. Bohemian caps were elaborately decorated with overall embroidery, frequently with some gold metal thread work included in the complicated patterning. (These caps were, later, to be replaced by the

53

ubiquitous printed headscarf of the 'industrialised machine worker of the world'.)

Embroidery in Moravia, with a hub at Brno, was accented with decoration of costume bodices, *fichus* (neck scarves) and long aprons. Bodice decoration was frequently in counted thread work, a major facet of Czechoslovak embroidery today.

In Slovakia there is still a predominantly peasant economy. Centuries of neglect and oppression alternating with covetous squabbling over her territories by her neighbours have resulted in a recently growing assertion of Slovakian nationality and language.

Slovakian villages are charming, with characteristic timbered one-storey long-houses set perpendicular to the one street. The traveller will see some use of daily regional costume, and on holidays and other special occasions he will be greeted with a riot of colourful dresses, similar to those of the neighbouring regions of Soviet and Romanian Moldavia, with red predominating and much floral patterning.

A survey of the embroidery of the whole country is roughly broken down into counted thread work, whitework, cutwork and satin-stitch embroidery with some French knot ornamentation. Design of the last category is flowing and gentle, with concentric lines adding a sense of organisation to the pattern. The overall impression is similar to Hungarian floral work, but less complicated in design.

In Prague and other major cities embroidery is still to be found utilised for traditional purposes. Though only a very few, and mainly the older, women wear full costume for everyday wear, household linen with delicate floral patterning, whitework or cutwork is still very much in use, and shops off Wenceslas Square have contemporary art. Embroidery is, in the main, still a peasant attribute, and in this Czechoslovakia adheres to the team of eastern, rather than western, Europe. Embroidery in Czechoslovakia is still rather a preconceived decoration, as opposed to the greater flexibility of original creation that is apparent in the West.

Dahomey

With its neighbour Nigeria, Dahomey possesses the arts of the Yoruba people, as is particularly evident in the appliqué to the south of the country.

Dahomey has a high level of education (one of the highest throughout West Africa) and a sense of thought shows through much of the appliqué design. The work of the Fon tribe, in particular, shows considerable sophistication in its simplicity, with clear-cut outlines forming caricatures of the animal and human figures involved.

Possibly French arts influenced the artists of Dahomey in expressing their feelings through their creations (until 1958, the country was under French administration). This could account for the combination of advanced ideas with basic theme.

Traditionally the use of appliqué through the west of Africa was associated with civil or military power and the ceremony connected thereto. Embroidered clothes were made by an exclusive family guild of artists who lived in a compound near to the chief's house, and they, and they alone, were allowed to fashion appliqué. It was purely a masculine skill. Motifs used were heraldic symbols and insignia of the chief: design could perhaps have been inspired by ancient bas-reliefs found on royal palaces.

Meyerowitz (in his *Tribes of the Niger Delta*, London 1932) believed that appliqué was first introduced in Dahomey by a Brazilian-Portuguese and it was asserted 'that the work was originally done on raffia cloth but that European cloth had been used since 1890'. Whatever the fabric of the ground, however, it was usually gold or black with applied motifs of red, black, purple, blue or green.

One contemporary appliqué artist is Abebisi Fabunmi, now curator of the Ife Museum in Nigeria. His works feature continuous strands of yarn closely worked in gorgeous colour combinations. He exhibited in the May 1973 International Monetary Fund exhibition in Washington DC.

DAHOMEY—*appliqué motif from the Fon tribe, Abomey region, showing a local chief with bestial strength. Detail of cloth, 69 × 42 in. (175 × 107 cm), in Musée Ethnographique, Porto-Novo.*

55

Denmark

One of the earliest known Danish embroideries is the braided hair-net, some 3,000 years old, found in a grave at Borum Eshøj in Jutland. Worked with a method known as *slynge* on a square block of wood with four holes through which threads were worked in a style similar to that of a child's 'knitting Nancy', this type of stitchery was practised in Denmark until about 1900, primarily for making garters.

Danish samplers present a variety of styles. Many make use of the country's pulled thread work (*sammentraekssyning*), sometimes adding to the confining discipline of the required exercise a more free-flowing floral or similarly individual motif. Such samplers were often worked in a squared frame, one type of pulled work to each window thereof.

Such squared samplers were alternatively embroidered in darning stitch or coloured cross stitching. There were whitework samplers showing the influence of lace of the 17th and 18th centuries. And map samplers were popular, perhaps intended to educate the embroiderers in the geography of the islands of their country and boundaries with their neighbours. An excellent representative selection of all types of Danish samplers is that of the Kunstindustri-museet, Copenhagen.

Tønder work comes from a small town of that name in Jutland, near the German border. Tønder has produced a range of laces since the early 17th century, but Tønder work as such is especially 18th century and is a pulled work of elaborate floral motifs on fine lawn or cambric. It is similar to the German Dresden work and is found on the points of 18th-century fichus, sleeve falls and similar delicate pieces. The connexion between Tønder work and Dresden work is an example of the considerable exchange of ideas that has been apparent between Denmark and Germany, particularly the Schleswig-Holstein area of northern Germany, typified in the close affinity of ecclesiastical embroideries of the two.

Amager, an island near Copenhagen which was the home of the finest linen of the country, was the centre of white linen embroidery. The apogee of the school was reached in the period 1760–1840. During this time the entire ground fabric was frequently covered with bird, animal, geometric and other motifs (there were few flowers in evidence). Generally white on white, there was also some black on white embroidery. Later, in the 19th century, Amager was reputed to have produced some splendid shoulder scarves, large kerchiefs with bright floral silk on silk work. It is now suggested, however, that these scarves were imported from Barcelona. There is today a delightful museum in a little farmhouse on the island, at St. Magleby, which traces local folkloric history.

The first three quarters of the 19th century were outstanding for

DENMARK—whitework edging, Tønder *work,* c. *1750.*
(Mrs. Marion Felix)

embroideries from all parts of the country. The increase in production was largely a matter of necessity. In Soelland, for example, caps of the 18th century had been of delicate silk brocade. But the poverty following the Napoleonic Wars had made it essential for the people to convert to less costly embroidery as decoration for their headwear. At first the ladies worked on a velvet ground with silk thread but, with confidence, they experimented with gold and silver threads as well until, after some decades, Soelland caps were splendid with overall closely-worked embroidery.

At first, too, only the more patrician ladies had dared to embroider their caps. But later all the female populace tried their hands. Soelland caps generally have a big central flower design from which emanates a bunch of smaller flowers and leaves, with five long leaves arranged to cover the five stiff folds forming the shaping of the cap. The embroidery was always done on a frame, and velvet shapes were sometimes fashioned over card templates.

There was at this time, too, much wool embroidery, with open patterns worked in wool thread on a ground of *wadmal*, a coarse weave wool.

Nineteenth-century embroidery of Denmark was summarised in part by C. S. Caulfeild in the 1880's under the too-embracing title of 'Danish embroidery . . . an embroidery upon cambric, muslin or batiste . . . suitable for handkerchief borders, necktie ends and cap lappets' (p. 141). This over-generalisation described what is now known as hedebo.

Dated roughly from 1800 to 1870, hedebo work is a white embroidery on a linen ground, embellishing bed and table linen, trimmings to clothing and, also, a decoration to the square pieces of linen (*knoedug*) that hung above Danish kitchen stoves.

Hedebo is a cutwork similar to *broderie anglaise* and it evolved from basic drawn work with the design worked in square meshes after the required number of threads had been withdrawn. At the beginning of the 19th century the design was transferred direct to the fabric ground and worked accordingly. Outlines were chain stitched and worked with spot or solid patterns of filling stitches. By 1840, however, open filling stitches similar to Italian reticella work were being much used for leaves and petals, but by the middle of the century the reticella influence was superseded by cutting holes which were then filled with delicate needlepoint laces.

As with many other embroidered arts, the industrial revolution throttled hedebo work which, from 1870, gradually succumbed.

Along coastal regions of Denmark's islands there has been some net embroidery, of a type similar to filet lace, and this is sometimes utilised by today's artists.

58

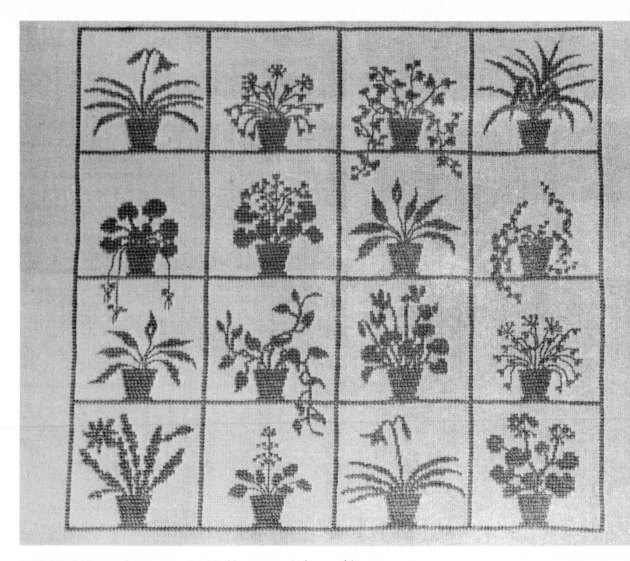

DENMARK—*cushion cover, 1958, blue cross stitch on white even-weave linen ground.*
(The Embroiderers' Guild, London)

The flower samplers of the past, too, with square neat frames and floral motifs in separate windows, are often recreated by contemporary embroiderers. Much of Denmark's embroidery is realistically floral. One design readily available and very popular is that of a wall cushion featuring the wall rue plants found on the walls of Hamlet's castle at Helsingør (Shakespeare's 'Elsinore').

One major asset of current Danish embroidery is the variety of stitches available, be they required for work on canvas, linen or cotton ground. A good mathematical brain is essential for the imitative addict when executing some of the more intricate designs on the market, and a general dexterity and accompanying patience are necessary too. Concentration on the balance of stitches, the correct placing of each insertion of the needle, is the quintessence of much Danish embroidery today.

Selskabet til Haandarbejdets Fremme (often known simply as 'Danish design') was founded in 1928 to protect and revive embroidery and other home industries in Denmark. Under the guidance of its President, Mrs. Gertie Wandel, the Guild has been instrumental in promoting Danish embroidery around the world.

Embroidery today, therefore, continues ancient tradition and incorporates modern innovation. Experimental artists like Maiken Berknov (who works appliqué of coils of metal filings, springs and electric cord into her 'embroideries') are evidence of the assertion that Denmark still plays a leading role in the embroidered arts world.

Egypt

It is thought that the use of needle decoration in Egypt dates back to the 1st Dynasty (*c.* 3000 BC) and by the time of the 6th Dynasty (*c.* 2500 BC) motifs were usually geometric, with bands, zigzag lines and lozenges. In the 18th Dynasty (*c.* 1400 BC), the period of Hatshepsut and Tutankhamen, design had progressed to vegetable motifs and flowers, rosettes and sphinx.

The adjective 'Coptic' is today synonymous with early Egyptian art, although oddly enough the word in fact only appeared with the advent of the Islamic age (derived from *Aegyptos* via *Gyptos* and *Kyptos* to *Koptos*). The Copts were the early Christians of Egypt, and though there were undoubtedly Christians from the 1st century AD it was not until the end of the 4th century that biblical motifs entered into embroidery design.

Early Coptic embroidery, on a linen ground (it is known that there was one important linen industry at Akhmin) consisted of decorative panels and bands woven on multi-shaft pit looms, possibly introduced from the Far East. The entire length of the finished garment was constructed from one width of the fabric.

More complicated patterning was attained with later Coptic embroidery. The Sir William Flinders Petrie collection in the Whitworth Gallery, Manchester, includes two works, both dated from 5th to 8th century AD. One is a cream geometric roundel motif on a dark brown ground, the other a similarly geometric panel, also worked with cream thread, from a robe.

Traditional *tissus coptes* (as they are often known) declined in production in the 10th century (during the Fatimid rule). During this time embroidery developed an exquisite quality with gold and red abstract patterning in which Arabic influence was sometimes apparent, no doubt as a result of the Arab conquest of the 7th and 8th centuries and, also, intense trading between Egypt and nearby countries of the Middle East.

Coptic embroidery was re-introduced to the arts world at the Paris World Fair in 1900 where it evoked much interest. It is today estimated that there are some twenty million fragments of *tissus coptes* in collections around the world, the greater part woven but many, possibly, with some element of embroidery.

Current embroidery production in Egypt is restricted mainly to cotton and silk thread decoration for clothing and domestic linens, with some additional cording. There is, for instance, no embroidery equivalent of the woven tapestry creativity of the engineer Wissa Wassef of Horraniya, whose marvellous contemporary hangings, obviously much influenced by an environment of 20th-century Egypt, are already known throughout many cities of the western world. And Egypt does not have, alas, the driving force of volunteer groups working in some other countries of the Middle East to sustain, and promote, indigenous embroidery tradition.

England

Although many facets of embroidery were commonly practised through the British Isles, the art can be legitimately regionalised. Under the heading of 'English embroidery' can be placed any form of embroidery that is not exclusively Scottish, Welsh or Irish either in origin or application.

It is known that Angle and Saxon women were embroidering in England as early as the 5th century and, possibly, Romans had been doing so for long before then. The earliest embroidery so far discovered is the 'Chasuble of St. Harlindis and St. Relindis', now at Stad Maaseik in the Province of Limburg, Belgium. Dating from the latter half of the 9th century, it is evident that the work (now in a barely-recognisable form) was embroidered in silks and silver-gilt thread.

With the Norman Conquest of 1066, Anglo-Saxon emotion was abandoned in favour of a more solemn and romanesque style of stitching. Gold work dominated, frequently on a silk ground. One of the first works to appear from the more dignified Norman school was the Bayeux Tapestry (p. 330), which alone would be indicative of the high standard of embroidery in the western world at that time. St. Dunstan was one gentleman involved with the art: apparently he supervised embroidery with fine detail (Masters, Ellen T., *The Gentlewoman's Book of Art Needlework*, p. 25). St. Cuthbert's stole, now at Durham, is early 10th century.

The zenith of early English embroideries coincides with that of English illuminated manuscripts (Jourdain, Margaret, *English Secular Embroidery*, p. 7), in the period of the 13th and 14th centuries. 'Opus Anglicanum' (English work) was widely exported during this period. It is known, for example, that both Edward I and Edward II presented beautifully worked copes to the Pope.

The term 'Opus Anglicanum' is in common use in embroidery terminology, but what exactly does it mean? Basically, it refers to embroideries from the early 13th to the latter half of the 14th centuries, and generally to elaborate ecclesiastical work. Threads used were coloured floss silks, a pure gold thread (often couched), silver (though to a lesser degree than gold thread) and pearls, stones and enamels which were often subsequently looted. Most surviving examples are on a ground of twill-weave silk (usually lined with

63

linen), of pure linen or, from the early 14th century, of velvet. Other ground fabrics included samit (the Byzantine *exsamit*) with a thick warp and flat gold-threaded weft combination, the traditional 'cloth of gold', cyclas (or siglaton), a lighter form of samit, cendal silk, buckram (also called fustian), much mentioned in inventories of the 12th and 13th centuries, satin (first mentioned in the 14th century), taffeta and camoca (forerunner of cashmere, being a combination weave of fine camel's hair and silk). Some of the gold work was diapered, a term which meant that the pattern of weaving the weft threads in and out of warp threads of the same colour resulted in a pattern produced purely by the weave (later the word 'diaper' came to be applied to any repeating motif giving a regular sprinkling or powdering effect). There was much couching, with surface and underside couching being particularly popular.

Many of the Latin names of Opus Anglicanum stitches have since been anglicised. Amongst the most commonly-used stitches were:

Opus conscutum—appliqué work, sometimes with painted features to the figures applied on to the main ground. Although the invention of this style of embroidery has been credited to Botticelli, *c.* 1444–1510, an overriding factor is the contradictory evidence that the method was already being employed in England.
Opus phrygium—gold work
Opus anglicanum stitch—split stitch (p. 437)
Opus plumarium—either general plumage or feather work or long and short stitch (p. 403)
Opus pectineum—woven or combed work
Opus filatorium—lace or darned work.

This, then, was a high point of English embroidery. A Vatican inventory of 1295 contained more items of Opus Anglicanum than of any other school of embroidery. It seems possible that the development was stimulated by the exorbitant cost of imported silk, a price which necessitated maximum skill in using each piece of thread. The professional embroiderers who produced true Opus Anglicanum were men. They served a seven years' apprenticeship.

There were a few notable female 'professional' embroiderers. Mabilia of Bury St. Edmunds, for example, produced many fine vestments for Henry during the period of 1239–44 and there are records of payments made to her during that time (Christie, Mrs. Archibald, *English Mediaeval Embroidery*).

Some of the most beautiful embroideries that have survived are chasubles and copes. The 'Clare Chasuble' (now in the Victoria and Albert Museum) is illustrated opposite.

▷ *CHILE – Isla Negra embroidery, "My kitchen" by Silvia Jofre, worked in chain stitch and back stitch, 1972.*
(Sociedad de Arte Contemporaneo de Santiago)

◁ *CHILE – "Wheat threshing" by Tato Dias, worked in back stitch and chain stitch. Isla Negra, 1972.*
(Sociedad de Arte Contemporaneo de Santiago)

▷ *CHILE – "The House in San Javier" by Elsa Araya, Isla Negra 1972. The artist has used running stitch and back stitch, with a free hanging plait for the mule's tail.*
(Sociedad de Arte Contemporaneo de Santiago)

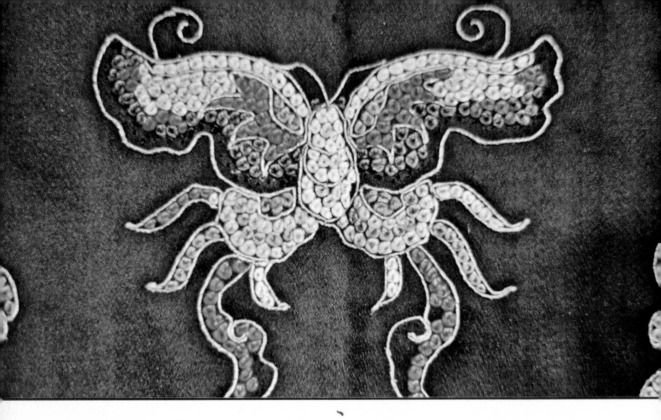

△ CHINA – motif in Peking knot on the imperial dark-blue ground, Ming dynasty.
(Gawthorpe Hall, property of the National Trust)

▽ CHINA – 19th-century dragon motif on imperial blue silk, collection of the 8th Earl of Elgin.
(The Earl of Elgin and Kincardine)

The back of the chasuble portrays (from the top) the Crucifixion, the Virgin and Child, St. Peter and St. Paul and the stoning of St. Stephen. Silver-gilt and silver threads and coloured silks have been worked on blue satin ground in underside couching, split stitch and laid and couched work. There is a 16th-century addition of blue and

ENGLAND—*late 13th century. The Clare Chasuble. A stole and a maniple which originally accompanied this work bore heraldic shields connected with Margaret de Clare, wife of Edmund Plantagenet, Earl of Cornwall. This dates the chasuble before 1294 (date of Margaret's divorce), as is also evidenced by the style of embroidery and the more elongated figures than those portrayed on earlier works. Silk and gilt on a blue satin and cotton ground, split stitch, underside couching and laid and couched work. 3 ft. 9½ in. × 2 ft. 2 in. (115 × 66 cm). (The Victoria and Albert Museum, Crown Copyright)*

gold lace on the front. Lion and griffin in foliate scrolls similar to those bordering either side of the chasuble have been found in the tombs of two French 13th-century bishops.

Figures throughout Opus Anglicanum tend to be short and stumpy, with large extremities. There is a vivacity of expression, an intense portrayal of emotion.

The 'Syon Cope', also in the Victoria and Albert Museum, dates from 1300–1320. Originally a chasuble, the fourth row of scenes was removed when the work was remodelled to its present cope form. Some of the omitted episodes were remodelled to the sides of the cope. On a faded red linen ground, with green between-quatrefoil applied ground bearing six-winged seraphs or angels, silver-gilt, silver thread and coloured silks have been worked in underside couching, split stitch and laid and couched work.

ENGLAND—*early 15th century. The Syon Cope. This work belonged to a group of nuns from the Bridgettine Convent in Syon, Middlesex, founded by Henry V in 1414. When the convent went into exile at the beginning of the reign of Elizabeth I, the nuns settled in Lisbon, returning to England in 1810. The cope finally came to the Museum in 1864.*
(The Victoria and Albert Museum, Crown Copyright)

The subjects of the barbed quatrefoils are, according to a key plan (reproduced by kind permission of the Arts Council of Great Britain and Mr. Donald King, author of *Opus Anglicanum*, the Arts Council, 1963):

1. Coronation of the Virgin.
2. Crucifixion.
3. Archangel Michael vanquishing the dragon.
4. Fragment of a scroll.
5. St. Philip with three loaves in a napkin.
6. Christ appearing to St. Mary Magdalene.
7. Funeral and assumption of the Virgin, with Jews attacking the bier and St. Thomas receiving the Virgin's girdle.
8. Death of the Virgin.
9. Incredulity of St. Thomas.
10. St. Simon with a club.
11. Small segment with no object.
12. St. Bartholomew with a flaying-knife.
13. St. Peter with keys.
14. St. Paul with sword.
15. St. Thomas with lance.
16. A segment of a quatrefoil.
17. Unidentified hand grasping a book.
18. St. Andrew with cross.
19. St. James the Great with pilgrim's staff and wallet.
20–22. Unidentified.

ENGLAND—*outline diagram of the Syon Cope showing quatrefoil representations. (Arts Council of Great Britain and Mr. Donald King)*

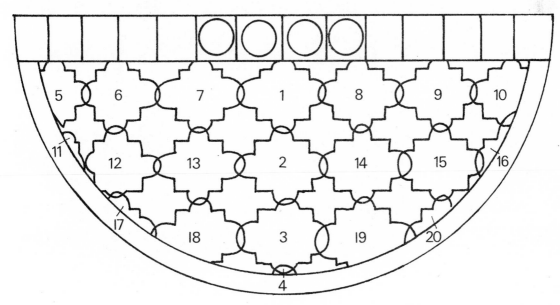

The cope measures 9 ft. 8 in. by 4 ft. 10 in. (2·9 × 1·4 m). Around the edge is a 3⅛ in. (7·9 cm) band of orphrey, remodelled from stole and maniple. The main orphrey, 9¾ in. (24·7 cm) wide, along the straight side of the cope, is in three parts—the two outer each have five lozenges of alternate red and green, and probably both come from the same alb, and the central part has four roundels on a green ground.

ENGLAND—*early 14th century. Detail of the Marnhull Orphrey, showing Christ carrying the cross. Silk, silver-gilt and silver on linen ground, split stitch, underside couching and laid and couched work. The orphrey bears the arms of the Wokyndon family and is probably 1315–35. 3 ft. 6¾ in. × 7½ in. (108 × 19 cm). (The Victoria and Albert Museum, Crown Copyright)*

68

A work from the same date is the 'Marnhull Orphrey', 1315–35, with scenes from the Passion beneath cinquefoil ogee arches, in the spandrels of each of which is a lion rampant of the Wokyndon family, benefactors of St. Paul's Cathedral. It was presented to the Victoria and Albert Museum in 1936 by the National Art-Collections Fund, who had purchased it from the Presbytery at Marnhull, Dorset. Its earlier provenance is not known.

Other outstanding examples of Opus Anglicanum include the 'Vatican Cope' (in the Museo Sacro, Rome), the 'Salzburg Cope' (the Abegg-Stiftung Collection, Bern) and the 'Pienza Cope' (Capitolo dello Cattedrale di Pienza).

The middle of the 13th century, therefore, was the high-water mark of early English embroidery. 1348 brought the invasion of the Black Death, and prolonged wars, both foreign and civil, of the latter half of the 14th century and the 15th century, meant a decline in quality of embroidery generally. Mass production became a necessity. Underside couching was replaced by the more speedy surface couching, and increasing use was made of pre-embroidered applied motifs.

This was a satisfactory and quick method of decorating church embroidery. On a ground of silk or velvet, the effect of the appliqué was usually heightened by superimposed couched silver-gilt threads around each motif. Most of the appliqué vestments and hangings that have survived bear a central motif surrounded by such designs as winged cherubs or lilies. *Or nué* (p. 183), a particular form of couching, was also common in church hangings.

Much Italian silk brocade was being used as ecclesiastical decoration and, with the increased availability of velvet, embroidery was less vital to the textile arts. Domestic embroidery, on the other hand, began to take on a new importance. Velvet decorated with coats of arms and similar heavy gold-work embroidery was extensively used for coverings for tables and benches. Above the main seat of honour in the dining hall would be a wall-hanging with elaborate embroidery.

Flowers, too, came into their own at this time. During the previous centuries floral motifs had played a minor role but, with the late 15th century, they were coming into frequent use. One 11 in (28 cm) high rose, silver-gilt and silk thread on linen, is applied as one motif to a dark blue velvet ground with split stitch, brick stitch and laid and couched work superimposed.

Some of the finest embroideries of this period are the great funerary palls commissioned by rich London merchants. On the whole, however, embroidery remained at a low ebb. There is certainly little information on work produced during the first half of the 16th century, either before or after the English Reformation of 1534–9.

Possibly some of the artistic skill was diverted to early lace production: the first lace patterns recorded date from 1523. This was a needle-made lace that does, in fact, come under the label of 'embroidery'. Fine needlepoint stitching, generally white on white, was used as decoration to collars, ruffs and caps. By the time of the Reformation, indeed, whitework cutwork was being produced by skilled amateurs as well as by the professional embroiderers. With the lack of washing facilities of the time, any well-dressed gentleman would have required more than one set of whitework trimmings such as ruffs and collars, and, doubtless, production was prolific.

Few domestic decorative embroideries survive, but there are records in such inventories as that of Katharine of Aragon, divorced wife of Henry VIII, of cushions and hangings of rich silks and velvets with embroidery and much ornament (1546).

Elizabeth I came to the throne in 1558, and in 1561 she refounded the ancient Broderers' Company, a band of some one hundred professional embroiderers, all men. Embroidery at this time was strictly segregated between the highly ornate work done by men and the more leisurely work of the ladies.

The life of the Elizabethan lady was well suited to the pastime of embroidering. New trade routes had brought silk direct from the East, and for some years steel needles, either from Germany or home-produced, had replaced the previous drawn-wire needles that were

ENGLAND—*16th-century black on white silk panel, 7 × 49½ in. (18 × 126 cm). Each motif has been individually applied to the main ground and there is a folded ribbon border. It is a delightful human work, with an air of surprise to many of the figures. Seeding is used throughout.*
(From the collection of Parham Park, Sussex)

70

difficult to manipulate. Improved economy and general interest in the arts also contributed to the upsurge of 'home embroidering'.

Flowers ('slips') dominate embroidery of the latter half of the 16th century. Motifs of a pansy and honeysuckle worked about this time show little technical difference from an earlier rose, although design is free-flowing and more alive. Sometimes the pattern was pre-traced, sometimes it was copied direct to the fabric from a similar work. With the more general impact of the printing press, too, pattern books began to appear. Illustrations from herbal, natural history, botany and other manuals were transposed for the needle. And samplers began to make their appearance.

The earliest dated sampler, now in the Victoria and Albert Museum, is that worked by Jane Bostocke in 1598, inscribed 'ALICE LEE WAS BORNE THE 23 OF NOVEMBER BEING TWESDAY IN THE AFTER NOONE 1596'. Coloured silks, silver and silver-gilt thread, seed pearls and black beads are worked on a linen ground, 17×15 in. $(43 \times 38$ cm) in Algerian eye stitch, satin stitch, chain stitch, ladder stitch, buttonhole stitch, coral stitch, two-sided cross stitch, couching and seeding.

Seeding (or speckling) was common throughout Elizabethan embroidery, and it is frequently found either as filling or ground covering. Much is done in striking black on white, as in the delightful panel at Parham Park, Sussex, where a veritable international zoological and botanical survey of individual black-worked motifs has been applied to a white silk ground.

Elizabethan blackwork was extraordinarily advanced: the design is never exaggerated, a balance of texture is maintained in the proportions of black silk to white ground of silk or linen. The work, heightened by use of silver or silver-gilt thread, was often used to embellish hangings, household cloths and articles of clothing.

Other Elizabethan decorative embroideries are less intricate. Canvas work made its début and tent or cross stitch was executed on a linen canvas ground. Hangings, valances, carpets and cushions were worked, examples of which are the famous Oxburgh hangings of Bess of Hardwick and Mary, Queen of Scots (p. 219).

Bess of Hardwick, 1520–1608, was successively Mrs. Robert Barlow, Lady Cavendish, Lady St. Loe and the Countess of Shrewsbury. She organised her life well. One of her staff reported:

Her 'waiting gentlewomen' were drawn from much the same class as the gentleman servants. They accompanied their mistress to prayers, helped her to embroider the enormous quantities of coverlets, bedcurtains, hangings and cushions which furnished the rooms and covered every available surface.

(Plowden, Alison, *Mistress of Hardwick*, BBC Publications, 1972)

As Countess of Shrewsbury, Bess was in charge of Mary, Queen of Scots (p. 219), for 15 years of her imprisonment, from 1569 to 1584, during which time the Oxburgh hangings, generally thought to be in the main Marian, were worked. The embroideries are now owned by the Victoria and Albert Museum and are displayed in Oxburgh Hall, Norfolk, owned by the National Trust. They are canvas work, with medallion motifs applied to a green velvet ground and outlined with couched silk cord. One panel is dated 1570. Some of the motifs are taken from one of the best-known contemporary books, *Devises Heroïques* by Claude Paradin (Lyon, 1557). Others are taken from Conrad Gesner's *Icones Animalium, Icones Avium and Icones Animalium Marino* (Zürich, 1554). A 'seele' panel, taken from page 164 of the latter work, bears the initials 'ES', for Bess. Other panels, such as 'Ivpitler' and the 'Eape panel', bear the royal monogram 'MR'. Others of their embroideries are in the outstanding collection at Hardwick Hall, Derbyshire.

Queen Elizabeth, too, had her own embroidery penchants. The Fitzwilliam Museum in Cambridge has a velvet canopy, 12 × 5 ft. (3·6 × 1·5 m) and richly embroidered on a red velvet trellis ground, that was carried over her head when she went to King's College Chapel in 1564.

Bed hangings from the latter half of the 16th century consisted, in their entirety, of four full-length curtains hanging from the top of the four-poster bed, short flounce to hang from the mattress around sides and bottom, valance to hang from the upper poster rail and, possibly, a coordinating bedhead. Wool on linen was worked into sprawling patterns of flora and fauna, with overall design still fairly simple.

This simplicity, though varied in form, is none the less characteristic of all facets of Elizabethan embroidery. The exact proportioning and repetition of a floral motif with surrounding scrolls on a blackwork coif, for example, convey the impact intended by the designer. The woman's hood from the Victoria and Albert Museum (p. 333) displays mathematical perfection of execution.

Hoods (coifs), men's caps, ladies' bodices and accessories such as purse bags were costume items often richly embroidered, with floral silk embroidery, with metal thread or with the omnipresent blackwork embroidery.

Metal thread embroidery was carefully controlled, as was the use of sequins and other addenda. Much of the gold, silver and silver-gilt thread used was couched in complicated scroll designs. (In 1548 the first recorded metal thread manual had appeared, *Moryssche and Damaschin renewed and encreased very profitable for Goldsmiths and Embroiderars*, by Thomas Geminus. It contained many arabesque designs popular with later embroiderers.)

72

Queen Elizabeth I died in 1603 and the embroidery of the 17th century can plausibly, therefore, be titled 'Jacobean' even though the greater part of the embroidered art thus generally labelled was not worked during the reign of either James. The Elizabethan embroidery tradition continued, in fact, throughout the first half of the 17th century. During the reigns of both James I (1603–25) and Charles I (1625–49), no new embroidery departures are noticeable, although the former king is known to have planted many mulberry trees in his continued efforts to further the country's silk industry, and certainly some beautiful work was produced, such as that of Edmund Harrison, principal embroiderer to Charles I and, later, to Charles II.

Clothing embroidery continued as before, although blackwork died out. Some embroidery patterns were copied from Richard Shorleyker's *A Schole-house for the Needle* (1624) and others from John Taylor's *The Needle's Excellency* (1631).

During the 'Commonwealth', the time of the Cromwells, from 1649 to 1660, there was a marked decline of imagination, colour and general sense of originality in all the arts, although Oliver Cromwell did institute a Guild of Needle-makers in 1656. After a decade of such sober rule, Charles II brought with him to the throne a sense of comfort, gaiety and overseas influences. He had travelled, he had many foreign friends, and increased trade with the Far East introduced a new oriental perspective into the decorative arts.

From India there were *palampores*, painted calicoes used for curtains or wall decorations. From Iran there was the 'Tree of life' motif which appears again and again in 'Jacobean' embroidery, usually springing from a stylised *terra firma* (mound of earth). The tree's branches, spreading in all directions, are laden with exotic birds and flowers. Playing and hiding around the foliage are lions, leopards, unicorns, stags, camels, elephants and more commonplace animals like squirrels, dogs and rabbits. No attention was given to proportionate sizing of these beasts: a dog might be chasing a rabbit the same size as himself.

Floral motifs include roses and lilies, harebells, tulips, hyacinths, pansies, honeysuckle, foxgloves, jasmine, shamrock, carnations, thistles and edibles such as wheat, vines, cherries and occasionally strawberries (the last a great novelty at that time).

'Jacobean' embroidery was generally worked with crewel or worsted wool on a twill ground of linen warp and cotton weft, and is, accordingly, also termed 'crewel embroidery', although crewel work as such did not make its appearance until 1689, with the accession of William and Mary. Queen Mary (who died in 1694) was another skilled embroiderer and did much to promote the art. Early

ENGLAND—*two examples of the 'Tree of Life' motif, taken from embroideries of the late 17th (top) and 14th centuries.*

73

wall hangings were worked in one colour, usually a shade of blue or green but sometimes red, and the overall designs were rather sprawling and indecisive. Later patterns became more solid with much in-filling, at first usually in long and short stitch. Subsequently, complicated filling stitches such as brick and cross filling, trellis work and 'squares and bundles' were utilised, often with one different complex method to each individual motif. The design was first outlined with chain stitch, with stem stitch (crewel stitch) for the rather serpent-like tree outlines. From 1689 on the appearance of such hangings veered away from the exotic approach to give a more domestic feeling. Isolated sprays of foliage began to appear and the overall pattern gave way to small 'spot' clumps. *Terra firma* mounds were less usual.

Samplers of the 17th century fall into various categories. They are all narrow, with widths varying from 6½ to 12 in. (16 to 30 cm), the length being determined by the width of the loom, usually 20–24 in (51–61 cm) but sometimes as much as 30–36 in. (76–91 cm) or more. Many 'Jacobean' samplers are decorated with spot motifs and overall patterns of flora and fauna, sometimes with gold and silver thread enlivening the silk on linen ground combination. They are rarely signed. Border samplers in silk on linen were perhaps the most common. Cutwork samplers and whitework samplers, linen on linen, were among the variety worked.

It is thought that by the time of Charles I, in fact, the making of samplers was an essential and regular part of some school curricula. From 1650 religious and moral inscriptions began to appear.

Stumpwork, or heavily padded embroidery on a ground of ivory-coloured satin, was practised in England only during the period 1650 to the 1680's. Raised metal thread embroidery had already been worked during the late 16th century and the 'Jacobean' embroiderers extended the three-dimensional effect in that the basic padding was sometimes further embellished with darned silk pile, metal strips, and faces and hands of carved wood or ivory. Stumpwork needlework boxes are delicately worked, often lined with pink silk. When the embroidered panels were finished, they were sent to a cabinet-maker who finished off the box, sometimes protecting the whole with transparent mica sheet.

Some stitches commonly used in the 17th century have since assumed noms-de-plume. John Taylor (1580–1653) in his treatise (*The Needle's Excellency*, 1631) spoke of:

Fine Ferne-stitch, Finny-stitch, New-stitch and Chain-stitch,
Braue Bred-stitch, Fisher-stitch, Irish-stitch and Queene-stitch,
The Spanish-stitch, Rosemary-stitch, and Mowse-stitch,
The smarting Whip-stitch, Back-stitch and the Crosse-stitch.

74

Metal work embroidery was couched as before, and beads, spangles, tinsel, jewels and even the occasional beetle wing are found incorporated into embroidery of this era.

There was increasing oriental influence throughout embroidery towards the end of the 17th century. Not only were patterns sent to India to be copied, or to be embroidered for re-export to the West, but designs from China and eastern Europe began to be noticeable.

ENGLAND—*17th century— oriental influence noticeable in the design and some of the stitching (Peking knots), appliqué on a bed valance or banker (bench cover). (City of Norwich Museums)*

75

Another innovation was the late 17th-century rage of 'knotting' which was sometimes coordinated with traditional embroidery to decorate household items.

ENGLAND—*17th-century christening cushion, 112 × 14 in. (284 × 36 cm), signed and dated "M.L. 1644', tent stitch, silk on fine canvas. The story of Moses in the bulrushes is played to a surrounding audience of animals, fish, flowers and butterflies. The cushion is edged with original lacing that includes strips of parchment or kid, bound in satin and folded in zigzags.*
(From the collection of Parham Park, Sussex)

Overall, 17th-century embroidery is more complicated, more
sophisticated than that of the previous century. A delicate overall
scroll patterning compared to work of a hundred years before shows
greater intricacy and, correspondingly, less effect as commendable
patterning. The complexity of the time, too, is shown in a delightful
christening cushion at Parham Park, Sussex, unique for its period in
that it is signed and dated (1644). It portrays the customary earthy
mound with a typical scene from the Old Testament, in this case
the finding of Moses in the bullrushes. Specimens of exotic fish,
animals, birds, flowers and fruits are neatly pushed into every available background space. It is a lovely work: the surprise on the face
of the ladies as they see the baby, the apparent cynical boredom of

77

the bird fishing at the bottom right-hand corner—all illustrate the wit and imagination that the 'Jacobean' embroiderer possessed.

The advent of the 18th century brought many important changes in the embroidered arts world.

The shape of samplers changed, for instance, from the former long narrow sampler to a square form on a woollen canvas ground. Samplers were sometimes purely inscriptional, others had motifs carefully duplicated in each quarter of the frame and, generally, there was a border surround. Map samplers came into popularity particularly during the 1780's and 1790's.

Household linen and articles of clothing were lush with rich embroidery, in silk or chenille worked with flat satin stitches and couched silver or silver-gilt thread. A stomacher dating from early in the century is of silk embroidered on a corded silk ground with much silver-gilt thread and applied cord. The satin and long and short stitching forms a delicate and precise floral pattern that typifies the love of chinoiserie that so affected the artists of this time. Other clothing embroideries included such useful extrava-ganzas as quilted satin petenlairs (hooded jackets with blouson back), often heavily worked with Italian quilting on a silk ground. Petticoats were also quilted, in silk or satin, with flowing curves of quilted lines. How practical and yet how attractive were some of the fashions of that time: decorative quilting had been in existence for some time, but in the 18th century it was used to great effect.

The middle of the century saw the peak of the London-based silk trade (during the last years of the 17th century French Huguenots had come to England to escape persecution and, also, the economic difficulties of their own country). Spitalfields, near Bishopsgate, London, had a high percentage of French immigrants and during the 1740's it was the centre of a unique brocaded silk which was some-times over-embroidered. This, too, was the high period of men's exquisite embroidered silk waistcoats, with metal thread and sequins as further embellishment. Not all such decorative work was in silk, however. Some crewel wool was used for more ordinary clothing.

Flowers bloomed everywhere in 18th-century embroidery. Whether this was an era of horticulture or not is irrelevant. What is notable is that the 18th-century designers added more realism to their floral motifs than had previously been achieved. Floral sprays trailed over designs for entire suites of chairs and settees, over wall-hangings and small pictures. Canvas work, in particular, was found to be a particularly agreeable medium for flower work, both in gros point and petit point, sometimes as fine as 40 stitches to the inch. Floral embroidery was sometimes allied with highly dramatic

ENGLAND—*detail of a screen worked by Julia, Lady Calverley (1686–1736), wife of Sir Walter Calverley (traditionally the original of Addison's 'Sir Roger de Coverley'). Lady Julia was a prolific needlewoman, and she is known to have produced the major part of ten wall panels and this screen, brought in 1755 from Esholt, Yorkshire, to their present home at Wallington, Northumberland. This detail, from the bottom of the third panel of the screen, tent stitch, wool and silk on canvas, illustrates the fine emotion of her work. Screen design derivation is thought to have come from the 1663 Ogilvy edition of Virgil's* Georgics *and engravings from the* Eclogues.
(The National Trust)

religious work, forming a border around, for example, a portrayal of the Crucifixion.

In the Needlework Room at Wallington, Northumberland, are the panels partly worked by Julia, Lady Calverley (1686–1736). One of the tent-stitch silk and wool on canvas pieces is dated 1717. Some oriental influence is apparent in the design of flowers, fruit, leaves and birds. Also in National Trust custody are the 'Stoke Edith embroideries', now at Montacute House, Somerset. The embroideries are considered early 18th century, although a belief that they were worked by five successive wives of one Mr. Foley is now discredited. (When the family house in Herefordshire was razed by fire in 1927, a later Mrs. Foley loaned the embroideries to the Trust.)

The embroideries from Stoke Edith consist of three works. 'The Orangery Garden' shows an ornamental garden with quartered *parterres*. The orangery itself is to the back and is, coincidentally, similar to that still to be seen at Montacute. Around the garden are

ENGLAND—*'The Orangery Garden', one of the 'Stoke Edith embroideries', now at Montacute House, Somerset. 20 × 11 ft. (6 × 3·3 m). Probably early 18th century. (The National Trust)*

cypresses, oaks and shrubs. There are tulips, the ubiquitous carnations, orange trees and a pair of King Charles spaniels. 'Alcove Garden' has more figurative play but is otherwise similarly photographic. Both panels are worked in wool and floss silk, tent stitch on single mesh canvas. The last panel, 'Hector and Achilles', perhaps a copy of a current drawing of the meeting of Aeneas and Achates, bears little relation to the other two works.

Whitework was popular. By 1750 delicate Danish Tønder work pieces were decorating the corners of *fichus* (fine white lawn neckscarves) with intricate chain stitching outlining motifs which were then cut away and filled with needlelace fillings such as hollie stitch (holy point). Throughout the century, too, whitework faced stiff competition from bobbin lace. Embroidered lace entered a losing battle. It was not until the Napoleonic wars and the economic depressions of the end of the 18th century that import of foreign lace was restricted and home whitework embroidery once more came to the fore.

About 1760 the tambour (p. 441) was introduced from China, by way of Europe. It very quickly gained a following and, no doubt, the speed with which hooked chain stitch could be worked contributed considerably to its appeal. It was generally worked on white muslin. About this time, too, patchwork and a combination of appliqué and patchwork came into vogue.

In 1768 Queen Charlotte assisted Miss Pawsey in establishing a needlework school at Ampthill, Buckinghamshire.

'Needlepainting', the art of transposing a painted or engraved picture with the needle, gained in popularity. One of the best-known exponents was Mary Linwood (1755-1845), who specialised in worsted embroidery on a linen ground. She had a permanent exhibition near Leicester Square and apparently possessed a first-class business brain (although she somehow managed to work in a state of utter chaos). She drew the outline of a painting by such a master as Stubbs or Sir Joshua Reynolds on to a strong backing cloth and then embroidered her design in irregular straight stitches, using specially dyed wool. Her portraits, in particular, are extreme examples of the patience and dedication needed for needlepainting. Napoleon is said to have been so impressed with her 'portrait' of him that in 1802 he conferred on the artist the Freedom of the City of Paris. The Empress Catherine of Russia also received her, and she bequeathed her copy of Carlo Dolci's 'Salvator Mundi' (for which she had once been offered 3,000 guineas) to Queen Victoria. Alas, on Miss Linwood's death the sale of her own personal collection realised less than 1,000 guineas.

By the end of the 18th century, quality of workmanship had

generally declined and creative inspiration was lacking. The tambour had brought speed too much to the fore. Embroiderers had a plethora of pattern books at their disposal and, also, they worked from pin-pricked pictures, with the design worked out on heavy paper or parchment and details such as faces and hands already painted.

Berlin wool work (see p. 112) seems to have arrived in England in about 1806, and started a craze. At first the designs reached England in small numbers, but in 1831 Mr. Wilks of Wilks' Warehouse, Regent Street, began to import them direct from Berlin, together with the materials for working the patterns.

Berlin wool work soon became almost synonymous with the entire world of embroidery. In 1847 Mrs. Henry Owen began her *Illuminated Book of Needlework* with the assertion 'Embroidery or as it is more often called Berlin wool work . . .'

Highly emotional and stylised scenes of mediaeval life, biblical stories, portraits of pet dogs on cushions and other fashionable 19th-century themes were popular subjects for this embroidery. In 1851 Sarah Francis of Chatham, then 17, worked the tragedy of Mary, Queen of Scots, lamenting and holding the body of Lord (Black) Douglas at Langside, scene of the Queen's defeat by the Regent Murray in 1568. This sad picture is now in the Eastgate House Museum, Rochester.

By the middle of the century beads were being added further to decorate the work, as was the raised pile of Turkey work (or plush) stitch. Berlin wool work continued its heyday until the middle of the 1870's when it was to be ousted by the 'Art Needlework Movement'. The main body of Berlin wool work in England, therefore, was worked in the four middle decades of the 19th century.

Beadwork had been particularly popular since the beginning of the century. Coloured glass beads from Germany and Italy, known as pound beads, were sold by weight, as were bugles (small tubular glass beads) and beads of cut-steel, jet, gold, silver and pearls. Roughly speaking, the size of beads grew as the century progressed. Opaque glass beads (known as 'OP' beads) came in about 1850 and were the most popular beads thereafter. Coral was much used during the 1860's and 1870's and in the last two decades of the century beads were sometimes backed with metal foil to give a jewel-like appearance.

All kinds of whitework had improved in quality throughout the Victorian era. Tamboured work on muslin was perfectly suited for the dresses, caps and accessories of its earlier years. (In 1829 an Englishman, Charles Walker, introduced tamboured net to Ireland and established his business at Mount Kennet, near Limerick, beginning the evolution of Limerick lace.) Hand-worked whitework, with satin, stem and overcast stitches worked in sprig or spray floral motifs, was known throughout as 'sewed muslin'. Such hand-embroidery declined in popularity, however, partly because of competition from Berlin wool work and from the new 'machine'.

Between 1810 and 1823 a Frenchman named Drago had settled in Coggeshall, Essex, with his two daughters. He introduced the use of a particular kind of tamboured embroidery and established a workroom in his house near the river Blackwater. 'Coggeshall embroidery' reached its peak around 1851, by which time 385 out-workers were employed (in 1901 there were only 149 on the books). The Spurge brothers were in overall charge of production in the middle of the century, and the family kept the industry alive throughout its wane until in 1939 a final lack of materials killed it.

Coggeshall embroidery is recognisable by a tamboured design of trailing wild flowers or similar spray motif (bluebells, primroses and sheep's parsley were particularly popular) on a net or muslin ground.

In 1829 Henry Houldsworth of Manchester took out English patent rights on the machine invented by Josué Heilmann of Mulhouse (p. 102). Houldsworth worked with coloured threads and specialised at first in sprigged dress fabrics. In 1851 he showed 'quilts, table-covers, curtains, panels and medallions' at the Great Exhibition and in 1855 he invented the mechanism for machine-embroidering scalloped edges (a technique the Swiss did not develop for another decade). Houldsworth, in fact, had a monopoly of the English machine-embroidery industry until the 1870's.

The 1851 'Great Exhibition of the works of industry of all nations', presented by the Society of Arts under its President, Prince Albert, was held in the original Crystal Palace, in Hyde Park. It was the forerunner of many exhibitions which promoted, encouraged and displayed the embroidered arts of the time. Section XIX of the official catalogue offered:

C. Tamboured work.
D. Embroidery.   (i) Gold, silver, glass.
　　　　　　　　(ii) Silk for shawls, dresses, mantles, tablecovers.
　　　　　　　　(iii) Machine embroidery.

as well as three sections for industrial embroidery. There was only one American item exhibited ('The raising of Jairus' daughter', from Boston, Massachusetts).

About the time of the Great Exhibition, a white cutwork known as *broderie anglaise* (p. 378) first made its appearance. Designs were either geometric or floral, with rather solid little sprigs of cut-out petals and leaves bound in buttonhole stitch. It was confusingly to

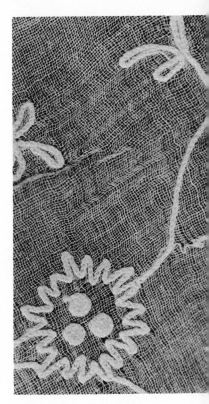

ENGLAND—*19th century—during the agricultural depressions of the middle of the century, Coggeshall embroidery, a tamboured whitework, was developed in Suffolk and Essex. Its attributes are flowing lines and patterns of local wild flowers.*
(City of Norwich Museums)

be known later as 'Madeira work' and was much quicker to work than the finer Scottish 'Ayrshire work'.

During the middle of the century, too, 'French embroidery' based on the needle-lace 'Point de France' (p. 400) and with designs similar to *broderie anglaise* but with the motifs heavily worked with padded satin stitch rather than being cut out, joined the whitework ranks, as

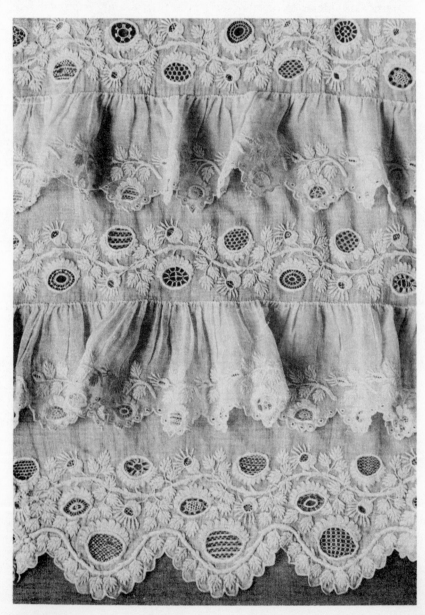

ENGLAND—*19th-century whitewaork on fine Indian muslin, showing a few of the many different in-filling stitches used, c. 1825. (Mrs. Marion Felix)*

did 'guipure work' (or 'Richelieu work'), a cutwork embroidery in which most of the ground was cut, leaving the pattern connected with narrow bars or 'brides'. 'Venetian embroidery', with particularly heavily padded satin stitching, gained its name from the former 'Point de Venise' needlepoint lace.

Dresses were sometimes decorated with coloured silk or metal thread work and later appliqué of ribbon work was utilised. Appliqué had previously been combined with Berlin woolwork and couched gold work, but was particularly dominant by itself during the 1850's and 1860's. Silk and velvet were often applied and the edges of the motifs were usually covered with beads or metal cord.

Metal thread embroidery had been used to great effect in such works as Princess Charlotte's wedding dress (1816), now in the London Museum. Silver spot motifs are worked all over the delicate low bodice and full skirt.

Embroidery of the 19th century ran the gamut from refinement to basic practicality. Smocking on rural shirts reached its peak about 1850. The basic cut of the Victorian smock was simple, with the fullness of the back and front of the garment held in place with 'tubing' of tight decorative stitching in rope stitch, basket stitch or chevron stitch. Smocks were usually worked in linen on a linen or twill 'drabette' ground, and designs were highly regionalised. Most shepherds wore blue smocks and best smocks throughout were usually white. In Essex and Cambridge, however, smocks were olive-green, in the Midlands a deep blue smock was known as the 'Newark frock', Dorset had a unique blue and white 'drab' smock and possibly the most beautiful examples of all were those from Sussex. Smocking designs were, also, often indicative of the wearer's profession— trade emblems might be embroidered on the 'box' either side of the main smocked 'tubing'. Motifs representing crooks and sheep-pens indicated a shepherd; a grave-digger generally sported crosses on his smock.

Rural smocking gradually died out with the influx of machines, but the skill reappeared for use in high fashion. In 1878 the first tennis dresses appeared with smocking decoration and shortly afterwards it was much used for tea-gowns, children's clothes and the like. It is thought that Oscar Wilde's mother had much to do with this adaptation of an essentially English 'peasant skill' and, certainly, smocking was to enjoy great popularity for many years.

Samplers throughout the Victorian era were much the same as in the 50 years before. There were only a few Berlin wool-work samplers, long and narrow and usually worked at first with wools, silks and beads on a fine single-thread white canvas ground. Later Berlin wool-work samplers were on a double-thread canvas with

10 squares to the inch, and designs throughout tended to be geometric and often of a highly three-dimensional affect.

The first aniline dyes (then called 'gas colours'), discovered and patented by Sir William Perkin in 1856, were manufactured in 1858 (Perkin's first dye was called 'Perkin's mauve' after the inventor). From this date, therefore, chemical dyes are to be found in all types of wool-work embroidery. Church embroidery, dormant since the Reformation, awoke from hibernation about 1835 (after the 1829 Catholic Emancipation Act, A. W. N. Pugin led a building pro-

ENGLAND—*19th-century hair portrait on silk of Heinrich Wilhelm Ernst (1814–65), worked by Miss Bernadine Gompertz, which was awarded a Bronze Medal in the Great Exhibition of 1851.*
(Whitworth Art Gallery, Manchester. Mrs. M. Meyers' Collection, 1934)

86

gramme which was to have much effect on church furnishings, and the Oxford Movement of the Church of England also stimulated a long-lasting interest in church arts). The Ladies Ecclesiastical Embroidery Society, founded in 1855, was only one group established to further church embroidery. Miss Street (whose brother, George Edmund Street, the architect, did some of the designing) and Miss Agnes Blencowe (her brother was actually in the Church) copied mediaeval motifs, floral, angelic or human. The Society amalgamated with the Wantage Church Needlework Association (of the Community of St. Mary the Virgin in Wantage) in 1863—the resultant collection has since been unavoidably scattered.

Pictorial embroideries continued to be popular. At the beginning of the 19th century 'printwork' had been highly fashionable. A monochrome embroidery, with copies of popular engravings copied in detail in silk on a taffeta ground, printwork maintained a following right through the century. The 1851 Exhibition included works by a Swiss artist, F. U. Tanner of Bühler, Appenzell, and from this time the name 'print work' gave way to 'etching embroidery' (it is interesting to note that contemporary American embroiderers, however, called similar work 'engraving embroidery').

'Camera work', another Victorian craze, originated about 1880 and consisted of ordinary photographs applied to cotton or linen ground and surrounded with an embroidered floral garland.

There was patchwork, but not on so wide a scale as in North America at the time. 'Appliqué patchwork', known as *broderie perse* or *cretonne appliqué*, dates from the time of the Exhibition. Motifs like birds and leaves were cut from printed cotton and applied to a plain ground of black, sewn on with buttonhole or overcast stitches. 'Mosaic patchwork', an inlay work with pictorial designs, enjoyed a short period of popularity at the same time.

'Japanese' or 'kaleidoscope' or 'crazy' patchwork originated in the last quarter of the 19th century, when everything 'in the Japanese manner' was very much in vogue (Thomas Jekyll had designed a hanging, embroidered by ladies from Norwich, for his 'Ironwork pavilion' at the Philadelphia Exhibition of 1876. This was one of the first embroideries described as being 'in the Japanese manner', and it was Japanese influence that introduced floss silk and oriental motifs into art needlework). Oriental traits were apparent not only in design but also in such features as voiding on some embroideries.

How did the Victorian embroiderers develop new skills and adapt patterns? In addition to the paper patterns and basic embroidery manuals, mid-century periodicals included such publications as *The Englishwoman's Domestic Magazine* and *The Young Ladies' Journal*. Vol. VIII, no. 371 (1871), of the latter magazine has, for example, two

ENGLAND—*printwork, 'A View on Windsor Forest', embroidered in shades of greys, blacks and browns. The oval picture measures 7 × 9 in. (18 × 23 cm).*
(Reproduced by gracious permission of Her Majesty the Queen)

88

ENGLAND—*19th-century polychrome silk on satin embroidery,
inscribed 'Ann Perry's Work 1820'. The funerary urn bears the
inscription 'To the Memory of/CAROLINE/of Brunswick/QUEEN/OF
ENGLAND'. The circular embroidery 14 in. (36 cm) diameter, is in an
$18\frac{1}{2} \times 18$ in. (47×45.5 cm) mount. It was a gift to the late Queen Mary
in 1950.*
(Reproduced by gracious permission of Her Majesty the Queen)

pages of detailed patterns for net embroidery, appliqué and guipure work.

The 19th century, too, was the era of the individual leaders of the embroidery world, of whom William Morris is foremost.

Morris (1834–96) met Edward Burne-Jones, Ruskin and such Pre-Raphaelite Brotherhood personalities as Rossetti and Millais when he was up at Oxford. After coming down he went to work for Street (the architect brother of the Ladies Ecclesiastical Society lady) and finally, in 1861, he and the group of friends he had gathered around him founded the firm of Morris, Marshall, Faulkner & Co.

Morris had been interested in embroidery since 1855 when, according to his wife Jane, he had an embroidery frame made to his own specifications. His first work was a repeating pattern hanging now at Kelmscott Manor, Lechlade. After their marriage in 1859, Morris taught Jane the art.

Besides Morris and his wife, the group included Burne-Jones, Philip Webb, Jane Morris's sister Elizabeth Burden, and the two Morris daughters, Jenny and May. Much of the embroidery attributed to the Morris School was in fact not the master's work. Burne-Jones designed the central figures and Dearle was chief of the designers who filled in the background.

The many Morris embroideries include the 'Red House series' (named after the house in which the Morris family lived from 1859 to 1865) and hangings such as 'Tulip and rose' and 'Vine and pink' designs.

One of the earliest ecclesiastical works was the altar frontal of Busbridge Church, Surrey. Morris sometimes sold the basic design with pattern already traced to canvas for the church worker to embroider himself.

It is, without doubt, for inspiration in design that Morris is chiefly remembered in the annals of the embroidered arts. The success of his designs depended on the skill of the executant, but Morris provided the incentive as well as the pattern. He infected the amateur needlewoman with his love of beauty through every facet of his life. It was Morris who first provided this degree of self-confidence to the ordinary embroiderer.

Through Morris came the terminology 'Art needlework', often misapplied but in fact indicative of the idea that art could be drawn with the needle and could be applied to all aspects of the home. 'Art needlework' or 'South Kensington needlework' (so called because of the part played by the South Kensington Museum, now the Victoria and Albert Museum) is usually associated with outline stitch in wool or silk on linen.

Another important movement in Victorian embroidery was the

POMONA

ENGLAND—*William Morris*—*Pomona, part of a full-length figure designed by E. Burne-Jones and background by H. Dearle, chief embroidery designer for Morris & Company. This is a copy of an original tapestry, 10 ft. × 7 ft. 6 in. (3 × 2·3 m), of 1891, first shown at the Chicago Exhibition in 1893. The original had a border inscription:*

> *I am the ancient apple green*
> *As once I was so am I now*
> *For evermore a hope unseen*
> *Betwixt the blossom and the*
> *   bough*
> *Ah! Where's the river's*
> *   hidden gold*
> *And where the windy grave*
> *   of Troy?*
> *Yet come I as I came of old*
> *From out the heat of*
> *   Summer's joy.*

This particular version, passed to the museum by the National Art Gallery, Wellington, is believed to have been worked by Lady Cory in 1907, and is the smallest of six panels.
(National Museum, Wellington, New Zealand)

Leek Embroidery Society, established in 1879 (although an 1873 altar frontal in St. Luke's Church in that Staffordshire town really signalled the conception of the society). The 'Leek Embroidery Society and School of Embroidery' was under the guidance of Elizabeth Wardle (1834–1902) who, after marrying her cousin Thomas (knighted in 1897 for his services to the silk industry) had 14 children and was for two years so ill that she could neither read nor write. She therefore learnt to embroider (William Morris was a friend of her husband). The Society was primarily important for its church embroideries, but it also sold designs, materials, silks and some completed domestic items. Leek embroidery is unique in that it was worked on a printed or brocaded ground with a beautiful colour scheme.

Elizabeth Wardle visited the South Kensington Museum in 1885 and was so impressed with the Bayeux Tapestry, exhibited there at that time, that she determined to copy it. Thirty-five ladies finished her facsimile by June 1886 and it was exhibited at the Nicolson Institute, Leek, with an admission fee of 1/–, from which a sum of £10 was raised. This copy, which has in its lifetime been shown to Queen Victoria, taken on two extensive British tours and cleaned twice, was last exhibited at Hastings in 1965.

Some overseas examples of more typical Leek embroidery can be seen in South Africa, in St. Mary's Church, Port Elizabeth, and in Grahamstown Cathedral. A 9 ft. (2·7 m) red altar frontal worked by Mrs. Warren, a member of the Society, for Zanzibar Cathedral is no longer in use as the Diocese of Zanzibar and Tanga has given up altar frontals. Mrs. Warren's son, the Reverend Hugh St. John Percy Warren, had worked at the Teachers' Training College in Zanzibar, hence the connexion. A similar frontal, which was sent to Lady Wingate in Khartoum in 1905, is currently being stored by His Grace the Bishop in Sudan. The former Anglican Cathedral of All Saints in Khartoum was recently incorporated into the grounds of the People's Palace, and the frontal, which had cost £21 when it was worked, has, alas, suffered some damage during the years.

The decline of production of Leek embroideries accelerated to some extent in 1902, when Lady Wardle sold her shop, a nucleus of the movement, to Mrs. Clara Bill. In 1930 Miss Sutton bought the premises and she, in turn, sold out to Miss Winnie Rawsthorne in 1937. The shop, in St. Edward Street, finally closed in 1939.

Another embroidery-oriented society was the Arts and Crafts Exhibition Society which strove, despite earlier fruitless efforts, to promote all decorative arts. Their 1888 Exhibition included embroideries by such artists as Lewis F. Day (1845–1910), a designer particularly associated with stained glass. Day, who came from

Peckham Rye, designed the floss-silk firescreen embroidered by his wife and exhibited in the Victoria and Albert's 'Exhibition of Victorian and Edwardian decorative arts' in 1952.

These, then, are some of the important names and bodies of embroidery of the Victorian era. The 19th century was prolific in different styles of embroidery, ranging from delicate to coarse, from sublime to ridiculous (there was, for example, 'écaille', quill embroidery, and some experimental work using human hair, butterfly wings and other exotica as embroidery media).

A somewhat freer style of embroidery developed at the end of the 19th century. The flowing lines of the Morris School had inspired artists to creative moving designs that had hitherto been denied the embroidered arts. Mary Newill (1860–1947), for example, was a follower of Burne-Jones and she in turn was the key figure in promoting early 20th-century embroideries in the Birmingham area.

One community of the time, the Fisherton-de-la-Mere Industry, was primarily concerned with whitework. Mrs. Arthur Newall took her first pupil in 1890 and the industry acquired its name when she moved to Fisherton-de-la-Mere in 1904. Mrs. Newall, who died in 1923, was influenced by Italian reticella embroidered work and she believed in starting her pupils with a simple pattern on linen ground and leaving them to continue, with infrequent criticism and advice from herself.

Important documentation of the early part of this century has been provided by Mrs. Archibald Christie. Her books, *Samplers and Stitches* and *English Mediaeval Embroidery*, are to some extent the authoritative tomes in this particular stage of embroidered history. Grace Christie was for many years in charge of embroidery at the Royal College of Art.

Mrs. Rebecca Crompton, one of whose best works is *The Creation of Flowers* (Victoria and Albert Museum), was similarly influential through her own embroideries, as was Louisa Pesel. Miss Pesel, sometime Director of the Royal Hellenic School of Needlework, returned to England and was commissioned to work a series of stitch samplers (now in the Victoria and Albert Museum) showing stitches used in early English embroideries. She was largely responsible for much of the ecclesiastical embroidery of the first part of this century. Amongst her many direct commissions she organised the making of four hundred kneelers, seat cushions and alms bags for Winchester Cathedral.

The low point of 20th-century embroidery has been, so far, the period of the Second World War and immediately thereafter. Materials were difficult to come by and, also, dressmaking and do-it-yourself were essential.

People generally had less leisure time in which to concentrate on the arts, although attention in Scotland was being given to embroidery by the Needlework Development Scheme (see p. 229).

In 1954 Olive Pass was instrumental in establishing 'Dorset feather stitchery' (p. 381), one of the few 'new' styles of embroidery to have appeared during the 20th century (though based on traditional stitches and motifs).

It is, however, really only in the last few years that a resurgence of involvement in embroidery has come about.

Where are the leaders of the English embroidery movement today? A few selected centres of influential creativity that are noteworthy to contemporary perspective include such bodies as 'The 62 Group', a select group of highly skilled embroiderers, men and women, who are all members of—though not necessarily connected with—the Embroiderers' Guild. 'The Textile Studio', in Beckenham, is another experimental group, founded in 1969. The memberships of the two bodies overlap, but fortunately embroidery in England has not reached the commercial need for self-preservation that it has in some other countries. Embroidery is still a friendly—and a positive—art form. Another group of enthusiasts is 'The New Embroidery Group', formed in 1968, which has regular working sessions (as does the Beckenham-based group). The Young Embroiderers Society, an offshoot of the Embroiderers' Guild, held its first and very successful exhibition in 1974.

It is probably safe to assert that today more people than ever before are involved in the embroidered arts. Specialist full-time and part-time courses are offered at many colleges and centres, some of the leaders in the field being Goldsmiths' College, the College of Fashion and Clothing Technology, and Manchester Polytechnic. Regular short-term courses are offered by the Embroiderers' Guild (founded in 1906) and the Royal School of Needlework. Residential courses are held in beautiful country houses such as West Dean College. Promotions by the National Federation of Women's Institutes, the Townswomen's Guilds, the Associated Country Women of the World, the Girl Guides Association and similar bodies help stimulate the individual embroiderer.

Embroidery in England is not perhaps recognised as the nervous and psychiatric therapy that it is in other parts of the western world. But it is, none the less, becoming increasingly popular with the busy Englishman and woman as a leisure time 'relaxer'. An unrivalled wealth of embroidery collections, both historic and geographic, Englishman and woman as a leisure time 'relaxer'.

Ethiopia

Ethiopia bears little embroidery relation to her neighbours in eastern Africa. Somalia, to her east, has no embroidery at all; there is little artistic interplay with Kenya, to the south; and motifs found in Ethiopia are dissimilar to the floral designs of the Sudan, to the north-west.

Foreign influence has probably been introduced mainly up the Nile, by the early Christians, and, more recently, through the trading centre of the French port of Djibouti. The Italian occupation of the country during the 1930's has left its mark on the arts of the country (as, for example, in rebellious interpolations depicting the occupying forces set into some of the grand frescoes decorating Ethiopian umbrella-shaped churches). Apart from some ecclesiastical robes, however, embroidery has retained its own geometric proportions and design.

Traditional dress of Ethiopian men consists of loose riding-breeches in white cotton with a toga (*shamma*) worn on top. At either end of the *shamma* is a woven band (*tibeb*, meaning 'art' or 'wisdom'), which frequently has embroidery superimposed in simple darning stitch. Women have similar *tibeb* bands around the hems of their very full white cotton skirts, with accompanying shawls (*netala*) which they shyly raise to their mouths when meeting strangers.

Shamma is an all-embracing term, generally used to denote any length of white openweave cotton with woven and embroidered motif bands. Frequently the cotton ground is of so poor a quality that it will not survive washing. Little such embroidery of any age, therefore, is found.

Apart from 'national dress', regionalised costumes feature printed textile design rather than embroidery. At the polyglot market in the walled city of Harar (about five miles from the little Italian hotel where Evelyn Waugh stayed when writing dispatches on the Italo-Abyssinian War and when collecting material for *Scoop*), the dress of the many unrelated groups who come to trade displays their scattered origin. Bold printed patterns abound throughout.

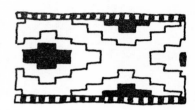

ETHIOPIA—*contemporary design motifs, embroidery superimposed on woven cotton* tibeb *borders. (Ethiopian Tourist Organisation)*

Finland

Embroidery of Finland has been most influenced by that of Sweden, evidence of the close association of the two countries being offered by the fact that since 1883 Swedish has been on equal footing with Finnish as the official language of the country and, today, over 7% of Finns still regard Swedish as their first language. With frontiers, also, with both Norway and the USSR (Russia was sovereign power as recently as 1917), additional inspiration is sometimes found from these areas too.

FINLAND—*19th-century* tykkimyssy, *an embroidered bonnet with lace trimming.*
(National Museum, Helsinki)

96

△ *CHINA – head of the dragon shown in black and white on p. 43.*
(Gawthorpe Hall, property of the National Trust)

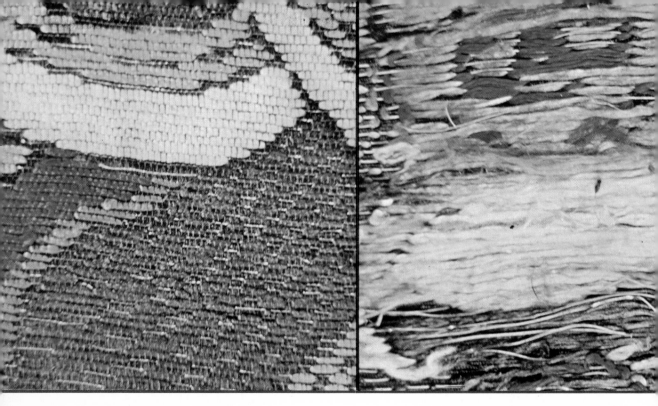

△ *CHINA – pattern darning, right side.*
(The Earl of Wemyss and March, KT)

△ *CHINA – pattern darning, reverse side.*
(The Earl of Wemyss and March, KT)

▽ *ENGLAND – canvas work, petit point with a count of 40 stitches to the inch, c. 1700. Also a detail of the same work.*
(Mrs Anna Younger)

There is a sizeable Lapp population in the north of Finland, and even today there is utilisation of tin or pewter thread embroidery. The traditional methods of 'Lapp tin thread work' are followed, as they are in Sweden. Hot strips of the required metal are pulled through the holes of *wortles*, reindeer horn gauges, to stretch the thread to the required size before coiling it around a cotton lining thread to form metal purl (or bullion).

As with other forms of Finnish applied arts, contemporary embroidery is colourful and design is often the predominant attribute. Both pulled and drawn thread work are particularly striking and delicate when executed by Finnish artists.

Wall-hangings are much in evidence. Appliqué, for example, is worked to feature a striking simplicity of outline with a combination of sophisticated balance. Karin Hellman's stitcheries portray a Picasso-like appearance which has an initial naïveté counterbalanced by exact proportion and use of space. Such apparently modern design, much admired in all Finnish products by visitors to Stockmanns and similar emporia in Helsinki and elsewhere, is in fact inherent in the country: until the middle of the 19th century, for example, married Finnish women wore neat little bonnets that were often highly embroidered in tamboured chain stitch to designs that were both flowing and freehand but, also, remarkably symmetrical and controlled.

France

Embroidery in France has a wide reputation of historical impact, in some instances possibly enhanced by mis-attribution of major works and schools.

Undoubtedly the most famous of all embroideries now in France, for instance, is the Bayeux 'tapestry', a misnomer since it is in fact an embroidery. Exact provenance of the work, to be seen in the Musée de la Reine Mathilde in Bayeux, Calvados, is in dispute. What is universally recognised today, however, is that it might have been worked in England. The 'tapestry' is here accorded a separate section (p. 329).

During the late 14th and 15th centuries, the House of Burgundy devoted particular patronage to all facets of the arts. Philip the Good, Duke from 1419 to 1467, founded the Order of the Golden Fleece to celebrate his marriage in 1429 to Isabella of Portugal. The famous 'Vestments of the Golden Fleece', known until 1477 as 'The Burgundy Mass Ornates', were probably used in the Duke's private Chapel. The entire set of vestments, now in the Treasury of the Hofburg Palace, Vienna, consists of two antependia, three copes, two dalmatics and a chasuble. The copes are each $51 \times 25\frac{1}{2}$ in. (130×64.5 cm), fastened with silver and enamel clasps. One antependium ($51 \times 18\frac{1}{2}$ in.—130×47 cm) has a central panel of St. Mary (Patron of the Order) with the baby Christ presenting St. Katherine with a holy ring. St. John the Baptist, holding the celebrated fleece of the Order, watches from the left. It is thought that perhaps the designer of both altar hangings was André Beauneveu, possibly advised by Jan van Eyck or his pupils. The oldest item connected with the Order's embroideries is the actual insignia, a golden fleece suspended from a collar of alternating flints and metal 'B' shapes, representative of the House of Burgundy. Attribution is further confirmed by the fact that one foreigner known to have been employed on the vestments, the Brussels *broderer* Jan van Maelborch, did also work in Dijon.

The Knights of the Order escorted Philip the Good's cortège in 1467. Burgundian art patronage continued for another decade: after the death of Charles the Bold in 1477, and that of his only daughter Mary in 1482, Burgundy passed to Mary's widower, a Hapsburg, and was added to the lands of that House.

Throughout the 15th century, too, Paris was an important centre of the embroidery world. From 1432 to 1434 it is known that Maître Thierry du Chastel, a leading artist, undertook many commissions (including several for Philip the Good).

It is difficult, in general, to dissociate the country of France from the city of Paris. The capital has, however, played a greater role in the nation's embroidery than has been the case in some other countries.

Anne of Brittany (1477–1514), queen to both Charles VIII and Louis XII, established a girls' school which taught needlework (Wilton, Countess of, *The Art of Needlework from the Earliest Times*, p. 379).

In 1551, Henry II and Catherine de Medici established 'L'atelier de la Trinité', for distressed children in the city. It was intended that pupils should be instructed in all types of textile arts: Catherine herself is known to have been particularly fascinated by silk embroidery and darned net embroidery. When she died in 1589 nearly a thousand squares of net embroidery (then known as *lacis* or *filet brodé*) were amongst her possessions.

The Cooper-Hewitt Museum of Decorative Arts in New York has a three-dimensional pictorial embroidery, $13\frac{1}{4} \times 11\frac{1}{4}$ in. (33 × 29 cm), that could possibly have been intended as a bookcover. It is dated 1525–50, and has coral beads embellishing a central oval in which a high-relief oak tree with metal trunk and silk lace leaves stands in front of a realistic landscape. At the foot of the tree is a salamander, the device of Francis I. Four serpents coil, one in each corner of the work. The embroidery is also exaggeratedly ornate, with maximum adornment of design and stitching achieved with no loss of uniformity or balance. For these reasons alone the work could, even without the distinguishing salamander, be ascribed only to French origin.

The period of *le grand siècle*, with Louis XIV, the glorious 'Sun King' (1638–1715), stimulating creative momentum throughout his long reign—he came to the throne when five years old—saw many changes in embroidery, as in all the arts of France.

Tambouring, the art of producing continuous chain-stitch embroidery, worked on a ground fabric stretched tightly over a circular frame similar in shape to the tambour drum, was introduced into France from China towards the end of the 17th century. It is suggested, indeed, that no less a person than Madame de Pompadour furthered the fashion for 'tambour work'. It was, certainly, an extremely lady-like attribute of the period, and for some time after, since embroidery worked exclusively in *point de chenette* (chain stitch) was to be particularly prevalent during the entire 18th century.

One important asset of the French embroiderer has always been

99

the interest and patronage extended to his art by royalty and other leaders. Louis XIV took a personal interest in the textile decoration at the forthcoming marriage, on 7th December 1697, of the young Princess of Savoy to his son the Duc de Bourgogne.

> He himself chose the design for the embroidery of the Princess. The embroiderer said he would leave all his other designs for that. The King would not permit this, but caused him to finish the work he had in hand, and to set himself afterwards to the other. (St. John, Bayle, *Memoirs of the Duc de St. Simon*, Batsford, 1964)

Metal thread work has played a vital role in French embroidery throughout the centuries. In 1973 there was an exhibition of early 18th-century purl work at Chez Victor Hugo in Paris. Worked about 1700, the five pieces, property of the Conservateurs de la Maison de Victor Hugo et de Hauteville House, showed a distinct oriental influence, introduced at the period of execution by increased trade with the East. Experts have in fact compared the actual designs of these hangings to those of Moghul empire works in India: there is similar work in the Guimet Museum which is dated early 18th-century, Indian. It is also suggested, however, that these panels had English association. One work contains the inscription 'Weston Favell 1698' and there is, still, a beautiful embroidered hanging, in excellent condition, in St. Peter's Church in Weston Favell, Northamptonshire. Victor Hugo and his wife are known to have spent five years in Jersey, in the Channel Islands, during their period of exile in the 1850's and 1860's, and it is possible the English embroidery is of the same school as those now in Hauteville House.

With overall backing of silver purl work, dominant colours in the five panels are brown and rust red. One work has a splendid rooster finding the proverbial egg at the bottom of a rather stiff and lifeless tree. It is a larger work, about 7 ft. 6 in. × 4 ft. (2·29 × 1·20 m) and rather immobile in composition. Another, more realistic, tree work has an eagle, wings outstretched, looking up from the ground to his eaglet perched, albeit somewhat precariously, on a branch with variegated russet leaves. The backing is similar silver purl, but with gold highlighting some of the foliage.

The largest, and perhaps the most alive, of the hangings has flowing lines and courageous composition. Two brace of pheasant intertwine around the base of the main tree, the leaves of which have been stylised to something rather like bats' wings. One male stands resplendent with his tail displayed, the other is more disarranged but none the less glorious with raised 'eyes' on the feathers. Raised zigzag, basket and other stitchery on feathers and ground leaves make

100

this work of particular interest. Some of the more realistic ground foliage has a russet carpet pile and there is superimposed gold purl to add highlights.

A delicate example of late 18th-century silk on silk embroidery is one isolated-spot motif work now in the Victoria and Albert Museum. The artist experimented with many different arrangements of floral sprays, each perfectly balanced and with a gentle curve to the stem. Perhaps she gained confidence as the embroidery neared completion: at the bottom of the panel is a row of grouped motifs

FRANCE—*late 18th-century white silk taffeta waistcoat embroidered in polychrome silks. The figures of Dido and Aeneas come from the opera by Piccini and Marmontel, produced in 1785. Dido herself is worked from a drawing by Gustave Moreau-le-Jeune for the costume worn by Mlle. de Saint-Huberty in the opera. Satin stitch, French knots and ribbon appliqué.*
(Cooper-Hewitt Museum of Decorative Arts and Design, New York. R. C. Greenleaf Collection)

associated with contemporary mourning embroideries. A memorial cupola, a tombstone, a garland entwined around a barren tree trunk, an elaborate garden grotto—all are finely worked.

It is possible to assert that the author of this dainty piece was a lady. Embroiderers of couture and other commercial works of the time were professional male artists. Ladies worked embroideries more suited to their status. They experimented, they sampled, they used their tambours, and later they were frequently to 'unravel', obtaining great pleasure from unpicking old embroideries as they sat visiting and conversing.

The first 90 years of the 19th century constituted an apogee of *haute couture* of the modern world. Paris was the hub of the continental changes and innovations that so excited and instructed the Beaux Brummells of western fashion. Following the Revolution of 1789, the experiments of the First Republic and of the Empire which followed it revitalised the inherent genius of French elegance. This was the time of long frock coats and of elaborate waistcoats. Of the latter, in particular, many fine examples are still to be found in major collections.

The Richard C. Greenleaf Collection, at the Cooper-Hewitt Museum of Decorative Arts in New York, includes several sophisticated silk brocade waistcoats with complicated silk and metal work embroidery, in panels to either side of the front opening and on the lower front diagonal pockets. Pocket buttons, too, were hand-stitched with painstaking care. Some items of the superb collection were included in the loan exhibition at the Victoria and Albert Museum in summer 1973.

There has been continual innovation in embroidery in France. It was, for example, a Frenchman who was initially responsible for machine embroidery.

In 1828 Josué Heilmann, a cotton manufacturer of Mulhouse, invented an embroidery machine which used double-ended needles with a hole in the centre. His first machine worked with 130 needles, all of which had to be individually threaded with short lengths of cotton thread. He could execute a simple sprig motif with a maximum width of an inch and a half (4 cm). The machine soon achieved recognition, and the following year it was awarded a medal by the Industrial Society of Mulhouse. Heilmann sold English patent rights to Henry Houldsworth of Manchester and Swiss rights to François Mange (who went on to initiate a prolific school of Swiss machine-embroidered whitework). Heilmann himself was awarded the Légion d'Honneur at the Paris Exhibition.

The growth of machine embroidery continued at a prodigious rate. In 1830 Barthélemy Thimonnier of Paris took out patent rights for a

102

chain-stitch machine which used a hooked needle similar to a hand-held tambour needle.

From this time on, indeed, much of the embroidery of France was worked on machines. But, as with all facets of the country's culture, French machine embroidery attained—and maintained—perfection in design and execution.

Machine embroidery was used specifically for the fine bed and domestic linens and for other forms of household embellishment. It was used, too, for basic dress embroidery, with repeating motifs on silk and satin grounds worked in floral or other designs to give greater luxury to the couture fabric. Such embroidery was generally white-work, or a polychrome work with convivial colour combinations.

Not all whitework was machine embroidered with *point de chenette* or general satin stitching. Particularly around the middle of the 19th century some whitework was carried out in a handwork padded satin stitch, similar to *broderie anglaise* in design but with petals finished with filling stitches (as opposed to the cutwork embellishment of the English counterpart).

In the 19th century, French samplers showed close relationship to similar works from Italy or the Benelux countries. They were usually square, worked in cross stitch and with a border around all four sides. Typical European motifs, such as religious symbols or a verse surrounded by a scroll, were popular.

Characteristically, however, French styles usually aid identification. The Whitman Sampler Collection of the Philadelphia Museum of Art includes a mid-century sample, 18 × 22 in. (46 × 56 cm), with cross and tent stitch in silk and wool on canvas. There is an elaborate leafy border all around. Across the centre of the panel three squat two-storey French houses, of the latest type found in the main square of any prosperous provincial town, stand amid trees. In front the family, with papa in his top hat utterly dominated by a gigantic mama in flowing crinoline and sheltering under her frilly parasol, stand admiring the view. The artist in this case doubtless furthered the cause of the matriarchal role: all the females of the group she portrays are exaggerated beyond the proportion of the rest of the work.

A similar leafy border, worked on two sides only, is found on Miete Cheilan's signed sampler (1847) in the Victoria and Albert Museum. Mlle. Cheilan's design, however, was less of a caricature and more experimental in involvement. She features alphabetical exercise, religious motifs (including a central altar) and a rather unnatural vase of flowers.

Some weird and extraordinary media were utilised during the 19th century by embroiderers with imagination and intuition. The

103

collection of the Smithsonian Institution in Washington DC, for example, includes an early 19th-century French dress belonging to Maria Hester Monroe Gouverneur, daughter of President Monroe (1758–1831). It was embroidered with straw, long stems of which were thoroughly soaked and, when pliable, were worked to naturalistic patterning in satin stitch and stem stitch.

In common with their English Victorian cousins, French 19th-century embroiderers experimented, too, with combinations of hair and silk embroidery, with much ribbon decoration and beadwork. They were not afraid to innovate to the extreme and generally, in the case of a French artist, the idea worked, although it can of course be argued that what did *not* work was usually destroyed before exposure to the general public.

In retrospect, therefore, embroidery in Paris and, to a lesser extent, in France continued to be influential throughout the 19th century. In all aspects of stitched textiles, exponents throughout the western world looked to their French colleagues for inspiration and theme.

In domestic embroidery, as in couture, French embroiderers took a lead. Why then did they later fall back?

The movement of 'Art needlework' was to some extent responsible. William Morris, with his involvement in the general arts world in England, was instrumental in taking the baton of leadership across the Channel. The concurrent troubles on the home front, with the 1870 Siege of Paris, resulted in an isolation of the French embroidered arts. And, in common with other countries with industrial potential, the onset of the machine age discouraged embroidery activity.

Not enough is known, alas, of outstanding individual embroidery designers of the last century. Hector Guimard, for example, an architect and leader of the general Art Nouveau movement, ignored his devotion to embroidery in his own writings. He went to painstaking lengths to promote his architectural conceptions in such works as *Le Castel Béranger* (Librarie Rouam et Cie, Paris 1898), but of his embroidery designs he made no mention.

An exhibition of the work of Guimard was held in the Museum of Modern Art in New York in 1972. After her husband's death, Mme. Guimard presented some of his work to the Cooper-Union Museum (now the Cooper-Hewitt Museum of Decorative Arts). Many of the embroideries were in fact executed by a leading contemporary couturier, Drécole.

Some of the innovations of French embroiderers are still apparent today. Some stitches are in general use: 'Basque stitch', for example, is a scroll stitch with prominent decorative merits, and 'barrier stitch', coincidentally similar to the Yugoslav 'Bosnia stitch', is equally effective.

During the last 300 years or so, too, French lace has frequently been in contest with embroidery in the field of superlative couture adornment. Laces such as Alençon, Calais and Point de France have been much used, and attained a justifiable fame. In some cases they have indeed been adapted to embroidery designs. Modern lace production at Calais today includes much machine-worked net embroidery, for example. One typical sample is a border net,

FRANCE—*early 20th century, part of a white silk collar designed by the architect Hector Guimard for his bride's wedding coat. Guimard was a leader in the Art Nouveau movement and is described as being 'dedicated to the creation of embroidered arts'.*
(Cooper-Hewitt Museum of Decorative Arts and Design. Mme. Guimard Collection)

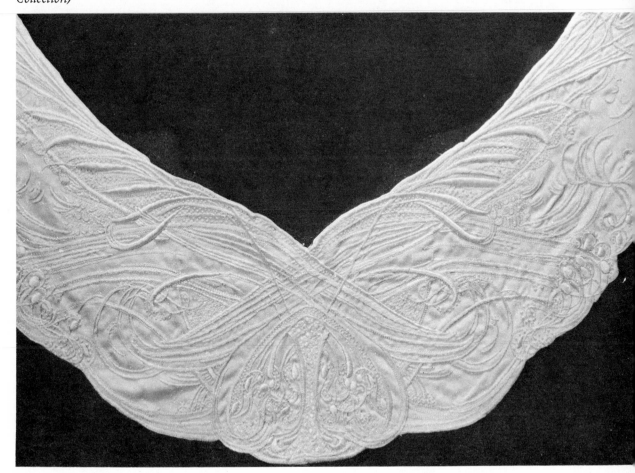

diamond-meshed with knotted junctions, with superimposed thick satin-stitched lily-of-the-valley sprig motifs.

One of the leading manufacturers of modern practical embroidery is the House of Pourthault, a family firm which designs and executes exquisite linens for customers around the world. Many of their delicate items feature machine or hand embroidery.

FRANCE—*contemporary scene 'The Port' embroidered by Felicia at her summer home on the Riviera. The artist started her own works after visiting Bayeux in 1967.*
(The artist)

There are still little 'embroidery houses' scattered throughout most of the *arrondissements* of central Paris. Listing of such establishments is to be found in that useful professional guide, *Bottin*. In some cases, however, the embroidery enthusiast should be wary: the *brodeur* may have moved, he may simply be concerned primarily with dress embellishment or, possibly, his *atelier* may be on the seventh floor of an inaccessible 'walk-up': it is, in fact, necessary to set aside some time when searching for one of those unrivalled embroidery specialists of whom the enthusiast has often dreamed.

From a more positive point of view, however, current French publishing devotes much attention to the embroidery arts. As well as the supreme example of the expansion of embroidery interest stimulated by the Dollfus-Mieg et Cie organisation of Mulhouse, arts organisations in general frequently cover stitched textiles. General and specialist arts magazines and newspapers offer news of creative embroidery as well as stitchery ideas for the practical follower. Embroidery collections in Paris include those of the Musée des Arts Décoratifs (retrospective collection of French embroideries from the 16th century to the present day), the Musée de Cluny (with a collection that includes some stylised 14th-century leopards *passant* on a millefleur ground in Room III, possibly a work of English origin), Musée de Costume and Musée de l'Homme (ethnographic collections from Greece, Italy, Portugal, Afghanistan, Nepal and Iran). Prices of available embroidery lots in the famous Marché aux Puces ('Flea Market') have, alas, escalated recently.

Germany

The Federal Republic of Germany and the German Democratic Republic, with their adherence to western and eastern Europe respectively, have only been separated since 1945 and, accordingly, their historical embroidery can plausibly be taken as one.

With a history of wars and disunity and the regrettable ravaging of many of her arts during the present century, few early German religious embroideries now survive. One example of German-produced ecclesiastical embellishment, now in the Museum of Fine Arts, Boston, is an early 13th-century mitre, $8\frac{7}{8} \times 11$ in. (23 × 28 cm), formerly from the Church of St. Peter in Salzburg. It is a rich work, on a ground of oriental silk. Two eight-pointed star motifs are applied, one to either side of the main panel.

During the 14th century there was a fluidity to some embroidery that was soon to be supressed by a manifestation of forcefulness typical of many other facets of German art. A simple silk on linen panel, for example, in the collection of the Cooper-Hewitt Museum of Decorative Arts, New York, shows the Crucifixion with surrounding scroll of trefoiled foliage and a dragon in each corner. It is, admittedly, unsophisticated both in design and approach, although it has humanity. A contemporary work probably worked by nuns and typical of north German embroideries from Westphalia, is the panel now in the Victoria and Albert Museum. It is an intricate and beautiful work, indicative of the skill of German needle artists.

Throughout the centuries, the tablecloth has been of great importance to the German family. As the household congregated for meals, the table around which they gathered held considerable import, and the cloth was often elaborately embroidered. (The importance of the tablecloth has, indeed, remained to the present time, and many current German embroiderers feel that table-linen embroidery is a satisfactory challenge to their skills.)

In the Victoria and Albert Museum there is a very large linen cloth dated 1585 with overall polychrome silk embroidery in tent stitch and long-legged cross stitch. In the centre of the work there is a quotation. Stitching is intricate but rather unbalanced. Close up the effect is not typical of much of the detailed workmanship usually seen in German embroidery.

GERMANY—*14th century, silk on linen embroidery.*
(Cooper-Hewitt Museum of Decorative Arts and Design. Elizabeth
Haynes Collection)

GERMANY—*part of a late 14th-century cover from Westphalia, typical of north German work of that time. Linen on linen with chain and braid stitch, 10 × 3 ft. (3 × 0.9 m). The main panels show the Visitation and the Coronation of the Virgin. Few examples of mediaeval ecclesiastical embroidery of this quality have survived as they were less prized than their more elaborate silk and gold counterparts. Such linen work was probably embroidered by nuns, and collections can be seen today at Kloster Wienhausen and Kloster Lüne. (The Victoria and Albert Museum, Crown Copyright)*

Some early 16th-century German embroidery is somewhat heavier in appearance than, say, contemporary Italian work. Both design, with unrelated religious and secular motifs utilising most of the ground fabric, and execution showed a frequent imbalance with too little thought given to planning.

In south Germany was worked metal thread embroidery couched in particularly distinctive circular whorls, an example of which is the altar frontal in the Marienkirche in Lübeck. It, too, is rather a heavy work, similar to the set of vestments now in Blairs College, Aberdeen, sometimes attributed to Mary, Queen of Scots but, more probably, of southern German origin.

Embroidery throughout the country has traditionally been organised rather than creative and experimental. The artist has often preferred to work to printed patterns, taking pleasure from the technical skill necessary for exact representation.

In 1604 Johann Sibmacher of Nürnberg published *Schön neues Modelbuch*, a work particularly instrumental in offering motif ideas. Similar publications followed, both in Germany and elsewhere in Europe. Design towards the end of the 17th century, for example, was influenced by Rosina Furst's *Modelbuch*, also from Nürnberg.

Since the middle of the previous century, Dresden had been a major centre of lace production. In the latter part of the 17th century the city evolved a fine pulled thread whitework similar in delicacy and realistic patterning to contemporary Danish Tønder work. Dresden work was used primarily for clothing decoration, and for embellishment of some exquisite whitework samplers, examples of which are to be seen at the Whitworth Art Gallery, Manchester, and in many other museums. The execution of this style of embroidery became very popular throughout the western world: it was, for instance, announced in Boston, Massachusetts, that schools of needlework were, in 1771, including it in their regular curricula.

The earliest dated European sampler was 1618. Throughout the 17th century, German samplers were often exaggeratedly rectangular. The Victoria and Albert Museum has one border sampler, date 1681, linen on a linen ground, that is $44 \times 9\frac{1}{2}$ in. (112×24 cm). It is a messy work, with little coordination to each band of embroidery, and the artist possibly possessed more technical than artistic expertise.

Another sampler in the same museum, however, portrays quite an advanced degree of designing skill. Worked in 1661, the 37×11 in. (94×28 cm) embroidery, silks on a linen ground, has complex outline block motifs worked within the confines of borders of varying widths. It is a fine example of the diversity to be found throughout embroidery. Another sampler, 1688, has the entire $23\frac{1}{4} \times 9$ in.

(59 × 22·5 cm) ground filled with exact block working of cross stitch, long-legged cross stitch, rococo stitch, Algerian eye stitch, satin stitch, tent stitch and eyelet holes.

Also representative of the fine embroidery of the 17th century are some of the *Paradenhandtücher* (show towels), elaborately embroidered and worked as coverings for the practical towels that were actually used. Embroidery decoration on *Paradenhandtücher* was frequently more or less identical to that worked on samplers, and examples are to be found today, particularly in areas of Pennsylvania, USA, and other regions with past German immigration.

In the second half of the 17th century, exaggerated sampler proportions were becoming somewhat less extreme. The Whitman Sampler Collection of the Philadelphia Museum of Art has one piece, dated 1663, which is $9\frac{3}{4} \times 6\frac{1}{8}$ in. (24·5 × 15·5 cm), silk on a linen ground. All-over spot motifs show a certain naïveté, with corresponding immaturity on the part of the designer, attributes shared by early 18th-century square samplers to be found in some museums today. Possibly the smaller sizing was indicative of sampler instruction in educational needlework: it would, after all, have been economical to give pupils a small square of fabric on which to embroider their sampling stitches and motifs.

The same heavy quality that has been noted in earlier German works pervades embroidery during the 18th and 19th centuries. This characteristic is exemplified by a $10\frac{1}{2} \times 10\frac{3}{4}$ in. (26·5 × 27·5 cm) sampler of the 1880's, silk on a wool ground. The overall cross stitching is worked in narrow border bands, in various alphabetical letterings and in complex motif forms of a tower with surrounding foliage, memorial plinth with garlands, lovebirds and an unseaworthy-looking ship. The work (now in the Victoria and Albert Museum) is, throughout, solid and earthy.

At the beginning of the 19th century one German initiated a style of embroidery, 'Berlin wool work', that was to become universally popular for many decades. Herr Philipson was a print seller in Berlin. In 1804 (according to the Countess of Wilton's *Art of Needlework*, 1840) or 1805 (according to Miss Lambert's *Handbook of Needlework*, 1843) he published some hand-coloured needlework designs on squared paper. His patterns were easier to follow than earlier monochrome designs, a comprehensible advantage to any embroiderer.

Within a year Herr Philipson's original designs were available generally throughout western Europe. Other entrepreneurs entered production. A leading publisher was L. W. Wittich, whose wife was herself an accomplished needlewoman; doubtless she suggested ideas.

'Berlin wool work' is a canvas-work embroidery, generally cross

112

or tent stitch, with clearly outlined motifs representative of the emotional and rather brash outlook of the arts of the time. Many designs are floral, with elaborate arrangements of flowers sometimes embellished with beading. Others are highly stylised pictorial scenes of historical events. And some are frankly sentimental, showing favourite lap-dogs on soft plush cushions. Most of the work was executed in wool, although sometimes silk and chenille were used. 'Zephyr yarn' (known as 'Berlin wool' in England) came from merino sheep in Saxony. It was spun in Gotha and dyed in Berlin.

The early 19th century was a time of some leisure. It was customary for affluent ladies of the western world to sit after dinner, and embroider as they conversed. Interest in 'Berlin wool work' continued to expand. By 1840 it was estimated there were over 1,400 different copper-plate designs on the market. Paper patterns and necessary materials from Berlin were challenged by those from Paris, but the embroidery was known throughout as 'Berlin wool work'.

The disturbances of 1848, with revolutions in many parts of Europe, possibly heralded the demise of this style of embroidery (contrary to supposition, the Crimean War would not have had direct effects on its decline in popularity as there was no German participation in the war). The Franco-Prussian War of 1870 and the concurrent advance of industrialisation in most countries of Europe further helped to bring about the downfall of 'Berlin wool work' production.

Embroidery in Western Germany today is largely confined to production of household items, some machine embroidered, others worked by hand. It is still a houseproud nation and, accordingly, the tablecloth and other decorative and practical works are much sought after. The tradition continues, therefore, of organised execution and technical skill taking pride of place over creativity.

Greece

The complicated history of Greece over the last millenium is echoed in the international influences to be found in her arts today. Influences from Byzantium, for example, introduced during her hegemony, show motifs such as the rose with serrated leaf. Oriental themes from Persia, with the 'Tree of Life' and that exotic flower, the carnation, have been introduced via the Turks, who bordered Persia and controlled Greece during the 15th to 19th centuries.

From the west, Frankish occupation by former and would-be crusaders from France, England and Germany occurred during the 13th to 15th centuries. Some of the Greek islands were particularly affected by homeward-bound Orders: Rhodes, for example, was under the sway of the Knights of St. John until they were expelled by the Turks in 1523 and beat a subsequent retreat to Malta. Venice, in particular, and to a lesser extent Genoa, disputed control of the islands with, in succession, Byzantines, Franks and Turks during the same period. And the spiritual empire of the Greek Orthodox Church continued to pervade the country even while both Greece and the 'Great Church' in Constantinople lay under Turkish rule.

This diversity of influence is typified by a cushion from Athens now in the University of Aberdeen, Marischal College, Anthropological Museum. It shows a squat 'Buddha-like' figure sitting cross-legged, surrounded by floral patterns worked in Romanian stitch.

Although cross stitch dominates throughout much of Greek embroidery, there are some unique forms of stitching. Astypalea, for example, has a threaded chevron stitch, worked in two stages, (p. 354). Rhodes has given its name to a step stitch (p. 438), and Crete to Cretan feather stitch (p. 370). Some pulled thread work is found on household linens and similar items, worked with a single or double faggot stitch (the design motif is sometimes left clear with surrounding background embroidery).

'Patiti stitch' (pattern darning) is found on examples like a beautiful early 18th-century hanging, in red silks on natural linen, now in the Whitworth Art Gallery, Manchester. There is some fine appliqué work, with edges of the applied motifs turned under before stitching, and in Macedonia tent stitch is sometimes worked with alternate horizontal rows facing diagonally to the left and to the right, a form of stitchery known as 'Macedonian stitch'.

114

Jannina, capital of Epirus, on the north-western mainland, was one of the most important international trade centres of the 17th to 19th centuries. Embroidery from this area was particularly prolific.

'Jannina work' shows certain Albanian attributes. The famous Ali Pasha, who held imposing court at the end of the 18th and beginning of the 19th centuries, was in fact an Albanian Moslem from Tebeleni and he recruited a band of Skipetars from Albania. Jannina embroidery shows much floral decoration, with the rose, the tulip and the hyacinth, and often with a vase of flowers worked diagonally in each of the four corners, with herringbone stitch and pattern darning.

Greek island embroidery dates mainly from the 17th century, although there are a few references to embroidery worked before that, and, with close connexions to the silk industry, it may be assumed that embroidered decoration did exist. Embroidery of the islands is practical work, made for the home. It is often highly individualistic, indicative of the independence of each insular community, and the most frequently used stitches are cross stitch, satin

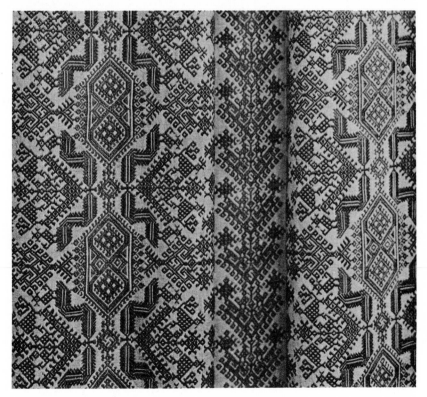

GREECE—*detail of bed-curtain, Melos, Cyclades, 18th century. Pattern darning in red silk on linen ground, 'Queen pattern'. (Whitworth Art Gallery, Manchester. Professor P. E. Newberry Collection)*

115

stitch, chain stitch, herringbone stitch and some Cretan feather stitching.

In the islands nearest the Turkish mainland, the Dodecanese and Rhodes, fine linen embroidery features particularly apparent Turkish design influence. Hexagonal and diamond border motifs, often incorporating small animals in the design, are indicative of Anatolian carpet patternings. Four of the principal Dodecanese designs, named by A. J. B. Wace in 1935 (*Mediterranean and Near Eastern Embroideries*), are the 'king design' (known also as *platyphyllenio*, 'the broad leaf'), with pairs of leaves coming off a central stalk at an angle of 45°; 'queen design' (known also as *kladhi*, 'branches', or *spitha*, 'spark'), a filled diamond motif; 'glastra design', a medallion with Tree of Life derivation; and *dixos*, a usually lozenge-shaped abstract pattern.

In Rhodes, the direction of cross stitching is important: cross-direction is not uniform and an apparently haphazard arrangement of direction is in fact designed to govern resultant patterning.

Crete, on the main Mediterranean trading routes, shows particularly strong Italian influence in her embroidery, exemplified by flowing and balanced Renaissance lines and, also, by 'gorgona', a double-tailed mermaid design, a motif which originated in Scylla with a woman's torso with double fish tail and dogs sprouting from her shoulders and waist. The design was a Venetian introduction to Crete. Motifs throughout, too, show oriental influence, with the Tree of Life design sometimes being featured as a large vase of flowers between a small pair of birds. The carnation occurs, as does the double-headed Byzantine eagle. Cretan embroidery is generally polychrome, although some monochrome work is found in dark red or dark blue silk, and some of the best examples are on skirt borders.

Mount Athos, a peninsula in north-east Greece which has nevertheless to be reached by boat, was established in 963 as an isolated monastic community, eventually with many national groups forming an exclusively male stronghold of various Eastern Orthodox religious orders. Priceless art treasures were brought by novices from all parts of the Eastern Christian world, many of which are still to be seen in the enclave, guarded by the sadly depleted ranks of the monks, for some communities are, indeed, now completely deserted and others are manned by only a few very old brothers.

Possibly some of the most outstanding 'art' embroideries of historical Greece are those worked, and signed, by religious artists themselves. Such an artist was the famous late 16th-century monk-embroiderer Arsenios, whose works are characterised by a symmetrical and classical composition with a resultant flat effect, by precise and detailed execution of workmanship, by lack of floral

116

ornament and by the bright reds and greens he frequently used. One of his masterpieces is the 'Epitaphios', $53\frac{1}{2} \times 63\frac{3}{4}$ in. (1·36 × 1·62 m), a gold thread embroidery inscribed 'at the expense and with the labour of the monk Sophronios of the Meteora in the year 7096' (i.e. 1587–8). It now hangs in the monastery of St. Nikanor at Zavorda in Macedonia. Evangelists, prophets, hosts of angels, with the sun, moon, stars and other cosmic symbols, illustrate the Ascension of the central figure of Christ. There is a noticeable and paradoxical feeling of glory and sorrow in the emotions displayed.

Some Greek metal thread embroidery can be identified by the fact that the gold or silver thread is worked right through the ground fabric (the more usual way is to lay the metal thread on the surface and couch it). Working metal thread right through the fabric does in fact often split the ground and this is one way of establishing Greek workmanship, although the same method has also been employed by Turkish artists.

Metal thread work has long played an important role in Greek embroidery. During the years of Turkish domination there were *Isnafia Syrmakesides*, gold embroiderers' guilds, with branches in Thessalonika, Jannina and elsewhere, fulfilling most ecclesiastical orders. It has been a tradition, too, for rich men's daughters to have gold-embroidered items in their trousseaux, sometimes with matching sets of embroidered quilts, covers and pillows. Gold thread embroidery during the 19th century included such items as ladies' fashionable short jackets and tasselled velvet berets, both items lavishly decorated.

In the Ionian islands, especially in Levkas, there are to be found today some of the finest contemporary cross-stitch embroideries. A typical feature of much Greek embroidery during the last three centuries has been the artist's fanatical desire to leave no clear spaces of ground, an attribute that is today being modified to conserve the time taken with each item. Much of the more beautiful work produced today is in decoration of blouses and other costume.

Traditional dress throughout Greece has understandably always been regionalised. In general, costumes from the lower valley areas have featured more embroidery than those of mountainous regions. General use of costumes declined during the 19th century, although the enthusiasm and interest of some individual patrons did infuse a certain resuscitating spirit into embroidery of Attica and other areas in an effort to keep the industry alive.

With a flourishing tourist trade, Greek embroiderers today are fully aware of the commercial value of their art. Bodies such as the National Welfare Organisation encourage and promote embroidery as a cottage industry. They develop new designs based on the arts and past motifs of the country, and produce large items such as canvas-work rugs and cushions, and miniatures such as detailed pictures of local flowers and birds. The National Organisation of Hellenic Handicrafts, too, has good material on different embroidery techniques.

One important promotional aspect of contemporary Greek embroidery is that her leading dress designers do incorporate the beauty of the art into regular collections. Yannis Travassaros, for instance, often includes exquisite embroidered panels and borders in his clothes. In his 1973 collection he showed a particularly stunning dress with front yoke panel, and matching handbag, made from fragments of *sperveri*, elaborately embroidered bridal bed curtains from the Cyclades and Dodecanese.

Hawaii

Hawaii became a full state of the USA in 1959. The islands' particular embroidery panache is in the field of quilting, and Hawaiian quilts are, to this day, easily distinguishable from contemporary work from other parts of the United States.

It is recorded that on 3rd April 1820 the American Board of Missions held its first sewing circle in Hawaii under the patronage of the dowager Queen, Kalakua. Needlework was not inherent in the culture of the islands: in common with other Polynesian peoples, Hawaiians had traditionally used as bedding layers of coarse pandanu leaf matting spread straight on to the floor: the higher the rank of the occupant, the finer the texture and the higher the pile of mats. Hawaiian embroidery can, therefore, be directly traced to that first sewing circle. Local women were obviously apt pupils. Lydia Brown, who came from New Hampshire in 1836 to teach the domestic sciences, noted that her students adopted needle and thread 'with surprising aptitude'.

By 1858, quilt-making had gained enough status for a prize example to be presented to the newly born heir of King Kamehameha IV and Queen Emma. Because there was no heritage of rag-bags in the islands, the development of quilts could not rely on utilisation of left-over scraps of fabric and, therefore, the mid-19th-century quilts began to acquire the flowing lines of bigger applied motifs with which they are today associated.

Hawaiian quilts are appliqué, with superimposition of one elaborate motif on to the main ground. Design is taken from the natural life of the islands. Breadfruit, pumpkins, paw-paws, figs and ferns, shapes of coral and outlines of turtles and octopuses, all appear frequently. The appliqué design is generally first drawn on a folded triangle of paper and opened out to form a template pattern, although some brave artists prefer to cut the fabric direct. Materials used include calico, percale and muslin and, after the motif has been applied to the ground, running-stitch quilting is worked in simple formations such as basic diagonals or, sometimes, spaced outlining, known as *luma-lau* ('wave-quilting').

Colour of the quilts is coordinated with design. A waterfall at Hanalei Bay (called '*No Molokama*') has been adapted into a graceful green-on-white applied motif: another green-on-white design is

'*Pahapaha o polihale*' ('seaweed at Kauai'). Some of the more famous red-on-white colour combinations originally portrayed rain on the individual islands: a stream on Waikiki, long since dried up, was first used as motif at the turn of the century for what is today known as '*Lihiwai o hanaha*' ('banks of a rippling brook').

Hawaiian quilting was a highly regimented pastime. It was forbidden for anyone but the artist to sit on a work as it was being stitched, and plagiarism of design was frowned on, and traditionally denounced in public songs at the next *luau* (gathering).

Queen Liliuokalani toured the islands shortly after her accession and a special quilt design, known as '*Ula hua i ka hapapa*', was evolved in her honour. She was later held captive in her royal palace, into which confinement she was voluntarily accompanied by a group of ladies who occupied their long period of enforced leisure by quilting.

Although Hawaiian quilts are associated primarily with two-colour flowing applied works, there were some exceptions. In 1893, for example, there was limited production of 'Union Jack' or '*Kuu hae aloha*' ('my love') quilts, with polychrome appliqué. The stimulus to the making of these quilts was the fact that at that time the 'Stars and Stripes' replaced the 'Union Jack', which had been incorporated in 1816 into the Hawaiian national flag. Intense adherence to the former flag prompted its incorporation on to quilts, worked more from a patriotic than a practical purpose since such quilts were seldom used.

Quilt-making is continued today. Sponsored classes are held in Honolulu and the work of individual artists is much encouraged. Mrs. Mealie Kalama, for instance, is one artist who both works herself and teaches traditional skills. Sometimes, however, contemporary quilting veers away from the main theme. Stephanie Cyr held a one-man exhibition at the Honolulu Academy of Arts in 1972 which included items featuring coordination of modern semi-abstract design with traditional local quilting styles.

HAWAII—*this 'Union Jack' quilt dates from 1893 when, for a short time, the 'Stars and Stripes' replaced the 'Union Jack' which had been incorporated in 1816 into the national flag of Hawaii (together with horizontal lines representing the eight islands of the group). Affection for the 'Union Jack' and intense patriotism and sorrow at its disappearance from their flag prompted the making of these particular quilts. (American Museum in Britain, no. 72.161)*

HAWAII—*typical 'Breadfruit' quilt design, yellow cotton appliqué on red ground.*
(Honolulu Academy of Arts, Hawaii)

Hong Kong

Hong Kong, a Crown Colony, consists of a number of islands and mainland territory bordering with China. Although Hong Kong is a truly international entrepôt, her arts are understandably inextricably associated with those of China.

Corollaries of the more general art connexions have been details such as production of minute embroidered buttons used on clothing, and quilting, purely practical in colder parts of China but, in Hong Kong, primarily as decoration.

There is today a prolific embroidery output catering for a ready modern market. Traditional forms of the art, too, are continued. An extravaganza of silk and metal thread, further embellished with sequins and beads, is worked in exotic decoration of ladies' robes (*cheong sam*), with full-length straight skirt and high-necked long-sleeved jacket with mandarin collar. Hong Kong is one of the increasingly rare caches of available talent and labour, both invaluable commodities that are utilised to maximum advantage.

Embroidery is worked on main panels of *mae dai* haversack-type papoose carriers in which the baby sits suspended from his carrier's shoulders. In Hong Kong, too, costumes for miniature Cantonese rod puppets are still often elaborately embroidered, with super-imposition of sequins, fur and tassel trimming.

The colony can in fact plausibly be described as one vast studio into which the foreign embroidery enthusiast will be warmly welcomed. Many of the embroidery concerns will undertake commissions, both personal or by mail order, and execute individually decorated wedding dresses, pictures, banners, altar cloths or whatever the patron requires. Most embroidery 'factories'—an exaggeration since in most cases the artist is a member of a small family business—turn out regular supplies of their items, either from designs of previous embroideries or worked from paper patterns, the outlines of which are pricked through to the ground fabric. Types of embroidery worked by such commercial organisations include basic silk satin-stitching, canvas work, cutwork, smocking, Assisi work, drawn thread work, quilting and appliqué.

An enthusiasm for the needle is nurtured at an early age. All primary and secondary school children have the art in their regular curricula. British-type General Certificate of Education 'A' Level Art includes an optional paper on embroidery: the 1975 regulations stipulate that the candidate may be expected to write for one hour on such diverse topics as couching, Italian quilting, needle-weaving and Assisi work. She is also expected to produce, within the remaining three hours of the examination, an actual piece of work, with suitable annotation.

The collection of embroidery at the City Museum and Art Gallery includes several Chinese coats and gowns of late Ch'ing Period (19th century). Two have *p'u-tzu* (p. 45) on both front and back. Embroideries from China are today imported continuously, especially after the biennial Canton Trade Fair. Old and new items, in the forms of panels, cloths or clothing, are on sale in most of the large Chinese department stores in Victoria. Many of the embroideries worked in outlying villages of Hong Kong are also available in the city, in the central Taipo market.

HONG KONG—*traditional design: detail of an altar frontal, 1973.*

124

Hungary

Towards the end of the 19th century 'Hungarian embroidery' usually implied appliqué of linen and other twill-weave fabrics, particularly in relation to covering household furniture. How this association evolved is uncertain.

Appliqué undoubtedly does constitute an important chapter of the embroidered arts of the country. It is bold in design and generally consists of felt, leather or heavy wool—or combination of these media—both for applied pieces and for ground. Appliqué is traditionally a man's craft and design features a correspondingly strong and forceful element.

Gay and colourful regional costumes, with exaggerated short full skirts, puffy white blouses and head garlands or caps, show more affinity to Romania than elsewhere. Traditional costume to the east often includes a small black cotton apron with concentrated satin-stitch embroidery panels around the bottom and sides, with repeating pattern of flower heads bordered to either side.

Hungarian colouring is red (in the artistic rather than the political sense). A typical traditional cottage at Mezokövesd, for example, has deep scarlet dominant colouring on the decorative plates hanging on the wall, as ground to printed fabric covering all bed linen and pillows, on the regional costume of the women—and in the embroidered bands of a table cloth.

There is, alas, a growing partiality to printed decoration. As so often happens, embroidery is therefore in a decline. This is a tragedy as Magyar design, in particular, with its elegant yet naïve floral shapes, is amongst the most attractive in Europe.

HUNGARY—*appliqué motif worked by a male embroiderer, red leather on natural coloured felt.*

125

Iceland

Although the Greeks and Romans long suspected that a land they called 'Ultima Thule' existed to the north-west of the British Isles, it is thought that the first visitors may have been Irish monks and hermits in the 8th century. The first settlers as such were the Norsemen, Ingòlfur Arnarson and his foster-brother Hjörleifur, who arrived about 871, and within the next few decades most of the island was ceded to various of their family and friends. Most of the original settlers were Norwegian, many of whom fled their homeland to escape the oppressive rule of King Harald Fairhair, and since Norsemen had already settled in parts of the British Isles and the Faroes, it is reasonable to assume that they also travelled on to Iceland from these points, bringing with them local wives and slaves. Some independent settlers, too, came from Scotland and Ireland.

From 1380 to the beginning of the 20th century, Iceland was under Danish rule (and a comprehensive collection of historical Icelandic embroidery is to be seen in the Nationalmuseet of Copenhagen). The island suffered considerably, particularly during the 16th and 17th centuries, at the hands of Spanish, English and Barbary pirates, and overall foreign effects on her arts, therefore, were varied.

Christianity was adopted in Iceland in the year 1000 and the first bishopric was established at Skàlholt in 1056. The Reformation came to the country in 1550, when Bishop Jón Arason of Hólar was beheaded without trial. Since that date the state church has been Lutheran.

Until the middle of the 16th century, church works such as altar frontals and antependia constituted the major part of the country's embroidered arts. Embroidery in general has been much favoured by Icelanders. With long and dark winters, creativity has been outstanding and production prolific in many fields of art.

ICELAND—*15th-century wool embroidery, 38 × 32½ in. (96 × 82 cm). Purchased by the owners from private sources in Westphalia, in 1933 or 1934, it is believed this embroidery was worked in Muli, in Suour-Pingey County, near Grenjaoarstaour. From the type of collar worn by the figure of God the Father, it appears that the work is after 1485. (Rijksmuseum Twenthe Enschede, Netherlands)*

126

127

One of the main facets of traditional Icelandic embroidery was *refilsaumur*, a laid and couched work with vertical and superimposed horizontal stitches couched. The term *refilsaumur* was used only after 1550, although the embroidery had been worked long before that time. It was generally in wool, with some blue or white linen and gold embroidery (*gullsaumur*). An altar frontal couched in this way is today to be seen in the Rijksmuseum Twenthe Enschede, Netherlands.

The National Museum in Rejkavik has an antependium of similar age, 3 ft. 3 in. × 6 ft. (99 × 182·5 cm), which shows three bishops, Gudmundur Arason (1160–1237), Jon Ogmundsson (1052–1121) and Thorladur Thorhallsson (1133–93), flanked by two angels with censers. All five frontal figures have their heads slightly at an angle. Hands are, in general, the dominating feature, set in bold relief against the dark embroidery of the bishops' 'Early English' chasubles and the angels' full-length robes. Wool, linen and metal threads have been worked in laid and couched work on an unbleached ground. The antependium came from the cathedral at Hólar, a church with other significance to embroidery. A 17th-century lady, Ragnheidur Jónsdóttir, was married in turn to two of the Bishops—the See was of course Lutheran after the 1550 execution of Bishop Arason—and she was known to have been active as a teacher and donor of embroideries. The National Museum has an altar frontal inscribed 'Ragneidur Ionsdotter 1694' that she presented to Laufas Church in memory of her mother. The work is $38\frac{1}{2} \times 49$ in. (98 × 124 cm) and is worked in *glitsaumur* (darning stitch) and Florentine stitch.

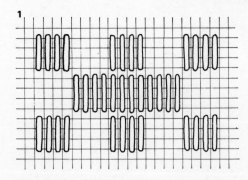 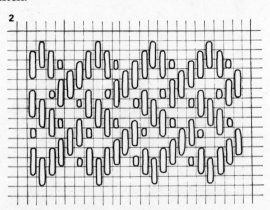

ICELAND—*diagrams of* glitsaumur *(figure 1) and* skakkaglit *(figure 2). See p. 130.*
(Reproduced by kind permission of the Needle and Bobbin Club, New York)

△ ENGLAND – late 16th-century forehead cloth, silk and gold on linen.
(City of Norwich Museums)

▽ ENGLAND – detail of late 18th-century embroidered picture, darning stitch, fine silk on silk.
(City of Norwich)

△ *ENGLAND* – *"Dido", a collage embroidery, worked with hand and machine stitching, by Richard Box, 1973.*
(The artist)

▽ *FRANCE* – *18th-century* – *gold perlé and silk on silk waistcoat.*
(Mrs Marion Felix)

ICELAND—*a typical feature of much Icelandic embroidery is the roundel (or hexagon or octagon) border framing each individual motif, as evidenced by this 15th-century antependium from Reykjavik. (Nationalmuseet, Copenhagen)*

Darning stitch embroidery has been worked from the 14th century, although the generic term *glitsaumur*, or '*glit* embroidery', was not in use until the mid-16th century. *Glitsaumur* today refers to square or rectangular blocks of pattern darning (fig. 1, p. 128), while *skakkaglit* (fig. 2), or slanting darning, implies diagonal blocks of pattern darning. Outstanding examples of *glit* embroidery include 17th- and 18th-century bed-hangings and valances, again with design motifs enclosed in geometric borders. Design shapes such as roundels, hexagons and octagons have, indeed, long been utilised in Icelandic embroidery as individual frames to biblical, saintly and human representations and natural motifs.

Krossaumur (cross stitch) was similarly brought into regular embroidery usage at the time of the Reformation of 1550. Coverlets of long-legged cross stitch, with additional eye stitch (*augnasaumur*) and other embroidery, were worked, particularly in the 17th century, with complicated figurative and geometric designs, each motif typically enclosed in its own border frame. One of the most famous examples of such a coverlet is the so-called '*Riddarateppid*' ('The coverlet of the knights'), in the National Museum, which has six motifs of mounted dignitaries in various garbs and an equal number of motifs of deer with flowering trees. The art of *krossaumur* has, today, evolved into what is known as *fléttusaumur*, or braid stitch.

Although 14th- and 15th-century church inventories did sometimes refer to *skorningur*, a term which might possibly have implied applied work, one of the earliest surviving examples of appliqué is an altar frontal, $38 \times 32\frac{1}{2}$ in. (96×82 cm), in the National Museum, which is thought to be early 16th century. In the 17th century there was much floral embroidery, *blómstursaumur*, worked with split stitch, stem stitch, long and short stitch and French knots. It was in general production until the 19th century and the term, as such, has come today to mean any split stitch embroidery.

Surviving Icelandic samplers are mainly of the 19th century, and mostly worked to designs popular throughout the western world. Stitches frequently used in sampler embroidery included cross stitch, darning stitch, Florentine stitch, stem stitch, satin stitch, buttonhole stitch and running stitch. Nineteenth-century regional costumes provided additional sampler grounds with the use of much delicate floral, silk and metal thread work on a dark ground.

Iceland's history of prolific embroidery continues, today, to fascinate students of the art. There is, for example, the definition of *sprang*, a type of embroidery mentioned in church inventories from 1318 onwards. Although it is suggested that *sprang* and *glit* are synonymous, separate references exist to both. By the 17th century, *sprang* certainly implied lacis or needle lace, and it may be that

130

earlier work of the same name covered any form of cutwork or whitework, few examples of the latter of which survive.

The history of Icelandic embroidery has been catalogued by Elsa Gudjónsson, and the best retrospective collection is in the National Museum at Reykjavik.

India, Pakistan and Bangladesh

It is impossible to divide the embroideries of the Indian sub-continent into what are, today, the political regions of India, Pakistan and Bangladesh. The arts have long been dominated by centres whose influences cross national barriers. It is therefore more accurate to look at the embroideries of the three countries under the artistic titling of 'The Indian sub-continent'.

By the time the first Portuguese traders arrived in the continent in the 15th century there was already a considerable Indian export trade of bedspreads and other embroideries. In 1603 that famed embroidery lady, Bess of Hardwick, signed an inventory of her household goods which included 'A quilt of yellowe India stuffe imbroidered with birds and beastes and white silk frenge and tassells, lined with yellowe sarcenet' (Victoria and Albert Museum, *Indian Embroidery*, 1951, p. 5). Embroidery workshops (*kharkhanas*) had been established in the country towards the end of the 16th century.

There are even earlier records of embroidery. At the Ajanta cave temples in Maharashtra, dating from the 6th century, there are embroidered costumes in the fresco designs. And the Venetian Marco Polo, writing in the 13th century, said of the city of Gujerat, 'embroidery is here performed with more delicacy than in any other part of the world.'

It is really from the middle of the 17th century, however, that the influence of Indian embroidery has been felt throughout the world. From 1650 on the East India Company was sending regular bulk shipments of chintzes and embroideries to England. And materials would be sent back, in return, to be embroidered in India for re-export to the western world.

There was some Portuguese and British influence in Indian embroidery from the 17th century and, also, some design ideas were carried from Italy to Portugal and thence to the sub-continent.

Dacca and Delhi were particularly noted centres of the embroidery market. In 1774 Abbé de Guyon noted that the best Indian embroideries in gold, silver and silk came from Delhi. It was the centre of the *choga*, the long-sleeved overcoat in cashmere, wool or satin, embroidered in gold, silver or silk. The older works have darn stitch panels. Newer works are couched with a chain loop.

Other older embroideries from Delhi feature a heavy ground, such

132

as velvet. Later embroideries have a finer ground (Dacca *muré*, cashmere, net) and brighter colours for the embroidery. Particularly fine pictorial silk embroidery from Delhi can still be found: the best pieces often have a luxurious red ground and all work is technically extremely fine.

One of the most outstanding of all embroideries from the Indian sub-continent is the 'Kurukshetra' hanging, a battle-action work that has something in common with the Bayeux Tapestry and other *tjells*. The subject matter is a recreation of the Kurukshetra battle in 3102 BC between the Kauravas and the Pandavas. Embroidered towards the end of the 17th century, the work was hung in the Raja's Palace at Chamba and presented to the Victoria and Albert Museum

INDIA—detail of the 17th-century 'Kurukshetra' hanging, depicting the Kurukshetra Battle of 3102 BC between the Kauravas and the Pandavas. Floss silk on cotton, 2 ft. 6 in. × 32 ft. 8 in. (0·76 × 9·9 m). (The Victoria and Albert Museum, Crown Copyright)

by Raja Gopal Singh in 1883. On a cotton ground, the polychrome floss-silk embroidery is primarily in satin stitch.

Collectors may at first have difficulty in distinguishing embroidery that comes from the sub-continent from imitations thereof that have gleaned ideas from the native original. There is in all facets of Indian art throughout the ages a distinct predilection for identification of man and life with nature, and this element of 'nature-identification' becomes more obvious to the practised eye. There is, throughout, a noticeably Persian influence in much Indian work, reflecting the origins of the Moghul empire.

Indian metal work, for example, is overall heavier and less flowing than that from China. Sequins are frequently incorporated into the design and there are palmettes in evidence.

The gold embroiderers (*zar-doz*) of India have traditionally featured the following stitches:

chain stitch (Kathiawar and, particularly, Bhuj, capital of Kutch)
couching
cross stitch (Sind)
cushion stitch
double chain stitch (Baluchistan)
Japanese stem stitch
knotted stitch
mirror work (Sind, Kathiawar and Kutch)
network stitches (Hyderabad and Madras)
split stitch
stem stitch
tambour work.

Traditionally much embroidery has been a male skill. Women did work the Punjabi *phulkaris*, the Bengali *kanthas* and tribal embroideries from the west and south-west of the country. But the really advanced embroidery—the Kashmir shawls, the elaborate metal embroideries of gold and silver wire, whitework, delicate tambouring—all these were male prerogatives (and, in fact, this division of labour still to some extent holds today).

Another traditional statement that still applies is that in Indian embroidery the needle is always pulled *away* from the embroiderer.

Whitework in the Indian sub-continent is principally *chikan* work, on muslin. Stitches used include the *bukhia*, an inverted satin stitch which is formed into knots, *katao*, a fine appliqué work, and *jali*, an open fret (drawn work) embroidery worked with fine buttonhole stitch. Worked with a cotton yarn and, sometimes, some yellow *muga* silk to relieve the colour monotony, the pattern was generally pre-printed. *Chikan* work originated in East Bengal and spread to

134

Lucknow in the early 19th century. This city—with Madras and Calcutta—is the centre of the art.

In the Moslem areas of East Bengal, particularly in Jessore, Khulna, Faridpur and Mymensingh, there have long been *kanthas* (*kantha* means 'rag'). Their forerunner was the *sanghati*, the patched robe of Buddha. Odd left-over scraps of cotton or remains, possibly, of the white saris of the Bengali women, were elaborately pieced together to the required size. Subsequent embroidery could have been worked with threads taken from those same saris.

A *kantha* is recognisable by the usual dark blue outlining of designs, with filling stitches of either the same or contrasting colour —all primary colours being popular. Back stitch is used for continuous lines and other stitching divides these quilts into three different groups. They can be worked with a much smaller running stitch, giving an overall dotted appearance. They can have close parallel lines of running stitch, giving a lined appearance. Or they can have running stitch worked into triangles, squares and other basic geometric designs.

'The vision of the embroiderer, which is spontaneous and primitive, is steeped in the tradition of India' (Kramrisch, Dr. Stella, *Kanthas of Bengal*, published by Mārg, Bombay, p. 21), and the artist portrayed the life around him, giving each motif traditional Indian grace. *Kantha* design was permeated by symbolism and association— the shape of the pattern, the triple shape found throughout (for example, three flowers on one stalk, three prongs to a trident and so on) and with much interlacing of motifs. It meant much to the artist. There is the lotus flower (always eight-petalled in Indian art) and the Tree of Life. And the massive cone shape or palmette (*kulka*, originally from Persia). Alas, no *kantha* examples earlier than the 19th century now survive.

The 18th- and 19th-century *rumal* embroideries from the Chamba district of the Punjabi hills are more sophisticated than the *kantha*. Whereas the *kantha*'s design is frequently conceived by the embroiderer as he works, the *rumal* is pre-designed and worked to a standard pattern. *Rumals* are coverings or hangings. They can be larger but are generally confined to a square with sides of 2 ft. (61 cm) or less and they are most commonly used for covering dishes of food to be offered to visitors. There is often an overall pictorial design in double satin stitch, silk on muslin. The style and subject matter of a *rumal* is similar to that of Pahari painting of the period. Traditional Chamba embroidery is always so neat on the reverse side that the work has a two-sided effect. And it was traditional, too, that a *rumal* was sent to a bridegroom as an indication of his future wife's domestic skill.

135

Silk on muslin is a textile combination found frequently in embroideries from the Indian sub-continent. S. A. Caulfeild, in 1887, referred to various Dacca muslins known as 'Evening Dew, Running Water and Woven Air' (*Encyclopaedia of Victorian Needlework*, p. 267). For many centuries Indian muslin has been far renowned.

Another Moslem area, Sind (Hyderabad, Karachi, Rohri, Shikarpur), has produced marvellous silk, gold and silver embroideries on grounds of silk, velvet, cotton or wool and with a dominance of geometric shapes to the design. Sind has some cross-stitch work and it is, also, a leading centre of mirror work (*shishadar*).

'Shisha' embroidery, as it is known today, is produced also in areas around Kathiawar and Kutch. It is worked with a border of strong cotton or silk holding down a mirror shape.

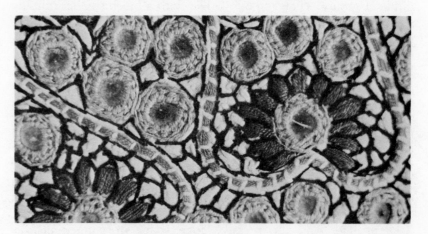

PAKISTAN—*detail of mirror embroidery with shisha stitch holding the glass in place. (Carla Hunt)*

Gujerat, another embroidery centre, has works that are distinguishable by their characteristic floral design, multi-coloured silk with predominant blues and reds.

In Peshawar and throughout the higher altitudes of the north, *sozni* work is found. *Sozni* quilts are usually made of several layers of cotton cloth (sometimes padded with cotton scrap) and stitched mainly with outline work such as back stitch and running stitch. The *sozni* stitch, accordingly, consists of rope-like threads, generally of silk, running in lines.

Kasida embroideries can be found from Dacca. These are distinguishable by all darn stitching and (in later works) some chain stitching.

Karnatak Kashida, from the former province of the 'Carnatic' and South India, is based on double running stitch. The embroideries, which include many traditional and symbolic patterns, look the same on both sides.

136

INDIA—*late 17th- or early 18th-century embroidery, chain stitch,
possibly to an imported western design. This 'export' embroidery, from
Gujerat, was worked for an eventual European market.
(Cooper-Hewitt Museum of Decorative Arts and Design, New York.
Au Panier Fleuri Fund)*

Phulkari ('flower work') has given its name, too, to a basic stitch, alternatively known as reverse darning stitch.

The best *phulkaris* come from the Indo-Aryan tribes of the Jāt people of the south-east Punjab, centring in Rohtak, Hissar, Gurgāon and Delhi. There are three basic kinds of *phulkari*:

1. All-over spot motif embroidery on *chaddars* (women's head veiling) or skirts. These are what are generally referred to by the term '*phulkari* work'.
2. *Kadr* covers, with a plain centre and embroidered border. These covers technically are known as *chobes* or *chops*.
3. 'Garden' *phulkaris* (*baghs*), with a connecting all-over pattern, generally worked in one colour only, embroidered by Moslem embroiderers in the Hazāra district.

Mirror work is often included in *phulkari* work and this is then known as *shishadar phulkari*. As well as the main *phulkari* stitch, stitches used include running stitch, satin stitch and herringbone stitch. And a *phulkari* can be recognised, too, by the floss-silk work on cotton ground (frequently the fabric is dyed indigo) and by the overall soft satiny effect of the stitching.

Quality in *phulkaris* is judged by the smoothness and regularity of stitching on the reverse side, by the pattern (the more simple and geometric the pattern, the older is the work) and by colour (ideally a *phulkari* should be worked in two colours only).

A particularly fine collection of *phulkari* work was that of Mrs. F. A. Steel, who wrote about her pieces in *The Journal of Indian Art* in 1888. It has not yet been possible to trace what happened to the Steel collection.

The term 'Indo-Portuguese' embroidery* (first referred to about 1870) is somewhat ambiguous. On the one hand it refers to embroidery worked in India under Portuguese influence. On the other, to Indian-style embroidery worked in Portugal. This latter section is extended, too, to include work in India produced by immigrant Portuguese and that produced by Indians under Portuguese patronage. The distinction can be drawn that work done in India is decidedly more artistic, more graceful, than that worked 'back home' in Portugal. See also section on Portugal.

This classification problem can be illustrated by the fact that

---

* 'Anglo-Indian' embroidery, it should be noted, was a 19th-century craze in Britain. Woven patterns on silk or furnishing fabrics and brocades were outlined and embroidered in crewel stitch, hem stitch, long and short stitch, French knots and couched work. It was also done on cheap Indian cotton handkerchiefs, lined with linen and then stitched to the woven pattern. This field of embroidery in no way enters the domain of embroidery of India.

the Metropolitan Museum of Art has changed titling as follows:

1. A 17th-century cape, quilted and embroidered with chain-stitched hunting scenes, silks on linen, has been changed from Indo-Portuguese to Indian (no. 23.203.1).
2. An 18th-century quilted white cloth, polychrome silks on cotton, chain-stitch floral embroidery, has been changed from Indo-Portuguese to Portuguese (no. 08.62.1).

With the arrival of the Portuguese traders, Indian embroidery began to adopt some Christian shapes and symbols in its design. Contemporary Portuguese records show that the Jesuit missionaries of that time were eager to welcome converted Hindu artists and craftsmen to their midst. But they were insistent that those converts break with their original Hindu traditional motifs. (John Irwin, in *The Burlington Magazine*, December 1955, tells the warning story of one of Vasco da Gama's sailors in India who thought he was worshipping a statue of the Virgin Mary—only to find it was in fact an image of the Hindu goddess Durga!)

The convert brought to western design his own inherent standard and skill. Bengal had been famous for bedspreads and hangings long before the Portuguese arrived. But Irwin dates the period of the particularly well-known *tussur* silk quilts from 1570 to 1650 (the Portuguese actually established their first settlements in the continent in 1537–8).

Tussur is silk from the cocoon of the wild silkworm *Antheraea paphia*, though legend had it that it was spun from a herb. When, from the 1680's on, it was regularly exported to England it was, in fact, known as '*tussur* or *herba*'.

Tussur quilts are sometimes labelled Goanese, but they are in all probability from Bengal. Irwin states that the quilt designs show them to have been worked in an area (such as Bengal) where embroidery was already practised, that they show traces of Vaishnava symbolism which precludes Goanese influence, and that *tussur* is only known to have been utilised in Bengal.

The quilts are recognisable by the yellow monochrome silk (sometimes faded to a brownish fawn) and by the invariably overall quality of the needlework. Stitching is chain stitch on a coarse cotton or jute ground, with back-stitch quilting. Average size is 9 ft. × 10 ft. 6 in. (2·74 × 3·20 m) and there are sometimes fringes and tassels. There may, too, be some appliqué.

Design is pictorial, with motifs gleaned both from Indian and European inspiration, including contemporary Iberian art. Motifs are stylised to the extent that their western template is often barely apparent.

139

In Kashmir there are shawls. The best, manufactured from the 16th century onwards, are of Tibetan goat hair. Sheep wool or common goat hair are also much used. Kashmiri looms were narrow so that, unlike the shawls of Norwich, Paisley and Paris, the twill-weave shawls were pieced. Embroidered shawls are called *amlikars* and were originally the poor man's substitute for the rich man's richly woven shawl. The older the shawl, the more simple the pattern (and, generally, only darning stitch—worked along the weft threads—was used). In later shawls there is tamboured chain stitch.

In the middle of the 19th century a variation of the cone design was presented in the form of pictorial designs. One particularly attractive example is the shawl in the Victoria and Albert Museum with a detailed city map of Srinagar, dated about 1870. It is suggested that this work was commissioned by the Maharajah of Kashmir, who was later, through financial difficulties, forced to sell it. On a cream ground, with patches around the edges, the all-over design shows city life. There is a company of soldiers, a walled cemetery complete with Moslem graves, a shepherd with his flock in a grove. The river Jhelum meanders across the embroidery. Fish swim and men row and birds fly overhead. Around the patched border of the whole work stands a series of young men, each in his own archway. The reverse side of this work is rough and obviously not meant to be on show.

One item fairly accessible to the would-be collector is the contemporary *namda* rug. Dating no further back than the last hundred years, most on sale today are very recent. They are not expensive to buy and, while of some interest to a decorating taste, are of no real collection value. *Namdas*—which are generally oblong but can be oval or round—are chain-stitched wool or wool felt and are from Kashmir. Silk on wool carpets from the same region are called *gabhas*.

Other embroideries to look out for include:

Chaupar boards—looking rather like ludo boards, and often embroidered.

INDIA—*map of Srinagar, c. 1870, possibly commissioned by the Maharajah of Kashmir. The catalogue of the 1902–3 Delhi Exhibition refers to a map of this city worked to a design 'as it stood in the time of Maharajah Sir Ranbir Singh GCSI, by whose order the shawl was made . . . designed for presentation to HM the King Emperor, then Prince of Wales'; it is possible this was the work. Sir George Birdwood (Indian Industrial Arts, p. 367 or 281) describes His Majesty being presented with such an embroidered map.*
(The Victoria and Albert Museum, Crown Copyright)

141

Koran covers from Hyderabad (all-over floral motif from Karachi).

Bengali *azamgani*—floral repeat-motif belts, some of which were shown in the Exhibition of Indian Art in Delhi in 1911 and which are no longer manufactured.

(Madras has produced some specialist beetle-wing embroidery!)

Glossary of embroidery terms for the Indian sub-continent

Ari—tambour hook

Azamgani—embroidered belts

Bagh—'garden' *phulkari*

Bukhia—inverted satin stitch, the 'shadow work' of *chikan* work

Chaddar—woman's head veil

Chaupur—Gujerat board game (also called *pachisi*), rather like ludo, sometimes reproduced in needlework

Chikan work—cotton embroidery on white muslin

Chobes
Chops } —cover with embroidered border

Choga—long-sleeved coat

Eri—one of the three main silks of India

Gabhas—silk on wool carpets

Jali—open-fret *chikan* work

Kalka—massive cone, palmette motif

Kantha—'rag work'

Kashida—embroidering with silk thread

Katao—fine appliqué work

Koran—holy Moslem book

Mochi—tamboured work, done with *ari*

Moonga
Muga } —one of the three main types of silk, a naturally bright colour

Nakli—'imitation' or drawn *chikan* work

Namda—wool on felted wool carpet

Phulkari—'flower work' embroidery of the Punjab

Rumal—coverlet

Sanghati—patched robe of Buddha

Shisha—mirror

Shishadar—mirrorwork

Sozni—quilts

Tussur silk—one of the three main types of silk, in a natural dull straw colour

Zar-doz—embroiderer working in heavy gold thread or wire

Zar-do-zi—embroidery in heavy gold thread or wire.

Iran

Iran, for long called Persia by the western world, takes great pride in her imperial past. Since before 500 BC her dynasties have for long periods ruled much of the known world of the times. The Achaemenians were overthrown by Alexander in 330 BC and the later Parthian culture (from the 2nd century BC to the 3rd century AD) successfully competed with Rome for dominance in western Asia. The Parthians were in turn followed by the Sassanids, all-powerful for four centuries from 224 until the tide of Islam swept them away in 642, to introduce what has been the apogee of Persian arts.

It is the dominance of Moslem heritage, admittedly interrupted by incursions of Mongols and Timur Lang ('Tamburlaine'), that has provided the major stimulus to the art of Iran for more than one thousand years, a heritage which continues today. Current population figures indicate a majority of Shi'a Moslems with minority, but often influential, groupings of Sunni Moslems, Jews, Bahais, Zoroastrians and Armenian and other Christians.

It has been forbidden under most Moslem doctrines to portray living things, and illumination has therefore utilised every conceivable and almost inconceivable variation of representation of non-living forms. Calligraphy has entered into all facets of Persian art, as is evidenced by the fine mosaic quotations from the Koran, the holy book, to be found in many of the mosques in Isfahan and throughout the country today.

Persian artists have for centuries produced exquisite and finely detailed miniatures and, on the reverse side of the coin, they have been equally unrivalled in their building of massive complexes of mosques and schools, embellished with fine decoration of brick and tilework completing the perfectly proportioned basic architecture. The decorative genius has been adapted to the medium, and embroidery has been but one of its manifestations.

It has been suggested that Persian influence is apparent in early Egyptian textiles (being shown in features such as swollen heads of men and animals). It is definitely known that regular trading routes were open through such Persian centres as Qum and Mashed. And as the merchants plied back and forth between Europe, North Africa and Asia they carried with them exchange of art forms. The *simurgh*

143

motif, for example, featuring an inventive hybrid of peacock and dragon, is found, though slightly altered in tone, in the arts of Byzantine and Islamic cultures.

In the main, embroidered art forms have always tended to travel from east to west. The *kulka*, the Persian palm-leaf, or palmette, motif, certainly followed the sun, from Persia to other parts of the Middle East, to south-eastern Europe and thence along the main trading routes to western Europe, to England and, with the first colonial settlers, to the New World.

One of the most copied oriental motifs has been the 'Tree of Life', a representation that has been utilised in embroideries in all parts of the world, particularly in the field of crewel and wool work. The twisting trunk of the Tree gives way to many branches, again with graceful curves to the lines and with a pleasing overall shape.

Sometimes the Tree rises from an earthly base, known in embroidery terminology as a *'terra firma* mound'.

Textiles of the Safavids (1500–1736) are today generally best known for their superb weaving, but some of the designs that permeated through to the West, such as the 'Tree of Life', were none the less equally applicable to embroidery. Designs of symmetrically paired animals, sometimes separated by 'the Tree', were popular in England, for instance, from the beginning of the 17th century. This

IRAN—*hand-embroidered whitework, cotton on cotton, Isfahan, early 20th century. Motif and detail. (Miss A. F. C. Williams)*

east–west progression of embroidery ideas was to continue: during the 19th century a Mr. Sepon Bezirdjian produced a portfolio of nearly a hundred different patterns for decorative needlework. He was himself responsible for introducing this publication to Europe.

Much 19th-century embroidery was brought back to the West by travellers from their Grand Tours. Examples are thus often to be found in Britain today in museum collections. The Whitworth Art Gallery in Manchester has one marvellous embroidery with arch-surround (the *mihrab* shape found in Islamic mosques and on carpets), presented by Sir Thomas Wardle, husband of the patron of the Leek Embroidery Society (p. 92). In such collections, be they in museums or in private homes, wall-hangings (*fallaks*) dominate, utilised by some western recipients as piano covers, table cloths and bedspreads.

This was a period of western fascination with anything oriental (a mystique that is apparent even today): there was, for example, a craze for *broderie perse*, a collage of applied patterned chintz fragments (p. 321), popular with some genteel European and American embroiderers.

From the 17th to 19th centuries, around Gonbad, in the east of the country, there was a delicate silk embroidery, called *kashedah*. The main centre of production was Kakhk, and the embroidery was used almost exclusively for ladies' trousers, illustrations of which are often included on contemporary miniatures.

The former area of Turkestan today straddles the Soviet Union, Afghanistan and Iran. In the Iranian province of Khorasan, to the north-east of the country, there are, accordingly, many Turkmen, now partially settled under the policies of the late Reza Shah, father of the present Shahinshah, Mohammed Reza Shah.

In their traditional nomadic life, Turkmen usually decorated the tents and clothing they designed to brave the extreme climates of the Central Asian steppes. It is plausible that the tradition of such embellishment is extremely old. The word 'Pazyryk' is known today to all carpet-lovers. In the Bzyryk excavations in Soviet Siberia, in 1947 to 1949, textiles were unearthed dating from the 4th to 3rd centuries BC. One item is thought to be the oldest knotted carpet in existence today and has since entered the main annals of floor coverings. This, and its companion pieces, belonged to the ancestors of the Turkmen.

Turkmen embroidery is recognisable by a brilliant colouring, with dense chain-stitched silk floral motifs, large circular flower heads and similar patterning, on a heavy white cotton ground. There is frequent appliqué, and colouring includes bright rose pink, bright orange and black outlining motifs and border edging. Many works,

146

indeed, have edges festooned with beads, buttons, ribbons or tassels.

Embroidery is found on large hangings, on animal blankets, bags, women's coats (the menfolk scorned similar decoration on their clothing) and on covers of many varieties.

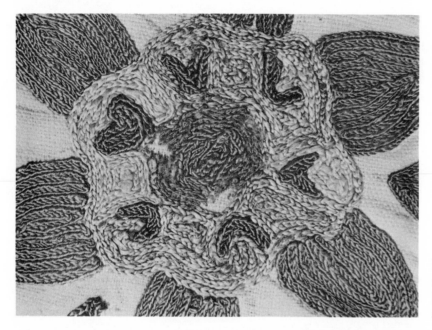

IRAN—*detail of Turkmen chain-stitch motif.* *(The Earl of Wemyss and March, KT)*

In many cases, as in all parts of the country, development of Turkmen embroidery has corresponded to that of knotted carpets. A large 19th-century prayer rug from Khorasan, for instance, now belonging to Mr. Albert Khoury of Beirut, has a dense patterning of satin and darning stitch *kulkas* on a coarse red cotton ground. Design is similar to many contemporary knotted carpets. Turkmen embroideries sport *gün* (sun) and *gül* (flower) motifs similar to those of knotted textiles.

Turkmen embroidery is, alas, becoming more difficult to find. The principal tribal embroidery production today is that of the Baluchi, a nomadic tribe and one of the last to make the twice-yearly trek between winter quarters and summer pastures. Such a tribe on the move is an awe-inspiring sight never to be forgotten: a complete community, spread over some three days' marching distance, moves in orderly groups. Small boys are in charge of flocks of lambs. Old ladies ride astride laden donkeys, cooking pots and tent equipment hanging on behind. Some small animals even ride on the backs of larger ones. Each night the entire procession pitches camp, and in the morning strikes it again to proceed further.

The Baluchi are mainly a weaving tribe, and their accoutrements include bright carpets and blankets, giving colourful decoration as they are 'on the move'. But they also produce fine embroidery, silk on a coarse linen, similar to that found in Swat and other regions of north-west Pakistan.

There is some appliqué to be found, on the south-west coast of the Caspian, around Resht, a felt on felt inlaid work, the joining seam often covered with rows of chain stitching, sometimes in gold or silver thread.

Iranian embroidery has, in the main, long suffered the fate of deference to other textile and applied arts. There is a plethora of information on both knotted and printed textile design, method and attribution but a dearth of comparable material on embroidery. The growth of specialist art tours to Iran is, perhaps, initiating some recompense for past lack of interest. Exhibitions in the West, too, are also helping to acknowledge the high quality of the country's past embroideries, although it is obvious that the embroidered arts will continue to play a subservient role in the Iranian textile world.

Ireland

The chronicle of unique Eire and Ulster embroideries today dates from the beginning of the 19th century, for before that the textile arts of the island had been closely related to those of England (see section on England). Many of the best metal embroideries of the 18th century were worked by artists in Dublin, but primarily for a London market. With the Act of Union in 1801, livery and other metal thread embroidery production moved across the Irish Channel to London. And the advent of peculiar schools of Irish embroidery occurred coincidentally at about the same time.

Throughout the 19th century the role of the 'agent' characterised Irish embroidery (as it did, similarly, much of that of Scotland). Middlemen sold and promoted whitework, drawn thread work, needle laces and, later, art needlework. An agent handed embroidery patterns with accompanying instructions to the embroidery out-workers on his books. The Ulster Folk Museum in Belfast has a half-worked linen collar with blue transfer design of leaves and flowers, late 19th century, stamped with the agent's briefing: 'Joseph Watson, Portaferry. If first class work and done in 8 days will be paid $\frac{1}{2}$' (half of what is left open to speculation).

The agents were based around the country: Rathfriland and Hillsborough, both in Co. Down, were, for example, two drawn thread work centres. Agents generally were responsible to firms in Belfast or overseas companies. Unfortunately many such men were preoccupied with financial gain and thereby did the art of embroidery considerable disservice. Their attitude, indeed, coupled with the continual natural, religious and political upheavals of the century, was partly responsible for much of the decline of Irish embroidery. For, although all facets of her arts are still executed, overall production is today but a fraction of that of the 19th century.

From a religious point of view, Catholic and Protestant factions have both helped to further all fields of the art. Catholic girls were generally taught their needlework in convents: their sisters in the Church of Ireland were instructed in parochial schools. Sometimes, however, religious cooperation encouraged embroidery advance. In 1846 'a Protestant lady' called Sainthill joined 'a Catholic lady' named McSwiney to found the Cork Embroidery School, which opened with a management committee under the Mayor of Cork,

149

a grant of £200 and 100 pupils. Even though further help was forth-coming from corporation benefactors and local Quakers, general local enthusiasm for the work produced did not parallel overseas interest in it.

Feudal tradition, with the responsibility of the landowner for his estates, often stimulated the involvement of benefactors. In 1822 Lady O'Brien of Drumoland, mother of the Young Irelander, William Smith O'Brien, organised an industry for about 400 children in Co. Clare, and the satin-stitch work produced was called 'Lady O'Brien's work'.

Lace and embroidery are particularly closely related in Ireland, with confusion of identity especially noticeable in the case of 'Limerick lace', which takes the form either of running-stitch work or tamboured chain stitch on a net ground. The tambour had been introduced to Ireland by an Englishman, Charles Walker, in 1829. He established a successful business at Mount Kennet, near Limerick, whence came the name of this work.

Limerick, a needle lace, unfortunately suffered the same fate as many other contemporary facets of the textile arts. It generally attracted greater foreign excitement than interest in home produc-tion and, although it is said that Queen Victoria was fond of the work, Irish connoisseurs were not enthusiastic. Apparently, too, at the Great Exhibition of 1851 and at the Dublin Great Industrial Exhibition two years later, the agents handling sales were too concerned with costs, ignoring the intrinsic value of the art.

Production of Limerick work therefore declined after the middle of the century, although it did revive considerably in 1883 when Mrs. Vere O'Brien opened a school. She is remembered today principally for her qualities as designer and teacher: in 1907 her work was accorded the right to the coat of arms of the city of Limerick as a reward for excellence. The 'O'Brien stitch'—a tambour stitch not to be confused with so-called 'Lady O'Brien work'—is named after her.

A later embroiderer influential in Limerick design was Helena Kelly who, in 1897, won a three-year scholarship to study at the School of Art in South Kensington. From 1900 until her death in 1936 she designed Limerick embroideries for the Kinsale Convent of Mercy. In 1884 the Convent had established a school with sections for art, crochet and cutwork. It is thought that by the beginning of the 20th century there were some 200 workers, and the subsequent decline was partly due to emigration of the local fishing community. Limerick embroidery production today is, alas, predominantly an occupation of elderly artists.

Ireland is famous, too, for many other kinds of whitework. There was, for example, limited production of 'Ayrshire work' (p. 224) in Northern Ireland during the 1830's: a group of Scottish ladies brought over contemporary designs and Messrs. Cochrane and Brown, of Donaghadee, even sent some of the resultant work to Glasgow to be re-exported as 'original Ayrshire'.

'Mountmellick work' is named after a town in Queen's County (now Leix) with strong Quaker traditions. In 1825 Mrs. Johanna Carter invented the combination of thick white cotton knitting yarn with a satin jean ground of even weave. It was very much a personal art, dependent on Mrs. Carter's inspiration, for when she died Mountmellick production declined considerably, although it was later revived both professionally to help gentlewomen of Ireland who had fallen on hard times, and also for the enjoyment of the amateur embroiderer. Mountmellick work is sometimes described as Moravian, for a 'Sister Carter' took whitework classes at the Moravian settlement in Co. Antrim, 150 miles north of Mountmellick, but the two ladies were probably not in fact one. ('Moravian embroidery' is a term more usually applied to a school of North American embroidery, p. 277.)

'Mountmellick stitch' has given its name to a regular embroidery stitch (p. 409). Mountmellick work designs were based on local fruits and flowers embellished with French and bullion knots. And although Mountmellick work is generally found on examples of heavy-duty linen such as thick bedspreads, it was also worked with more delicate materials to produce fine baby clothes.

The period before the famines of 1845–50 saw the spread of what is now known as 'Carrickmacross work' or 'Carrickmacross lace', an embroidered cutwork fashioned by sewing through three layers of paper pattern, muslin ground and machine-made net. The design is completed to the outline of the paper pattern, which is then torn off and the muslin ground underneath cut away around the design outline to reveal the net. It can be worked, alternatively, by omitting the bottom net ground and cutting away the muslin to produce a cutwork known as 'Carrickmacross guipure'.

'Carrickmacross' was named as such following the Dublin Exhibition of 1872, although the Irish introduction of this field of embroidery took place some 60 years earlier. The Rev. and Mrs. John Grey Porter, of Donaghmoyne, Co. Monaghan, went to Italy on their honeymoon in 1816 and took with them their sewing maid, Annie Steadman. There the two ladies saw applied embroidery on net, and brought with them to Ireland the basic ideas and designs.

Mrs. Grey Porter had before her marriage already been teaching some needlework and she instituted the manufacture of this 'new' appliqué, with Annie Steadman conducting the classes. John

151

Heathcoat's 1809 patent for a bobbin-net machine had expired in 1823 and machine-made net accordingly was cheaper. Production of the work expanded until Mrs. Grey Porter died and Mr. Grey Porter left Donaghmoyne in 1842.

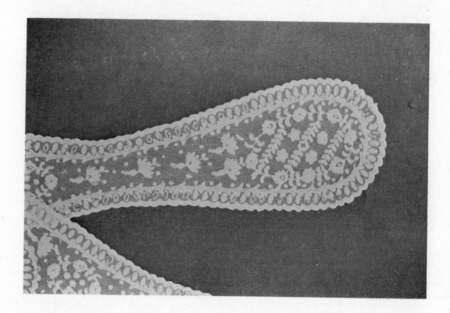

IRELAND—*detail of a Carrickmacross bonnet, mid-19th century. (The Valentine Museum, Richmond, Virginia)*

Their neighbour, Miss Reid of Rahans, furthered the cause. She opened classes for local girls of slender means in the outhouses of her brother's estate. Miss Reid, and her sister Dora, adapted Mrs. Grey Porter's patterns and built a special schoolhouse for the study of lace and appliqué on Castleblaney Road, Cullaville. In 1846, Tristram Kennedy, manager of the Bath estates, established the 'Bath and Shirley Lace School'. Realising the usefulness of the Misses Reid's work, he obtained a public relief grant of £100, and the agent of the neighbouring Shirley estate, Captain Morant, donated an empty house in Carrickmacross for a central base to supply designs. Kennedy became Member for Louth in 1852, but even during his subsequent long career in Parliament he was responsible for promotion of the school's work. The first teacher, Mrs. Keiler, adapted many Brussels and Brabant designs, and during the coming decades new variants were continually incorporated. In 1890, for example, the teacher, Miss McKeon, was buying patterns from young designers at Dublin Art School.

The eventual demise of the Bath and Shirley School was due to the concurrent rise of similar institutions. The Crossmaglen School attracted many of the embroiderers. And towards the end of the 19th century the Sisters of St. Louis came to Carrickmacross. The Convent's first two outstanding embroiderers were Miss Rose Carolan and Mrs. Bridget O'Brien, both of whom are still remembered in the history of Irish embroidered arts. Excellent teaching and good design stimulated interest in the embroideries worked at the convent. With an average of 130 workers at any one time, production in the first ten years earned a total of £20,000, and demand for the St. Louis Lace School's work spread abroad.

In 1907 lace and embroidery had the main central stand of the Irish International Exhibition. But with subsequent political upheavals, culminating in the Rising of 1916, production of Irish handwork waned rapidly. Some appliqué is still worked today, mostly through a cottage industry organisation, with embroiderers working in their own homes under the supervision of the Convent, which still maintains a high standard of design and workmanship in all the embroidery it produces.

The famines of 1845–50 were followed by the arrival of mechanisation and industrialisation, and the failure of the 1879 Irish potato crop, a harvest vital to the survival of many of the people. Many socially minded persons and organisations instituted relief programmes, which included setting up employment for workers and subsequent sale of their products. Mrs. Ernest Hart, of the Donegal Industrial Fund, instituted in 1883, helped adapt patterns from the 'Book of Kells' and other early Irish manuscripts. These, together with art needlework designs, were worked on grounds of linen, wool or flannel.

In 1886, for the last few months of Gladstone's premiership, the Earl of Aberdeen was Viceroy of Ireland. His Countess helped organise the Irish Industries Association (later the Royal Irish Industries Association), and continued her chairmanship after her husband's brief term of office had ended. After its considerable success at the Chicago World Fair in 1893, the Association held regular exhibitions in England. It existed until 1914, thanks largely to the continuous patronage of such concerned parties as Lady Aberdeen, Lady Cadogan, Lady Londonderry, Lady Abercorn and Mr. H. Gordon Selfridge, who had first become involved when he was a partner of Marshall Field in Chicago.

The Royal Irish School of Art Needlework in Dublin had been established in the 1870's and the universal vogue for 'art needlework' was to become popular throughout Ireland, thanks partly to the following of the Dublin school. In 1887, William Morris's daughter May (p. 90) had given lessons to Lily Yeats, sister of the poet. Miss Yeats returned to Dublin in 1901 and herself taught

153

embroidery at the Dun Emer Industries in Dublin, founded by Miss Evelyn Gleeson. She and her sister Elizabeth later had their own studio, the Cuala Industries, at Dundrum, five miles from the capital. Apparently W. B. Yeats was worried about the lack of business acumen in the venture and he was continually suggesting his poems, and other themes, as subjects for their embroideries.

Lily Yeats's best works were her banners, most of which were worked in the late 1920's, about tea-towel sized. Twenty-five such works designed by another brother, the artist Jack B. Yeats, and worked by Lily with the help of Pamela Colman-Smith, are today in Loughrea Cathedral, Co. Galway. Another banner is in the National Museum of Ireland in Dublin.

Israel

The *de facto* frontiers of Israel since 1967 encompass all the Palestinian lands, formerly Turkish and under British Mandate from 1917 to 1948, territory which includes the West Bank of the Jordan river, home of the most celebrated Palestinian embroideries through the ages.

To consider Israeli embroidery first: there is a resurgence of keen interest in all the textile arts. Since the formation of the State of Israel in 1948, the many Jews who have converged on the area from all parts of the world have brought with them their artistic skills and traditions to add to those of earlier arrivals and the existing populace.

Before the First World War, Russian Jews came, including those from the Ukraine. Between the wars, there was German Jewish immigration. Immediately after the Second World War, Poles and other displaced persons arrived, and since then there has been especial immigration of Iraqi, Yemenite, Moroccan and other Jews from the Arab world, some from western Europe and the United States and, lately, from the Soviet Union.

Many of these groups brought with them their heritage of embroidery. The Yemeni Jewish immigrants, for example, introduced their traditional gold work. Yemeni embroidered trouser legs and leggings have become a noticeable feature in Israeli work, with cross stitch, herringbone stitch and laid and couched work, embroidered by the 'oriental Jews' in clear-cut geometric patterns.

Israeli embroidery today is encouraged by influential patrons such as Mrs. Ruth Dayan, President of MASKIT, the Israel Centre of Handicrafts. Pattern books with designs of interest and deep meaning to Jews all over the world are increasingly popular.

Jerusalem today is a bustling city with many elements contributing to its overall prosperity. The old walled city is largely Arab, though sacred Jewish sites as well as Christian and Moslem are there. In the *soukh* (market) areas there are some embroidered costumes to be seen, and bought, but the greater part of traditional dress remains in the outlying villages.

The Palestinians of the villages are *fellahin*, settled Arab farmers, Sunni Moslems in the main but with some Christians and Druses among their numbers. One of the treasures of each Palestinian girl

155

has been her wedding dress, particularly beautiful examples of which have come from the Bethlehem area, long famed for its couched work (*tahiri*), similar to that of Greece, Turkey and Persia: Bethlehem dresses and accompanying jackets were highly prized items in most Palestinian trousseaux (it was expected that the groom offer these pieces as his contribution to his bride's wedding chest). In villages where Bethlehem dresses were not traditionally worn, a heavily embroidered *djillayeh* dress was the custom, to be brought out after the wedding only very rarely for special occasions.

Apart from Bethlehem couching and the drawn thread work of Galilee and some of the coastal regions, most common stitches found in Palestinian embroideries are cross stitch and satin stitch (although Louisa Pesel's early 20th-century sampler in the Victoria and Albert Museum includes more than ten different stitches purportedly regularly in use in Palestine).

ISRAEL—*detail of cross-stitch counted thread motif of the Kennedy Memorial from Ann Roth's* Jerusalem in Needlepoint and Embroidery. *The monument, 23 ft. (7·0 m) high, stands near the village of Aminadav, near Jerusalem, and was designed by the Israeli architect David Reznik. It is constructed of 51 vertical concrete pillars, representing the States of the United States with the District of Columbia.*
(Reproduced by kind permission of Massada Press Ltd., Jerusalem)

Southern Palestinian embroidery can be divided into the following areas: Bethlehem, Ramallah, Beit Dajan, Ashdod, Hebron Hills, and Falujeh and Tell es-Saffeh. Each region has its own peculiar styles and designs.

Ramallah embroideries are particularly well known, thanks to the devoted cataloguing that has been done on the subject. Ramallah (meaning 'Hill of God') is, like most of the embroidery centres, predominantly Christian. It stands about 12 miles north of Jerusalem. Its inhabitants came from Shobek, in Trans-Jordan, in 1680, and tradition has it that their particular costume style was introduced by Crusaders (although the Crusaders could equally have been influenced by their hosts' robes).

156

Phyllis Sutton, an English lady from Nottingham, first came to Palestine in 1921 and, although she was at the Quaker School in Ramallah for only eight years, from 1927 to 1935, her knowledge of embroidery of the area is unique. Together with Grace Crowfoot, a British archaeologist, to whom she was introduced by Lady Flinders Petrie, she, more than anyone, is responsible for keeping alive the interest in, and understanding of, Palestinian embroidery throughout the Middle East. Her subsequent years in Amman, in fact, strengthened her determination to keep in use some of the ancient embroidery motifs. She is still today, in Beirut, enthusiastically preserving her own collection of samples and styles.

Embroidery has generally suffered through lack of written history. Apart from recorded patterns and pattern books in the western world, embroidery has been continued and passed on by example. In many regions these samples have been lost and succeeding generations have not been amenable to having local motifs taught them by their elders. Ramallah work is one facet of the embroidered arts that has been preserved, much of it as costume decoration.

Unlike most Palestinian dresses, which have a black or dark blue ground, the Ramallah robe is traditionally deep rose pink silk (from Damascus) on a white or unbleached linen ground, called *roumi*. It is a full-length robe (*khalaq*) with deep batwing sleeves with an extra 'wing' added underneath, and has applied vertical skirt panels back and front and bracing the frontal neck opening. This frontal applied breastplate (*kabba*) is in one piece, similar to Greek and Dalmatian styles. Today such costume is not commonplace wear, although on Palm Sunday it is still customary for many of the girls in the area villages to put on their best robes.

Ramallah designs show some Moroccan and considerable Persian influence, the latter in such aspects as a recurrent cypress motif. There is an eight-pointed star, called *ain el-baqqar* ('eye of the cow'), similar to those that were found on prehistoric pots of Egypt and Ur. Motifs have names, too, such as 'road to Egypt'. This is a Greek-key pattern with many turnings worked in a single cross stitch, and described by one embroiderer as typical of the windings of the way between Palestine and Egypt, recalling the words of the early pilgrim Sylvia who had herself described the Israelite wanderings as continually weaving from left to right and back again (*The Pilgrimage of S. Sylvia of Aquitaine*, Palestine Pilgrims Texts, Vol. 1). 'Old man upside down' is worked half in red and half in black, and the 'baker's wife' motif looks rather like trays of *farrane*, Arab bread. 'Bachelor's cushion' has seats for two and 'pattern of the heart' is complicated enough to set the cardiac pump beating at an alarming rate. It is

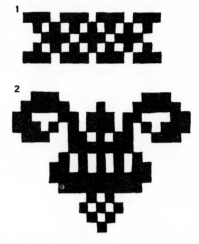

ISRAEL—*Palestinian embroidery motifs*: el farrane, *'the baker's wife', a narrow border which could have been named after a baker's tray (figure 1), and* erq el-tajat, *'a crown' (figure 2).*

157

alleged that if a lazy Ramallah embroiderer failed to cross a stitch 'it may be taken for granted that she has fallen into the sin of sloth'.

Considerably less embroidery is found in the north of the country. Around the Galilee area, where many of the embroidery techniques died out at the beginning of the 20th century, drawn thread work, satin stitch, hem stitch and stem stitch and cross stitch are found.

It is difficult for an amateur to date and place old Palestinian embroidery. Most vendors will automatically say any item for sale is 'old'. One reliable test is to hold the piece up to the light. The more uneven the weave of the ground, the older the piece might be. And, as for carpets, chemical dyes for thread did not come into general use in the Middle East until about 1930. The earlier natural dyes often produced an *abrash* (fluctuation of colour) to the embroidery thread.

Italy and the Vatican

The history of embroidery in Italy has for centuries been influenced to a major extent by the Catholic Church and some of the finest works have been ecclesiastical robes and decorations.

The Holy See has historically been so interrelated with the rest of the Italian peninsula that it is often erroneously incorporated with Italy: it has since 1929, in fact, been a fully independent sovereign

ITALY (Sicily)—the oldest and most significant piece of the many splendid vestments which the Norman kings commissioned in Sicily is the 'Coronation mantle' from the Royal Workshop in Palermo, 1133–4, probably made for King Roger II. 11 ft. 2 in. × 4 ft. 5 in. (342 × 135 cm), gold work, silk and pearls on scarlet silk. A second inner lining, of Italian damask worked with gold and silver, is thought to have been added at the coronation, in 1520, of the Emperor Charles V at the nunnery of St. Clare in Nürnberg. It is believed that the mantle has been in regular use since 1220 for coronations of the Holy Roman Emperors.
(Kunsthistorisches Museum, Wien, Weltliche Schatzkammer)

159

state. Vatican City has an unsurpassed cultural ratio of nine official museums for its population of only just over a thousand!

Church and other ceremonial embroideries in the peninsula have been more exaggerated, and have often had more finesse, than other contemporary European work. Religious fervour contributed dedication and the necessary patience to the execution of fine vestments, altar cloths and robes for cathedrals and cardinals, as well as for tiny churches. Nuns have generally been connected with exquisite handwork: in Italy, in particular, the convent-produced embroideries have set high standards of perfection.

In the 12th century there was particularly outstanding embroidery from the Palermo workshop in Sicily. Lush ecclesiastical and regal vestments were produced, some of which still survive. In the Kunsthistorisches Museum in Vienna is the 'Coronation mantle', worked for the Norman King, Roger II. A border inscription on the mantle is dated 528 of the Sicilian Hedschra, or 1133/4 AD, and it is the oldest example in existence today. The mantle is on a scarlet silk ground, richly outlined with gold. It has two symmetrical lion motifs, originally outlined in dark blue silk with double rows of pearls. There is superimposed gold enamel filigree work and some precious stones.

Another 12th-century Sicilian embroidery, equally extravagant, is the silk chasuble from the Church of St. Peter, Salzburg, and now in the Museum of Fine Arts, Boston. It is $60\frac{1}{4}$ in. long (153 cm) with embroidered inscription around the hem.

Gold metal thread embroidery has been lavishly used both in Italian religious and secular embroideries. The exquisite mosaics in the Church of St. Vitale in Ravenna bear evidence of extensive gold work through the elaborate clothing decoration of both the Emperor Justinian and his Empress, Theodora, and their retinues. Also in the Boston museum is a 14th-century antependium, 'The Crucifixion', $11\frac{1}{4} \times 16\frac{1}{2}$ in. (28·5 × 42 cm), a silk and gold embroidery that has tremendous realism and depth. And in the Cooper-Hewitt Museum of Decorative Arts there is a late 16th-century linen border, heavily embroidered in gold and silks. The metal thread is thickly laid and couched with overall delicacy of execution, the patterning throughout of scrolls and waves. It is inherently difficult to achieve a lightness of touch with the usually weighty medium of metal thread but, in this case, the artist attained an easy fluidity.

During the period of High Renaissance in the 15th century, Florence was an especially prolific centre of all the arts. There was much communication with similarly creative havens (such as Ofen, later Budapest), and it is suggested that what is now known as 'Florentine work' (p. 391) may have originated in Hungary. One

160

△ FRANCE – wedding urn picture, satin stitch and French knots on silk ground, presented to President and Mrs Woodrow Wilson. The work is inscribed "PS.ES. en avril 1815".
(Woodrow Wilson House, Washington D.C. Photo: Norma Papish)

△ FRANCE – a modern appliqué of Jonah by Claudie Tardits. (The artist)

▽ GREECE – detail from 18th-century cushion cover, possibly from Epirus. Wedding scene, silk and gilt embroidery on linen ground.
(Whitworth Art Gallery, Manchester. Sir Jospeh Lee Collection)

△ *GREECE* — *fragments joined to make a long cushion cover, Jannina. Silk on linen ground, mostly double running stitch.*
(Whitworth Art Gallery, Manchester. Professor P. E. Newberry Collection)

Medici did indeed bring home a Hungarian bride, who is known to have had 'Florentine work' decoration on some items of her trousseau. Whatever its exact siting of conception, however, Florentine artists like Antonio Pollajuolo designed variations on the theme of the basic wave, or flame, motif, the most famous examples of which are the chair coverings in the Bargello Palace. Amongst its many other names, 'Florentine work' is also variously termed 'Bargello'—or 'Hungarian point'.

ITALY—*Assisi work band, possibly 17th century, $16\frac{1}{2} \times 7$ in. (42 × 18 cm). The background is heavily embroidered, generally in long-legged cross stitch, so that the design is heightened by the linen ground showing through the motifs. This band portrays (from the top) the story of the Creation and Adam, Eve and the temptation of the Garden of Eden, the expulsion from the Garden and the story of Cain and Abel (the last two not shown here). (The Victoria and Albert Museum, Crown Copyright)*

161

One of the main facets of Italian embroidery has always been *punto tagliato* (cutwork) (p. 378). In 1542 Mathio Pagan published, in Venice, the first patterns exclusively for this type of work, included in his book *Giardinetto nuovo di punti tagliati*. Venice was a main centre of such delicate embroidery, and from the basic cutwork there evolved *reticella*, or *reticello*, geometric-pattern embroideries based on the earlier *punto tagliato* and, also, on *punto tirato* (drawn thread work).

Reticella, in turn, gave way to *punto in aria* ('stitches in the air'), first described in 1587 with the publication of Federico de Vinciolo's book, later known as *New and Singular Patterns and Workes of Linnen*. *Punto in aria* was a needle lace free of all cloth foundation, with stitches worked on parchment paper to a pre-drawn pattern: it was known also as *Point de Venise* or *Venetian point*. Marco Polo had sent oriental gifts from his travels, but in return Venice sent out to the world new and exciting embroidery patterns such as Giovanni Ostaus's *La Vera Perfettione del Disegno* (1561). The new Venetian cutwork, therefore, was soon exported widely, to be received with much appreciation (Vinciolo is supposed to have taken the designs in person to Catherine de' Medici in Paris). And, as the cutwork became increasingly ephemeral, so it evolved into a true needle lace and, accordingly, out of the technical jurisdiction of 'embroidery'.

Italian lace continued to be germinal to the adoption of new types and themes of work throughout the western world. And as lace grew in popularity, embroidery association similarly lessened.

One form of traditional embroidery that has remained popular is 'Assisi work', a counted thread embroidery with a background embroidered and the foreground motif left unworked, to give a 'negative' effect, in contrasting relief. Two-sided Italian cross stitch was worked, as in *punto tirato*, to form overall cross stitching. Designs of trees, animals and similar subjects were thus outlined on a fine or medium weight linen ground.

Throughout the 16th and 17th centuries, Italian samplers were long and narrow, although wider than some contemporary examples from England and Germany. Much drawn thread embroidery was worked, on a linen ground, and there was spot motif embroidery in cross stitch, back stitch and satin stitch. The Victoria and Albert Museum has a 16th-century sampler, $30 \times 15\frac{3}{4}$ in. (76×40 cm), worked throughout with outlines of motifs embroidered in back stitch, satin stitch and long-legged cross stitch. Only one of the motifs has been filled in and, obviously, the embroidery is unfinished (there is a blank space in the middle of the ground). But it is none the less clear that the artist intended a comprehensive study

162

ITALY—*late 18th- or early 19th-century sampler, 9 × 9½ in.*
(22·5 × 24 cm), silk on linen, worked in cross stitch and back stitch.
(The Victoria and Albert Museum, Crown Copyright)

of various scroll and naturalistic foliage border patterns of the time, featuring some gargoyles, many vines with laden bunches of rich grapes, and elaborate diagonal patterning.

A 17th-century sampler, from the same museum, 32 × 18 in. (81 × 46 cm) and signed 'Givllia Piccolomini', is intricately worked in a complicated border patterning of complex *reticella* and other styles of cutwork, with accompanying drawn and pulled thread work. True to her country's religious affinities, however, the artist has included the Christian cross motif in one corner.

In comparison with earlier works, samplers of the 18th and 19th centuries are somehow rather unnatural and contrived. They are often of landscape form, with a small border around each side. Cross stitch predominates, with frequent satin stitch, double-running stitch, chain stitch, feather stitch and stem stitch. Maria Moratti's 1807 embroidery, in the Whitman Sampler Collection of the Philadelphia Museum of Art, is 14 × 27½ in. (35·5 × 70 cm), in black, green, red, brown, white, tan, blue and pink silks on a tan linen ground. The artist worked a narrow zigzag border surround and on the right of the main central panel is overall spot motif representation of religious symbols such as Holy Water jugs, the Crown of Thorns, Jacob's Ladder and the inscription *'Passio Christi Conforta Me'* ('Passion of Christ, comfort me'). The rest of the panel is taken up with different alphabet letterings, samples of vertical line embroideries, floral spot motifs and one rather delightful complex grouping of a small girl by a chair, her pet bird on a table and a poodle, or similar quadruped, chained to an ornamental wrought-iron gate.

Samplers throughout Italian embroidery history have, in fact, often included symbols of the Passion, a feature which can help to identify national provenance.

Embroidery in Italy has always been noticeably regionalised. In the area of the Marches, for example, particularly under the sway of Papal rule, very fine white stitchery was usual, with designs less angular and far more solid than in other parts of the country. In the Abruzzi region, cross stitch in coarse red cotton on a rough linen ground was utilised for trimming aprons, pillow-cases, sheets, towels and altar cloths. Locally woven fabrics, such as the fine linen ground from Bologna, were used in many such 'peasant works'.

Folk embroideries are today to be found in all regions: although traditional dress is no longer commonplace, an Italian love of ceremony preserves the occasional use of such regional costumes. Cross stitch dominates, often Italian two-sided cross stitch, in decoration for full-sleeved blouses, skirts and other clothing items. And the further south, the more exaggerated is the use of bright red thread. Much contemporary folk embroidery is copied from mediaeval art, embroidered or otherwise. By counting blocks of threads or tiles, embroiderers facilitate pattern transposition. They tend to prefer, on the whole, to execute designs that are associated with their environment. But such regional embroideries are not, unfortunately, in prolific supply: old ladies still, in some parts of the country, work the three items traditionally associated with their advancing age (namely a shroud, a pillow-case and a napkin), but their younger countrywomen tend to turn their skills in other directions.

Drawn thread work today is confined, for example, almost exclusively to bed-coverings worked in Sardinia and Sicily. In Sardinia the entire background of the typical rust-coloured fabric is withdrawn and re-formed with stitching. In Sicily, embroidery on a ground of red, blue or green fabric frequently has a background to the main design left clear.

Overall, in fact, with a continuing lace industry of some prominence (in 1878, after some disastrous floods, the needle-lace industry in Burano had been revived by the inspiration of Queen Margherita, assisted by Paula Fambri and the Countess Andriana Marcello), a plethora of embroidery is not today immediately evident. Some modern work is being carried out, to designs that are, in the main, derivative of those of the lace industry. But, more often, what work is being produced now is either for a specific church intent or for a generally undiscriminating tourist market.

Japan

Japanese embroidery is often less complicated in design than other oriental works. Frequently the pattern is not so full, not so organised. Japanese needlepainting appears overall to have a more feminine association than has, for example, contemporary work from China.

One distinguishing factor may be the custom, in Japan, of embroidering on to Japanese silk that has previously been painted. Another may be the design. S. F. A. Caulfeild (*Encyclopedia of Victorian Needlework*, 1887) stated categorically that 'their geometrical and conventional designs are not so good as those produced in China and India', a pronouncement that seems rather dogmatic and, in fact, inaccurate.

Much Japanese design has been derived from wildlife of the country, the sacred stork being particularly favoured. There are flora such as the double anemone, iris, chrysanthemum and cherry blossom. Figures are often caricatured, worked by someone with a decided sense of humour.

It is necessary to realise the close association of embroidery in Japan with Buddha. It was devotion to the deity that first encouraged the embroidered arts in the country. One of the first records of embroidery is that of the portrait of Buddha worked in AD 605 by court ladies to imperial command.

An important early Japanese embroidery is the *Tenjukoku mandara* in the Chūgūji Temple in Nara. This *mandara* (prayer work) is one of a pair executed in 621 by ladies of the court at the order of Tachibana-no-Ōiratsume, consort of Prince Shōtoku, as a prayer for her late husband's spirit. The work portrays the *Tenjukoku*, the Buddhist paradise ('Land of heavenly longevity'), whither his spirit was reputed to go. Designs of people, a phoenix and the legendary hare living in the moon decorate the small fragment, about 3 ft. (91·5 cm) square, that remains of this embroidery. Similar fragments also survive of the other hanging.

The zenith of domestic stitchery in the country was in the Nara Period (710–94), due in large part to the introduction of the T'ang crafts from China and, also, to the late Prince Shōtoku. In 646 the *Taika-no-Kaishin* (Great Reformation) had, under his posthumous ideals, centralised land and government under the leadership of Crown Prince Naka-no-Oye. The Crown Prince had organised textile industries, in which embroidery played a key role that was to diminish in importance only with later improved dyeing techniques. Until the end of the 18th century (the middle of the Edo Period, 1603–1867), graphic designs were customarily embroidered rather than dyed.

Embroidery was frequently allied with *surihaku*, appliqué of gold or silver leaf. This combination of embroidery with the appliqué (*nuihaku*) was worked in perfect balance, as is illustrated by a delightful *noh* robe in the Tokyo National Museum. The gold leaf of the *haku* was pressed on to patches of starched or glued fabric of the ground cloth.

Occasionally embroidery was similarly paired with tie-dyeing, with some interesting and intricate results.

About the time that dyeing began to take over the former importance of embroidery in the textile industry, foreign influences in embroidery as clothing decoration were introduced by overseas traders, and embroidery as an art form began to develop. *Obis* (wide sashes holding in the waist of the *kimono*, a full-length robe) had been decorated with some embroidery since the early 8th century, but gorgeous decoration with metal work and jewels did not appear on the *obi* until the 18th century. Costumes for *noh* and *kabuki* plays became more elaborate and, accordingly, more use was made of extravagant embroidery.

A centuries-old tradition amongst the farming communities of the Honshu island is *kogin* embroidery, or Japanese pattern darning. By working long darning stitches with only a few threads of fabric caught up at each entry of the needle, minimum embroidery yarn was displayed on the wrong side of the fabric, which meant maximum overall impact of thread. Today Mrs. Misao Kimura's students at the Technical School of Embroidery in Sendai are adapting some of the old *kogin* patterns, often working with traditional unbleached cotton yarn on an indigo cotton ground.

Kogin patterns displayed many diamond motifs and variations thereof. The effect is simple yet striking.

Appliqué work was not necessarily the metallic *surihaku*. Much heavy padding was used, but always, when worked with the exquisite movement of an oriental artist, the lightness of the finished pieces belies the strong techniques used in the making.

An example of deep padding is the series of wall panels now in the Huis ten Bosch Palace in the Netherlands. In 1791 Prince William V of Orange had been presented with two sets of complete room fittings, one Japanese and one Chinese, by the United East India Company in Canton (see also pp. 46, 184). Each embroidered panel combines realism of natural life with a delicate handling and

167

JAPAN—*in 1791, four years before the arrival of the French in the Netherlands, Mr. Hemmingson (Merchant-in-chief of the United East India Company in Canton) presented Prince William V of Orange*

168

and his Lady, Princess Wilhelmina of Prussia, with the fittings for the
Japanese Room of the Huis ten Bosch Palace. In 1808, during the
reign of Louis Bonaparte over 'The Kingdom of Holland', the
embroidered panels were superimposed, under the direction of
Pieter de Swart, over the room's original Louis XIV panelling.
A detail of one panel is shown below.
(HM the Queen of the Netherlands)

approach. Padding is skilfully used to heighten the three-dimensional effect.

With the growing importance of East–West trade in the 19th century, Japanese arts in general had a noticeable effect in western Europe. Japanese embroidery, in particular, was popular during the last quarter of the century (see p. 170).

A major result of the interest in Japanese embroidery was the use in England of floss silk instead of traditional crewel wools. With the new 'silk embroidery' ladies concentrated on a general oriental approach in their needlepaintings, an example of which is a trio of iris, $17\frac{1}{2}$ in. (44·5 cm) tall, satin, long and short and outline stitches on a satin ground, in the Victoria and Albert Museum. Worked in 1899, there is oriental voiding to the petals and a strength in fragility to the outline that betrays inspiration from the east (acc. no. T.270-1927).

Satin stitch, French knots, long and short stitch—these are all much used in the home embroideries of Japan. Voiding (the art of working a motif to an exact edge with no 'bleeding' to the next motif, making a tiny void between the outlines of each motif) is indicative of Japanese origin. Gold and silver thread is much used in the embroidery of the country, frequently painstakingly couched and sometimes superimposed over floss-silk embroidered ground. Hair was often used to effect a more realistic picture, and glass eyes enlivened the faces of some heavily padded animals.

What can collectors look out for on the market today? Embroidery on old robes (*noh* robes and *kosodes*, the customary dress of both men and women from all strata) would be valuable items, as would a *ban*, the embroidered pennant used in Buddhist temples.

Japanese hangings are often gems of photographic collage. The Embroiderer's Guild in London has an example, item no. 3477 in its permanent collection, partly stitched through paper to protect the blue cotton ground. The 64 × 40 in. (162 × 102 cm) panel is a typical example of 19th-century wall-hanging embroidery, showing the floss-silk and couched Jap-gold embroidery worked in straight stitch, French knots, long and short stitch and with much voiding throughout.

One of the best collections of Japanese embroidery, as would be expected, is that of the Tokyo National Museum in Ueno Park. Rotating embroidery exhibitions feature aspects of the history of the art.

Glossary

Haku—gold or silver leaf

Jap gold—Japanese is the highest-quality gold thread: the magnificent colour does not easily tarnish. It is expensive—it is made from thin sheets of pure gold beaten to tissue thickness, cut into narrow strips and coiled around a core of floss-silk thread.

Kabuki—classical play, a combination of words, dancing, music with gorgeous costumes in a spectacular setting. In true *kabuki* the female roles are played by men. A single performance can last five hours.

Kimono—full-length robe

Kogin—Japanese pattern darning

Mandara—prayer work

Noh—highly stylised drama, with the masked actors in symbolic costume

Nui—embroidery

Nuihaku—embroidery with *surihaku*

Obi—*kimono* sash

Surihaku—appliqué of gold or silver leaf.

Jordan

If one is to continue defining embroidery within the perimeters of current boundaries, Jordanian work suffers from the exclusion of embroidery from the West Bank of the river Jordan, traditionally one of the most interesting centres of the textile world (p. 155).

The territory today to the east of the river has operationally communicative borders with Syria (to the north), Iraq (to the east) and Saudi Arabia (to the south and east). With a narrow strip of coast and its one port, Aqaba, on the Red Sea, embroidery in Jordan has lately remained free of added outside influences and therefore continues much as in the old tradition. Painstaking geometric counted patterns, in red and other coloured silks on a dark heavy cotton ground, adorn clothing and cloths.

One of the most outstanding collections of embroidery of the region is that of Mrs. Widad Ka'war of Amman. She has complete outfits, with dresses, headwear and accompanying jewellery, from all village and other communities of Jordan and elsewhere in the Arab world.

The definitive display of costume is in the new Jordan Museum of Popular Traditions, in the Roman Theatre of Amman, near the Philadelphia Hotel. It was opened by Mrs. Saadiyeh Tell in 1973.

Amman, the capital of Jordan, is still a haven for finding Palestinian and other Arab robes. Although the *soukhs* (markets) are becoming increasingly well known to travellers, second-hand dresses that have long been worn and loved are still available.

The most usual local dress found on the market is full length, with wide sleeves. It opens all the way down the front or has a short frontal neck opening. Embroidery is most commonly found around the neck opening, on the hem, cuffs and in a wide front yoke panel (or breastplate). Deep triangular panels inset into the skirt side front are often heavily embroidered, as sometimes is a wide V-panel across the back of the shoulders.

Many of the dresses have been remade over the years and this in fact adds to their appeal. Applied scraps sometimes adorn the inside of the skirt. On a heavy cotton ground, generally black or dark blue, cross-stitch embroidery is worked in thick cotton thread in patterns that are both indicative of regional origin and symbolic in motif.

There is some beadwork: turquoise beads (reputed to ward off the

172

evil eye) are often added as picot-ornamentation to a finished embroidery panel.

Panels alone frame beautifully. With intricate overall cross-stitch patterns, bright and colourful wall panels can be made from Jordanian embroideries without cutting or damaging the fabric. Generally, the more faded the ground and the more muted the colours of the embroidery threads, the older is the work. This can of course be offset by the fact that a particular piece has received little wear over the years and therefore looks comparatively new. Most traders automatically say that every piece they have to offer is 'a hundred years old' or 'real Phoenician' but, in fact, few embroideries are older than the beginning of this century. Embroidery is to be found, also, in Christian markets in such places as Madaba, south-west of Amman, a town perhaps better known for its unique 6th-century tessellated floor map of contemporary Jerusalem and the lands of the eastern Mediterranean.

Kenya

There is Arabic and Persian ornamentation apparent in many of the applied arts of the East African countries. In Kenya, today, the only traditional stitchery practised, along the coast, shows primarily Swahili culture with Arab influence. There is bead stitchery and some shell work.

Modern embroidery centres on Nairobi. In Parliament House are hangings designed and worked by ladies of the East African Women's League, portraying the history of their country.

Outside the capital, one of the main aspects of stitchery is the bright-coloured beadwork of the Masai, whose tribal lands overlap the border with Tanzania. Men, women and children—the women with closely shaven heads—beautify themselves with wide flat neck-collars built up with many concentric rings of fine beading. Both sexes wear complex earrings, sometimes more than one pair at a time, sometimes hanging right down to their waists, with equally fine beadwork decoration. But, alas, Masai beadwork has become a magnet to the safari seeker and general tourist, and as prices have soared there has been a corresponding decline in quality.

Lebanon and Syria

Because of the intertwined relationship of the arts of the two countries, political frontiers are not strictly relevant to the study of the embroidery of Lebanon and Syria.

The arts of Lebanon are, basically, a casserole of heritage from different religions and from many parts of the world. With a population that includes Christians and Moslems in more or less equal numbers, there are sub-groups of Maronite and Orthodox Christians, Sunni and Shi'a Moslems, Druses and other factions, all contributing their own symbolism and design to the culture of the country. Lebanon was in fact ruled, by the Turks, as part of Syria (albeit with French and American missionary influence) until 1917, and as a French mandate from then until the Second World War. Today foreign trends are still being introduced. Beirut, the capital, is a busy international transit stop and, also, the centre of much Middle Eastern trade. With excellent communications, the cosmopolitan foreign population has time, and inspiration, to instil its own arts into the country.

Syria, on the other hand, is predominantly Moslem and there is noticeably a more Turkish aspect to her embroidery. Most of her arts are found in the west and south of the country, and, therefore, her border with Iraq does not contribute much oriental influence. An eastern European dimension is coming to the country, particularly around the Euphrates, through extensive trade and aid projects.

Lebanese and Syrian embroideries are in the main similar and in many cases it is difficult even for an expert to distinguish them. Embroidery is often termed simply 'Palestinian' (p. 155), and, indeed, some of the countries' finest works have been produced by the Palestinians who have come into both Lebanon and Syria since 1948.

Embroideries that are historically indigenous are generally either domestic or ecclesiastical. Decoration is practical. 'Robes' (the local name for gowns, be they long, short, open or closed) can be completely covered in bright cross-stitched patterning on a heavy cotton ground. Sometimes such robes are lined, either in one piece or patched with bright coloured scraps left over from satinised cotton clothing. Most of the ground is black or a very dark navy blue, cotton or linen. But striped unbleached cotton and a patterned ground of

175

tiny spot motif flowers are also found. Around Bosra, in south-eastern Syria, one dress of the Druse chiefs was an English-type smock with brilliant gold silk embroidery, cross stitch, on the front yoke panel and around the cuffs of the double sleeves and collar.

Gold on white embroidery is also found in Damascus, and there is an excellent collection on view at the Azam Palace Museum off the Street called Straight. This form of 'Damascus embroidery' has intricate cross-stitched patterns, and is often found on cuffs, collars, bookmarks and similar small items. 'Damascus embroidery' refers, too, to machine-embroidered tamboured table linen, produced in vast quantities and in a range of qualities. Working to a block-printed pattern of all-over doodles, the embroiderer generally works one colour on the cotton ground. More expensive cloths can be specially ordered with polychrome embroidery, and retailers, often in minute and chaotic attics in a side street reminiscent of bedlam, recount with delight how one particular embassy has just ordered three cloths each 10 m long, each with matching table napkins. . . .

The traveller has a particularly good chance of seeing embroidered costumes being worn if he is away from the main coastal region (Latakia to Tyre) and away from the main truck routes of Beirut to Damascus and Damascus south to Deraa (of Lawrence fame). Once inland and off the beaten track, permanent or nomadic communities still wear traditional costumes. In eastern Syria, in particular, Bedouins sometimes have striking embroidered edges to the long flowing robes of the women (women with proud, dark faces and with gold sovereigns rustling from forehead bands as they wear their fortune for safe keeping).

An example of the variety of costume found can be seen, for example, at such a gathering point as Al-Rasafa, near the gigantic ruins of a Byzantine city, some 100 miles east of Aleppo. Lonely in surrounding desert space, the site nevertheless has magnetic attraction, in the spring when flocks can graze, for many people over a remarkably wide area. Some walk miles to get to it; other come by donkey or horseback, and keffired (head-scarved) enthusiasts on highly decorated motor bicycles arrive to join the mêlée. Everyone puts on his best outfit and the embroidery on view ranges from delicate shadow patterning on a silk ground to heavy appliqué work on coarse cotton.

Religious embroideries have tended, in the past, to be highly ornate, and this tradition is continued in the Christian areas of Lebanon. Convents produce a regular and prolific offering of domestic embroideries, too, with fine stitching and patient workmanship the two dominant attributes.

Embroidery, alas, is not yet an established part of the arts world

176

either of Lebanon or Syria. *Kaftans*, full-length coats or dresses with wide sleeves and embroidery around the cuffs, neck and front openings, are decorated with laid and couched work and a plethora of gold and silver thread. And there are embroidered accessories, such as purses and cushions, designed by relief organisation volunteers and worked in Palestinian refugee camps for foreign markets.

Mexico

Although so many other artistic facets have been discovered, little textile information has survived from Pre-Columbian Mexico, with its succession of distinctive cultures based around such centres as Teotihuacan, Tula and Monte Alban.

The sudden and dramatic overthrow of the Aztec rulers of the region by Cortes and his Spaniards in 1519 brought with it Iberian influence in the arts, as in most aspects of life. The Spaniards wantonly, or accidentally, destroyed much pre-existing art, of which one of the few textiles to survive is the plumed headdress which was sent to Cortes, whom many believed to be the god Quetzalcoatl. (In 1520 Emperor Charles V gave the headdress to his son, Archduke Ferdinand of Tyrol, and it is now in the Oesterreichisches Museum für Volkskunde in Vienna.)

There is great similarity between Spanish and Mexican samplers. Patterns and designs followed by schools of the religious orders in Mexico were identical with those taught in Spain.

Early Mexican samplers were usually oblong, with border design and accompanying scattered spot motifs. A 29 × 18 in. (73·5 × 46 cm) silk on linen sampler, 1794, in the Whitman Sampler Collection at the Philadelphia Museum of Art, is intricately worked with little space between each border band.

Later samplers were more often square in shape. There are two outstanding examples in the Victoria and Albert Museum. One (late 18th or early 19th century) is 12 × 15¼ in. (30·5 × 38·5 cm) in silver-gilt thread, purl, spangles and silks on a linen ground. It features large spot motifs, highly representational, with an oriental delicacy of execution. A 17¼ in. (44 cm) square post-Colonial sample, on the other hand, worked by Virginia Samtibañes in 1870, is detailed and organised, with formally worked strips of different border designs combining together to form a 'log cabin' pattern around the central inscription, with satin stitch, cross stitch and drawn thread work.

The standard of embroidery in Mexico since the beginning of the 16th century has been excellent. A combination of Spanish administration and design with local labour and time has produced such panels as the city life scene, 29 × 80 in. (73·5 × 203 cm) now in Parham Park, Sussex, formed from three narrow strips of linen with geometric border bands in between. The spot designs are entirely

178

representational and the comparative scale of motifs is not as exaggerated as that of some contemporary work. It has a generally photographic appeal, and in minutiae and characterisation is comparable with the famous Srinagar hanging from India (p. 140).

Embroidery worked on bands of fabric in this way is found throughout Mexican textile production. Ingenious artists utilised

MEXICO—*detail of late 18th-century border embroidery with four bands of embroidery showing men and women, in carriages or boats, dancing and playing musical instruments. Silk and silver thread (wound on silk) on silk ground; darning, satin and outline stitch. 7 ft. 9 in. × 1 ft. 6 in. (236 × 45 cm). (Philadelphia Museum of Art. Given by Mrs. George W. Childs Drexel)*

what scraps of left-over fabric they could find and, frequently, an embroidery ground has been constructed from remnants with subsequent embroidery covering the joins.

Gold and silver metal thread embroidery was particularly popular during the 17th and 18th centuries. Patrician gentlemen were presumably partial to metal work adorning their fashionable jackets, doublets and *ropons* (capes). As the hemlines lifted in the 18th century, elegant ladies sported footwear extravagant with metal decoration. (As was so often the case, the dress of the colonial *élégant* was more lavishly decorated than that of his home-based brother.)

Today such embroidery is worn mostly on regional costume. Women wear the *huipil*, a simple rectangular garment of cotton or wool. It can be long or short, loose or tight-fitting. The *quechquemitl* is a triangular poncho with neck opening, usually made of wool. Both items can be roughly embroidered. One 1969 *huipil* bought in Mexico City has a grass-green satin-stitch pattern of two leafy sprays, one running up each side of the front of the shirt. Overall design is lively and balanced, the workmanship excellent (the inside of the garment is as perfect as the outside).

Similarly admirable in technical application is a 1973 cushion cover, embroidered in Mexico to a design by Nancy Hemenway, the American artist whose own works echo Pre-Columbian American culture.

The influence of its northern neighbour on Mexican art today is more than balanced by the Mexican design and ethnological attributes found throughout the southern United States. Arizona, New Mexico and Texas, in particular, have been generally receptive to themes from south of the border.

Morocco

Embroidery tradition in its present form in the north-west of Africa dates back in the main to the dominance of the Moors, who had since the 8th century occupied much of Spain. The last were only finally expelled to their original homeland by Philip III in 1609.

They took back south with them their arts and skills. Much of the work was blackwork, with intricate and demanding motifs painstakingly embroidered on a linen ground. The minutiae of overall design continued through to the 19th century, as can be seen from the extremely complex sampler in the Victoria and Albert Museum. This work is in fact typical of Moroccan embroidery. A Moslem country, no figurative representation has been allowed and therefore motifs are largely based on stylised floral or geometric forms. The central cypress design is similar to that found throughout the lands of the eastern Mediterranean, a not surprising affinity since trading from Phoenician times has connected countries around that ocean.

Some influence from 19th-century Turkish and Greek embroideries can also be traced, a fact that can also be attributed to trading connexions.

Darning stitch was used by Thérèse de Dillmont for her generalisation of 'Moroccan embroidery' (*Complete Encyclopedia of Needlework*). She stated that 'clear-cut designs, consisting of the material left bare, and standing out sharply against a background of encroaching flat stitch, are characteristic of Moroccan embroidery'. This is perhaps too incomplete a view, but darning stitch and pattern darning are, it is true, to be found on many works, particularly decorative cloths, from north-west Africa.

Design is to some extent regionalised. Around Fez, Rabat and Meknes, monochrome plait stitch is frequently worked; south of Casablanca, outlinings and details are generally worked in line or cross stitch; and around Marrakesh polychrome plait stitch is worked alternately, with one row going from right to left and the next from left to right.

Morocco is today continuing her trading heritage and offering her wares to the tourist. The growing numbers of visitors to Tangier, Rabat, Casablanca and Marrakesh buy *ghallabejehs*, full-length robes of flowing proportions, and *kaftans*, often elaborately embroidered or decorated with cording around the front neck opening, the sleeves

181

and the hem. Modern Rabat embroidery is usually worked in dark red silk satin stitch; Tetuan embroidery is outlined with a black running stitch and filled with darning stitch.

MOROCCO—*part of a late 18th- or early 19th-century sampler, 41½ × 30 in. (105·5 × 76·5 cm), silk on a linen ground, worked with long-legged cross stitch, double running stitch, back stitch, buttonhole stitch, satin stitch, stem stitch and plain cross stitch.*
(The Victoria and Albert Museum, Crown Copyright)

The Netherlands

Perhaps more than some other western European countries, the Netherlands long acted as a staging post in the various routes of the embroidered-arts world. The country has herself been reluctant host to other powers, notably Spain and France. In return she has passed her embroideries to former settlement areas such as the Atlantic seaboard of the United States, and to South Africa, where elements of her embroidery influence, first introduced with the Boer settlers in 1652, have still remained.

One of the most influential Dutch innovations has been *or nué*, the technique of laid and couched work that originated in the Netherlands in the 14th century and passed quickly to the ecclesiastical and other lush embroideries of Belgium, France and England.

There has, in fact, always been speedy transmission of embroidery ideas between the Netherlands and her neighbours. Samplers, for example, have generally echoed contemporary works. An intricate square sampler, 1663, in Het Nederlands Openluchtmuseum, Arnhem, has a finely worked band of 22 different border motifs, all geometric and mostly based on dominant diagonal lining. The rest of the sampler ground is worked in spot motif formation with lettering surround.

The Victoria and Albert Museum has two contrasting 18th-century samplers. One, signed and dated 'Gerarda Gerritsen, 1763', features different darning patterns in block form. It is $14\frac{1}{2}$ in. (37 cm) square, silk on linen, and worked in cross stitch, chain stitch, Algerian eye stitch and pattern darning. The other, anonymous but dated 1798, is also silk on linen, $21\frac{1}{4} \times 18\frac{1}{2}$ in. (54 × 47 cm) and worked throughout in cross stitch. The patterning is symmetrical, with vertical reversion, except for a brilliant peacock with outspread tail to the right side. Each element of design is perfectly executed: carnations and other flora are life-like and generally more realistic than earlier representations.

Ground fabric for embroidery during the 18th and 19th centuries was not cheap and maximum utilisation resulted. School samplers and embroideries from orphanages frequently bear particular evidence of frugality. The Whitman Sampler Collection in the Philadelphia Museum of Art has, in its Dutch selection, one 1812 almost square sampler, $22\frac{1}{4} \times 21\frac{3}{4}$ in. (56·5 × 55·5 cm), cross stitch in

NETHERLANDS—*embroidered bookbinding, 1606, 6¾ × 4⅜ in.*
(17 × 11 cm), covering a New Testament and a Dutch Psalter,
both printed at Delft in 1594. The cover might have been
commissioned for the marriage of Ernest Casimir, Count of
Nassau-Dietz, Stadholder of Friesland, to Sophia Hedwig, niece of
Anne of Denmark, in 1607: there is allusion to marriage in the
water-colour painting around the edges of the embroidery. Pearl work
adds glory to the embroidery. Motifs of carnations, roses, pansies and
a tulip are indicative of Elizabeth influence. It will be noted that
the spine is very worn.
(The Victoria and Albert Museum, Crown Copyright)

silk on a linen ground. An outer surround of zigzag floral sprays is filled with dense motif working. A recurrent theme seen here is the neat three-storey house, with fence and looped chain in front. Once again the motif is completely symmetrical and balanced, indicative of the orderliness and fastidious outlook of the young lady who worked it. Other motifs include a cynical-looking reindeer, various Trees of Life and many other floral and animal groupings.

Nineteenth-century samplers often featured similar borders, with small leafy or floral repeating spray designs. Predominant stitching was cross stitch and there was, in the main, little personality apparent through the execution of rather formal designs. This adherence to convention showed, for example, in the working of some darning samplers. Unlike contemporary works in other western European countries, Dutch darning samplers, as evidenced by a piece also in the Whitman Sampler Collection, tend to be rather unexciting.

The artists of the Netherlands showed evidence of oriental influence, partly due to Dutch rule of the East Indies, in all facets of the arts ('willow pattern' Delft dates from the early 18th century). The fittings for a 'Japanese Room' and a 'Chinese Room' in the Royal Palace of Huis ten Bosch (pp. 46, 167–70) may have contributed design inspiration to Dutch embroiderers.

Contrary to popular belief, there is no such thing as a national costume in the Netherlands. Clothing has traditionally been regional, with specific textile interest in some of the headdresses. Not all examples feature embroidery, but typical regional head-coverings include the popular 'Dutch bonnets' from Volendam, whitework headdresses from Zeeland, flower and ribbon ornament from Brabant, ostrich-feather work from Veesen and pill-boxes from Marken Island. The last named, a tourist haven near Amsterdam, also features a polychrome wool embroidery.

Dutch 'blackwork' is often executed in red wool, particularly in Zeeland. Whitework and cutwork feature in embroidery of all regions. There is a very fine example of the latter form, called *snee werk*, similar to much Norwegian cutwork: it is found decorating aprons, blouses, pillowcases and similar items of personal and household wear.

There is in embroidery today a certain blending of the ancient and the modern. Frequently, indeed, both aspects are combined to produce traditional items—such as a sleeveless woollen waistcoat embroidered in a thick wool chain stitch—in an extremely modern colour scheme. Sometimes, too, contemporary stitchery bears direct comparison with other northern European work: stark outlines with minimal execution aimed at maximum effect certainly resemble

185

embroideries of northern Germany and, indeed, those of Scandinavia today.

NETHERLANDS—*Gunila Edwall's collar incorporates appliqué and 'Lapp tin thread work' (see p. 97). (The artist)*

New Zealand

New Zealand is one of the most embroidery-conscious countries of the world. Main historical influences have been English, Scottish, German and oriental (particularly Chinese, dating from the days of the gold rushes of the late 19th century). Original New Zealand embroidery stems from the beginning of the 19th century: although Captain Cook had first visited the islands in 1769 the first missionaries did not arrive until 1814.

The missionaries, who preceded later settlers, brought with them their household pieces, including items such as the silk and cotton

NEW ZEALAND—*'Our Kitchen', a pen and ink sketch by William Bambridge, 1819–73. The artist sailed from England in the s.s.* Tomatin *on 23rd December 1841, and became 'writing master' at St. John's College, Auckland, until 1848, when he returned to his homeland. During his time in New Zealand Mr. Bambridge kept a detailed diary with sketches such as this one, which shows Mrs. Bambridge sewing, her embroidery frame clamped to the table. (Alexander Turnbull Library, Wellington)*

patchwork quilts still treasured in many homes today.

Missionaries are rightly famous for the skill and diligence with which they spread the arts. Mrs. Marianne Williams, wife of one such ecclesiastical settler, was instrumental in teaching embroidery to Maori girls in her husband's mission at Paihia soon after her arrival in the country in 1823. (And, in fact, Mrs. Williams's descendants still play a large part in the fields of embroidery and general arts.)

When the Maoris first came to the islands in about 1350, they brought with them from the Polynesian Islands no specific embroidery heritage per se. The women's bodices (*pari*) did sometimes have basic interlacing set as a decorative horizontal band and there were stitched feather cloaks (*kahu huruhuru*). Auckland Museum has a modern example of the latter, worked by Mrs. Rangimakehu Hall of Utihina.

The Maoris have, however, handed on a tradition of *taaniko* weaving design. Although a woven art, the geometric designs are important to embroidery. *Taaniko*, a form of finger weaving, is best described as macramé with the various threads interwoven rather than knotted together. Using threads of flax, the weaver produces a narrow border to the required length to decorate clothing or stand by itself as headband or similar decoration.

NEW ZEALAND—*workbox by Joan Forsyth, 1972. Cotton on red linen, $8\frac{3}{4} \times 4\frac{1}{2}$ in. (22·5 × 11·5 cm). Featuring traditional Maori design interpreted in cross stitch, the motifs are (from left)* taaniko *design on the needlecase, Maori carved head on the pincushion, interpretation of carved Maori figure with protruding tongue on the left face of the box, traditional Maori 'rafter' design on the right face. (The artist)*

Apparently before the arrival of the missionaries, *taaniko* (or *taniko*, depending on the tribe) had had some men artists, but from 1814 on it became exclusively a woman's work.

In 1960 W. J. Phillips (*Maori Rafter and Taaniko Designs*) categorised these *taaniko* designs relevant to embroidery as follows:

Aronui—triangle-based designs
Aramoana ('ocean path')—simple zigzag designs
Tukemata ('eyebrow')—comprehensive zigzag designs
Whakarua koopito—diamond designs.

All variants of these four styles are traditional, and although they are too basic to be readily adapted by the enthusiastic needlewoman, they have been transposed to cross-stitch work on canvas.

The embroiderers of New Zealand have, more often, interpreted figures from the traditional Maori wooden carved figures (the Maoris themselves tend not to adapt their own symbolism to needlework).

Unlike settlers in some other parts of the world, the pioneering lady arrriving in New Zealand in the 19th century did not have services or luxuries to allow her freedom of time and ideas. There is not, therefore, a considerable history of show embroidery in the islands during the last century. What art was embroidered was generally governed by the needs of the home and of the family.

One form of decorative embroidery that was highly popular, however, was Berlin wool work, worked either with or without beads. It is impossible to segregate those pieces that were originally brought from Germany from those brought from Britain or worked in the islands themselves. There is a wide range both of Berlin wool work and Ayrshire whitework (introduced by Scottish settlers) in the collections of the National Museum in Wellington.

Wellington Cathedral plays a dominant role in current embroidery. The St. Paul's Cathedral Guild has, since 1964, produced fine sets of vestments combining ancient and modern styles and design. Dorothy Zohrab and Mary Walker have steered the group since its conception, and, with initial help from their first designer, Cynthia Marks, the group keeps to a universally noted standard of professionalism. Pulled and drawn work is used throughout for most of the whitework, and most of the hand stitching is embroidered on a white German linen, 'Odessa', with coarse thread weave of 29 to 30 stitches per inch. Vestments feature gold work and appliqué with fine stitching. Some of the imported brocade used has been specially woven to the Guild's specification.

The inspiration of the embroideries of Wellington Cathedral has acted as stimulus nationally and further afield. There is New Zealand ecclesiastical embroidery in the chapel of the Lolowal

189

Hospital in Melanesia (a set of linen burses, veils and stoles) and in the Chapel of the Tower of London (a whitework altar cloth worked by Ina Thornton and similar to an earlier piece of hers in Napier Cathedral).

The current interest in embroidery is typified by the working group established in Wellington between the National Museum and local ladies. The volunteers are helping with conservation of some of the nation's embroidered treasures. And one of their briefings is to undertake research into embroideries such as the William Morris 'Pomona' wall-hanging, worked by Lady Cory in 1907 (see p. 91). One of six such panels, the piece came to the Museum via the National Art Gallery. But beyond this routeing, little is known of the history of the work. Such research should produce not only information on the Morris movement but also on the recent history of embroidery in New Zealand.

An outstanding individual Wellington embroiderer is Beverley Shore Bennett, a 'Renaissance' designer with many of the facets of her talent associated with the arts. She often combines hand and machine stitching in her embroideries. The design of works such as 'Nova' and 'Wave' typifies the strength and personal aspect of her art. In the latter work, particularly, the surging crest of the incoming sea speaks with an onomatopoeic tone.

The newly formed Association of New Zealand Embroiderers' Guilds has branches in Auckland (2), Palmerston North, Wanganui, Wellington, Christchurch, Dunedin, Balclutha, Invercargill and Timaru. Throughout the entire country there is a growing awareness of the international importance of embroidery.

One of the largest embroideries in the entire country, however, is in the Town Hall at Christchurch, in the South Island. A wool on wool *tjell* panel on a brown ground of men's local suit cloth, the 37 ft. × 2 ft. 8 in. panel (11·28 × 0·81 m) portrays semi-abstract motifs of the city's life. Designed by Colleen O'Connor and worked by ten other ladies, it was unveiled March 1973.

Fields of embroidery particularly popular in modern New Zealand work include blackwork, canvas work and Hardanger. Embroidery in the islands is universal: the artists are enthusiastic to adapt to new designs and ideas. New Zealand has a wealth of embroidery talent and technical skill, and in this aspect of the art it is probably one of the leading countries in today's embroidery world.

Niger and Nigeria

The four main embroidery tribes of this West African region are the Yoruba (to the south-west, around Ibadan), the Ibo (to the south-east, around Enugu), the Nupe (to the central-west, along the banks of the river Niger) and the Hausa (across the north of the region, encompassing Kano and Zaria). Yoruba territory extends across Dahomey. Hausaland carries on into northern Dahomey, too. There is throughout, in fact, interchange between the arts of Dahomey and Nigeria, particularly in the field of appliqué. Samuel Ojo Omonaiye is one artist whose design from both countries is already known in Britain and America: his appliqué and patchwork stitcheries were included in an exhibition at the International Monetary Fund in Washington DC, in summer 1973.

Niger, to the north of Nigeria, is more or less dependent for all embroidery inspiration on her southern neighbour. For that reason, therefore, Niger and Nigeria are here described together.

There is much interplay of design between Hausa and Yoruba embroidery, as there is of all the arts, although patterns have been more likely to travel from north to south, to the coast. Design has thus gone from Hausaland to Yoruba territory, sometimes to be modified for re-export north. On the whole Hausa motifs tend to be flat and abstract, whereas those of Yoruba arists are representational and three-dimensional.

The main centres for embroidery (*dinki*) are in the north, in Hausaland. Hausas are travellers and traders. Their embroidery is creative and imaginative. Men embroider: the women spin, weave and have to suffice with occasionally being allowed the privilege of embroidering the skull caps that their menfolk wear.

Typical kinds of embroidery practised today throughout Hausaland are braid and metal thread work, whose design indicates inspiration from the robes of the *Hajji*, Moslem pilgrims returning from Mecca, cotton thread embroidery and machine stitchery. Cotton thread embroidery is, perhaps, the most fascinating of these movements. Buttonhole stitch, running stitch and chain stitch are most frequently used. Artists work on an imported or local cotton ground: traditionally the local fabric, generally white or indigo, was woven in strips 2 in. (5 cm) wide, which were then sewn into panels prior to stitching.

NIGERIA—*a copy of six versions of Hausa embroidery design by Alhaji Sanni of Yalwa, Kano, 1971, collected by David Heathcote. The knife motif (aska) is recurrent throughout Hausa design but has no known symbolism. The knot motif (dagi) is found in many fields of Nigerian art. This drawing was first produced in Mr. Heathcote's article 'Insight into a creative process: a rare collection of embroidery drawings from Kano' in* Savanna, *Vol. 1, no. 2, December 1972. (Reproduced by kind permission of* Savanna)

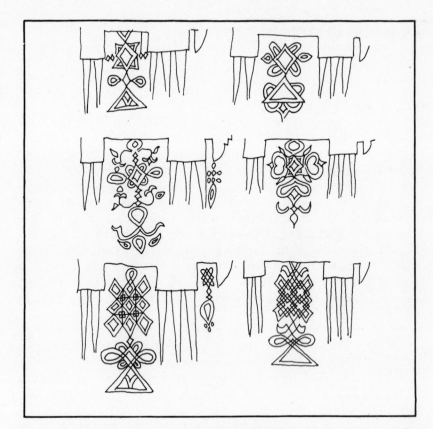

Dress has played a symbolic and important role in the life of the Hausa and there has been extensive embroidered decoration. Even now, apparently, men are to be seen wearing more than one robe with elaborate embroidery design. David Heathcote, author of several works on Hausa arts, suggests that embroidery has its beginning in the area in the 19th century, but more exact dating is impracticable. One of the earliest known robes can be accurately traced to mid-19th century.

Designs on *riguna* (gowns) and *wando* (trousers) are often of the spot motif category, with various small emblems apparently unconnected to any overall theme. Repetition of combination of emblems is not apparent. It is thought, therefore, that the embroidery artist works to original association of such emblems. Influence can be definitely ascribed, however, to Islamic architecture in the region. Mosques and the interiors of palaces have provided ideas for the artist. The Hausa has an exceptional memory and he often incorporates symbols from his childhood into his embroidery patterns. Throughout his drawing there is a fluidity of conception, and he is

192

△ HONG KONG – mod-
ern appliqué hanging on
velvet by a student from
the Sir Robert Black Tea-
cher Training College.
(Mrs Wong Tam Man-So)

△ INDIA – detail of embroidered houserobe made
in Kashmir, c. 1930, by artists employed by one
"Suffering Moses", a textile entrepreneur known
to be continuing in business in recent years.
(Mrs Naomi Micklam)

▽ INDIA – modern Indian shishadur ("mirror work").
(Author's collection)

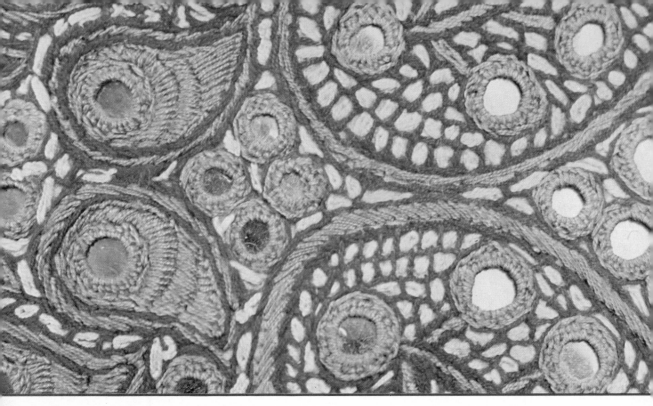

△ *INDIA – modern Pakistani* shishadur *("mirror work")*.
(Author's collection)

▽ *PALESTINE – panel bought in a Jerusalem* soukh *(market) in 1972. The muted colours and faded ground help to date it as a late 19th-century work.*
(Author's collection)

fond of *dagi*, the complicated knot designs found throughout the arts of Hausaland.

Most motifs are considerably stylised. Indigenous animals are represented continually, but in varying guises. The lizard, for example, has been among the most popular subjects in many art fields, possibly through the association of that reptile with beliefs concerning fertility and love. Lizards have been used for many forms of body decoration (such as body painting) and are found in typically stylised form on embroideries.

Aska, the Hausa knife, is another recurrent design, but this has not yet been proven to have definite symbolism. Comprehensive cataloguing of possible connexions of embroidery motifs to the cultural beliefs of the people is currently under way at the Ahmadu Bello University in Zaria.

Norway

From 1397 to 1814 Norway was united with Denmark: she was then under the protection of her neighbour Sweden until she regained complete independence in 1905. And, with northern lands bordering Finland and the USSR, with whom she shares responsibility for the Lapp people of the Arctic, Norway's embroidery affiliations are varied. There is also a recognisable British connexion, for example, in some aspects of her work, a heritage that can be traced to the era of the Vikings: a lettering sampler in the Norsk Folkemuseum in Oslo has an English-type alphabet, indicative of that sea communication.

Much of Norway's embroidery today shows close association with that of her Scandinavian neighbours. Whitework and wool work, canvas work and modern creative stitchery do, in many instances, resemble embroideries from Denmark and Sweden and, to a lesser extent, those of Finland.

An early example of truly indigenous Norwegian stitchery is the 'Høyland tapestry', now in the Museet Universitetet i Trondheim. It was dated in 1952 by Helen Engelstad to the second half of the 12th century (although A. M. Franzen has since suggested the early 13th century). Apart from the fact that it is from the church at Høylandet in Nord-Trøndelag, little is known of the history of the work, which tells the story, from St. Matthew's gospel, of the Magi riding to Bethlehem to present gifts to the Child. From unfinished edging at either end, it is reasonable to suppose that the embroidery

NORWAY—*the Høyland tapestry, 13th–14th century, telling the story of the coming of the Magi to Bethlehem. (Universitetet i Trondheim, DKNVS, Museet)*

NORWAY—*detail of the Høyland tapestry, showing the middle King.*
(Universitetet i Trondheim, DKNVS, Museet)

was originally longer than it is at present—15 ft. 10¾ in. × 17 in. (485 × 43 cm): it is worked in double running threads on a warm red woven ground, now faded to a yellow-brown hue. There is a somewhat stilted rigidity about the overall appearance, a typical attribute of arts of the time, but, as the detail of the central king shows, the artist had an undoubted sense of humour which was employed when he was working the facial details.

There was much folk embroidery, particularly during the 17th and 18th centuries, and high standards of design and execution were maintained. The 19th century featured embroidery on a baize ground, with woollen flowers, highly stylised, worked in split stitch. Edgings were of braid or velvet.

'Hardanger work', a form of drawn thread work (p. 382) with roots around the fjord of that name, evolved about 1780. Hardanger has been instrumental in the progress of other forms of cutwork, particularly those of Italy, and it has also promoted the use of *kløster* stitch (satin stitch), used for the *kløsters* (blocks) in its execution.

With her more extroverted embroidery counterparts in other areas of Scandinavia, the Norwegian embroiderer tends today to be somewhat overlooked in the contemporary arts world. Individual artists are not as well known as they should be. There is outstanding embroidery being created, both by the independent artist and by groups of church embroiderers who produce stunning vestments with subtle texture combinations and bright colour schemes.

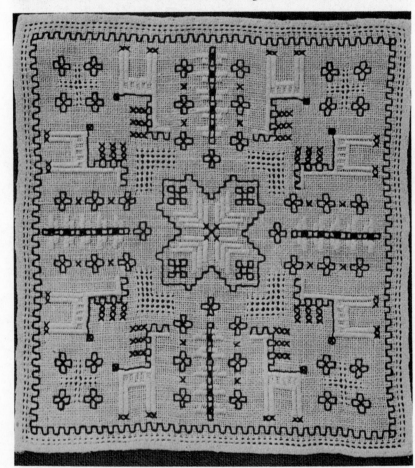

NORWAY—*small white linen mat from the west coast, 1949, the white thread worked in satin and four-sided stitches, the black thread in Holbein and cross stitches. (The Embroiderers' Guild, London)*

The Pacific Islands

There is no long-standing embroidery tradition in the numerous smaller Pacific islands. Many of the insular communities have, until the last 150 years, been entirely self-sufficient, with little contact with the rest of the world. The advent of missionaries from the beginning of the 19th century introduced embroideries such as patchwork, Hawaiian quilting (p. 119) and the appliqué found in the Cook Islands and Tahiti.

Traditional island fabric was constituted from beaten bark decorated with stencilled designs. In Fiji, today, there is wool stitching on such a ground fabric. Embroidery stitches are taught in some schools throughout the islands: the girls of Queen Salote College in Nuku'alofa, in Tonga, for instance, sell samples of their work at their annual bazaar.

Panama and Central America

With a highly complicated and interrelated history, the countries of Central America can justifiably be classified in one section of the embroidered arts of the world.

Guatemala, Honduras, El Salvador, Nicaragua, Costa Rica and Panama were under Spanish rule from the early 16th to the early 19th centuries. Spanish influence is directly felt in national costumes like the *pollera*, a full-length dress with some ten yards of material in a full skirt with layers of flounces. It is claimed that this Iberian-looking garment is in fact, however, of native Central American origin, possibly inspired by the robes of black slaves of the past.

Of the three categories of *pollera* (*pollera montuna, pollera de gala* and the wedding *pollera*), the two last are the more special, and therefore the more heavily embroidered. Each garment has two or three petticoats, hand-made of fine white linen and embellished with much cutwork and fine embroidering. The outer skirt, too, frequently has embroidered motifs on the wide flounces. Appliqué is common and the combined appliqué/embroidery motifs are often floral, bright and colourful. The wedding *pollera*, however, is traditionally white on white.

General embroidery motifs are the balanced, soft designs found throughout Central America, less rigid and geometric than those of central Europe. Geometry is confined to simple bands of diagonals, for example, forming the border of a man's shirt (*montuno*). There is also oriental heritage in some stitchery design: the *kulka* (palmette design) found in so many places of the world is in Central America too, though in one particular instance the proportions appear more fish-like than palmette-like.

Other embroidery influences have been imported by the complex immigrant structure of Central America. Panama gained independence from Colombia in 1903 and there is some Colombian element to design today: Panama was not, in fact, considered part of the 'Central America' group as such until the beginning of the 20th century. Chinese immigration occurred particularly in Panama. The US-administered Canal Zone constitutes another source of external influence, and neighbouring Costa Rica is a heterogeneous result of various European immigrations.

It must have been difficult for colonial settlers and immigrants of the past sometimes to obtain the embroidery materials they required in Central America. The British writer Emilia Ross Bell (who married Gustavus Ferdinand von Tempsky, to play a leading role in the New Zealand Maori wars) wrote to her sister, Mrs. Jane Bogle in Glasgow, from Bluefields, Nicaragua, on 21st August 1845:

> . . . We always share in things sent from home . . . you may see one tearing over in a frantic manner to the residence of the other to borrow a needle or to beg in a humble manner for the loan of two pins.
> (Reproduced by courtesy of the Alexander Turnbull Library, Wellington, New Zealand: *Tempsky MSS.*, correspondence 1840–1880 of Emilia Ross von Tempsky (Bell).)

Guatemala is dissimilar to her Central America neighbours in that a large proportion of the population is descended from the Mayas. The country, therefore, has a correspondingly lively tradition of colourful weaving.

Guatemalan embroidery today is customarily largely reserved for additional clothing decoration. In the famous market of Chichicastenango can be seen wide tubes of thick cotton fabric with vertical and horizontal woven bands of decoration (this entire tube is wrapped around and tucked in to form a skirt). Accompanying blouses, woven in three panels, frequently have an embroidered square on the front yoke and there is often a woolwork rosette on each shoulder.

The term 'Panama embroidery' is applied to simple canvas work on 'Panama fabric', a Java canvas that can be either linen or cotton, with an open weave and four warp or weft threads forming each strut of the 'basket weave'. The fabric is suitable ground for simple geometric motifs and is widely used in basic western embroidery.

Panama does have embroidery unique to its own territory, however. The most frequently encountered contemporary embroidery is the *mola*, produced exclusively by the Cuna Indians of the 386 atolls of the San Blas Islands off mainland Panama. The *mola* is a form of 'reverse appliqué' worked by cutting down through various layers of fabric, a complex and fascinating art with no similarity to any of the arts from the rest of Panama. San Blas is, in fact, noticeably independent in outlook: in 1925 the 26,000 Cuna Indians declared themselves to be an independent state, and although they are today legally part of the Republic of Panama, they are none the less a comparatively separate community.

A *mola* is an oblong panel some 18 in. (46 cm) long and 12 in. (30·5 cm) high. It is still worn sewn on to the front of the Cuna woman's blouse, and is thought to have evolved from early body paintings of the islands. (Lionel Wafer, in 1699, described Cuna women with painted bodies. . . . 'The women are the painters, and take great delight in it. The colours they like and use most are red, yellow and blue . . . they make figures of birds, beasts, men, trees or the like up and down in every part of the body, more especially the faces.')

The derivative 'body painting' of the fabric *mola* is, therefore, less than two centuries old. Possibly fabric clothing was imposed on the people by prudish missionaries of the last century. Captain Kit S. Kapp, one of the first foreigners to recognise the collecting value of the *mola*, has several robes (*nimatra molas*) from the nearby Colombian villages of Arquia and Rio Cariman that are, with their coloured and decorated bands on the lower hem of the full skirt, possibly Victorian forerunners of today's *mola*.

PANAMA—*a traditional Cuna Indian* mola *from San Blas, the thin cutwork appliqué derivative from the coral of those islands.* (Carla Hunt)

Dating a *mola* involves consideration of various factors. There is some element of definite timing, whether by the inclusion of the actual year of execution or by some 'pegged' motif such as President Kennedy, with rocking chair and his son John, that was included in the 1973 exhibition of *molas* at the Textile Museum in Washington DC. Technical dating includes the guideline that patterns and stitching were cruder and less sophisticated during the 20's and 30's and the width of strips of appliqué was often $\frac{1}{2}$–$\frac{3}{4}$ in. (13–19 mm). In later *molas* the spaces were reduced sometimes to a width of $\frac{1}{4}$ in. (6 mm) and design became more complex. Within the last few years, alas, the

200

progress has been reversed towards a wider space between applied cuts, which admittedly is quicker to work but produces a *mola* with less resultant appeal.

Cuna Indians adhere to a matriarchal society. Women design the *molas* and women make them (and of course wear them). Some of the designers are skilled artists with an advanced sense of balance, and many have a considerable sense of humour.

Inspiration today is sometimes gleaned from advertisements. One *mola* inscribed 'King size WINSTON filter cigarettes—finer filter for finer flavor—made in USA' was included in the 1965 exhibition at the Museum of Contemporary Crafts of the American Craftsmen's Council, New York.

The *mola* now usually consists of three or four layers of light-weight cotton, often with a thicker layer at the bottom to act as substantial backing ground. The layers are tacked together with rough stitching (sometimes left in). A design is marked on the top layer of fabric and cut out, in step form, through the various layers of fabric to the bottom ground. Cut edges are turned under and sewn down. A design can also be built up from the exposed bottom ground, giving a finished cross-section similar to that of a contour map. As well as the hemming and running stitches used to hold down main pieces of the design, superimposed cross stitch, back stitch, chain stitch, straight stitch, buttonhole stitch and couching are sometimes added for details such as animal eyes, facial expressions and similar personal characteristics.

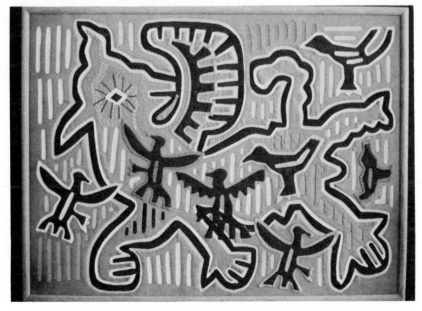

PANAMA—*a modern Cuna Indian* mola *from San Blas, with wider cutwork appliqué strips showing fierce bird-planes.*
(Carla Hunt)

201

Since the introduction of the domestic sewing machine, an advent hastened by recent social volunteers to the San Blas Islands, some machine sewing is taking over from hand stitching. Since each *mola* is so personal a work, and so very human in effect, machine embroidery is not really suitable to the medium.

There are many schools of thought as to symbolism of design. A two-headed bird, fierce and watchful, appears again and again, sometimes with a fledgling in her 'womb'. There is mythological foetal representation with some human association. A long-clawed jaguar devouring a rough-shaped moon is said to symbolise the local reasons for an eclipse. Iguanas, pelicans, palm trees, rattlesnakes and the shapes of coral around the islands' reefs are all much-used motifs. But whether they do in fact have anthropological meaning is not yet definitely ascertained.

Certainly some of the *molas* produced today have little symbolic significance. With a growing number of cruise ships putting in at Panama, local traders (and the Cunas themselves) are supplying a ready and eager market. *Molas* are produced to demand with whatever design the collector wants, though the finished product still features the omnipresent styling of the embroiderer.

There were no *molas* on the regular embroidery stalls until a few years ago. Now they are to be seen framed on walls or gracing tables in many parts of the world. The supply will, however, continue to be necessarily restricted by the fact that the Cuna woman is a talented artist and proud of her skill.

Much interesting research on *molas* is now being carried out by Mrs. Herta Puls.

The Persian Gulf
(*or* The Arabian Gulf)

The country most prolific in embroidery, bordering the Gulf, is Iran
(p. 143). The others, Saudi Arabia, Kuwait, Bahrain and the newly
formed Federation of Arab Emirates, do not have such production.

Iraq produces some outstanding 'Kurdish rugs', worked by the
Marsh Arabs of the Tigris-Euphrates delta. Bright yellow, green,
pink, black and white designs are worked in thick woollen yarns on
a dull red wool ground. These embroideries are, at the moment, in
regular supply, but they are already becoming much prized as collectors' items.

Kuwait epitomises the region's oil-based prosperity and corresponding rapid disappearance of traditional culture. Some of the
dresses still worn today feature embroidery, particularly on costumes
such as the *addar'ra*, a full-length dress, the *athoub* or *mantua*, a long
cloak or gown worn over the *addar'ra*, and the *al-bakhnak*, a child's
dress. Embroidery is mostly in chain stitch, sometimes with the
addition of spangles, wire thread and *athuria*, inserted metal shapes
similar to the Indian *shisha*. Much of the work is today machine-
tamboured, as are the bed and other domestic linens that are becoming increasingly popular with house-proud Kuwaitis who are now
well aware of the luxury consumer products of the West.

Peru

In common with the rest of western South America, Peru came under the domination of Spain after the arrival of Francisco Pizarro (1478–1541) and the other *conquistadores*. Examples of the arts immediately prior to this time—the arts of the Chimu and the Inca—were in large part destroyed.

It is the earlier embroideries and applied arts that have survived, probably because much of the creative output of the Paracas, Nazca, Ica and Tiahuanaco artists had long since been buried, in necropolis bundles or some other form, and remained preserved in the sands of the dry coastal region, undisturbed by the fury of Pizarro and his men.

From about 1400 BC Chavin de Huantar was a leading cultural and religious centre of what is now known as the Paracas culture (named from the 'Paracas open winds'; to escape them the people lived partly underground, based around the mouth of the Pisco river). Early Paracas dating is divided into Early Horizon and Early Intermediate periods, each sub-divided into epochs. The greater part of Paracas textiles, of which the majority were woven, today date from the end of the Early Horizon and beginning of the Early Intermediate periods, roughly 500–200 BC, and embroidery as such became the preferred medium for much textile decoration from this date until about Epoch 3 of the Early Intermediate Period. Most early items were burial shrouds elaborately worked with motifs and symbolism.

Design found in Paracas embroidery frequently includes the 'Oculate being', a flying anthropomorphic figure with flowing appendages and big eyes. Early Paracas figures have an element of fun about them, with wide smiling mouths, a misleading and paradoxical attribute since the figure often also carries a knife or spear, sometimes with a severed head as trophy. Many embroideries from Epoch 9 featuring this dramatic being were found, for instance, during the Cerro Colorado excavations of Julio C. Tello in 1925. Sometimes the figure is falling backwards, his chest arched and his head flung back.

Paracas embroidery was exclusively a male art: the womenfolk were employed in other directions. Embroiderers used mainly stem stitch, satin stitch and running stitch, generally on a ground of local cotton or alpaca wool. They had more than 190 different colour shades from which to choose, obtained through their natural dyes.

Some of the best complete items of Paracas embroideries are in the Museo Nacional in Lima. Mantles, shirts, loin-cloths, turbans in vivid reds, blues, yellows, greens and browns come from the funerary bundles which have revealed so much of the burial procedure of the people. A complete bundle consisted of many concentric layers of cloth, sometimes charred and much weathered, indicating that the compiling of the whole took place over a period of time. Besides the customary mantle, the bundle contained a feathered cape, possibly worn by a 'bird man' similar to the 'Oculate being' and some bundles, too, contained complete sets of clothing, with skirts, ponchos and mantles embroidered in the same motif. Necropolis bundles can be dated by the number of wrappings (the later the

PERU—*detail of burial mantle from a necropolis bundle. The embroidery, 114 × 53¾ in. (290 × 136·5 cm), is Paracas style, possibly from the Early Intermediate Period, c. 4th century BC. (Courtesy Museum of Fine Arts, Boston. J. H. and E. A. Payne Fund)*

bundle, the fewer the layers) and, also, later designs featured elaborate detailing to the lower face of any figures, whether human or anthropomorphic.

By Epoch 10 of the Early Horizon, embroidery had become more dominant over the textile ground and motifs were often outlined by a number of thin lines rather than by the single heavy outlining of earlier works. The first eight Epochs of the Paracas Early Intermediate Period correspond more or less to the eight Epochs of the Nazca culture, most of the first examples of which have been found in Cerro Colorado and the Cabeza Larga. Nazca culture soon held sway over the entire coastal region, displacing not only the Paracas culture but also that of the Topara at Ica.

Nazca embroidery was similar in design to that of Paracas, with the 'Oculate being' once again, with bird, feline and killer-whale features. Stem stitch was used throughout, occasionally with some two-sided stitch. Later there was much black outlining, some of which has since rotted away.

Following the Nazcas were the Huari and Tiahuanaco empires of the Middle Horizon Period (c. AD 550–900). The Huaris were from the central Peruvian highlands; Tiahuanaco was further south, and stretched into what are now Bolivia and Chile. Both cultures had similar art styles and both adopted designs from their predecessors. Stone monuments at the ruined city of Tiahuanaco, in Bolivia, show motifs similar to those of embroidery: designs are formal, with band embroideries separated by plain strips between, on a cotton or alpaca wool ground.

The Late Intermediate Period (c. AD 900–1476) saw the rise of the Chimu and, from 1350, the Inca. Embroidery of the time is characterised by step-patterning throughout, and sometimes bird motifs were incorporated into the design. It was indeed an ornithological era: 'feather embroidery', in which whole quills were stitched to plain-weave fabric, was used to form garments such as the poncho now in the Linden-Museum, Stuttgart, which has feathers stitched to the base and is thought to be from the central highlands or southern coastal regions of Peru.

With the arrival of Spanish settlers from the 16th century onwards, Peru's embroideries fell more or less into line with those of other Spanish colonial areas, with the greater part of the work produced closely allied to Spanish convent embroideries and work of the home country.

The recent awareness of the magnificent arts of the pre-Columbian civilisations in Peru has stimulated foreign embroiderers, and artists today are adapting ancient motifs to 20th-century media. Obviously the symbolism of the zoomorphic and anthropomorphic figures of

206

the Paracas cannot carry meaning to the modern embroiderer, but the intricate connexion of line, balance and humour has much to appeal to current thought. In Peru itself, embroidery has generally become a typical folk art, with chain and cross stitch patterns, but with an inherent humour still noticeable in much of the design.

There are many outstanding collections of early Peruvian embroideries of the pre-Columbian cultures, as, for instance, those of the Museum of Fine Arts, Boston, the Textile Museum of Washington DC, the Museum of Art of Rhode Island School of Design and the Eugene Fuller Memorial Collection of Seattle Art Museum.

The Philippines

The turbulent history of the Philippine Islands has imparted varied qualities to her arts. The Portuguese navigator Magellan arrived in 1521 (and was slain by natives of Mactan Island): subsequent Spanish conquerors, in 1565, named the islands 'Filipinas' after the son of their king. The islands were Spanish colonies from then until 1898, when, in a Treaty of Paris, they were ceded to the United States. After Japanese occupation in the Second World War independence was finally gained in 1946.

Added to this active history is the multi-stranded religious heritage of the Filipinos themselves (they may be Christian, Moslem or pagan). Despite such a multiplicity of invasions and conversions, however, they do maintain certain unique facets to their arts.

The Philippines are primarily famous for their fabrics. *Piña*, a gossamer-fine pineapple cloth, for instance, has long been used as an embroidery ground. The leaves of the plant are scraped and the resultant fibres spun and woven. Production of this cloth is very much a family affair, and *piña* embroideries, worked into runners, handkerchiefs and other delicate items, are therefore today becoming increasingly rare.

There is a local cotton material—the early Spanish settlers wrote home of native islanders in cotton clothing—and, since 1935, *ramie*, originally introduced from China, produced from a perennial grass with quarterly harvests. *Buri* is a raffia from the most tender leaves of palms found in Luzon and southern Quezon, and *jusi* is fabric woven from raw silk imported from China. On such grounds, therefore, embroidery has been worked to specific requirements, sometimes to those of foreign traders. There is much self-coloured embroidery, particularly on the off-white *piña* cloth.

PHILIPPINES—*detail of pulled thread embroidery on piña ('pineapple cloth'). The stitching is reminiscent of much Tønder work and was probably influenced by foreign settlers in the islands. (Honiton and Allhallows Museum, Devon)*

Poland

From 1795 to 1918 Poland was partitioned, lying within the confines of Prussia, Russia and Austria-Hungary, and there still remains much inter-action between the embroideries of Poland and her neighbours.

Few complete examples of pre-18th-century Slav embroidery exist, but leather embroideries dating back to the 10th century have been found in excavations at Opole and, also, fragments of an embroidered ritual handkerchief of 1686 have been found in Bobrek, near Cieszyn.

Embroidery has traditionally been a feminine occupation (*švadlena* or *švajka* is the embroiderer herself), thought to be becoming for those who could not undertake heavier physical work. Sometimes the art was taught in convents, but, more usually, apprentice embroiderers learnt from those already masters (mistresses) of their trade.

Working on home-woven linen or wool, the artist gave particular importance to embroidering near to the seams and openings of clothing (this is in fact a peculiarity of Slavonic countries: embroidery is always found near to the edge of the fabric).

Stitches used in this peasant dress embroidery include chain stitch, cross stitch, square stitch, raised stitch and various bilateral stitches such as *zawolocz* in which stitches run alternately vertically and horizontally. Earlier dress embroidery was worked mainly in one, two or three colours, but today more variety is employed.

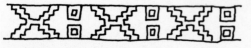

POLAND—*border motifs from Kosow.*

Cross stitching is particularly characteristic of folk embroidery of the region of the Beskidy Mountains of Silesia. In this area, too, there is much background embroidery, with the main motif left clear in sharp relief. Apparently young girls tend to wear red (for innocence) and older women wear black. Around Cieszyn violet signifies either widowhood or the fact that the wearer was about to marry for the second time—or the loss of virginity.

Metal thread embroidery developed largely through ecclesiastical vestments (Poland is to this day predominantly Catholic). Symbolic designs are often religiously related. Others include motifs of one- or two-headed eagles, stags, horses, lions and geometric forms such as squares and rhombuses. Gold-embroidery centres were Krakow, Zywiec, Gdarsk and Jablonkow, in Silesia.

One school of embroidery unrelated to the peasant cross stitching is the floral satin-stitch work, with delicate sprigs and individual flora on a cotton ground, either plain or patterned. This, and a white-work similar to *broderie anglaise*, has no direct relationship with what is generally thought of as 'Polish peasant embroidery'.

In the Gorce region of the Polish Carpathian Mountains—in north and north-west Gorce and parts of Wyspowy Beskid, but not in the Silesian Beskid area—is found *parzenica*, a traditional form of decorative embroidery on men's trousers. This form of embroidery is first known towards the end of the 19th century when two-opening trousers came into fashion (previously trousers had only one opening). The edges of these openings are extravagantly embroidered with elaborate motifs in shapes peculiar to a particular village community. Stitching used is generally chain stitch, satin stitch and herringbone stitch. Common designs found in many local variants of *parzenica* are the heart and a chevalier's knot. Early *parzenicas* were worked only in red and dark blue, but to receive acclaim today the embroiderer should use a minimum of seven colours.

The traveller to Poland will find embroidered blouses and cross-stitch bookmarks and mats available in most of the main cities. Traditional dress is, alas, fast dying out for everyday wear, and, although it is to be seen east of Warsaw, as the farmers' wives and children join their men to ride on long low bullock wagons to and from market (an uncomfortable journey that, since the wagon may have no springs) it is generally only the older ladies who wear *dirndl* skirts and white blouses with gay cross-stitch embroidery decoration. Embroidered shirts for men, known as *barongs*, are sometimes worn for full-dress occasions.

One of the best museum collections of historical Polish embroideries of all regions of the country is that of Muzeum Przyrodnicze in Krakow. Other collections are in the Pánstwowe Muzeum Ethnograficzne in Warsaw and in the regional museums of Lowicz and Rzeszów (Muzeum Okręgowe).

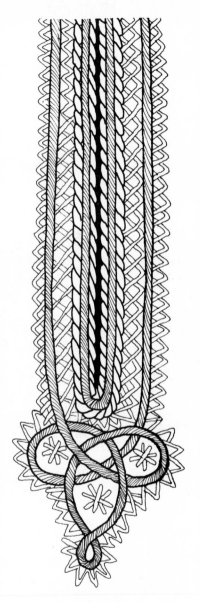

POLAND—parzenica, *detail of embroidered motif with 'chevalier's knot' design. Jan Ploskonka, Kasina Mala (Limanowa district). (Polska Sztuka Ludowa)*

Portugal and Madeira

PORTUGAL—*part of a 17th-century quilt, silk on linen, mainly chain stitch, with Indian influence in design throughout.*
7 ft. 3 in. × 7 ft. (2·21 × 2·13 m).
(Museu Nacional de Arte Antiga, Lisbon)

PORTUGAL—*part of a 17th-century Indo-Portuguese quilt, embroidered in Portugal, red, white and yellow silk on linen, back stitch dominating. 9 ft. 5 in. × 6 ft. 7 in. (2·87 × 2·01 m). (Museu Nacional de Arte Antiga, Lisbon)*

Portuguese influence stretched far across the known world of the late Middle Ages. In 1498 Vasco da Gama reached India via the Cape route, and Portuguese expertise in maritime navigation forged the links of her chain of trading posts strung around the coasts of Arabia, India, Malaya, China and the islands of the East Indies.

From the early 16th century, therefore, Portugal's own colonial connexions afforded a valuable insight into embroidered arts of other

213

parts of the world. The first Portuguese settlements on the Indian sub-continent, for example, were instituted in Bengal in 1537, and the newcomers carefully noted, and copied, the intricacies and finesse of the arts of their host country. A missionary, Sebastien Manrique, who visited Bengal in 1629, wrote:

> Amongst the more important commodities dealt in by the Portuguese in Bengal are very rich back-stitched quilts (*riquissimas colchas, en las pespuntadas*), bed-hangings, pavilions and other curious articles worked with hunting-scenes.
> (from *Itinerario de las Missiones que Hizo el Padres F. S. Manrique*, Rome 1649)

It follows, accordingly, that much home-produced Portuguese embroidery from the late 16th century is so closely allied to what is called 'Indo-Portuguese embroidery' (p. 138) that it is often difficult to differentiate between the possible provenances of a piece of work of this time, and positive identification is possible only with practice. In the main, however, Portuguese-produced embroideries are more static and less flowing than their Indian-produced counterparts which, also, have a unique element of nature-identification.

Less exotic embroidery production in Portugal has, as in many countries, been mostly regional. The Royal Scottish Museum in Edinburgh, in its collection of items from the former Needlework Development Scheme, has a 19th-century shirt, from Guimaraes, in the north of the country. It is $37\frac{1}{2}$ in. (95 cm) long and bears relation to contemporary British rural smocks, with a similar 'tubing' of embroidery on the front yoke panel, although—unlike British works —it is not smocked but embroidered straight to the linen ground with white cotton panels of wheel-motifs, quatrefoils, loops, rosettes and foliage. At the bottom of the 'tubing' is a horizontal band, with red cotton lettering 'FIRONI'. The Museum has another Guimaraes work, dated 1935–40, a tray cloth ($20\frac{1}{2} \times 14\frac{1}{4}$ in.—52×36 cm) with red cotton on a linen ground, worked in similar vein, with quatrefoils and floral sprays in the border.

Also to the north, in Viana do Castelo, north of Oporto, there is a costume embroidery with wool threads of yellow, purplish-pink and green coordinated with cotton threads of white, blue, green and yellow on a red flannel ground. Flat strips of gilt metal thread, sequins and glass beads further embellish the work, which is predominantly executed in herringbone stitch, satin stitch and laid and couched work. In Vila do Conde, near Oporto, there is a local needlelace with particularly heavy *cordonnet* and *toile* on a diagonal-mesh ground: motifs are scrolled, with some *kulka*, indicative of Persian

214

PORTUGAL—*part of a modern* colcha *(quilt) from Castelo Branco.*
(Secretaria de Estado da Informacão e Turismo)

influence, apparent also in the *colchas* (quilts) worked in the Castelo Branco area of the country.

Some of the finest embroidery from Portugal today is found in the beautiful cross-stitched carpets and rugs worked by women prisoners in and around Lisbon. Under the guidance of skilled designers, they work to required patternings. There is reputed to be a three-year waiting list for these custom-worked embroideries, which enjoy a ready sale in North America and elsewhere.

One of the best representative collections of Portuguese embroideries is that of the Museu Nacional de Arte Antiga in Lisbon, which features frequent embroidery exhibitions. Some embroidery is to be seen, too, at the annual *Mercado de Primavera* ('spring market'), also in the capital.

The island of Madeira, in the Atlantic Ocean some 520 miles southwest of Lisbon, is under the administration of metropolitan Portugal. Main foreign embroidery influence in the island was in the middle of the 19th century. Phylloxera, a ravaging disease, attacked the vineyards and, to help relieve the resultant distress, the daughter of a wine shipper, a Miss Phelps, paid for a Scottish expert to introduce Ayrshire whitework (p. 224) to Madeira ladies. Unfortunately the temperature and humidity of the island made embroiderers' hands very 'damp', a natural occurrence which quickly discoloured white embroidery yarn. A pale blue thread was therefore substituted and, although the colour did lessen with frequent washing, Madeira 'Ayrshire' can sometimes be distinguished by its blue hue.

'Madeira embroidery', a cutwork, was often worked under the supervision of Catholic nuns in the island's convents. It was similar to *broderie anglaise* (p. 378), which was, in fact, sometimes known as 'Madeira work' from the 1880's.

Romania

Romanians reputedly have a nomadic past and, indeed, even today large bands of gypsies can be seen, each family grouped around its own fire with curling smoke, a gaily decorated caravan behind, a horse grazing nearby . . . a whole community, self-sufficient from the rest of the world, settling for the night in a forest field high in the mountainous Carpati region.

More to the point, what has—since 1947—been 'The Romanian People's Republic' has had a constant history of invasion. Greeks, Romans, Turks, Hungarians, Poles, Germans and Russians have in turn occupied the land and large areas have changed nationality in the recent past.

With troubled life around them, the peoples of Transylvania, Wallachia and Moldavia have led a necessarily transient existence. Home pride and domesticity, when coupled with a temporary base, resulted in decorations that could be moved. Embroidered rugs, carpets and hangings were both portable and personal and, therefore, in Romania today can be seen examples of embroidered 'house decoration'.

Foreign influence has been felt not only through occupant nations. Traders from Venice, for instance, brought glass beads which were utilised as decorative addenda to blouses from Muntenia or Moldavia.

Ground fabric throughout has usually been wool or *pansa*, a hand-woven crêpe-like material of cotton or linen. Stitches most frequently used are Romanian stitch, fly stitch, Holbein stitch, line stitch, straight stitch, chain stitch and satin stitch. Buttonhole stitch is sometimes used as an edging.

Although it is the women who embroider in Romania, the art nevertheless has universal association. To take one example: Capus is a small one-street village some 100 km east of Oradea in Transylvania (once part of Hungary and today still peopled by the large Hungarian minority in Romania). Even the local architects have contributed to the overpowering embroidery connexions of Capus. Each garden fence has a tall seat let into it, long enough for half a dozen women to sit and talk as they stitch. And they do so. Girls from the age of 9 to 90, the older ones in gay kerchiefs and full regional dress, sit and sew, glancing up at the passing lorry drivers and

217

sometimes offering their wares. Capus is, alas, on the main route from Bucharest to Budapest and the resultant awareness of the handwork of the village has forced a regrettable decline in quality both of design and workmanship.

Design throughout the country is highly regional. To the east of the country, in Moldavia, there is bright-coloured wool embroidery on leather, with occasional inserted black borders. Overall colouring is darker than in some other parts of the country and there is less delicacy and sophistication to ground fabric and technical skill of the embroidery.

In the north, in Bukovina, blouses are similarly heavy and un-sophisticated. Transylvania, to the north and west, has much black or white wool-on-wool embroidery and, also, dense overall embroidery on a thick cotton ground.

The most advanced and refined embroidery is that of south-western Wallachia, around Oltenia. Bright red dominates, with much fly stitch. Throughout the rest of Wallachia there is evidence of Greek and Bulgarian influence: flat metal bars are sometimes folded into a motif.

Apparently no design was ever repeated exactly and, certainly, there is more slightly differentiating detail of comparable em-broideries than in other eastern European countries.

One of the best representative collections of Romanian embroidery is that of the Muzeul de Arta Populara in Bucharest.

Scotland

Despite pronounced interrelationships with the rest of the British Isles, there are important elements of the embroidery of Scotland that have remained national. Scotland is unique, for instance, in the number of superb retrospective collections of her embroideries. Traditions of baronial patronage of the arts, and current facilities for storage, are apparent in many of the castles and houses of Scotland today.

Little embroidery exists that was executed prior to the 16th century. Some of the earliest Scottish pieces are the narrow strips of petit-point canvas work, sometimes embroidered in wool or silk to a length of 6 ft. (183 cm) per band, that embellished decorated appliqué or petit-point bed hangings, possibly worked from a practical necessity of keeping out the bitter northern winters. The petit point showed French influence in detail of design and workmanship and, indeed, Franco-Scottish affinity had been apparent in the arts from the 15th century or before.

Another outstanding example of finesse in 16th-century canvas work is a $13 \times 47\frac{1}{2}$ in. (33×121 cm) valance, in the Burrell Collection of the Art Gallery and Museum, Glasgow. It is one of a set of three, worked in coloured silks and wools on linen canvas. The arms of Campbell impale Ruthven with the initials 'CC' and 'KR' separated by a lover's knot, a ram's head above. The initials are those of Sir Colin Campbell of Glenorchy and his wife Katherine, daughter of Lord Ruthven. They married in 1550 and, since Sir Colin died in 1583, it is plausible to date the valance to that span.

Foremost of the names of Scottish embroiderers is that of Mary, Queen of Scots (1542–87). Accompanied by her ladies-in-waiting, Mary Seton, Mary Beaton, Mary Fleming and Mary Livingstone (a quartet known as 'The four Marys'), she was sent to France at the age of six to be educated with the children of King Henry II.

During the period of her association with the French court, Mary probably became involved with all facets of artistic and cultural life. Contemporary court fashion was grandiose and exaggerated: her own personal tailor, Nicolas de Moncel, for example, is recorded as having made her a silver dress with silver lace edging and a green satin hem, further decorated with 120 diamonds and rubies sewn to the sleeves and white satin yoke. And an engraving of 1558, at the time of Mary's marriage to the Dauphin, shows her wearing an elaborate trellis-work hair net with jewelled decoration and a tight-fitting dress with rich patterning and shoulder ruffs.

Mary became Queen of France when her husband, as Francis II, succeeded to the throne on the death of his father in 1559. The following year she lost both her mother, Marie de Guise, Regent of Scotland, and, shortly after, her husband. Thus orphaned and widowed, she returned to Scotland to assume a second throne, this time in her own right.

There followed a second marriage, to Lord Darnley, the birth of her son (later James VI of Scotland and James I of England), a second widowhood, a third marriage, to the Earl of Bothwell, and imprisonment on the island of Lochleven in 1567.

Whilst in Lochleven Castle she asked her captors to provide her with 'an imbroderer to drawe forthe such worke as she would be occupied about' and it has been variously suggested that this request was filled by one Ninian Millar, or, more probably, Pierre Oudry, whose name is on the portrait of the Queen now hanging at Hardwick Hall, Derbyshire.

For 15 years, from 1569 to 1584, Mary was in the custody of the Earl of Shrewsbury, first at Tutbury Castle, Staffordshire, and then at Sheffield.

Most of Mary's embroideries that survive today were worked during the first years at Tutbury. She was then on very good terms with the Countess of Shrewsbury, more generally known today as 'Bess of Hardwick' (p. 71), herself a keen needlewoman. Mary obviously utilised her initial period of captivity: in 1569 Shrewsbury reported to Cecil of 'daily resorts to his wife's chamber where, with Lady Leviston and Mrs. Seton, she sits working with the needle'. In 1571, Mary's Ambassador at the English Court, Bishop Lesley, recorded a cushion with the Queen's Arms—a symbol of a hand with a knife pruning a vine, all made by the Scottish queen's hands.

Embroidery inspiration came partly from books available at that time, such as Conrad Gesner's four folios. *La Nature et Diversité des Poissons*, by Pierre Belon (Paris, 1551), was another source book. J. L. Nevinson traces some illustrations, too, to the works of an Italian botanist, Pietro Andrea Mattioli (1500–77).

Mary, Queen of Scots, was a generous lady and, despite a lack of reciprocal attentions, she plied her cousin, Queen Elizabeth, with presents. A skirt, thought to have been embroidered by her for the English queen, is delicately worked with coloured silks, gold and silver on a red satin ground, with an overall design of honeysuckle, daffodils, lilies and roses. It is known that she sent a New Year's present in 1575 of a piece of needle lace, delivered, as were her other gifts, through the good offices of her French maid and the French Ambassador.

An inventory of Mary's few possessions in 1586 included many unfinished embroidery panels, such as '124 birds of different kinds in petit point'. In her retinue she had an embroidery adviser, Charles Plouvart, whose services were, soon after the inventory, deemed to be superfluous and he was dismissed.

It is possible that some of her bird panels went into the final composition of the 'Oxburgh hangings' (p. 72), on loan to the National Trust from the Victoria and Albert Museum. Many of the panels in the hangings bear a crowned initial 'MA' superimposed on the Greek letter Φ, initial of Mary's first husband, Francis II of France.

The main Marian hanging, the 'Norfolk panel', has a square centrepiece of the same hand carrying down a vine with the motto 'Nirescit vulnere virtus' ('Virtue flourisheth by wounding'), with Mary's cipher and the Royal Arms of Scotland. It is surrounded by 8 octagonal and 28 cruciform panels, all of petit point, wool on canvas. The panels are all applied to a green velvet ground. In all, 30 panels include the royal cipher: motif designs include some, such as that of a lion, instantly identifiable as deriving from Gesner.

Corresponding to the 'Norfolk hanging' are the 'Shrewsbury' and 'Cavendish' panels, the latter with a central square of mourning symbols, Cavendish arms and motto, 'Cavendo tutus' ('By guarding safe') and the initials 'WC' and 'EC', signed and dated 'ES 1570'. It was worked as a memorial to Lady Shrewsbury's former (second) husband, Sir William Cavendish, whom she had nursed with much devotion before his death in 1557.

Despite her own Catholic faith, Mary's embroideries were usually secular. One set of vestments, now at Blairs College, Aberdeen, is sometimes attributed to her needle, but it is now thought unlikely that they were actually worked by her (Margaret Swain, in *The Needlework of Mary Queen of Scots*, 1973, associates the couching of metal thread patternings with contemporary works from South Germany, possibly influenced by French design). Examples of secular embroidery that are ascribed to Mary can be seen in the Victoria and Albert Museum, Hardwick Hall, Derbyshire, and Parham Park, Sussex.

Just before her execution, at Fotheringhay in 1587, Mary handed a list of items she wanted safely kept to her French maid, Mlle. de Beauregard. Heading that list was a set of elaborate needlework bed hangings.

Large embroidery panels and hangings continued to be very popular in Scotland. In the collection of needlework at Traquair

House, Peeblesshire, is a petit-point panel, *c.* 1600, with 42 small motif representations of blackberries, carnations, roses and other local and exotic flora. It is a beautiful work, with much attention to detail. Sometimes such panels were adapted from former bed curtains, as may have been done with the 1683 petit-point hangings, for example, in Malcolm's Room at Glamis Castle, Angus.

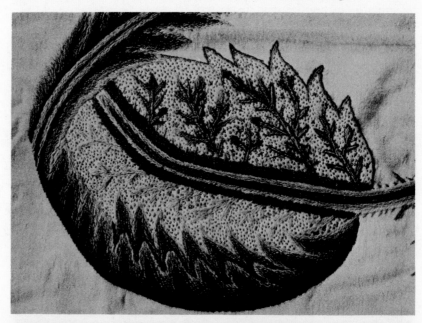

SCOTLAND—*detail of the 'Jacobean' bed-hangings worked in 1700 by the daughters of the 2nd Earl of Kincardine.*
(The Earl of Elgin and Kincardine)

SCOTLAND—*in 1700 the daughters of the 2nd Earl of Kincardine worked a set of delicate crewel bed-hangings, and, when they had finished, they embroidered a whitework caption to hang by the bed.*
(The Earl of Elgin and Kincardine)

In many cases, demands of heraldry have provided the *raison d'être* for Scotland's best and most rich embroideries. The 1966 National Art-Collections Fund's exhibition, 'Needlework from Scottish country houses', in Edinburgh, included a mantle of a Knight of the Order of the Thistle (now the property of the Earl

222

of Ancaster). The Order was revived in May 1687, one of the original eight Knights being the 4th Earl of Perth whose induction mantle this was. It has a powdering of gold thistles on a green velvet ground, and a silver and blue shoulder badge of 'St. Andrew the Apostle . . . bearing before him the cross of his martyrdom'. (When the Order was again reformed, by Queen Anne in 1703, the present plain green velvet ground with accompanying shoulder badge was ordained.)

By the beginning of the 18th century, keen Scottish needlewomen were, like embroiderers elsewhere in the western world, copying patterns and designs from available literature. The interest of the delightful 'Mellerstain panel', 1706, for example, is further enhanced by the accompanying book (*A Booke of Beasts, Birds, Flowers, Fruits, Flies and Wormes, exactly drawne with their Lively Colours truly Defcribed,* by Thomas Johnson, 1630) from which the design was taken. The panel, $13 \times 19\frac{1}{2}$ in. ($33 \times 49 \cdot 5$ cm), tent stitch in polychrome silks and wools on canvas, has a central motif of an august lady, in a wide-brimmed picture hat, holding a basket of flowers, her dog sitting faithfully at her feet. The border surround has a wealth of natural exotica such as rhinoceros, peacocks, kingfishers, rabbits and carnations, grouped on a dark blue ground. The panel (at Mellerstain House, in Berwickshire) is initialled 'GR', 'RB' and 'MM', for Lady Grisell Baillie (born 1692), her sister, Lady Rachel (born 1696), and their governess, Miss May Menzies. The main central motif was copied from an engraving 'Smelling', one of the 'Five senses' bound into the Thomas Johnson book, which belonged to Miss Menzies. The surrounding flora and fauna were copied from motifs throughout the book.

Association with European embroidery continued to be apparent, probably nurtured by constant visits across the North Sea. In about 1710, one of the daughters of the 4th Earl of Traquair returned from the French Ursuline Convent of St. Jacques, for example, and brought with her a *colifichet* panel (p. 344).

Towards the end of the 18th century, an Italian, Luigi Ruffini, set up an embroidery workshop in Edinburgh. He had arrived in the country in 1782 and the following year he was granted the sum of £20 by the local Board of Trustees, who had in 1707 been delegated parliamentary monies of £2,000 a year to aid fishing and linen throughout Scotland. Ruffini's grant, initially for one year, enabled him to employ 20 children mostly aged between six and ten. His work expanded: by 1785, after assorted financial difficulties, he had 70 apprentices on his books and he moved to a more fashionable part of the city.

Ruffini's contribution to embroidery in Scotland was considerable: he introduced tambouring and Dresden work (p. 111). He was, also, ahead of his time in recognising the essence of good design in any embroidery, be it artistic or commercial, although he himself is reputed to have been highly talented in the former but not the latter capability.

The first cotton mill in Scotland had been set up at Rothesay in 1775. Cotton became extremely popular and, indeed, Scottish weavers were soon producing some of the finest cotton muslin available in any market. The bulk—and some of the most delicate—of the muslin was woven in the west of the country, manufacturers gaining inspiration from imported Indian fabrics introduced by the East India Company.

Ruffini had 100 apprentices by 1790. They were aged nine to twelve and served a four-year indenture: for the first year they were paid 2/– a week, for the second 2/6d. and for the last two years, 3/– a week. Ruffini followed the European practice of having the designs transferred to the ground fabric before handing any commission to his apprentices. He gleaned designs from imported fabrics, a source of inspiration that declined in part during the Napoleonic Wars and the subsequent lack of French lace.

Motifs for cotton muslin work were influenced, too, by the Drawing Academy in Edinburgh. In 1796 they advertised a post for a qualified person with 'Designs or patterns for Linen and Cotton and Flowered muslin manufacturers' included in his briefing. Fashion similarly governed embroidery design: flowing classical lines were in vogue, and embroiderers, therefore, adapted floral and twig designs to accommodate current thinking.

Scotland is famous the world over for its 'Ayrshire whitework', practised from the middle of the 19th century. A fine tambour embroidery, cotton on a cotton ground, it has a delightfully delicate and crisp overall look. The fillings to the tamboured outlines of a motif show a wide range of stitches: one sampler is said to have contained 80 different filling stitches. This variety of stitching is, indeed, one of the chief features of Ayrshire work, and typical, also, is the flower patterning, from which the alternative name, 'Floo'erin'', is derived.

Ayrshire work is typified in babies' long christening robes and bonnets. The robes, of a vintage when infant costume necklines were straight across and very wide, and the delicate puffed sleeves incredibly tight for even the smallest of babies, often have an inverted triangle of embroidery from the front neck to the waist and, also, a highly embroidered panel from the front waist to the hem, widening at the bottom. Babies' bonnets, too, were outstanding for the minutiae of embroidered floral motifs set into the crown.

224

△ *JAPAN – detail of panel, with heavy thread and cord embroidery, c. 1900.*
(Auckland Institute and Museum, New Zealand their no. T319)

▽ *JAPAN – detail of hanging, silk and metal threads and applied satin motifs on silk ground, 8 ft*
2 in.×6 ft (2.49×1.83m).
(Auckland Institute and Museum, New Zealand their no. T2)

△ *NETHERLANDS – traditional embroidery from the island of Marken.*
(Vermande Zonen, Holland. Photo: Marijn ten Holt, Amsterdam)

▽ *NIGERIA – embroidered cap, early 20th-century.*
(The Embroiderers' Guild, London)

▽ *NIGERIA – detail of embroidered cap, early 20th-century.*
(The Embroiderers' Guild, London)

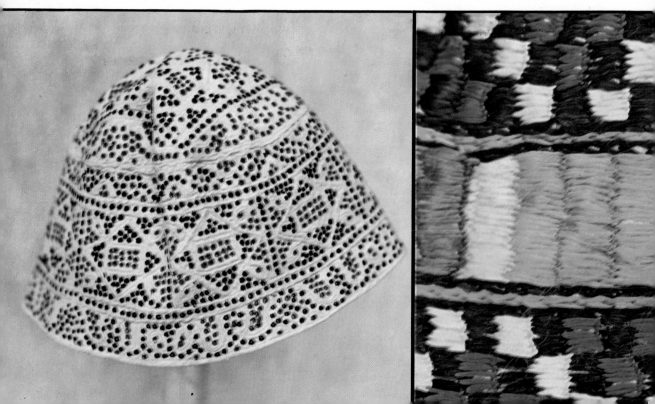

Ayrshire work was instigated primarily through the efforts of two mentors. At the beginning of the 19th century Lady Mary Montgomerie accompanied her husband (her cousin)—at one time aide-de-camp to the Duke of Wellington—when he was posted to the court of the King of Naples at Palermo. The Earl died in 1814 and Lady Mary returned home to Ayrshire. Amongst her luggage were some French baby clothes for her two small sons.

When she reached Scotland she lent some of these delicate

SCOTLAND—*Ayrshire whitework, mid-19th century, on the yoke of a baby's robe.*
(Mrs. Marion Felix)

garments to a Mrs. Jamieson, wife of a cotton agent in Ayr. Mrs. Jamieson, who seems to have been atypically business-like and opportunist for a lady of those days, had already organised a cottage industry for house-bound ladies to embroider fabrics supplied by her husband. She recognised the need to switch from the flowing sprays and classical motifs of the Regency period to a French inspiration, and although she was helped by her two daughters it was she, alone, who was responsible for the ultimate introduction of needlepoint fillings and the strong overall design found in Ayrshire needlework. She was responsible, too, for getting annual prizes for such 'sewed muslin' established in Edinburgh.

Ayrshire whitework continued to receive the high accolades that Mrs. Jamieson had sought. Queen Victoria accepted a robe made for the birth of her son, the Prince of Wales, in 1841. And in 1863 that same gentleman was given an Ayrshire bedspread as a wedding gift on his marriage to Princess Alexandra of Denmark. The spread was a gift from the Countess of Eglinton, daughter-in-law of Lady Mary Montgomerie, and the family has retained its interest in Ayrshire embroidery. Lady Mary's son, for instance, ordered three bedspreads, two of which are still in his descendants' possession. One work bears the Earl's coat of arms with a shamrock and thistle

226

in each corner (as well as being a Knight of the Thistle he was Lord Lieutenant of Ireland and awarded the Order of St. Patrick).

For those who wanted to copy Ayrshire whitework, designs were generally available from Glasgow already stamped on muslin. By 1845 Ayrshire work, either completed or in basic design form, was exported regularly to North America, France, Russia, Germany, Dublin and, of course, sent south to London. As well as the main Scottish centres in Ayrshire, it was produced in Lanarkshire, Renfrewshire and Perthshire.

A group of Scottish ladies taught embroidery in the 1830's to areas of northern Ireland (Messrs. Cochrane and Brown, of Donaghadee, sent some of this work to Glasgow to be re-exported as the 'original' Ayrshire). The story of the introduction of Ayrshire work to Madeira is told on p. 216.

In Scotland, Ayrshire whitework was, after Mrs. Jamieson's time, always in the overall charge of men, who employed both men and women as agents to liaise with the workers, who were women.

It seems, in retrospect, unbelievable that the industry did not continue to expand. With the increased overseas trade of the latter part of the 19th century, Scotland could have expected long to continue this unique form of embroidery. Such handwork was original. But, alas, Swiss manufacturers were copying Ayrshire designs and their machined imitations were undercutting the hand-made originals. The blockade by the North of the ports of the South during the American Civil War completely disrupted exports of raw cotton, another crippling blow to the Ayrshire industry, for imports of cotton to Glasgow fell from 172,055 cwt. in 1861 to 7,216 in 1864.

Towards the end of the 19th century, Mrs. J. G. A. Baird and Mrs. Vernon of Auchans, wives of Ayrshire landowners, tried to revive the Ayrshire whitework industry, but Madeira work was underselling the Scottish embroidery and there was at this time, in any case, a greater market for coloured embroidery.

The effects of the industrial age had forced a decline not only in the whitework industry but in all forms of handwork. Efforts were made, as they were in other parts of the British Isles, to keep alive the skills and traditions of all needleworkers. In 1877, for instance, Lady Henry Grosvenor started a School of Needlework at Wemyss Castle, in Fife. Some 30 girls, mostly adolescents, were taught to sew and execute fine needlework. Eventually smocking and embroidery entered the curriculum and, in fact, during the last few decades, the Wemyss School of Needlework has been exclusively known for its elaborate and complex embroideries. The school today is a delightful and personal entity: an open fire warms an office stocked with French canvases and wools of every imaginable shade.

As far as individual designers and artists were concerned, however, the most influential movement at the end of the 19th century was the so-called 'Glasgow School', which revolved around the Glasgow School of Art. Francis H. Newbery was principal from 1885 and under his guidance embroidery was prominent in the arts produced. Newbery's wife Jessie (born 1864) was an embroiderer: the daughter of a manufacturer of Paisley shawls, one William Rowat, she taught at the school from 1894 to 1908, including amongst her pupils such artists as Frances Mary Templeton.

A fellow embroidery lecturer at this time was Ann Macbeth (1875–1948), actually in charge of the Needlework Department. She felt strongly that embroidery must be within reach of every woman: it should be quickly worked, and on an inexpensive material. She instituted classes in decorative stitchery and utilised such unlikely media as hessian, unbleached calico and greenhouse sheeting.

One of Ann Macbeth's finest embroideries is the hanging in St.

SCOTLAND—*cushion cover, 2 ft. 3 in. (68·5 cm) square, designed by Jessie Newbery and embroidered by Edith Rowat in pink, green and yellow wools on a linen ground, stem stitch, satin stitch and French knots, 1899. (The Victoria and Albert Museum, Crown Copyright)*

228

Patrick's Church, Patterdale, Cumberland, whither she retired in later life. The embroidered panel depicts Christ as the Good Shepherd on a hillside with a background of Hartsop, Deepdale, Caudle Moor and Kirkstone, the view around her in Patterdale. It is a soft work, full of a naïve compassion, possibly inspired by the fact that Miss Macbeth lost the sight of one eye in early childhood. Another Macbeth embroidery, on loan from the Trustees of Glasgow Art Gallery and Museum, is on display annually from Whitsun until October: it shows the Virgin Mary with an angel adoring the Infant. Once again the artist has set the representation in her own surroundings. Helvellyn and Grisedale are in the background, Patterdale Township is to the fore.

In 1933 the McLellan Galleries in Glasgow held an exhibition of the works of Charles Rennie Mackintosh (1868–1928) and his wife, Margaret Macdonald Mackintosh (1865–1933). With Margaret's sister, Frances Macdonald (1874–1921), and her husband, Herbert Macnair, the Mackintoshes were half of a creative and influential quartet known as 'The four', all leading lights of the Glasgow School. Mackintosh had been one of the foremost decorative architects of his day, one of his masterpieces being the School of Art buildings. Margaret, with her then unconventional head attire of long side plaits with Indian forehead band, was a similarly highly skilled artist.

Another name of significance in embroidery innovation of this period is that of Louisa Chart, who in 1913 came north to teach embroidery at Edinburgh College of Art. Her own embroideries include a set of canvas-work chair covers for the Palace of Holyrood House.

In 1934 the Needlework Development Scheme was formed, to encourage 'greater interest in embroidery and to raise the standard of design', through stimulation and through the Scheme's own collection of embroideries. The organisation was centred in the four art schools of Aberdeen, Dundee, Edinburgh and Glasgow. By the time of the outbreak of war in 1939, when it was decided temporarily to close the scheme, more than 900 embroideries had been catalogued.

The Scheme was revived in 1945 on a new basis, to enable it to extend the scope of its operations to art schools and other centres throughout the whole of the United Kingdom. In 1946, an Advisory Committee was formed, consisting of representatives of the Scottish Education Department, the Ministry of Education and the Victoria and Albert Museum. Miss E. K. Kohler was appointed as the Scheme's first embroidery expert (to be followed in 1948 by a Swede, Miss Ulla Kockum, in 1950 by Miss D. A. Allsopp from West

229

Hartlepool College of Art and, from 1955 until 1961, Miss Iris Hills of Bromley College of Art). In 1947 the Scheme commissioned Mary Kessell to prepare promotional designs, a project termed 'The Kessell experiment'.

During the 1950's the Scheme continued to expand, extending its coverage throughout the British Isles. Besides the main collection of embroideries, there was a central reference library with a collection of slides and photographs. The Scheme also sponsored lecture tours by embroidery personalities such as Mrs. Rebecca Crompton, Madame Pavlu of Czechoslovakia and Gertie Wandel of Denmark. It held regular exhibitions (two of which, in 1950 and 1955, were held in conjunction with the Arts Council of Great Britain), and it produced its own publications.

The Needlework Development Scheme was wound up in 1961, partly because it was felt that the original aims of the experiment had been achieved. The valuable collections of British and foreign embroideries and related literature were divided in the main part between the Victoria and Albert Museum and the Royal Scottish Museum, Edinburgh, and, to a lesser extent, between the four original art schools involved in the scheme. The remainder was distributed to interested centres around the British Isles.

There is commendable recognition in Scotland today of the part that embroidery can play not only in contemporary arts but, also, in commercial aspects of life. In 1966, for example, the Tay Road Bridge Joint Board commissioned Kathleen Whyte, head of embroidery at the Glasgow School of Art, to work a stole for H.M. Queen Elizabeth the Queen Mother to celebrate the official opening of the new road bridge linking the northern shores of Fife with the city of Dundee. The stole, on a cream and gold handwoven pure silk ground, is illustrated here.

SCOTLAND—*embroidered detail of a stole presented to Her Majesty Queen Elizabeth the Queen Mother when she opened the Tay Road Bridge in 1966. The stole was commissioned by the Tay Road Bridge Joint Board and the embroidered panel, 15 × 3 in. (38 × 7·5 cm), was designed and executed by Kathleen Whyte. The design is bisected by a representation of the bridge's shape and to either side are feathered arabesques reminiscent of swirling waters, with symbolic devices of the crowned heart of Glamis, lilies in a vase of Angus and a knight of Fife. The artist worked in Jap gold thread, white silk and with appliqué of forty pearls from the river Tay.*
(Reproduced by gracious permission of Her Majesty Queen Elizabeth the Queen Mother)

230

SCOTLAND—*one of a set of canvas-work chair backs, tent stitch in wool on linen canvas, being worked by the Earl of Wemyss and March, KT. (The artist)*

Sierra Leone

Embroidery in Sierra Leone today is foremost in the ranks of work from West Africa if not, indeed, from the whole continent.

In 1787 the country was ceded to Britain by the native chiefs to be used as an asylum for freed but destitute ex-slaves. The resultant negro migration from the British Isles, North America and the Caribbean meant the import, also, of styles of art.

The Creoles brought with them, for example, a love of samplers. One modern version, featuring flowers, emblems, leaves, fruits and local proverbs, was worked by Granny Niger, of Percival Street, Freetown, who is also a particularly skilled slipper maker. Creole slippers are still worn, worked in wool on cheese-cloth ground. The women embroider geometric patterns to the required shape and size and take their finished work to a local shoemaker to be made up.

SIERRA LEONE—*stitchery on the head of Goboi, a devil of the Pore Society, who runs amok in the local streets and scatters irritative herbs as he goes. Mende tribe, Nigerian cowrie shells and local raffia work.*
(Sierra Leone National Museum)

Traditional patterns have names such as 'Ladies wrapper' or 'Walk for no man after four'. The *'tabaka* leaf' is a half-soled mourning slipper worked in black and white. In all slippers, Florentine work is popular, and cross stitch and tent stitch are used.

SIERRA LEONE—
bambada *cap worn exclusively by the native doctor of the Galenese tribe. Satin stitch, interlaced band, arrowhead stitch, double herringbone stitch with white cotton crocheted edging. Worked by the Jessi. A similar doctor's cap is worn by the Lemba tribe.*
(Sierra Leone National Museum)

233

Map samplers, with the flags of the African countries added to the geographical outline of the continent, are effectively worked in canvas work and appliqué, a form of needlework that has a long history in Sierra Leone. Traditional ankle-length cotton print dresses worn by local women often have an applied yoke known simply as 'stitches'. One variation is composed of $\frac{3}{4}$ in. (19 mm) wide strips of contrasting fabric in a trellis pattern on the main ground. Other yoke decorations are worked with tiny tucks, piping, cutwork in the shape of local fruits such as the paw-paw, or with an overall design of machine stitching.

Cotton is the main ground fabric for all clothing. 'Country cloth', a gingham fabric, is produced mainly among the Mendes of the South. 'Gara cloth', another locally woven fabric, is tie-dyed and generally not embroidered. Chain-stitch, cross-stitch and stem-stitch decoration is found on bed linen and handkerchiefs, the edges of which are generally crocheted. Some drawn thread work is practised.

There is beadwork throughout the three provinces of the country. Initiation bangles and *yavasahs*, the frontal apron worn by girls during the customary post-initiation dancing festivities, are highly decorated: examples of both items can be seen in Sierra Leone National Museum in Freetown.

South Africa

South African embroidery is important in that some of the works being created today are the most outstanding in technical skill of any contemporary embroideries.

The heritage of such devotion to the needle came with the Dutch settlers when they first came to the region in the 17th century. They brought with them their love of beauty and fine decoration. English immigrants came with their smocking designs and *broderie anglaise*. Italians came with Assisi work. French Huguenots brought their designs—as did the Germans and the Scandinavians, who introduced Hardanger.

Dutch settlers brought their *kappies*, traditional white caps later favoured by the South African Voortrekkers. Making such a cap was a demanding and lengthy process. Each section of the bonnet had three layers, the two outer of linen and an inside lining on to which the design to be quilted was applied. It is suggested that leather templates were used to facilitate exact proportioning, and the design lines were then laid with thick piping cord, stitched either side through the three layers. The whole surface was eventually covered with fine quilting, often in feather and scroll patterns and to the embroiderer's own design. *Kappies* are particularly associated with the period of the Great Treks from the Cape to the interior of the country in 1836–38.

The story of the Trekkers is told on the Voortrekker tapestry at the Voortrekker Monument outside Pretoria. An emotional and awe-inspiring work, it was first hung in 1960. Members of the Vrouen Moederbeweging van die ATKV had decided, in 1952, to undertake the work and the sum of R26,000 ($40,000) was collected within a year from women's organisations, municipalities, Afrikaans churches, schools, firms and other bodies. The 13 panels, designed by Mr. W. H. Coetzer, vary in length from 6 to 9 ft. (1·83 to 2·74 m). Each is 32 in. (81 cm) wide. Eight embroiderers used 130 different coloured wools and 3,353,600 stitches to complete the series.

The panels tell the story of the Great Trek: the journey to the unknown north, crossing the Orange River, battles with Zulu warriors and, all the while, normal domestic life somehow continuing. It is a moving series. One panel depicts the burial of a small girl, Anna Philippina Susanna Scheepers. Around her rough coffin stand the

235

diarist Louis Trichardt, his sons Carolus and 'Pieta' (Petrus Frederick) and other persons mentioned in accounts of the Trek.

The exacting journey continues throughout the tapestries. One work shows a desperate attempt manually to haul a wagon over the

SOUTH AFRICA—*whitework* kappie, c. 1800, made by Mrs. de Klerk in the Tarkastrad district, whence came many Voortrekkers. The bonnet features traditional shirring and, in between the lines of cording, fine stitching through the three layers of fabric. (National Cultural History and Open-air Museum, Pretoria)

Drakensberg Mountains. Wheels have come off and people use their own backs to balance the fallen vehicle. Vultures circle overhead. Balancing this panel of hardship is a peaceful representation of the arrival in Natal: sheep graze and a small boy waves the Voortrekker flag. Another such domestic panel shows the devotion of the travellers. A group sits around the table to hear a white-bearded elder reading from the Bible. A slight breeze blows the candle flames illuminating his book towards him and, in effect, thus directs the eye of the viewer around an oval arc of the heads of the assembled company to the reader on the right of the panel (a movement similar to that of Salvador Dali's 'Last Supper').

Unlike other former colonial countries, South Africa does not have a proliferation of historic samplers. The Oude Kerk Museum in Tulbagh does, however, have a collection.

The major output of embroidery in the country stems from the

SOUTH AFRICA—*'The Storm', twelfth of the 14 'Voortrekker tapestry' panels, presented in 1960 by the Vrouen Moederbeweging van die ATKV. Designed by Mr. W. H. Coetzer, this panel was worked by Mrs. A. W. Steyn. The photograph shows the painted canvas with only a small area to the left already worked. Representation is of a hailstorm in Colenso, below the Drakensberg Mountains.*
(ATKV and Mrs. A. W. Steyn)

237

end of the Boer War. In 1902, after peace negotiations at Vereeniging, the time was opportune to initiate an interest in the art. Miss Katie Neethling, in the Cape, taught appliqué, *broderie*

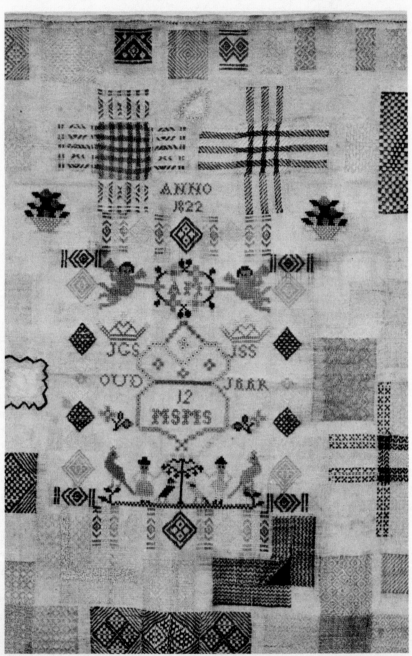

SOUTH AFRICA—*part of a darning sampler worked by 12-year-old Maria Susanna Magdalena Stegmann in 1822. 20 × 18 in. (50 × 46 cm). (Stellenbosch Museum, South Africa. Photo: Image Studios, Stellenbosch)*

anglaise, broderie suisse, Hardanger, silk work, drawn work, shadow work, hedebo, *reticella* work and other stitcheries, drawing for help on foreign books. In that year, also, Emily Hobhouse founded a school of lace and embroidery in Koppies, in the Orange Free State. Examples of her work can be seen in the Museum of the Vroue Monument in Bloemfontein.

Bantu and other geometric designs have had considerable influence on embroidery design. African beadwork, from which much of that inspiration was gleaned, can be seen in the East London Museum (Xhosa work), the Natal Museum in Pietermaritzburg (Zulu work), the Cultural History Museums of Cape Town and Johannesburg, the Africana Museum in Cape Town, the Old House Museum in Durban and elsewhere.

Dr. H. S. Schoeman (in *Lantern: Journal for Knowledge and Culture,* Vol. XXI, no. 1, and Vol. XXI, no. 2, September and December 1971) has expounded the social and anthropological connexions and import of beadwork in Southern Africa. Since the earliest times beads have had considerable signficance although, today, the well-used patterns and designs have less direct relevance on South African embroidery than in the past.

From where, then, do the designs come? The countryside provides inspiration. Protea, disa, zebra, kudu and other flora and fauna appear again and again. And some ideas are brought back to South Africa after visits by embroiderers and interested persons to Europe and America. South African embroidery design today is similar to that found elsewhere in the western world: the artists are quick to adapt new motifs and designs which they hear about. What causes the South African embroidery to stand out, however, is the enviable patience of the artists themselves when creating their beautiful and delicate works. Many of the domestic embroideries are evidence of months and years of continual work, evidence of time and loving concentration.

Much of the internal design worked today stems from the studio of Hetsie van Wyk, herself surely one of the most prolific embroiderers working anywhere in the world today. Trained first at Stellenbosch and then in England (under Constance Howard in Cambridge and, also, in Birmingham) and Switzerland (in Geneva and Lausanne), she now runs her own school in Bloemfontein. Her book *Borduur Só,* published in Afrikaans in 1969, offers a complete course of most usual facets of embroidery and is, in fact, the most widely used embroidery source in the country today. The designs and stitches are easy to follow, running the needle's spectrum from beginning stitch to advanced design, and they form a useful portfolio for the embroiderer of the flora of Southern Africa.

SOUTH AFRICA—*cloth in old Hedebo and pulled work,*
Hetsie van Wyk.
(Courtesy of the artist. Photo: Christo Photographers)

240

Mrs. van Wyk also designs patterns for lace, an art that is closely associated with embroidery throughout the country.

Other popular facets of stitchery entered in the *Standard Encylopaedia of Southern Africa* (Vol. 8) include carding, crochet and tatting. It is reported that shells from Jeffreys Bay, near Cradock, were used to make fine stitched mantelpiece covers, but whether or not this art is still practised is not certain.

There are many devoted societies and associations fostering embroidery. The South African Women's Agricultural Union, with branches in Cape Province, Natal and Transvaal, plays a vital role in promoting embroidery interests. Since 1949 they have included in their regular scheduling the fields of Assisi work, blackwork, cross stitching, Dorset feather stitchery, drawn work, Florentine embroidery, Hardanger, hedebo, Italian and English quilting, needleweaving and shadow work.

Exhibitions throughout South Africa often marry the supposedly masculine world of agriculture with the feminine-oriented art of

SOUTH AFRICA—*runner with local flowers executed in pulled thread work by Ansie Heyns, 1970. (Courtesy of the artist)*

241

embroidery. These exhibitions are judged by home economists from the Department of National Education, or similarly qualified persons, whose criticisms are attached in writing to the work on view.

An itemised guide is produced for the direction of the judges. It includes the duties of the 'office bearers' who have to 'place the

SOUTH AFRICA—*bullion work on filet lace by Hetsie van Wyk. (Courtesy of the artist)*

following in readiness before the judging of handwork—a comfortable chair and large table, in a good light'. A breakdown of suggested marks for handicrafts is as follows:

'General Appearance and Usefulness
    General design and size: balance, proportions and suitability
    Materials: suitability and durability
    Colour: Suitability, variation and balance
    Aesthetic value: Overall attractiveness of the article
    Method of exhibiting the article..........60 marks
Workmanship
    Neatness and skill as regards construction
    Correctness and durability of construction
    General finish.............................40 marks.'
(Department of National Education Cultural Advancement Branch, Home Economics Section, *Guide for Exhibitors and Judges*, Pretoria, p. 27).

As a typical example of the range of classes in an embroidery exhibition, the programme for the Royal Agricultural Society of Natal's 1973 Annual Show had 16 sections (Division H—Embroidery) for counted thread, 11 for needle tapestry and 20 for general embroidery, including one for an 'Article embroidered in Chinese style'. Entrance fee was 10c. per work, and besides the Savilles Floating Trophy, the 'Bobs' Forsyth Floating Trophy and the Embroiderers' Guild of South Africa Trophy (for blackwork), the highest cash prize was 4 Rand ($6, or £2·50).

The Embroiderers' Guild of South Africa, founded in 1955, was commissioned in 1968 by the City Council of Pietermaritzburg to work the coat of arms that can be seen hung above the Mayoral Chair in the city's Council Chamber.

Embroidery, therefore, is practised throughout the country. It is included in regular school curricula from primary days on. Technical colleges in Bloemfontein, Cape Town, Durban, Johannesburg and Pretoria offer final diploma courses. The Universities of Pietermaritzburg, Potchefstroom, Pretoria and Stellenbosch include it as a minor subject in their main Home Economics courses. European embroidery is taught to Herero, Sotho, Xhosa and Zulu women in their villages, and the resultant work is sometimes marketed in the cities.

The do-it-yourself aspect of embroidery is well nourished with regular articles in such magazines as *Farming in S.A.* The English–Afrikaans *Dictionary of Embroidery* has a comprehensive listing of about 5,000 embroidery terms. Foreign specialists are a welcome source of inspiration.

In fields such as Assisi, drawn and pulled work and whitework, South Africa is undoubtedly one of the main world centres of embroidery today.

SOUTH AFRICA—
wall-hanging with symbols from the Old Testament (to left), the three crosses of the Transition (centre) and the parables of the New Testament (to right), appliqué and embroidery, 8 × 16 ft. (2·44 × 4·88 m), 1968. Group-work under the guidance of Lyda van Rensburg.
(Kroonstad East Dutch Reformed Church, Orange Free State)

South America

Despite a fierce pride of culture, race, religion and nation it is plausible jointly to consider those countries of South America not prolific in unique embroidery. On the whole there is, throughout South America, an inherent and noticeable predominance of weaving. Bright colours and gay designs are incorporated in any textile that can possibly be so embellished, but where there is a weaving tradition there is not, usually, an embroidery tradition, a generalisation that is certainly true in South America.

There are exceptions. Chile has contemporary Isla Negra work (p. 39) and Peru's history of embroidery dates back well over 2,000 years (p. 204).

Direct Iberian influence throughout South America from the 16th to the 19th centuries has resulted in some uniform features of embroidery around the continent. In convents, for example, Spanish and other nuns taught their pupils fine needlework, instilling into them a heritage of precise and detailed patterning with a disciplined attention to detail. Convent-inspired embroidery included fine and luxurious underwear and baby clothes (examples from Brazil are particularly elaborate).

In Colombia much of what embroidery is today to be found has such convent provenance. Although there is a weighty history of various forms of handwork in the country, other embroidery tradition is sparse.

There has been Portuguese embroidery influence, particularly in Brazil. Much of the embroidery available there today is imported from the Portuguese Atlantic island of Madeira.

Influences on the whole, however, have been varied and short-lived. Although waves of immigration, such as that of Italians to Argentina, Lebanese to Brazil and Chinese to Peru, have become assimilated, the immigrants' own embroidery traditions have generally not continued after the first generation.

There are contemporary projects throughout the continent to pursue all forms of the arts. In Guyana, where the indigenous Amerindian had beadwork decoration to his clothing but little other stitchery, there is now a national drive to place emphasis on the use of local materials. Apparently there is a project in Georgetown to incorporate into stitchery local beads, called 'Job's tears', each $\frac{3}{8}$ in. (9.5 mm) long and formed from dried grass seeds.

Much of the modern embroidery of Ecuador comes from Azuary, in the south, or Zuleta, in the northern province of Imbabura. Spot or border motifs are handworked around the edges of skirts, shirts and on cushion covers. Surface satin stitching, long and short stitch, stem stitch, back stitch and the occasional spangle are employed in neat, if rather unoriginal, designs.

SOUTH AMERICA (Ecuador)—*diagram of a modern Riobamba pillow cover, 15 in. (38 cm) square, worked in satin stitch, feather stitch and back stitch.*

South-East Asia

Many countries of South-East Asia have a long history of weaving and other textile skills such as batik dyeing. Where other forms of fabric art are rife, embroidery is not immediately obvious. In some countries, indeed, the art is not found at all; it is authoritatively declared today that 'embroidery is considered alien to Indonesians', possibly in reaction to many years of Dutch rule. In the late 17th and early 18th centuries, chain-stitched pictures in coloured silks were made and exported as 'Dutch East Indies work'.

In Cambodia, Laos and Brunei, similarly, there is no tradition of embroidery. Vietnam has had considerable French influence, introduced by nuns who taught 'fine needlework' as a suitably lady-like accomplishment. Many countries of South-East Asia have in fact assimilated ideas and arts of the peoples with whom they have traded, or by whom they have been settled. A Malay lady, Davang Hajjah Dara, for instance, won an international prize in 1972 with a filet drawn thread work embroidery, obviously not an indigenous art form. Singapore, particularly, has especial cosmopolitan talents, with a notable degree of Chinese-style production.

Atypical in her artistic self-sufficiency is Thailand, which was, unlike her neighbours, never colonised by a western power. She has therefore received little foreign arts heritage and influence, other than that from China, brought by immigrants now largely assimilated. Thai textiles are largely concerned with production of the fine and colourful silks so much prized throughout Europe and North America, and pride of place has therefore justifiably to be accorded to this facet of the textile arts. Some tribal women from the hill regions of the country do, however, have an element of embroidery in their culture—Yao ladies, for example, embroider panels for trouser legs, work which is similar to that found today in Yemen. Motif emblems are geometric, either in repetitive spot or border form.

Spain

Unlike some countries of the western world there has not, in Spain, been so noticeable a dichotomy between weighty religious embroidery and secular 'folk stitching'.

Admittedly there has, throughout the Iberian peninsula, been a tradition of outstanding ecclesiastical embroidery inspired by the Catholic Church. There has also, however, been unsurpassed heraldic and ceremonial embroidery associated with the Spanish empire through the centuries. A love of ornate and complicated detail has therefore correspondingly filtered down, with little attenuation, to the ordinary person.

There is some affinity with the arts of her neighbours, particularly in the northern Basque region, an area which has oscillated between French and Spanish rule. This is the home of the 'Basque stitch' (p. 329), a complicated scroll stitchery with associated knotting that is highly decorative.

Generally, though, much influence on Spanish embroidery has been gleaned through trade with Arab and other merchants through the centuries. They imparted their own Moslem design and, also, ideas from Persia and other eastern centres. Such oriental inspiration included a disregard for exact proportionate scale, and geometric designs of stylised flowers and birds such as the two-headed Hapsburg eagle.

From the 8th century to 1609, when Philip III expelled the last remaining Moors back to their original North African homeland, there was Moorish dominance in embroidery as in many fields of Spanish art.

Christian influence, too, is apparent in design motifs such as the Lamb of God, the Dove of Peace and other religious representations found in similarly high Catholic areas of the world. Gerona Cathedral in Catalonia, in the north-east of Spain, has a superb 12th-century hanging, 14 ft. 9 in. × 13 ft. 1 in. (4·5 × 3·9 m), with the entire ground embroidered. It features the story of the Creation.

A recurrent attribute of Spanish embroidery throughout the last 400 years has been the intricate counted thread work known universally as 'Spanish blackwork'. The progress of this form of embroidery around art centres is sometimes attributed to Katharine of Aragon, who crossed the English Channel in 1501 to marry Arthur

248

Tudor, elder brother of Henry VIII whom the widowed Katharine was later to marry. The future queen did certainly have in her inventory in 1501 'One paire of shetys of fyne Hollande clothe, wroghte with Spanysshe worke of blacke silke upon the edgies', but black-

SPAIN—*blackwork runner, wool on linen, 18th century. (Cooper-Hewitt Museum of Decorative Arts and Design, New York. Frederick Splint Collection)*

work was already well established in the British Isles by that time.

The true provenance of blackwork must surely go back to the influence of the Moors in Spanish arts. The complicated wrought-iron effect of colouring and design found throughout this type of embroidery is justifiably associated with design and outlook along the north-western African coast today.

Early blackwork in Spain was embroidered in natural wool from black sheep, on a linen ground. The chiaroscuro of colour and diversity of texture available to the blackwork embroiderer were immediately acceptable to the Spaniard with his love of detail, his intense emotion and his tradition of ceremony.

SPAIN—late 16th-century cartouche, one of a set of three showing the arms of a Knight of Santiago, probably of the House of Guzman, surrounded by scrolling foliage. Crimson satin appliqué, silk cord and silk in satin stitch and couched work on a cream satin ground, shadow-painted yellow.
(Whitworth Art Gallery, Manchester. Robinson Collection)

This was the height of Spanish dominance in the western hemisphere, the period of Cortes, Pizarro and other intrepid conquistadores. A waxing empire often produces outstanding arts, both direct and applied, an assumption that has been verified in cultural epochs throughout history. And, therefore, the 16th-century embroidered art production in Spain was both prolific and spectacular.

In the Victoria and Albert Museum there is a late 16th-century band of net embroidery, 7 ft. 8½ in. × 2 ft. 1 in. (234 × 64 cm), on a square mesh with knotted junctions. Around the edges is a small outer surround with, inside, borders of lions alternating with flowing arboreal motifs. The central panels portray 'family groups'. In one such representation an august gentleman holding a vertical stick sits, with trepidation on his face, astride a bloated and elongated steed, his lady (who has lost her legs to the customary artists' licence) sitting behind him. A dutiful page boy stands behind. In another panel, a similar gentleman, equally pompous in appearance and holding a flowering carnation, is accompanied by an adult foot-follower. The panels are separated by more lions with alternating motifs. Despite the unnatural rigidity and proportions of the main human and equestrian representation, there is in the work an advanced degree of complexity of design and diversity of stitches. The only inexcusable error, indeed, is that the embroiderer inexplicably worked the surrounding border of lions facing the opposite way from the central panels.

An inventory of Queen Joanna, 1479–1555 (known as 'La Loca' ('The Mad') after the death of her husband, Archduke Philip, in 1506, deranged her), in 1509 mentions samplers, but few pre-18th-century examples have survived.

Spanish samplers are often larger than similar contemporary works from other European countries. Geometric and floral patterning is common: lettering samplers with texts and verses are less usual. A typical example of intricate Spanish workmanship, illustrating concentration on shape, line and a balance of colour and texture, is Gertrudes de Opasyo's sampler (1729), in the Victoria and Albert Museum. It has overall border patterning on a linen ground. Many 18th-century Spanish samplers were extremely elaborate and, indeed, by this time balance had sometimes given way to exaggerated fussiness and an unnecessarily fanatical dedication to execute maximum patterning within the confines of one area of ground. Doña Isabel Eulogia de la Espada's 1756 work, 30 × 28 in. (76·5 × 71 cm), in the same Museum, has a typical border surround with nine central panels which contain a feast of design with no corresponding idea of restraint to the embroiderer's enthusiasm.

A 1762 sampler, 31 × 37 in. (78·5 × 94 cm), in the Whitman

Sampler Collection of the Philadelphia Museum of Art, has an exquisite and perfect border edging of complicated Hapsburg eagle design, with a clear foreground and worked background. Inside, nine equally sized square panels feature different border motifs, with emphasis throughout on diagonal patterning. One panel includes exaggerated drawn thread work. Only the central panel of all has

SPAIN—*18th century, silk on linen sampler, 36 × 26½ in. (91.5 × 67.5 cm), worked by Gertrudes de Opasyo in 1729. Hem stitch, back stitch, satin stitch, diagonal chevrons, four-sided stitch, outline stitch and bullion knots.*
(The Victoria and Albert Museum, Crown Copyright)

pictorial representation, with a tiered cupola—reminiscent of a wedding cake—surrounded by religious and ornithological motifs.

By the 18th century, too, many of the regional costumes still occasionally found today had reached their present advancement. Colouring of costumes is highly regional. Red and green dominate in the Sierra Morena area, honey-brown and blue in Toledo and blue by itself in Galicia and the Basque region.

In Andalusia, shirts similar to the *huipil* taken by conquistadores and subsequent settlers to Central and South America, and still found today in Mexico and elsewhere, had brilliant silk embroidery on a linen ground, with cross stitch (*al pasado*), coral stitch (single and double), braid stitch, Italian cross stitch and back stitch dominating.

Embroidery in the Archipelagos of the Balearic Islands and the Canary Islands, and in Spanish settlements on the Moroccan coast, is—as was former colonial embroidery—in some cases only distantly connected to that of the home mainland. As time passed, original conceptions of the art have been necessarily affected by indigenous workmanship. Spanish themes have, for example, often been softened by Mexican embroiderers until only the source of white-work and drawn thread work is immediately recognisable.

Sri Lanka

Sri Lanka, or Ceylon, as it was more generally called until 1972, has a comparatively recent history of successive domination. The Portuguese arrived early in the 16th century and established a rule that was to last some 150 years: Portuguese influence was noted to some extent in all facets of life. In 1658 administration passed to the Dutch East India Company, who introduced contemporary modes from the Netherlands. British influence was introduced when she was ceded the 'Maritime Provinces of Ceylon' in 1798 and it was not until 1968 that the country finally achieved her independence.

It is little wonder, therefore, that today Sri Lanka has no immediately evident peculiarity in the embroidered arts world. She has given her name to an embroidery stitch (p. 348) which closely resembles knitting. But most of her embroidery today is machine-chain stitched, lacking the grace and finesse of neighbouring Indian work and yet, none the less, with unmistakably oriental traits.

SRI LANKA—*early 20th-century work, detail of a tablecloth.*
(Cooper-Hewitt Museum of Decorative Arts and Design, New York.
Mrs. Daryl Parshall Collection)

255

Sweden

Embroidery in Sweden is closely connected to that of other Scandinavian countries, but it does have some characteristic areas of stitchery. Hälsingland, for example, is the home of 'Delsbo work', with floral motifs in stem stitch and surface satin stitch on a cotton ground. This style of embroidery dates back no further than the middle of the 19th century: the early examples were less elegant and more often in rose or blue than works of today, which are generally monochrome red. Delsbo work was purely domestic in use, confined primarily to bed-linen.

Hälsingland also produces 'Järvsö work', a variant of Delsbo. Järvsö is chiefly worked with rose-coloured thread and is easily identified by the little tassels that often hang freely from stems, flowers and leaves of the main design. Satin stitch is worked throughout: if the stitches are too large they are couched.

Swedish embroidery today tends to be typified by neatly executed design and skilful use of colour and stitches to obtain maximum impact. One exception to the bright colour usually associated with much Swedish work is 'blekinge work', a completely free style of embroidery that could have gained inspiration from the vogue in western Europe for oriental embroidery in the 17th and 18th centuries (Sweden had territories in northern Europe at that time and was involved in frequent wars). Blekinge work hangings date from the end of the 17th century to about 1850 and the designs are those of the Swedish countryside, with flowers and birds. Satin stitch, filling stitches and stem stitch are most frequently employed, with an oriental lightness throughout.

Historic embroideries in Swedish museums also include examples of some intricately worked carriage seats such as the 'Adam and Eve' seat, in the Nordiska Museet, Stockholm, from the Skåne district. This rough-wool 18th-century embroidery, worked in back stitch, indicates a degree of—contemporary!—censorship in the form of two large fig leaves covering vital parts of the biblical couple.

Long narrow wall-hangings are found throughout Scandinavia. Called tjells or refills, they date from the time when Swedish travellers carried their arts around with them. The tjell shape was easily accommodated in the narrow Scandinavian long-boats of these sea-rovers. Swedish houses, too, were once shaped like upturned

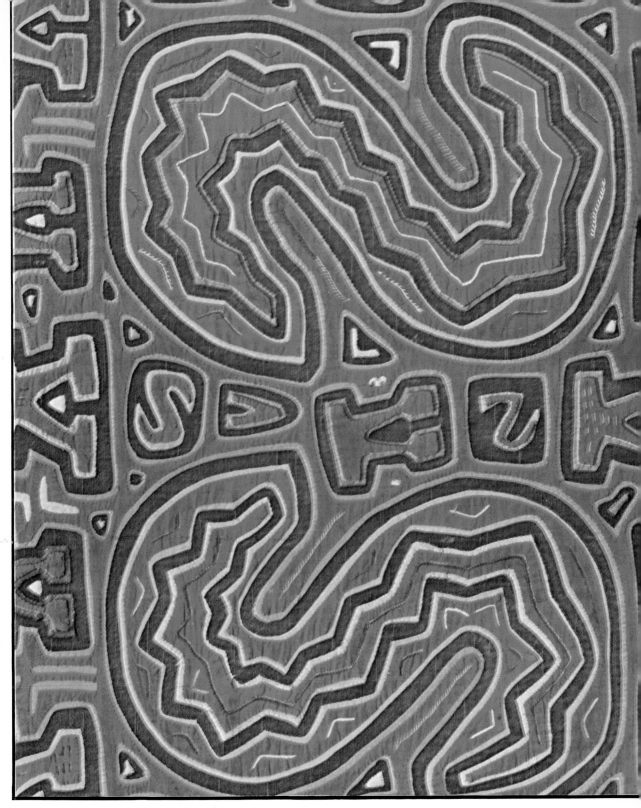

△ *PANAMA – Cuna Indian* mola *from San Blas with design adapted from the coral reefs of the islands.*
(Author's collection)

△ *PANAMA – the* mola *is today somewhat modified in intricacy: this work was bought in Panama City in 1974.*
(Author's collection)

△ *SCOTLAND – 18th-century fire screen, silk and wool on canvas, tent stitch with cross stitch surround. Dated 1754 with the initials, "HG" it is probable that it was worked by Henrietta, wife of the second Duke of Gordon and mother-in-law of the seventh Earl of Wemyss.*
(The Earl of Wemyss and March, KT)

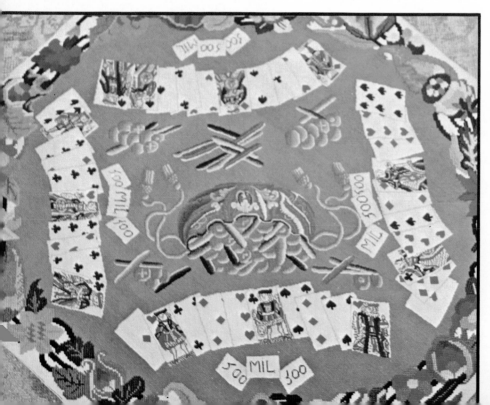

◁ *SCOTLAND – octagonal card-table cover, set for the game of Quadrille, silk and wool on linen canvas, 37×36 in. (just over 91 cm square). One of a pair, both unused. Research undertaken by the Imperial Chemical Industries showed yarn to have been dyed with Orchil or Cudbear, a natural lichen dye which was used in this country until late 19th-century. It is difficult to date this work more exactly than middle 18th to end 19th-century.*
(The Earl of Wemyss and March, KT)

boats, with low walls underneath, and the *tjell*-shaped embroideries correspondingly fitted into the décor in the form of narrow embroidered bands running around the outside walls.

'Halland work' is generally found on such *tjell*-shaped wall-hangings. Red, and sometimes blue, cotton thread on a white linen ground is worked with satin stitch, cross stitch and herringbone stitch to graceful yet geometric design. A motif frequently used is that of a tree with pointed leaves.

Hölesom (cutwork) is believed to have been worked in the country for many centuries and has been much used for household linens and decoration. Drawn thread work (*näversöm*, meaning 'birch bark embroidery') has been worked in the northern provinces since the 17th century. Ground linen was originally stretched over a frame of birch bark or, alternatively, warp and weft threads were woven direct to such a frame to build up the ground fabric direct from the bark. Early drawn thread work, too, had simple geometric shapes, squares, triangles, generally worked in white thread in the

SWEDEN—*'Adam and Eve'—embroidered carriage seat from Skåne, in the south of the country, 1814. Chain and cross stitches and seeding on a black wool and linen ground, $19\frac{1}{2} \times 59$ in. (49·5 × 150 cm). (Nordiska Museet, Stockholm)*

257

more southern provinces, in pink, red or blue in the northern provinces. Such drawn thread work embellished domestic and church textiles: bier bands (generally 9 ft. 9 in. × 15 in.) (320 × 38 cm), with which coffins were lowered into the earth, often had a narrow border of exquisite drawn thread work.

SWEDEN—*detail of an embroidery from a chasuble made in the latter part of the 15th century by Albertus Pictor, an embroiderer and painter from Stockholm. (Rikstantikvariembetet, Stockholm)*

Unlike some other European embroideries which are winter occupations, Swedish drawn thread work is one form of embroidery that has traditionally been a summer occupation. An annual migration of female labour at the end of the 18th century found girls spending their winters in Hälsingland and Medelpad, carding, spinning and weaving, and their summers in the meadows of Jämtland and Härjedalen whilst looking after cattle. This is when the embroiderers worked on their bands of embroidery, an art which has, in Sweden, until now been primarily a peasant pastime.

Towards the end of the 19th century, Augusta Gripenberg, of Judiksvall, revived the old drawn thread works. She brought back the former patterns and developed new ones, with names like 'Crown robe', 'Evening star', 'Margit's rose' and 'Joy'. Her niece carried on the cataloguing and general promotion of her work. There are today outstanding examples of drawn thread work both in the Nordiska Museet and in the Jämtlands läns Museum Och Fornbyn Jamtli, Östersund.

Embroidery with real tin thread or pewter is a traditional art of the Laps. Today Swedish embroiderers are continuing this metal thread work, although it is becoming increasingly difficult to obtain real tin thread. Narrow coils of hot tin are pulled, prior to use, through a *wortle*, a reindeer horn studded with holes of varying sizes, rather like a knitting-needle gauge. Drawing the tin thread at an even pace through the required hole stretches the hot metal to the desired thickness. It is coiled around a fine cotton inner thread to form a typical metal 'purl' thread. Lapp tin thread is worked like any other metallic embroidery yarn, held down with couching, and it was traditionally used to decorate Lapp costume, reindeer harnesses and belt pouches.

In every province of Sweden today there is a handicraft society, and the Association of Swedish Handicrafts and the ICA Publishing Company are particularly active in promoting the art. There are excellent handicrafts magazines giving good coverage to embroidery. Counted cross-stitch work, often on a fairly coarse-weave canvas, is particularly popular. So, too, are the creative stitcheries featured by outstanding modern embroiderers, who juxtapose exaggerated textures with daring combination, all carefully pre-planned and skilfully executed.

Switzerland

Embroidery in Switzerland in the past has often been so closely allied to that of her neighbours that it is difficult sometimes to confirm its heritage. Much was worked on a wool or linen ground. Composition of design is often more ornate and more complex than that, say, of contemporary works from England. There is a renaissance aspect to some of the work of the 16th and 17th centuries.

Influences have been closely governed by geographical region. In the west of the country (Geneva, Lausanne) there is French association. To the north (Basle, Zürich) there is a noticeable German association. To the east (St. Gallen) there is Bavarian connexion, and to the south (Locarno) a resemblance to Italian work.

Switzerland has unique facilities open to the embroiderer and to the lover of the arts. The paradox of a cosmopolitan country with a fiercely guarded self-reliant identity enables embroidery to fall into the distinct categories of that which has been brought into Switzerland and that which is originally Swiss.

When the Constitution of 1847 encircled the 22 major cantons with one political flag, many of the symbiotic groups brought with them their own 'national' costume, some of which was embroidered.

The Canton of Berne, for example, is famous for 'Berne embroidery', formerly used on the national dress of the region. Laid work of threaded beads, couched at regular intervals with Romanian couching, is worked into small spot motifs on a dark velvet ground. Traditionally the designs are of realistic floral sprays. Tendrils and some outlining are worked in gold thread, mostly in satin stitch.

Swiss whitework is known to every lady who blows her nose on soft white cotton (although today, admittedly, suppliers in the Far East are amongst those who can undercut the prices of the better-quality manufacturers). Extremely detailed motifs and borders are worked, sometimes with *broderie anglaise*, occasionally with *broderie suisse*. There is less pulled work than in comparable whitework from Italy.

Swiss whitework, always very delicate, was worked on a ground of Swiss cambric, a fine Victoria lawn cotton from the Zürich and St. Gallen areas. One such example of delicate embroidery is a handkerchief in the collection of the Embroiderers Guild in London. Buttonhole stitch, seeding, satin stitch, eyelets and

SWITZERLAND—*detail of 1601 hanging, dated and signed 'BP'.*
Barbara Peyer, daughter of David Peyer (1549–1613), probably finished
the work shortly before marrying Hans Im Thurn (1579–1648),
Burgomaster of Schaffhausen, whose subsequent family tree can also
be seen in the same museum. This hanging tells the story of Tobias,
who is here, at the bottom left corner, taking leave of his parents.
14 × 69 in. (36 × 175 cm), coloured wools, silk and some metal thread
embroidery on white linen, kloster *stitch and simple knotting.*
(Musée National Suisse, Zürich)

trailing are combined with pulled work to execute the floral
border. This particular piece, 11 in. (28 cm) square in white Victoria
lawn, comes from the Canton of Appenzell.

And then came the embroidery machine . . . in 1829 Josué Heilmann of Mulhouse was awarded a medal by that city's Industrial
Society for his 'embroidery machine' and, shortly after, he sold the

261

basic rights to a Briton and to François Mange, a Swiss businessman.

This sale marked the demise of hand-embroidered Swiss white-work. Swiss manufacturers worked on—and perfected—the machine, and although they did not fully develop the finesse of machine-stitched scalloping until 1862, they were, by the late 1850's, already exporting throughout Europe and to North America a vast quantity of machine-embroidered muslin in the form of handker-chiefs, edgings and the like. In 1863 they invented machined *broderie anglaise* and this extra facility further accelerated the decline in handwork.

J. J. Sutter of Buhler exhibited some fine hand-worked cushions in the London Great Exhibition of 1851.

Exquisite Swiss machine-embroidered baby clothes, table linens and other domestic embroideries can, therefore, be dated back over a century. They were the forerunners of modern commercial em-broideries and they maintained an undisputed high standard in whitework embroidered by machine.

As if to break away from some of the neat and orderly aspects of embroidery in the past, Swiss embroiderers today are concentrating on boldness of design and the individuality of their conception of that design. As they try in the main to swing the mood of embroidery to personal creation they do, however, still adhere to past devotion to organisation. A modern Swiss wall-hanging or collage is recognis-able by the fact that it is so finished, so perfect. The piece is balanced. Mood and theme often play supporting fiddle to the lead of the technical quality of the work.

An example of domestic and decorative wall-hanging embroidery is the work of Lissy Funk of Zürich. Bold patches of colour form mood designs, each hue—if taken separately from its companions—standing by itself to form a solid and definite shape. A Funk is a pleasing decoration and easy to live with.

From the big to the small . . . Swiss embroiderers are also produc-ing some outstanding miniatures. Liselotte Siegfried of Zürich is one such artist who uses her needle to execute highly detailed and com-plex works in minute scale. Rosemarie Winteler of Zumikon works to both scales. A herb garden scene in delicate appliqué with super-imposed stitching, 1960, measures 59 × 47 in. (150 × 120 cm). A 1971 roundel, noticeably advanced in intent but none the less as technic-ally organised as the earlier work, is only 12 in. (30 cm) square.

Much of contemporary Swiss embroidery is good exhibition material. Wall-hangings are serviceable in design and they generally hang well together with similar works. By and large the modern embroideries are not of the dominating category that can—and needs to—hang alone with no supporting pieces around. Perhaps

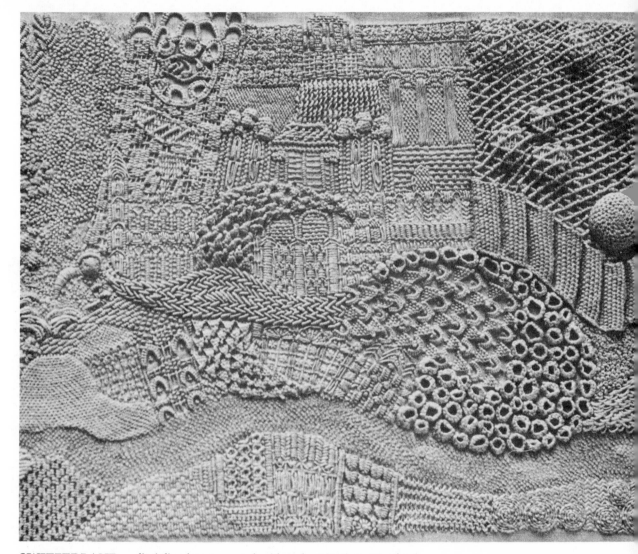

SWITZERLAND—*disciplined texture embroidery by Lieselotte Siegfried of Zürich. 14½ × 8½ in. (37 × 22 cm), 1970. (Heidi Baumann)*

this aspect of today's embroidered art is governed and encouraged by the market that exists. Embroidery is more readily accepted into the general art field than in some other parts of the world.

Organisation of Swiss embroidery extends to the promotional and commercial opportunities of the art. Biennial competitions of the

Schweizer Heimatwerk, open only to amateurs, act as a stimulus to the needlework artist. The simplicity of two of the 1972 prize-winning pieces is typical of one element of current embroidery in the country. A net work of the Nativity is executed in the stark confining lines of the vertical, horizontal and diagonal. Yet because no one line is the least out of order the overall design, with four individual scenes, is human and simply moving.

Heimatwerk's publications have designs and articles which are also undoubtedly instrumental in shaping channels of embroidery ideas throughout the country, and offering critical advice to embroiderers who need guidance.

The Abegg Foundation, 12 miles from Berne, opened in 1967. Although it is open to the public in the summer months, the main aim of the Foundation, established by Dr. Werner Abegg of Zürich,

SWITZERLAND—blackwork from the Textilklasse der Kunstgewerbeschule, Zürich, 1922. 46½ × 44 in. (118 × 112 cm). (Collection of the Kunstgewerbemuseum at the Museum Bellerive, Zürich)

264

is twofold: to set up a laboratory to evaluate and preserve the price-less collection of woven textiles and other applied arts and, also, to provide study facilities in those fields.

The Foundation's two regular publications centre on the main collection, which does not actually include any embroidery in its

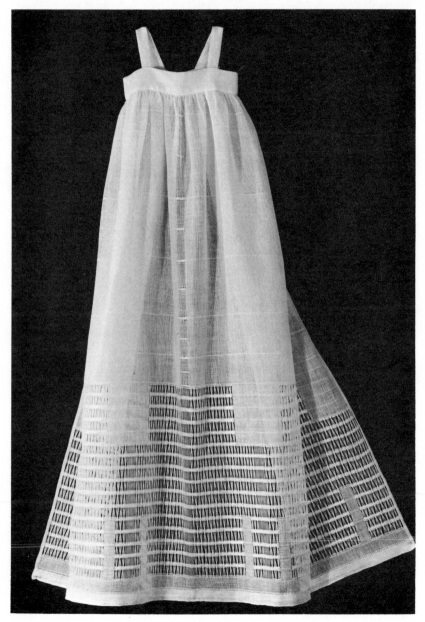

SWITZERLAND—
christening robe by Heidy Gutzwiller, Liebefeld-Bern, one of the main prizewinners in the 1972 Schweizer Heimatwerk competition. (Schweizer Heimatwerk. Photo: Peter Gruenert)

inventory. *Schriften der Abegg-Stiftung* is a general magazine with articles about Dr. Abegg's collection. *Monographien* is a discussion publication with international expert participation.

It is in the conservation of textiles, however, that the Abegg Foundation plays a particularly vital role in the embroidery world. Mme. Mechthild Flury-Lemberg, with her brother, Rolf Lemberg, an architect, designed the Foundation's outstanding laboratory which is used not only for conservation of the centre's own textiles but also for intensive training of specialists. They can take only three apprentices at a time, plus one research assistant from a Swiss museum. They are so inundated with museum commissions for many years ahead that there is no immediate opportunity of the laboratory being able to cope with requests from the individual collector. The special study collection of the conservation laboratory does include much embroidery.

Taiwan

TAIWAN—*'Rendering of the Spirit of the Verse of "Potted Chrysanthemums", an embroidered hanging, 76 × 25½ in. (193 × 64·8 cm), taken from a popular poem from the Sung Dynasty (960–1127). (Collection of the National Palace Museum, Taipei)*

267

When General Chiang Kai-shek retreated from the Chinese mainland to the island of Taiwan (Formosa) in 1949, he took with him not only half a million Nationalist supporters but, also, an invaluable retrospective collection of Chinese embroideries from the Ming Dynasty onwards.

Many of these works are now in the National Palace Museum in Taipei, and are beautifully illustrated in what must surely be one of the world's most lush and extravagant books, the Museum's *Kokuritsu kokyū hakubutsuin*, published in two volumes in 1970 at a retail price of N.T. $12,000 (£800)!

TAIWAN—*embroidered hanging, 85 × 18½ in. (216 × 47 cm), with assemblage of various contemporary objects from the Ming Dynasty (1368–1644).*
(Collection of the National Palace Museum, Taipei)

Turkey

Straddling Europe and Asia, Turkey today is as much a crossroads for trade and influences as it ever has been. Basically, the Turks are a Turanian race, ethnically related to the Manchus and Mongols of northern China, to Central Asian people and to the Finns. By continuous blending and permeation, too, Turkey's people and customs today derive to some extent from those of most of the countries of the European and Middle Eastern world.

The Seljuks established the Kingdom of Rum, with a centre at Konya (the biblical Iconium), in about 1092–1106, and they encouraged all forms of literature and the arts. With the collapse of the Konya kingdom on the death of Kai-Kubad II in 1307 there began a struggle for supremacy, resulting in annexation in 1472 by the Osmanli Muhammad II. Thus the Osmanlis (or Ottomans) made their début, to begin a rule of over four centuries.

Ottoman power expanded, reaching its zenith in the 16th century under the great Sultans Selim I (1512–20), Suleiman I, known as 'The Magnificent' (1520–66), and Murad III (1574–95). It was not, in fact, until defeat outside Vienna in 1683 that the graph of the Empire's fortunes entered a long downward curve, in which the lands of the Turks were finally reduced after the First World War to their present vestigial form. The perimeter of Ottoman supremacy at its height, however, was far-flung. It spread from Central Asia and the borders of India through Arabia, the north-east and north coastal regions of Africa, Greece and most of south-eastern Europe. The main sphere of textile concern of this period is restricted to those works of art from the Balkans and Asia Minor, one of the major cultural centres of which continued to be Konya.

One of the first references to embroidery as such is that of Nicolai de Niicolay in 1568. He mentions the 'artistic women of Karamen with their embroidery'. The Ottomans were itinerant warriors, traversing their wide territories, and they took with them rugs and coverings embroidered by their womenfolk to make their journeys seem more palatable. Many such rugs and prayer rugs were hooked, from which the embroidery 'Turkey work stitch' (p. 445) probably evolved.

Turkish embroideries are generally floral in design, for the Turks, as Sunni Moslems, have always been adverse to the representation

269

of human and animal figures. Frequently used motifs have also included crescents and stars. Early works were on a velvet or silk ground (the Emperor Justinian had established a silk industry in Constantinople during his reign, 527–65) and, even at that stage, there was much metal thread embellishment.

Concurrent with the inherited influences of the Byzantines and the Ottomans there was foreign inspiration to some native Turkish embroidery, despite—or possibly due to—continual border harassment both on the part of the Turks and the Persians during the 16th and 17th centuries. Oriental influence is in evidence in such motif forms as the *kulka*, the cloud scroll and, also, in a design of three balls. European fashions in the 18th century ousted some traditional floral design, and colouring became more naturalistic: individual floral stems began to grow from flower pots. Architectural motifs made their first appearance, to be much used for towel and sampler decoration. Foreign travellers brought with them their own techniques of embroidery, with a partiality for stitches such as the French knot and satin stitching.

In return, Turkish silk continued to be exported along all the main trade arteries. Some of it, for example, was handled by Armenian traders for sale to merchants and diplomats in Hungary. Gold and silver thread was similarly transported, as is shown by the number of churches in Hungary that have embroideries worked in Turkish thread.

By the end of the 17th century new colours had entered the Turkish embroidery palette; delicate shades of mango red, blue and green were often used, on such exquisite items of embroidery as the *obi*, the show-towels used as carry-cloths by ladies and gentlemen to hide their washing necessities as they progressed to public bathhouses. The shaping of these towels (similar to the German *Paradenhandtücher*) was sometimes exaggeratedly long and narrow, an outstanding example of which can be seen in the Whitworth Art Gallery, Manchester. Towels were, alternatively, used at table as napkins: Lady Mary Wortley Montagu, harbinger of so many female explorers, described going to have dinner with the Sultana Hafiten in 1718 when the napkins were all 'embroidered with silks and gold, in the finest manner, in natural flowers'. Such embroidery was, at that time, worked on a frame, and main stitches employed were double-running, a basic pulled thread work and tent stitch transposed from its general canvas ground to a linen ground. In addition to basic floral designs, fruits such as wild pear, pomegranates and strawberries were sometimes worked.

Turkish metal thread embroidery has played a key role throughout the centuries of textile arts. One of the earliest examples is a 16th-century red velvet quiver to be seen in the delightful Topkapi Palace Museum in Istanbul. Some such embroidery can be identified by the peculiar feature of the metal thread passing right through the ground fabric (as opposed to the more usual form of metal thread embroidery

TURKEY—*18th- or 19th-century sampler, 26 × 16½ in. (66 × 42 cm). Silk on linen worked with double running stitch and eye stitches. (The Victoria and Albert Museum, Crown Copyright)*

in which the thread is surface-couched). The Turkish method of working, similarly employed by Greek artists, tends to split the threads of the ground fabric.

In the same museum there is a typical example of 19th-century gold work, heavily padded with both vertical and horizontal under-laid threads, on a light velvet ground. Artists frequently used paper templates to achieve exact proportioning. Gold-work motifs were again floral, crescent-shaped, arabesque or in complex formations such as those worked at the beginning of the century on the saddle-cloth made in Constantinople for the 7th Earl of Elgin when he arrived to take up his office as Ambassador to the Sublime Porte.

Equestrian apparel and accoutrements such as overnight tents had, as befitted a travelling race, been close to the hearts of Turkish artists throughout the history of their country's imperial eminence. An appliqué tent captured from the Turks in 1683 by the Austrian armies at the gates of Vienna is evidence of the elaborate workman-ship that went into both the design and execution of so utilitarian a structure.

Most Turkish embroidery styles today employ counted thread work, often using triangular Turkish stitch to work the designs. There is still, too, some leather embroidery, on the soft local hides that are possibly better known when fashioned into the coats and jackets sold in the markets of Istanbul and Izmir and around the world.

United States of America

American embroidery, as such, really began about 1725, but it is necessary, in order to gain a comprehensive picture of work produced in the United States, to start with the 'stitcheries' of the American Indians.

In 1492 Columbus wrote that when he landed at Watling Island he won the confidence of Indians with 'friendly gifts of red caps and some strings of glass beads', and established peoples in North America must have been wearing beads long before that. Beadwork was either loom-woven on small box or bow looms or, alternatively, it was roughly stitched. Ojibwa, Sauk and Fox were some of the tribes around the Mississippi river who specialised in outstanding sewn beadwork, often held down with the 'lazy squaw' method by which several beads were threaded on to the needle before the holding string entered the ground fabric. The basic Indian method of stitching beadwork was to take a near-surface stitch, not going right through the buckskin or other ground fabric (although complete stitches were fastened on through some softer leather grounds).

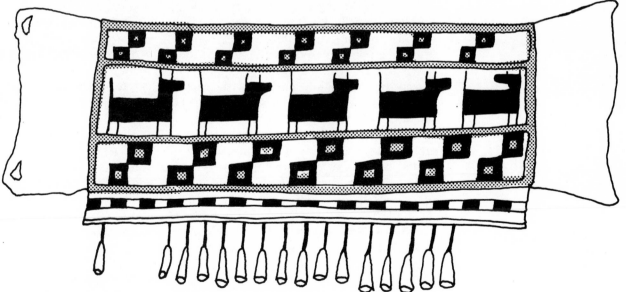

USA—*diagram of a North American Indian quilled deer-hide decoration for a baby-carrier.*
(Museum of the American Indian, Heye Foundation, New York.
No. 24/2011 in the Andrew Foster Collection)

Buckskin, a pure-white leather, deerskin, buffalo and other skins were also decorated with primitive quilting, dangling addenda such as bells—and quill work. Sometimes beadwork and quill work were combined with pleasing results.

It can be reasonably suggested therefore, that Indian quill work, beadwork and Alaskan fish-skin needlework (dried seal intestine and fish-skin appliqué worked on to skin in traditional Aleutian fashion) were some of the earliest stitcheries found in North America.

By the 17th century colonists were already establishing strong communities along the eastern seaboard and in the south of the country. Embroidery influences were, accordingly, English (especially in New England and Virginia), Dutch (along the Hudson river), Swedish (in the Delaware Valley) and Spanish (the east coast of Florida, in Louisiana and Mississippi). Later in the century French Huguenot influence was apparent in South Carolina, Pennsylvania, New York and Virginia, and German in Pennsylvania. Scottish and Irish influence followed, apparent in Pennsylvania, Maryland and Virginia.

Besides enough stocks of household linen and clothing brought (forewarned by various colonising companies) to last some time, good settling ladies brought with them their embroidery heritage and some of the necessary materials. John Hall, a London businessman, wrote to his mother, Rebeckah Symonds, in Ipswich, Massachusetts, for 20 years following 1663, giving her revealing pictures of the fashions in England at the time and thereby stimulating her to produce the same beautiful items. Linen, twill and broadcloth were imported, but homespun, much used throughout American embroidery, implied colonial origin. Equally, local cotton embroidery thread was available, although the early thread was very thick, almost like string. Cotton and wool were the most popular embroidery media throughout: silk was extremely expensive.

Apart from ideas sent by relatives overseas, early American embroiderers had a wealth of inspiration available. As well as imported works that could themselves be copied, there were paintings and wallpapers with suitable motifs. The colonists had their own magazines and newsletters and there were published patterns such as the book now in the Valentine Museum in Richmond, Virginia. The Museum's Textile Center, with its Consulting Curator, Mildred J. Davis, is paramount in serious study of embroidery.

USA—*Samuel Adams's christening blanket, crewel wool on linen and cotton twill ground, embroidered in Boston, c. 1700–1713, by his mother, Mary Fifield (born 1694). 78¾ × 56 in. (200 × 142 cm). (Courtesy Museum of Fine Arts, Boston. Gift of Miss Mary Avery White)*

275

One of the earliest American samplers is that of Loara Standish (1623–56), whose embroidery, now in the Pilgrim Hall Museum, Plymouth, Massachusetts, bears the words:

Loara Standish is my name
Lord guide my heart that I may do thy will
And fill my hands with such convenient skill
As will conduce to virtue devoid of shame
And I will give glory to thy name.

The greater part of early American samplers in fact came from New England and the surrounding area. The embroideries were influenced by the heritage of the artists' backgrounds, and samplers are, accordingly, often very little different from contemporary English, Dutch or Scandinavian works (although the very long and narrow shape characteristic of English samplers of that time was not so exaggerated in American versions). It was not until the 18th century that a truly American sampler evolved.

One of the outstanding sampler collections in the United States is that started by the Whitman Candy Company. Pet Incorporated, controllers of the Company, presented the 30-year-old collection to the Philadelphia Museum of Art in 1969. A Pennsylvanian sampler (1754) from the collection, $22\frac{1}{4} \times 17\frac{1}{4}$ in. (56·5 × 44 cm), is typical of the age in that it has a landscape view along the bottom. Sheep and other domestic animals are scattered on hills and under two weird and imaginative trees. Later these landscapes were to expand and fill more of the available sampler space so that, by the 19th century, a complete landscape sampler was quite common and views were more realistic.

From the earliest days, American settlers' children were enjoined to learn how to sew, for the desirability of self-sufficiency was stressed at an early age. The working of samplers was a necessary part of most girls' upbringing. Some schools had their own colour combinations, and motifs and samplers can be recognised accordingly.

Feelings of tenderness for their original homeland often show through these early samplers. Sometimes the artists stitched their family trees, remembering relations who had perhaps stayed the other side of the Atlantic. The genealogical record was usually surrounded by a border of flowers or similar garland. On the whole, however, early American samplers are not so abundant as contemporary embroideries from England or Europe. There were some map samplers, occasionally with detailed outlining to the then map of America. Detail was stressed throughout: during this period much energy went into the embroidering of 'architectural' or 'landscape'

276

samplers, with recognisable views. Houses, churches and complete landscapes were often portrayed with minute exactness.

German settlers arrived in Pennsylvania between 1683 and 1775 and usually stayed in a fairly restricted area with less assimilation than some other immigrant groups. Pennsylvanian German or so-called 'Dutch' samplers are amongst the easiest to identify. A few had figures with painted faces and hands, others had sequins and metal thread adding further ornamentation. But, basically, a Pennsylvanian sampler is worked in bright colours with such stitching as satin stitch, cross stitch and rococo stitch. Sometimes, particularly from the mid-18th century, there are squared motifs of geometric patterns along the top and down the sides of the work: sometimes there are pairs of birds worked with the inscription 'An emblem of love', or similar wording, in an octagonal surround (although this motif also appears in work from Trenton, New Jersey). Dark green canvas grounds, as in Anzolette Hussey's sampler in the Smithsonian Institution, Washington DC, are peculiarly Pennsylvanian, and there is often a ribbon binding around the edge of the work.

The earliest Pennsylvanian sampler known to have survived is the 1724 work of Susanna Painter, of Philadelphia, aged seven. She embroidered two alphabets and the inscription 'The blessing of the Lord: it maketh rich and he addeth no sorrow with it' in cross stitch and eyelet stitch.

The first sampler known to have been worked in a Pennsylvanian school, however, is that of Lydia Hoopes, aged ten, in Mrs. Hollis's School in 1765. Apparently Mistress Hollis ran a small school in her own home which, though it lacked literary opportunity, produced a great deal of fine needlework. Lydia's border sampler, wool on linen, again used cross stitch and eyelet stitch.

Many samplers, in design and colouring, are similar to *Paradenhandtücher* ('show towels') of the time, which were often highly decorated, a form of 'practical sampler' that was also evidence of the cleanliness and prosperity of the embroiderer's home. Motifs used in America were similar to those of German *Paradenhandtücher*. The earliest dated American example is 1820 and, in the main, later works are longer and thinner than their predecessors.

'Moravian', or 'Bethlehem', embroidery, which evolved in Herrnhut, Germany, in 1722, traces its American origins to 1741 when Herr Nicholas Lewis of Zizendorf arrived in the country. The following year his daughter Benigna, helped by two ladies and three gentlemen, started a school for 25 pupils at Ashmead House in Germanstown. Two months later the school moved to Bethlehem, Pennsylvania, then to Nazareth and, finally, back to Bethlehem in 1749.

Apparently it was part of their education that the young ladies be taught 'plain and fancy needlework' amongst other feminine accomplishments. According to William C. Reichel and William H. Bigler (*A History of the Moravian Seminary for Young Ladies at Bethlehem*), the students had two hours of tambour work and music most days and, in 1790, the school prospectus announced annual

USA—18th century—whitework sampler, silk on linen, satin stitch, buttonhole stitch, eyelet work, drawn work and hollie point. 13 × 15 in (33 × 38 cm). Jane Humphreys, aged 11, 1771.
(Philadelphia Museum of Art. Gift of Miss Letitia A. Humphreys, 114–307)

fees of two guineas for instruction in 'fine needlework', to include use of the tambour.

One of the oldest surviving Moravian embroideries is the 1778 banner worked for Count Casimir Pulaski, who smoothed communications between American soldiers and Bethlehem inhabitants. In 1826 some of the students worked an elaborate embroidery of ribbon and silks for Mrs. John Quincy Adams.

The Bethlehem establishment was the first Moravian school: another opened in Warwick Township, Lancaster County, in 1846. Here the girls learnt sewing, knitting, darning and the ornamental needlework for which the school was famous.

'Bethlehem embroidery' or 'Moravian embroidery' as such often refers today to mourning pictures, in silk on a silk ground. Highly emotional in effect, the features of persons portrayed are exaggerated to achieve maximum impact. During the 19th century, ribbon, silk and crêpe were applied and added to the more traditional silk on silk composition. Moravian embroidery is recognised by the fluidity, though not the complete realism, of the design. Outlines are frequently simplified to facilitate effect and, as such, natural representation gives way to balance of shape and colour. Moravian embroidery is, therefore, particularly associated with religious work, be it in the form of mourning picture or a more happy subject. It also includes some beadwork, taught by the Sisters of the establishments of Bethlehem, Nazareth and Lititz.

Eighteenth-century embroidery design in general often included animals, either real or imaginary. Floral motifs, sometimes worked in monochrome, were popular—ships, on the other hand, were seldom portrayed, a surprising absence since many of the embroiderers had themselves travelled by sea. Most-used stitches of this time include straight stitch, chain stitch, outline stitch, Romanian stitch (particularly on canvas work), French knots, buttonhole stitch, satin stitch, tent stitch, cross stitch, eyelet holes, herringbone stitch, fishbone stitch, seeding and feather stitch. Surface satin stitch ('economy stitch') was very common, a useful innovation since its use meant more mileage from precious imported yarn. There was appliqué but little padded work.

Whitework embroidery in the 18th century was generally worked with wool or cotton thread on a ground of cotton, linen or wool. Delicate 'Holy point' or 'Dresden work' became fashionable towards the end of the century: the sampler worked by Jane Humphreys in 1771, in the collection of the Philadelphia Museum of Art, is an exquisite example of the fine work produced. The advent of this more dainty whitework coincided, too, with the arrival of lighter-weight dress fabrics.

Quilting was worked on some clothing. As in Europe, practical and decorative quilted skirts, in satin or silk, were high fashion between 1770 and 1775.

In 1790 a census of the foreign background of American settlers showed that 61% had English origin, 19% had Scottish, Irish or Welsh origin, 9% German, 3% Dutch and 2% French. This is indicative of the variety of types and styles of embroidery of the time.

There were, for example, bed hangings, although today few complete sets survive. One beautifully embroidered set is that of the Old Gaol Museum in York, Maine. Sets consisted of the basic curtain (hangings), valances (vallens), base pieces (or flounces), counterpane (or coverlet) and head cloth (or tester). Many sets were whitework, others were embroidered in blue and rose pink. There was little wool work in the warmer and more humid South where cotton was a more practical medium and, also, being locally produced it was considerably cheaper.

In the main, bed hangings were in 'crewel' work, similar to foreign contemporary work, but, in New England for example, never quite as heavy as the English counterpart. Once again, the American embroiderer had to economise on thread, and the resulting design was simple, with fewer stitches used. Some of the best surviving New England pieces are worked solely in surface satin stitch. Others employ herringbone stitch, buttonhole stitch, running stitch, outline stitch and French and bullion knots.

Because imported twisted worsted yarn was in such short supply, many embroiderers dyed their own. Some of their dyes, such as the 'tag locks', yellowed ends of sheep's wool, used to produce a blue-green hue, have remained fast to this day. Artists used black walnut to get brown yarn, sumac and golden rod to achieve yellows which have not, admittedly, proved to be fast.

Mary Fifield Adams, born in 1694, worked a christening blanket for her son, Samuel Adams, early in the 18th century. She also worked, in partnership with her daughter, an elaborate full-sized bedcover with an oriental approach to the motifs, indicative of the universal scope of design of the time. The coverlet, crewel wool on cotton with a linen warp, is embroidered and quilted. Both embroideries are in the Museum of Fine Arts, Boston.

Martha Washington, wife of George, is one of the most famous embroiderers of the late 18th century. In 1765 she ordered canvas and worsted yarn from England and worked 12 cross-stitch cushions in a shell motif since copied by many enthusiastic embroiderers. Six of these pieces are still in the collection of the Mount Vernon Ladies' Association of the Union. Mrs. Washington also worked a small drawstring bag, with appliqué and embroidery, for one of her granddaughters, Eleanor Parke Custis Lewis.

George Washington was a popular subject of many needlework portraits and, obviously, a pattern was quite generally available since many of the canvas-work pictures are taken from the same design. (From 1789 on, in fact, the President of the United States has continued to be a popular portrait subject, both in America and elsewhere—lurid silken mats with stylised heads of President Kennedy are to be found even in the smallest bazaar in a side street of Shiraz, in southern Iran.)

The delectable-sounding 'fishing lady' and 'Boston Common' embroideries are portraits worked by daughters of prosperous New England families. Six examples are at Winterthur, Delaware.

Embroiderers of the late 18th and through the 19th centuries were particularly fond of working such embroidered 'portraits', possibly to replace wall-hangings they had left behind in their homeland. Copies of engravings were worked in detail, in monochrome silk on a taffeta ground. Unlike their British counterparts, the 19th-century 'print works' and 'etching embroideries', however, contemporary American embroideries of this type were called 'engraved embroideries'.

By the end of the 18th century the United States had several highly productive textile factories, an industry which meant the gradual demise of home-spun and home-dyed textiles.

An outstanding feature of American embroidery and stitching throughout the ages had been the unrivalled quality of all her bed coverings and quilts. The actual process of quilting (p. 419) is a universal art. But many of the fine bed coverings, such as bed rugs, patchwork quilts, applied quilts and the like, are peculiarly an attribute of North America.

Not all bed coverings were in fact embroidered. Of the Indian *palampores* or chintzes (brought from England), the brocades and velvets from Spain or the silks and damasks from France and Italy— many were made into striking coverings as they were, without further embellishment. Or, alternatively, such beautifully lush grounds would be worked with some superimposed embroidery, such as the 102 × 90 in. (2·59 × 2·29 m) overall floral printed pattern on cotton twill spread, at the Colonial Williamsburg Foundation, Virginia, that has a fine chain-stitch embroidery.

Generally printed coverings were in themselves splendidly decorative and usually rather patrician in appeal (many examples were found in the Boston area). More rural—and more practical— were the plain-ground quilts of, for instance, linsey-woolsey that have provenance mainly in Connecticut and throughout New England.

Linsey-woolsey, peculiar to quilts from North America, gets its name from mediaeval 'lynsy wolsye' ('lynsy' from Lindsey, Suffolk, England). Technically the words mean a 'coarse fabric of cotton or linen woven with wool', although today the term is generally applied to a thick quilted bed covering, usually hanging to the floor and with corners cut to accommodate bed posts.

Linsey-woolsey automatically implies a wool work and, generally, the item concerned is a country quilt. Such a piece is one-colour, with a linen warp and wool weft. Most that survive today are quilted in matching thread. Colouring is indigo blue, brown, red, deep turquoise, yellow, pink or a light blue. Linings are of contrasting colours, and the two layers are sewn together with a layer of natural unwashed padding between. Linsey-woolsey quilting patterns feature particularly a central design that stands out from a trellis or other quilted 'ground'.

Whitework quilts were generally worked in *trapunto*, Italian quilting, or in candlewicking. The Henry Ford Museum has a *trapunto* coverlet, about 1820, 60 × 32 in. (152 × 81 cm), with an intricate design of central floral pattern in lozenge border, with outer border of similar floral band and geometric trellis as main ground. Most examples of quilting on American bed coverings are from the first three-quarters of the 19th century, although the San Antonio Museum Association has a piece worked shortly before the Chicago World's Fair of 1893, in which it gained a first prize.

The earliest form of American candlewicking was woven in rather a rigid and formal pattern. Later, French knots and darning stitch took over and the candlewicking as we know it today evolved. The Metropolitan Museum in New York has one fine example of candlewicking, signed and dated 'TD 1825', with two American eagles and stars close to a large eight-pointed central star.

Quilts have long been cherished and passed down from generation to generation. Since each dutiful American bride was supposed to have some 13 different quilts in her marriage chest, there is today an entire gamut of quilts that have been worked down the years with incredible patience, for the quickest and most skilled needlewoman takes a long time, working single-handed, to complete even a comparatively small quilt.

That truly American innovation, patchwork quilting, dates back to about 1775. At the time of the War of Independence the shortage of fabric would have been particularly acute and from necessity came forth art. Many of the names of the early quilts spring from events or personalities of the war. Until about 1875, patchwork quilts occupied a leading role in the field of American stitchery. The art of patching fascinated and inspired girls as soon as they could hold a needle.

There are, also, a great many beautiful appliqué quilts from the same period, 1775–1875, again springing from the need to 'make do'. The earliest applied quilts had printed motifs sewn to plain grounds of white cotton or linen which were then covered with quilting.

One of the earliest examples of applied quilts is the 'Westover-Berkeley' coverlet in the Valentine Museum, Richmond, Virginia, which is in fact thought to have been even earlier than the main period of applied quilting. It was worked on alternate fortnights at the Westover Plantation, Virginia, home of William Byrd II, and at the neighbouring Berkeley Plantation, owned by Benjamin Harrison IV. Evelyn Byrd, who died 'beautiful and single' in 1737, was reputed to have worked on the quilt, but it is now generally supposed that the embroidery was executed in the decade immediately before the Revolution. The quilt was passed down through the Harrison family until it was given to the Museum by Mr. and Mrs. Tazewell Ellett in 1946.

Some appliqué quilts were dated, as was the 'E.W. 1818' quilt with an 'orange slice' design now in the Henry Ford Museum. But, generally, it is difficult to trace the origin of many quilts unless they have been inherited through a fairly traceable family line or unless there is accompanying documentation.

Making a quilt was usually a highly sociable affair. A 'freedom quilt', for example, was made for a man's coming of age. On the afternoon of his 21st birthday his mother (or sisters) would ask suitable girl friends to come to help. Each brought left-over scraps of dresses from her own wardrobe and she would make her section of the quilt with patches of her own personal mementoes. The finished quilt was then put aside for the lucky man's future fiancée to put in her dowry chest (complete with such souvenirs of her love's past!) This form of quilting 'bee' (as this busy sewing gathering was called) went out of fashion about 1825, although the name 'freedom quilt' re-emerged during the Civil War when it was applied to a patriotic quilt with relevant flat motifs.

A similarly communal festivity was the 'friendship medley party' for the making of a 'friendship quilt'. Generally after the announcement of a girl's engagement, a good friend would host the party and each guest would, again, bring her favourite 'pieces' to work into the quilt.

Not all quilt-making was joyfully inspired. 'Memory quilts' were fashioned from scraps of the wardrobe of the recently departed, a macabre remembrance of a Loved One.

A 'crazy quilt' is, paradoxically, not technically 'quilted' at all. The top covering is in fact usually 'caught' through middle layers of padding to the inner lining with small stay stitches placed at irregular intervals. 'Crazy quilts' were a basically mid-19th-century phenomenon, typical of the outrageous over-decoration of that time. Any pieces, be they fabric, ribbon, cord or a similarly soft substance, were worked in a usually unreasoned sequence to produce the 'crazy' effect. Some, to be fair, were in fact governed by a semblance

USA—*women's pockets, showing patchwork, appliqué and crewel embroidery. New England, early 19th century.*
(Old Sturbridge Village, Massachusetts)

of design, though in fact the more realistic a crazy quilt became in design, the closer it got to the perimeter of the territory of the 'appliqué quilt'.

'Hawaiian quilts' (p. 119) are recognisable by flowing design and characteristic colour combinations.

Another form of bed covering, the rug, is generally associated with

USA—detail of a bed-rug, polychrome wool on natural homespun tabby-weave wool, signed and dated 'HM 1833'.
(American Museum in Britain, no. 60.243)

285

American origins, but this is in fact a falsification. There are bed rugs to be seen on display in Norway. And in 1636 one ship, the *William and John*, is reputed to have crossed the Atlantic from England with 240 yards of rugs. Imported examples were known as 'Biscay' or 'Bilbao' rugs.

What is unique, however, about the purely American bed rug is that it is generally signed and dated. One of the earliest examples is the 'M 1722 A' work, 98 × 88 in. (2·49 × 2·24 m), at the Essex Institute in Salem, Massachusetts, made by Mary Avery in wool on a home-spun linen. Six hearts in the design suggest that it may have been part of a marriage chest.

Most rugs were worked with multi-ply yarn in running stitch or a plush stitch, which gave the effect of pile when cut. Unlike patchwork coverings, the bed rug was a pre-conceived accomplishment: materials used were specially designated and prepared, with no leftover scraps utilised as in patchwork.

Many rugs show some *abrash*, variation of shade of one colour used, evidence that in some cases the artist underestimated the amount of wool needed. Connecticut was the chief centre of rug production, although many examples today have come from New England. Many rugs have diagonal slits in the bottom two corners to accommodate bed posts as they lay in place, covering the bed.

Unfortunately not enough bed rugs have survived to ascertain exact provenance of a particular design, but it is possible that some were worked to oriental inspiration. By the middle of the 18th century the familiar oriental Tree of Life motif appears constantly. Other contemporary rugs featured a flowering bush pattern dissimilar to the more common Tree of Life design. One outstanding piece is the 1773 rug, 7 ft. (2·13 m) square, worked by Polly ('Molly') Stark, now the property of the Daughters of the American Revolution Museum. A comprehensive retrospective exhibition of bed rugs was held at the Wadsworth Atheneum, Hartford, Connecticut, in 1972, entitled 'Bed Ruggs 1722–1833'.

Berlin wool work arrived in the United States shortly after it reached English shores and, as in other places in the world, immediately became very popular. Patterns were imported, as were many of the canvases, from England, France and Germany, from 1805 on. The first volume of *Godey's Lady's Book* (1830), one of the handbooks of the American embroiderer in the 19th century, stated that 'patterns for working may be purchased at most of the fancy shops . . .'

Of all the Berlin wool-work patterns available, floral designs were the most frequently followed. Wreaths of flowers and bouquets

adorned screens, bags, purses, blotters and all kinds of knick-knacks.
In the 1830's and 1840's the design was generally on a light ground:
by the following decade a black or dark-coloured ground had become
more usual. There were, too, many bird motifs, possibly suggested
by Audubon's *Birds of America* and similar ornithological works.
Berlin wool work with superimposed beads, silks and chenille thread
has been called 'German embroidery' and, as the 19th century
developed, so did such embroidery grow in scope and imagination.

Some of the smaller Berlin patterns could be worked on perforated

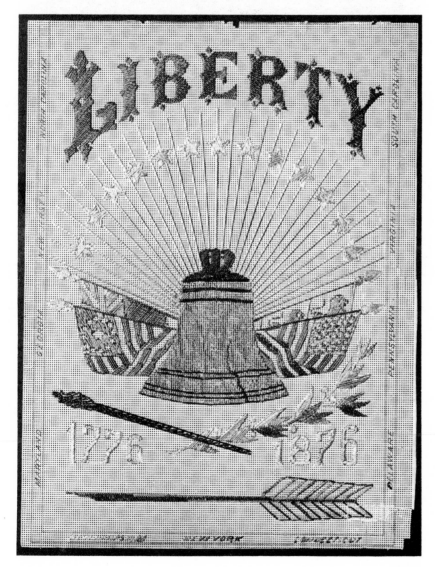

USA—*19th century*—*silk on card work, with blue, brown, tan, yellow, grey and green thread worked in satin stitch and tent stitch. 14 × 10¾ in. (35·5 × 27·5 cm), 1876. (Philadelphia Museum of Art. The Whitman Sampler Collection given by Pet Incorporated, 69-288-204)*

card. This was an era of much emotion and, accordingly, embroiderers went overboard with needleworked entreaties such as 'Love thy neighbor' and reminders of 'Home sweet home'. An 1876 sampler in the Philadelphia Museum of Art, celebrating the centenary of the War of Independence, silk on card, satin stitch and tent stitch, is evidence of the patience which the artist was prepared to devote to 'paper work'.

USA—*19th-century 'memorial picture' worked by Ann Lovett, January 1809. (Schenectady Museum, New York)*

Embroidery in general, however, faced a severe decline in popularity with the Civil War of 1861–5. The effects of industrialisation, too, were widely felt, although fortunately the mechanical advance and its slow poison were counterbalanced to some extent by such events as the Philadelphia Centennial Exhibition of 1876, which included a special exhibition of embroidery. The same year the Decorative Art Society of New York was founded. Mrs. Candace Wheeler (author of *Development of Embroidery in America*) and Louis Comfort Tiffany organised a chapter to provide a unifying core for ladies who wanted to make use of their artistic talents.

In 1879 the Needlework School of the Museum of Fine Arts in Boston evolved from the local chapter of the Decorative Art Society. It was set up under the guidance of William Morris (p. 90), with Mrs. Oliver Wendell Holmes Jr. as a worthy leader, to try to revive the beautiful 'crewel' embroideries of the past. The School reiterated

288

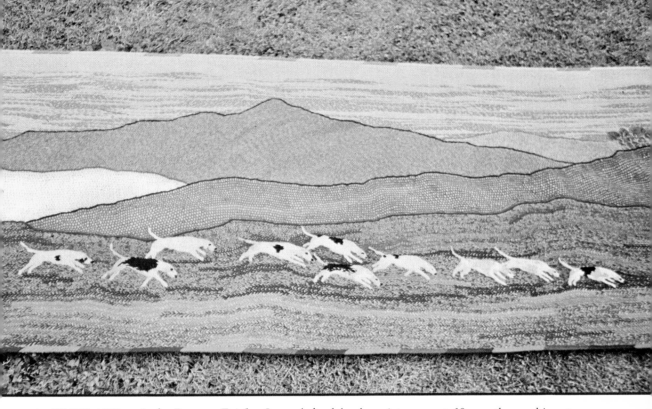

△ *SCOTLAND – Lady Ramsay-Fairfax-Lucy, helped by her sister, spent 18 months working a portrait of the Jedforest Hunt. Tjell-shaped, 30 × 3 ft (9.14 × 0.91 m), on a coarse linen ground, it shows 13 mounts, 5½ couple of hounds, and the fox. Finished in January 1958, it hangs annually at the Hunt Ball. Each hound is recognisable. Illustration shows a detail.*
(The artist)

▽ *SYRIA – a detail of Damascus gold work – gold silk thread on fine cotton ground.*
(Author's collection)

△ *SYRIA – another detail of Damascus gold work – gold silk thread on fine cotton ground.* (*Author's collection*)

the aims of the Boston Women's Educational and Industrial Union which had also been formed a few years previously.

In Chicago Mrs. Potter Palmer founded the Needlework and Textile Guild at the Art Institute. She was in charge of the Women's Pavilion at the Exhibition in 1893.

The Litchfield Historical Society started a collection of old needle-work. Mrs. Emily Noyes Vanderpoel was instrumental in initiating this collection.

There was, too, a plethora of printed publications and patterns to tempt the would-be embroiderer. The Butterick Publishing Co.'s *Artistic Alphabets for Marking and Engrossing* (1893) has every type of script imaginable (and, to judge by one particular grasshopper-like alphabet, hitherto unimaginable), expressly designed for embroider-ing monograms on fine bed-linen and handkerchiefs. As well as the well-known *Godey's Lady's Book*, 19th-century embroidery enthusiasts were tantalised with magazines such as *Leslie's Ladies' Gazette*, *Petersen's Magazine* and, later, *Harper's Bazaar*.

The late 19th century was certainly a time of experiment. Although earlier examples of American stumpwork are rare, Anna Lippincott (born 1848) of Chester County, Pennsylvania, worked a picture, $22 \times 15\frac{1}{2}$ in. (56×39.5 cm), now with the Chester County Historical Society, that combines a fussy contemporary approach with 'Jacobean' features to the people. There was, too, hair embroidery and, as in England, occasional use of beetles wings and other exotica.

Samplers of the 19th century were larger than those of the 18th century. It had become customary for the embroiderer to work her name as a statement of her proficiency: often she would also work the date of completion and other personal details.

Candace Wheeler, writing in 1921, said she remembered her grandmother showing her a 'huz-if', a sampler-container that held sewing equipment (a descendant of the housewife's 'pocket' of former days). Pockets of different Indian chintzes were sewn to a linen ground, each pocket holding thread and other necessary needlework accessories.

Blue and white, in embroidery language, is often synonymous with the work of Deerfield, Massachusetts. Around 1890 two families, the Whitings of Holyoke and the Millers of Hatfield, moved in from their nearby former homes. Each family coincidentally con-sisted of a widowed mother and two unmarried daughters and possibly this composition drew them together. At any rate, Ellen Miller had studied in Springfield and Margaret Whiting at the New York Academy of Design and both were then 30 years old.

Both were also highly artistic and, through their interest in their new environment, they became involved in local needleworks that had not been practised for many years. They started a collection of the old patterns and, by buying up pieces and copying examples of others, they compiled a thoroughly comprehensive catalogue of New England embroidery. They also analysed the stitches used, realising that the main stitch had been Romanian stitch (in Deerfield always formerly called 'New England laid stitch').

In 1896 Ellen Miller (who was shy and introverted) and Margaret Whiting (who was an articulate and witty woman) took in their first pupils and formed the 'Deerfield Society of Blue and White Needlework' (blue had been a favourite colour in the original work). Although neither lady was a trained scientist, they dyed their own blue yarn, a painstaking chore which involved pounding down lumps of indigo to powder form. Their white linen threads were imported from Scotland and, possibly, their linen ground fabric from Russia, via a New York supplier.

At first the Society produced small mats, but with practice they embroidered larger items such as coverlets and bed hangings. Of the retail price of any particular piece, 'five parts (or ten) go to the embroiderer, two parts to the designer, two parts to the fund which is used to pay running expenses of the Society and the one remaining part covers the expense of materials used'. This was, then, a truly cooperative venture. Patterns were pre-drawn, all drawn threads were prepared and small work plans completed before each commission was delivered to the embroiderer. Patterns were individual and once-offs.

Later other colours relieved the original two-colour scheme. The Society was expanding and remained fully operational until 1926, when it was finally disbanded. Ellen Miller was ill (she died soon afterwards) and Margaret Whiting was losing her eyesight. Their patterns and notebooks survive today, as do many pieces of the Society's work.

In order to gain overall views of American embroiderers since the beginning of the 20th century it is necessary to consider some germinal figures and movements of the recent past.

At the end of the First World War, Mariska Karacz (1898–1960) came to the United States from her native Hungary. She studied dress designing and it was not until her marriage broke up, during the Second World War, that she diverted her talents from dressmaking to embroidery *per se*. Her early works show a definite Hungarian influence and, also, a certain caution as she experimented with use of different textures and styles. Gradually her embroideries took on a new import. They were unique in an original approach whereby theme and subject were dominant over method of working and technical skill. She alone is responsible for many schools of creative stitchery in the country today.

One famous American 20th-century embroidery is 'The legend of Czar Saltan' in the Smithsonian Institution, Washington DC. It was worked by Mrs. Theodore Roosevelt, who took her design from a painting by a 19th-century Russian artist, Ivan Bilibin. The original embroidery design had been transferred to fabric by Mrs. Roosevelt's son, Cornelius, in 1937, but it was not worked until 1951–53.

USA—*embroidered picture of 'The Legend of Czar Saltan' worked by Mrs. Theodore Roosevelt in 1951–3 from a design, drawn in 1937, by her son Cornelius from a 19th-century Russian painting by Ivan Bilibin. Mrs. Roosevelt worked on a special frame, also made by her son, and completed one vertical strip before proceeding to the next. Her 'daily stint was an area equal to seven square inches'. Area of picture 5 × 4 ft. (152 × 122 cm). (The Smithsonian Institution, Washington DC)*

The picture is particularly outstanding for its perspective and corresponding three-dimensional effect, and for the symbolic expressions incorporated in the three faces. Mrs. Roosevelt, apparently, was herself very pleased with the realism of the folds of the turban. She used gold and silver threads, copper, wool, Lurex, floss silks, glass beads, plastics and jewels on a linen twill ground. Her stitches were split stitch, satin stitch, long and short stitch, outline stitch, stem stitch, loop stitch, oriental stitch, knotting, seeding and couched work.

In 1916 the Needle and Bobbin Club was founded, included amongst the original members of which organisation was Richard Cranch Greenleaf. Lace was Mr. Greenleaf's main textile love and it was in an effort to preserve some of the Flemish treasures during the

291

First World War that he instigated a collection of both needle and bobbin laces from western Europe.

Richard Greenleaf was first editor of the Club's *Bulletin* and he continued to take an active part in the embroidered arts world in New York. After his death in 1961 his own personal collection of priceless examples of 16th- and 17th-century English caps and coifs, and of men's 18th-century French silk waistcoats, needle and bobbin laces and sundry other items, went to the Cooper-Union Museum in

USA—*20th-century whitework 'White Elephant' was designed and worked by Merry Bean, of Arlington, Va., using nylon trolling line on Plexiglass (chain, heavy chain, buttonhole filling, knotted buttonhole, trellis, spider web and darning stitches).*
(The artist. Photo: Charles Photographers)

292

New York (now the Cooper-Hewitt Museum of Decorative Arts).

Today the Needle and Bobbin Club continues to flourish. Its main contribution to embroidery has been, throughout its existence, to nurture serious attention to the art. With its own nucleus of experts, visits to unique and outstanding personal collections and regular coverage of many international aspects of embroidery, it is responsible for much of the truly artistic value of the needle today.

Obviously not all States are today similarly active in embroidery. Some contemporary work is highly regionalised. In the South-west, within a radius of a hundred miles or so around Santa Fé and Taos, New Mexico, *colcha* stitching (p. 359) is very popular.

New Mexico and Colorado are two very prolific embroidery areas today: Denver, for example, has many artists who work together and stimulate interest in stitchery.

Two dozen exquisite canvas work chair seats for the official dining room of the Governor's Mansion in Little Rock, Arkansas, were presented in the summer of 1973, worked to individual heraldic design by ladies of 'The order of the scissors'. Each embroiderer worked approximately 110,000 stitches into her particular chair seat (see p. 341 for an example).

The 'Flying Needles Club', in Texas, has provided a core for enthusiastic embroiderers since the early 1960's.

In California there is, understandably, considerable and exciting experimentation taking place in the embroidered arts. The market is aware of, and conducive to, creativity, and needle artists respond accordingly. There is corresponding opportunity for those who want to participate and for those who prefer simply to look at other people's work. The 'Golden Thimble II Exhibition' in Los Angeles, in the spring of 1973, had no fewer than 1,076 items exhibited, several of which were worked by men. Experimental workshops in all fields of allied embroidery and stitchery are constantly being offered, and embroiderers and teachers are not only abreast of current thinking but, in many cases, way ahead of their counterparts in the rest of the western world.

None but the completely isolated could, indeed, fail to be aware of the tremendous enthusiasm and publicity that is connected with the whole field of embroidery today. Newspapers, magazines and books galore offer an endless variety of ideas and styles: television reiterates the message (Erica Wilson's excellent programmes have regular viewers of all ages and both sexes). Visual promotion of embroidery in this way enjoys a heterosexual audience, no doubt partly due to personalities involved but, also, to the widespread interest in embroidery.

Whereas in the past, too, foreign influences have been apparent

293

throughout embroidery of the United States, today the tide has turned and much American-inspired work has filtered through to similarly inventive embroiderers around the world. True there is still an element of plagiarism (as in the Mexican-inspired work found in New Mexico, and the Indian motif works used throughout the country) and there is comparison with other contemporary designs (such as those from Scandinavia). But in general foreign innovations are on the wane, and although leading English embroidery personalities are prize guests of honour at conventions and exhibitions throughout America, the country's own designers are coping well with an incessant demand for new ideas and new suggestions for stitcheries.

There are exhibitions all over the country. In New York, for instance, biennial exhibitions are held alternatively by the Amateur Needlework of Today Inc. (who had 500 items listed in their 1973 exhibition) and by the Embroiderers' Guild of America Inc. The latter body, originally founded in 1958 as an affiliate of the London group, achieved self-reliance and independence in 1970. It has over two dozen functioning and livery chapters throughout the United States and, besides its regular exhibitions and participation in general arts activities, encompasses the entire country with its annual seminar, an important event in the world of embroidery. Specialist groups such as the 'Colcha Club' (p. 359) and the Counted Thread Society of America further particular facets of the art.

Most towns and some smaller communities throughout the country have their own museum. *The Verlag Dokumentation Museums of the World* (Munich, 1973) has 3,970 museums listed in the United States, ranging from Aberdeen, South Dakota, to Zolfo Springs, California, and many of these have made a point of collecting local memorabilia, including embroideries.

In New York, superb comprehensive collections of historical embroideries are in the Cooper-Hewitt Museum of Decorative Arts and the Metropolitan Museum of Art, and there are many outstanding specialised collections as well. In the Boston area are the Museum of Fine Arts and the Peabody Museum at Harvard. In and around Washington DC are the Smithsonian Institution, the Textile Museum, Woodrow Wilson House (particularly interesting for its First World War Belgian embroidered flour sacks), the Woodlawn Plantation and Mount Vernon. In Philadelphia there is the Museum of Art (with its sampler collection) and the University Museum (with Chinese embroideries). Elsewhere in the East are the Indian and Tibetan embroideries of the Newark Museum, New Jersey, and the colonial examples of the Shelburne Museum Inc., Vermont, and Old Sturbridge Village, Massachusetts.

Embroidery 'tours'—lectures illustrated with coloured slides—are becoming increasingly popular. The Washington DC 'tours' conducted by Norma Papish, a docent at the Smithsonian Institution, include illustrations from many hitherto undiscovered collections in the capital.

At Winterthur, in Delaware, there is a comprehensive range of crewel work, canvas work, samplers, quilting, tambour work, candlewicking, Berlin wool and bed rugs. From a conservation viewpoint, too, Winterthur is one of the centres of the embroidered arts of America.

There has been a heritage of fine needlework in the South. On big estates there was time, and inclination, for the ladies of the household to produce delicate work. The Textile Center of the Valentine Museum, Richmond, Virginia, has a particularly fine collection of southern embroideries, including a delightful sampler worked by Elizabeth Ellett of Virginia in the early 19th century. She used cross stitch, satin stitch and outline stitch on a linen ground and, with contemporary floral motifs in a large border underneath, she wrote on virtue:

Virtue's the chiefest Beauty of the Mind.
The noblest Ornament of human Kind:
Virtue's our Save-guard and our guiding Star
That stirs up Reason when our Senses err.

An all-round selection of 18th-century American needlework is particularly well represented at the Colonial Williamsburg Foundation in Virginia. Their samples of crewel work, Florentine work, bed rugs, appliqué, wool and silk embroidered pictures, silk bed covers and cotton whitework covers are truly representative of much excellent work that was being produced in the early days. Further south there is the Henry Morrison Flagler Museum in Palm Beach, Florida, with embroideries of similar local interest.

In the 'mountain states', Denver Art Museum, Colorado, has a particularly notable embroidery collection: on the west coast, there is the Los Angeles County Museum of Art . . . the list is endless. In addition to the purely secular collections, ecclesiastical needleworks of many churches all over the country are outstanding. The National Cathedral in Washington DC, for example, has much marvellous needlework executed, and supervised, by the Needlepoint Committee of the Cathedral at the original instigation of Dean Sayre in 1955. The high-altar rug, designed by the four Misses Tebbets from Connecticut, was worked by 23 ladies from Pittsburgh. In St. John's Chapel, canvas-work kneelers depict lives of famous Americans (and one honorary citizen, Winston Churchill). The War

295

Memorial chapel has a 'Tree of Jesse' hanging, with applied motifs of canvas work (similar in make-up to the Oxburgh hangings of Mary, Queen of Scots, p. 219). Many other churches have equally fine embroideries, indicative of the close affiliation of religious and secular art that has been established in the traditions of the United States.

Union of Soviet Socialist Republics

An enormous diversity of traditional arts is to be found in what now forms the USSR. Although it is technically incorrect, for the sake of convenience the description 'Russian' is often applied to the arts of the entire Soviet Union unless they can specifically be documented to a particular republic. Undoubtedly much of the embroidery that has reached the West in the last few decades comes from the western republics of the Russian Federation (RSFSR) and White Russia (Belorussia).

Generally, embroidery of the western areas of the Soviet Union can be distinguished either as secular or religious, and both categories have a long history. The earliest surviving fragments of gold embroideries, dating from the 4th century BC, were excavated in the Crimea and are now in the State Hermitage Museum, Leningrad.

Christianity was introduced from Byzantium in AD 988, and Russian embroidery gained early heritage both from this influence and that of the Orient brought in by invading Tartars. A winding sheet dated 1399, worked by Princess Mary, widow of Simeon the Proud, shows a central frame of Christ, hesitatingly moustachioed and with a small beaded halo. Around him are St. Mary, St. John the Baptist and a chorus of cherubim. The work features typically Byzantine elongated figures and emotion displayed in two-dimensional stylised tones. (A similar work, dated 1555 and in the White Lake Monastery of St. Cyril, has acquired Renaissance attributes of depth and movement.)

Until the end of the 16th century, very fine and detailed design was apparent through Russian ecclesiastical embroideries. In the 17th century, however, a tendency to exaggerated show of richness led to preference for precious and sumptuous materials, with corresponding decline in subsequent embroidery thereon. By the 18th century there was noticeable influence from the West and, from that date, Russian Orthodox embroidery shows less unique expression.

Materials used in early religious embroideries were silks (from Persia, China and, later, from the West via Novgorod), homespun linen, gold and silver thread and some pearls. Stitches were satin stitch, split stitch, chain stitch and, particularly in vestment

USSR—*15th-century Russian embroidered motif from the Grand Chasuble of the Metropolitan Photi (1414–17), now in the Armoury Palace of the Kremlin, Moscow. The embroidery is worked in zigzag, satin and back stitch, with superimposed pearls and gold purl.*

297

embroidery, slanting satin stitch. Cross stitch, two-sided stitch, buttonhole stitch and pulled thread work were also utilised.

With the pomp and detail of the Eastern Orthodox Church, including the *pokrov* (winding sheet) and *pelena* (stitched icon), embroidery production must have been prolific and beautiful. Many early pieces were taken by novice Russian monks to the monasteries of Mount Athos, on the Greek coast. Some of the works still remain today, guarded by the now depleted ranks of brothers.

Secular embroidery is linked in its early career to the rise of Moscow in the early 14th century, when independence was gained from the Tartars. St. Sergei founded the Troitsa Lavra at Zagorsk, and he and others embellished 'art workshops', many of which were renowned for their embroidered arts. Most of the work produced was on a silk ground, rarely on cotton or wool. An embroidery would first be designed by an established icon painter, making his lines with white paint straight on to the silk ground. The design was then outlined with dark silk and subsequently filled in. Colours do not blend. They are generally light and brilliant in overall effect.

USSR—*early 20th-century cross stitch on canvas, Russian.*
(Miss Anabel Boome)

298

In the north-west of the USSR today are the Republics of Estonia, Latvia and Lithuania, sometimes referred to collectively as 'the Baltic States'. Throughout the embroidery of these regions there is a prevalence of red-on-white cross stitch, with a coarse linen ground, with resultant conventional and formal effect and little naturalism.

Estonia has a particularly strong tradition of needlework. During the Middle Ages the Estonians, together with their Baltic neighbours, traded and had contact with other Nordic coastal peoples. They therefore incorporated into their arts a certain element of foreign influence. Despite such incessant contact, however, Estonia did maintain unique characteristics in her own embroidered arts. A snowflake motif, for example, is frequently portrayed, either singly or in groups.

Estonians are hardy people. During their brief return to independence (1918–39) there was a general resurgence of national dress. Shirts, blouses, jackets, aprons, shawls and other items of national costume are often richly embroidered. Stitches used included cross stitch (though not in the north of the republic), slanting gobelin, eye stitch and satin stitch. Beads and sequins embellished net

USSR—*modern Armenian embroidery to traditional design, silk on black velvet. (Author's collection)*

299

USSR (Ukraine)—*detail of
nyz embroidery, a form of
pattern darning. Close parallel
lines of vertical stitches are
first worked in black thread
from the wrong side of the
fabric, and a subsequent design
of coloured threads (here the
thicker threads) added from
the right side.*

embroidery; appliqué was used for coats and similar heavy garments, and hanging ribbons were always an essential finale to a finished costume.

Whitework is geometric and bears distinct affinity to that of the Scandinavian countries: design is orderly and symmetrical. Many plant forms are used, generally in repeating patterns.

Drawn thread work, which is overall similar to that of Sweden and Finland, includes much knotted stitching, a speciality of Slav embroiderers. The chief characteristic of Estonian drawn work, however, is the fineness and detail of work, which may sometimes be incorporated with a contrasting texture such as wool.

Pulled thread work, found particularly on items of household linen, features simple and naïve design, frequently with a background of single or double faggoting on a coarse linen ground.

In the south-west of the USSR lies the Ukraine, the embroidery of which region features highly coloured floral motifs in red, browns, blues, yellows and oranges. There is less dominance given to subtlety than to contrast. The most beautiful historic embroideries date to before the advent of industrialisation in Kiev and other centres (in other words, pre-1850). Today exquisite work is produced by expatriate groups such as the Ukrainian National Women's League in the United States. They embroider particularly attractive *rooshnicks*, narrow cloths about 48 in. (122 cm) long with embroidered bands at each end, traditionally wrapped around the family icons and deemed to ward off evil.

To the central south of the USSR is Turkestan, a region which today straddles the political border with Iran. Since the greater part of information of Turkmen embroidery today comes to the West via Iran, it is therefore described under that heading (p. 146).

Folk embroidery is, therefore, regionalised across the country. But, as is found throughout the more affluent centres of the world, sophisticated embroidery of the élite was cosmopolitan, influenced particularly by the mentor of French refinement.

Some collections of such 19th-century Russian 'sophisticated stitching' have reached the West, many brought around the time of the Revolution of 1917.

The Princess Zeneide Warvatszy, for example, came to Bournemouth, England, at the beginning of the 20th century. The Princess, born in 1840, had inherited her family's vast estates in southern Russia and ruled them with an iron hand. She met her future English companion, Miss Soffe, through the then British Ambassador in Moscow and it was to the Soffe home that she accordingly came, complete with her personal bedroom furniture and other household effects. (The Princess is buried in Wimborne

Cemetery: shortly after her death her devoted companion married a lifelong admirer called Felix-Jones.)

Only a few items of Princess Zeneide Warvatszy's personal linen remain today. There were originally complete sets both of day and night bed-linen. The day linen was particularly ornate, with complicated overall whitework so delicate and so intricate that it would have been impossible actually to use. Each pillowcase was numbered. Night bed-linen was slightly more practical, even though the fine white cotton sheets and pillowcases were embellished with padded satin-stitch monograms, cyphers and other motifs.

What is particularly remarkable about this collection is the fact that, although her own personal linen was highly refined and delicate, the Princess did also possess numerous items of folk embroidery. The collection today still includes table and cushion covers, perhaps cross-stitched by workers on her estate.

USSR—*early 19th-century sheet border, cotton and metal thread on cotton.*
(Cooper-Hewitt Museum of Decorative Arts and Design, New York. Au Panier Fleuri Fund)

Despite the vast span of the USSR (some 7,000 miles from west to east), it is, none the less, possible today to acquire a cursory representative introduction to the embroidery of the entire country. Standing in Moscow's Red Square in the height of summer, queuing for an hour or more to enter the pallor of Lenin's mausoleum, the tourist sees around him peoples from all the republics, including those of the Far East. Uzbek men from Central Asia wear tight-fitting black felt skull caps with white back-stitch and satin-stitch outline embroidery. Armenians, from around Erevan in the south-west, sport a complicated knot embroidery, lush and pompous on a velvet ground. These are just two of the examples that could be cited.

Wales

WALES—*bedspread worked by Theodosia Henry, 1708–86, daughter of the Rev. Matthew Henry. The work is a combination of applied patterned motifs and superimposed embroidery in crewel wools.*
(National Museum of Wales, Welsh Folk Museum)

Although there is no definite assertion of a tradition of embroidered art in Wales, there is poetical reference to work from the 14th to 17th centuries, and St. Helena, held by some to have been a Welsh princess, and mother of the Emperor Constantine, is supposed to have embroidered a vestment with an image of the Virgin in about AD 293.

There has certainly been no traditional embroidery in many rural parts of the country. The ladies of Wales have, instead, a heritage of partiality to weaving, and to their knitting needles.

WALES—*sampler worked by Margaret Morgan, aged 14, from Westbrook's School, Pontypool, Monmouthshire, 1839. Main representations include Elijah being fed by the ravens, the finding of Moses in the bulrushes and the Flight into Egypt. Contemporary detail is added with the central air balloon. Polychrome silks on woollen ground.*
(National Museum of Wales, Welsh Folk Museum. Gift of Sir L. Twiston Davies)

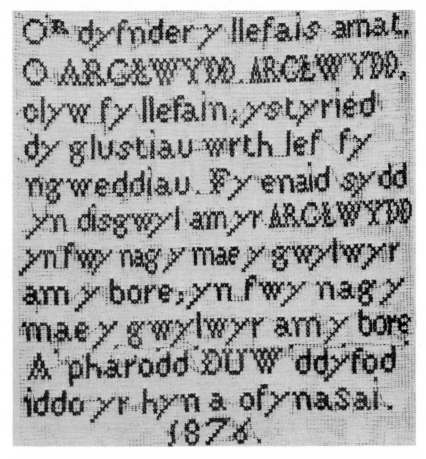

WALES—*sampler from Llannefydd, Denbighshire, 1876. The biblical verse, in Welsh, was worked at home during a period of official opposition to the Welsh language.*
(National Museum of Wales, Welsh Folk Museum)

Historic stitcheries that do exist are usually either in the sampler, smock or quilt category. In general, samplers from Wales seem to have kept their original colour better than contemporary works from other parts of the British Isles (it has been suggested that this preservation has been partly due to the small windows traditionally found in Welsh cottages). The major output of samplers was from the 17th to the 19th centuries.

One interesting item is in the collection of the Welsh Folk Museum of the National Museum of Wales, at St. Fagan's Castle near Cardiff. The sampler is dated 1739 and the design has been drawn on a linen ground with ink: obviously ordinary writing ink was used as it has run in several places.

Biblical themes recur in samplers of all ages. Margaret Morgan, of St. Westbrook's School in Pontypool, Monmouthshire, worked her sampler in 1839 when she was 14. She showed different biblical scenes, including Elijah being fed by the ravens and the finding of Moses in the bulrushes. She expressed typical contemporary sentiment, too, in her accompanying verse:

> There is an hour when I must die
> Now can I tell how soon twill come.
> A thousand children young as I
> Are called by death to hear their doom.

What makes this rather detailed and instructed work utterly personal and delightful, however, is the original inclusion of a central air balloon motif, so inappropriate to the general subject matter and yet so revealing of the excitement of a young adolescent of the day.

Reaction to continual suppression of the Welsh language in the past has provided a stimulus to many fields of the arts. A simple lettering sampler, 1876, black silk on a linen ground, features a biblical verse in Welsh. Because of the oppression in public places, such a Welsh language treatise was obviously worked at home. There is complete lack of superfluous decoration, resulting in an appearance of strict Puritanism. This sampler, like that of Margaret Morgan, is at St. Fagan's.

The oldest quilt in the collection of the Welsh Folk Museum is 18th century, with double diagonal trellis stitching on a white ground with printed rosebud motif. There is also an early 19th-century example with similar stitching, known to have been worked in Newport, Pembrokeshire. Other frequently used stitching styles are overlapping circles and plain spirals, as worked by another Victorian quilting specialist, Margaret Richards of Abergwili.

Sometimes quilts feature more complex stitching patterns. In 1929 Mrs. M. Thomas of Gelli, Rhondda, worked a pale yellow and green quilt with central motif of the national dragon with the legend *'Amgueddfa Genedlaethol Cymru'* ('The National Museum of Wales') and surrounding border of leaves and spirals.

Some of the most outstanding stitcheries of Wales, however, are the rural smocks. As with smocks from other parts of the British Isles, they are highly regionalised and the profession of the wearer might be established by the motif displayed on the tunic.

An early 19th-century Brecknockshire smock, supposed to have been worn first by Squire Vaughan of Llanfilo and then by a carter of Bronllys, has a four-leaf clover design worked in chain stitch on the collar.

Most workers had both everyday and 'Sunday best' smocks, the latter generally featuring the more complicated embroidery. A farm labourer of Llansilin, Denbighshire, for example, had a 'Sunday best' smock with 7 buttons down the front opening and elaborate panels of embroidery on both shoulders and in the embroidered 'box' to either side of the central panel of smocked 'tubing', both front and back.

Some blue linen smocks, with white linen embroidery, were probably also worn only on the Sabbath 'day of rest' and other holidays.

WALES—*20th-century copy of traditional blue smock with central 'tubing' of smocking and 'boxes' either side embellished with floral and scroll patterning.*
(National Museum of Wales, Welsh Folk Museum)

Generally, alas, embroidery has experienced a fall in output in the 20th century. It is recorded that quilts from Glamorgan and elsewhere in South Wales have featured a ground of flower-printed sateen but, as with all embroideries, quilt-making in Wales declined in popularity during the generally depressed years after the First World War. In the 1930's, there was a conscious effort made to reintroduce the craft to women in many parts of the country, and in 1951 the Welsh Folk Museum held an important conference on quilting with a corresponding competition, won by Miss Emiah Jones of Crosshands, Carmarthenshire.

One excellent ground medium for some types of modern embroidery is Welsh flannel, a soft openweave wool. The Rev. D. W. E. Brinson of Swansea is one artist who uses a great deal of local Welsh flannel for his works. After his ordination in 1955 he started making his own vestments, having studied the talents of the Sisters of the Priory at St. David's, Pembrokeshire. Mr. Brinson now has suitable sets of vestments for all seasons of the church year. He machine embroiders, applying motifs of soft gold kid and other fabrics to his chosen ground.

Yemen

Traditional embroidery in Yemen has been reserved almost exclusively for domestic use. In the past, along this part of the Red Sea coast, such decoration, mostly done by the once-large Jewish community of Yemen, was splendid and full of pattern.

Today, alas, one sees pairs of trousers with the ends slightly gathered into an embroidered band, or a child's cap, almost Dutch in style with embroidery on the flaps—but little else. Special clothes are still embroidered in the old style. A typical bridal gown has elaborate embroidered panels on the trouser cuffs.

Traditional design has been geometric with some complicated patterns based on a central frame of square, zigzag or border of circles. Motifs were often tribal. Today, however, embroidery has little organised design other than the simplest of geometric shapes. Colours used are generally red, green, white and yellow on a heavy cotton ground (black, red, green and white are Yemen's national colours).

Since 1920, and with much larger volume during the last 25 years, Jews living around Sana'a have been moving to Israel. Apart from a community around Sa'da in the north of Yemen, there are today few Jews left in the country. It is, in fact, as if the most highly talented embroiderers have now left and taken their Yemenite arts to Israel. The Israel Museum in Jerusalem has several outstanding examples of Yemeni-inspired trousers, more ornate than the practical counterpart, glistening with embroidery in chain stitch, cross stitch, herringbone and laid and couched work.

Some pieces of the imported embroidery are worn in Israel as decoration to current western dress. The imported and the home-produced 'Yemenite' embroidery are distinguishable by design motif, with the indigenous Jewish work featuring more prominent Jewish symbolism.

YEMEN—gargoush
mezzahar, *ceremonial
headgear of Jewish women of
Sana'a, Yemen: cord, coins,
chains, silver and gilt on a
brocade ground.*
*(The Israel Museum,
Jerusalem)*

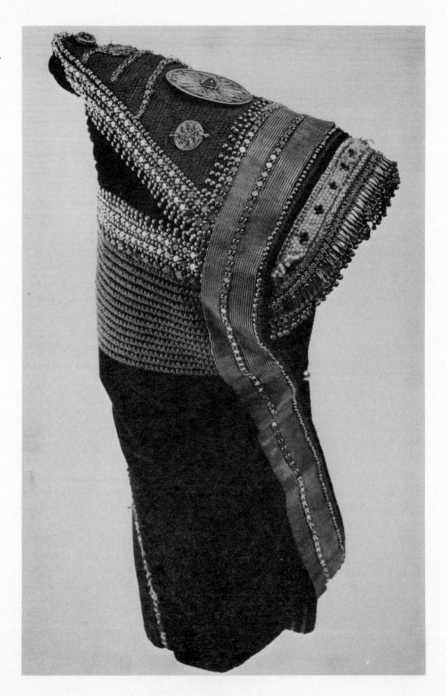

Yugoslavia

Yugoslavia gained her independence in 1918. One-third of her current population is Serbian and, generally, Orthodox Christian; there are Catholics from Croatia, Slovenia and Dalmatia and, also, a Moslem minority in the south, in Montenegro, Yugoslav Macedonia and parts of Serbia. With the country's chequered and unquiet history, the resultant factions of her populace today not surprisingly exhibit few elements of national uniformity in the arts, or in any other facet of life.

YUGOSLAVIA—*embroidery designs on tourist postcards.*
(Author's collection)

In general, however, embroidery from all regions of Yugoslavia can be distinguished by a density of stitching, with a concentration of embroidery more apparent than in other Balkan and eastern European countries. In all regions there is counted thread embroidery, worked in wool on a linen ground: in the south of the country there is silk embroidery thread; near the Bulgarian border, cotton thread.

Cross stitch predominates. Other stitching frequently used includes line, satin, chain, stem, double back and Romanian. 'Yugoslav border stitch' is a zigzag stitch with alternating diagonals. 'Bosnia stitch' is an 'N'-shaped filling stitch, like Yugoslav border stitch but with one of the alternate stitches at right angles to the main direction of working, found particularly on embroidery from the area of that name.

Colouring throughout is highly regional. Red is found particularly around Prilep, Bitola, Debar and Ohrid. Black is dominant around Dolni Polog and Skopska Crna Gora.

YUGOSLAVIA—*detail of early 20th-century coat, Serbia. Coloured cotton embroidery (back stitch, chain stitch, buttonhole stitch and herringbone stitch) on a glazed linen ground. (Whitworth Art Gallery, Manchester. Miss G. Johnson Collection)*

312

Some parts of Yugoslavia, such as Bosnia and Herzegovina, were Turkish provinces until as late as 1878 and there is, in urban areas of these regions, still a tendency for townswomen to include Turkish elements in their embroideries. Sumptuous fabric with elaborate stitching is often more decorative than work from other parts of the country.

Design from all regions tends to be formally organised, with repeating motifs featuring basic geometric and stylised floral patterns. Much of design from the Serbian region around Belgrade shows Greek influence and, also, some heritage from the arts of ancient Byzantium.

YUGOSLAVIA—*typical border motifs.*

In the Etnoloski Muzej, Skopje, there is a late 19th-century bridal smock from Skopska Crna Gora. Thick black wool gives relief outline to discreet dark blue square motifs around the hem, with characteristic vertical embroidered panels on the back. The work has an oriental affinity.

In many Yugoslav museums, too, there are examples of metal thread embroidery. Strips of gold or beaten silver and brass are sometimes worked into braids. Much of the embroidery existing today, however, is clothing decoration. In Bosnia, Mediterranean, central European and Balkan cultures are apparent in the regional costume of a married woman, who wears a shirt with edging embroidery, a long full skirt and a sleeveless jacket (*jelek*) and apron (*pregaća*). Most shirts have a frontal neck panel, the *oshvitza*, similar to the Chinese *p'u-tzu* in concentration of embroidery, a flat panel, often solidly worked and among the most beautiful and intricate examples of workmanship from anywhere in Yugoslavia.

313

Headwear is sometimes embroidered. Particularly in the early 19th century, both Moslem and Catholic women used to wear a large veil of lace or embroidered net or muslin, with floral satin-stitch decoration in floss silk, similar to contemporary net embroidery in England, Austria and Hungary.

Of interest, too, are the *marama*, show towels, frequently showing Turkish influence. It is thought that such towels were often fashioned from wedding outfits taken from a bride's coffer, a combination of economy and remembrance of an important day past.

There are many excellent collections of Yugoslav embroidery, one of the most outstanding of which is the Durham Collection at the Bankfield Museum, Halifax, Yorkshire (p. 20).

Zaire

Some of the most beautiful West African embroidery is the raffia work from the area around the confluence of the Sankuru and Kasai rivers in the central region of Zaire (formerly known as 'Belgian Congo' and then 'Congo-Kinshasa').

In many cases the raffia stitching is cut close to the ground fabric to ensure a thick, close pile. Designs are geometric, with much emphasis on a square shape. Before stitching raffia, loose-woven ground fabric, also of raffia, is pounded by hand, either in water or dry, to make it soft and supple. Colouring is either left natural or dyed with indigo to varying shades of blue or pink. Raffia stitchery thread is split as fine as possible and similarly pounded or worked to ensure maximum pliability, and several strands are then twisted together. Thread colouring is generally red, yellow, purple, black or brown.

It has been thought that Bushongo raffia work was first adopted in the 17th century when Shamba Bulongongo, a famous Bushongo king who reigned from 1600 to 1620, learnt the art from the Bakele or Pende tribes. Today, however, it is suggested that the craft originated in the Lower Congo, or with the Egyptians of the Nile Valley.

Zaire also has fine surface satin stitching, often with black outlining around a motif, an example of which is a pile cloth from Boma (now in the Pitt Rivers Museum, Oxford) which is pre-1910. In the Mbala regions there is some stem stitch or chain stitch: such tribal embroidery has traditionally been a woman's work.

The beautiful past embroideries of the Bakuba are today, alas, on the decline, although since 1970 the Institut des Musées Nationaux in Kinshasa has been reorganising its collections of all forms of textiles, paying particular attention to the ornate velvet embroidery of the Kasai.

PART II
The Stitchery

This section is concerned primarily with universal forms of embroidery—where a type of needlework is unique to one country it is included within the confines of its homeland, in the first part of the book.

The types of embroidery, and the stitches connected to them, are here catalogued from an identification viewpoint as well as from that of the practising embroiderer. There is basic cross-referencing within the section: detailed cross-referencing is provided by the main index.

A few essential reminders to facilitate execution of the stitches:

Canvas-work stitches need an open-mesh canvas, and the stitches are not always transposable to a woven ground.

Drawn thread work stitches and **pulled thread work stitches** should be worked on a loose open-weave ground such as linen scrim, and stitches should often be pulled tight.

Explanatory diagrams are drawn as work charts and are not indicative of the appearance of the finished stitch.

Many of the method rules are by no means mandatory—the route to a finished stitch is ultimately largely the choice of the artist.

△ *SYRIA – 19th-century gold work on silk ground, indicative of Turkish domination until 1914. Notice the heavy padding under the metal thread.*
(Author's collection)

▽ *TURKEY – 18th-century gold work on purple velvet: detail of a saddle-cloth made in Istanbul for the seventh Earl of Elgin.*
(The Earl of Elgin and Kincardine)

△ *SYRIA – modern waistcoat, the bright colour scheme typical of today's work.*
(Carla Hunt)

ALGERIAN STITCH

A pulled thread filling stitch (which should be pulled tight for maximum effect).

Another 'Algerian stitch' is an eight-pointed eye stitch, (p. 388), sometimes called **Algerian eye stitch**.

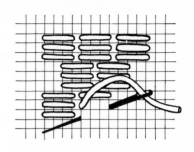

APPLIQUÉ

Appliqué—from the Latin *applicare* and the French *appliquer* (to put on, attach) is, quite simply, the art of applying one layer of fabric upon another. It is not restricted to any particular facet of embroidery and has long been practised the world over. Lewis F. Day (*The Art of Needlework*, Batsford, London 1901) even went so far as to say 'it is almost as much a man's work as a woman's . . .' and, indeed, some of the most skilled appliqué artists at work today are men.

The earliest and most simple appliqué consisted of the superimposed piece of fabric 'put on' to the main ground fabric, secured with stitches around the edge. This process, when decorative pieces are put on, is **overlaid appliqué** and is known colloquially simply as **appliqué**. Other forms of the art include:

Broderie perse, or **cretonne appliqué**, which probably originated about the middle of the 19th century and barely falls in

APPLIQUÉ—*panel, 11 × 17 in. (28 × 43 cm), worked in fabric collage and hand and machine embroidery by Richard Box, 1973. This is part of a work consisting of 16 panels and depicting the legend of Perseus. In the panel shown here, Pallas Athene and Hermes are presenting gifts to help Perseus in his task of slaying the gorgon Medusa. (The artist)*

the category of 'embroidered' appliqué since it consists of printed fabric motifs cut out and stitched to a ground fabric with minimum needlework.

Broderie suisse is an applied piece inserted between a front ground of muslin or similar semi-transparent fabric and a more solid backing ground (such as satin). The design is then stitched around, holding the inserted motif to both front and back grounds. It shows through as a shadow.

Inlaid appliqué. The piece to be applied is set into a prepared hole of exactly the right size and shape, like a jigsaw piece. The joining seam may then be hidden under rows of stitching or couched work. This form of appliqué was much found during the Middle Ages when ecclesiastical woven textiles sometimes had embroidered figures inlaid and stitched with feather stitch (**opus plumarium**) or split stitch (**opus anglicanum**). It is found, too, amongst embroideries from India and from the Recht area of Iran.

Net appliqué—a particularly detailed version of which is Carrickmacross lace from Ireland—has the appliqué fabric tacked to the net ground. The outline of the design is then tightly stitched with satin stitch or buttonholing and surplus fabric cut away.

Padded appliqué can be worked either from the front or from the back. In the case of padding from the *front*: the area to be thus padded is applied to the main ground, leaving a small area open. Padding is then pushed in, with tweezers or a small pair of scissors, and the appliqué sealed. In the case of padding from the *rear*: a lining of muslin or similar fabric is tacked to the rear of the main ground. The outline of the area to be padded is stitched through both layers (from the front), the lining slit from the rear and the padding inserted. The slit is then sewn together.

Reverse appliqué, most commonly employed today by the Cuna Indians of the San Blas islands of Panama, is a cutting-down rather than a putting-on technique. Several layers of cloth are held together and the pattern is cut down through the various layers, each layer forming a 'step' to the pattern. When the bottom layer is reached, the pattern is sometimes built up again, like a contour map, with ordinary 'put on' appliqué. A simpler form of reverse appliqué, when one extra fabric layer is stitched to the back of the ground which is then, itself, cut away from the front to reveal the applied backing, is known as **découpé.**

322

APPLIQUÉ—broderie perse *or cretonne appliqué on an*
American quilt, c. 1800. The large size, 96 × 90 in.
(2·44 × 2·29 m), indicates Southern handwork.
(Ginsburg & Levy, Inc.)

Shadow appliqué is a whitework technique when either a piece of the main, semi-transparent ground fabric (like fine lawn) or a contrasting fabric (such as satin) is stitched to the reverse side of the ground and sewn around. The appliqué appears as a 'shadow' from the front of the work. (Shadow appliqué sandwiched between two layers of ground is, of course, **broderie suisse**.)

Appliqué can be worked by hand (with or without a frame) or on a machine. Stay-stitching, often done today with a machine, can become an essential part of the overall effect of the work.

If a domestic sewing machine is used it is necessary—for greater flexibility of movement—either to have an embroidery foot or to remove the ordinary foot altogether. Machine appliqué work for the beginner should definitely be worked on a frame, to avoid buckling.

One of the advantages of appliqué to the embroiderer is that it can cover a large area of ground in a short time. Most fabrics (from shiny kid to softest silk) can be used, but it is advisable to avoid a combination of natural and synthetic fabrics. The former stay taut. Synthetics, on the other hand, tend to buckle when being worked. Fabrics that do not fray (such as felt, leather and net) are particularly easy to work with, although raw edges of other fabrics can be controlled either by running a brush with glue over the cut threads or by backing the entire cloth with an iron-on lining.

Having chosen the fabrics and design to be applied, it sometimes helps to work with a template. This ensures that the design keeps to the original shape. Some artists today temporarily hold their appliqué patches in place with glue, but this does tend to wrinkle the fabric. A few stay stitches are more satisfactory.

The edges of the applied piece are, if necessary, turned under before being sewn down. An alternative method of finishing raw edges is to cover them with cord, braid or further stitching. Machined zigzag (either open or closed) is a particularly effective operation to hold down an applied piece and decorate the resulting 'seam' in one motion.

Appliqué can be combined with other forms of needlework: with embroidery in general (most stitches can be used with appliqué), with patchwork (appliqués are sewn on to the patches) and with quilting. No mention of the subject is of course complete without due reference to quilts. Amongst well-known patterns of North American appliqué quilts are album

324

quilts and chintz cutouts (similar to **broderie perse** but, in this case, the entire appliqué shape is sewn firmly down). Hawaiian quilts, too, are invariably appliqué.

APPLIQUÉ—*applied motifs on a leather collar with superimposed gold thread work. By Stina Carlstedt-Duke.*
(The artist)

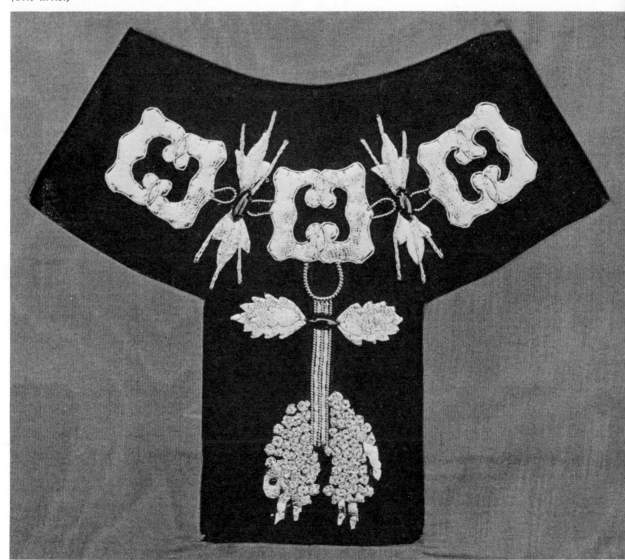

325

ARMENIAN EDGING STITCH

Most effective if pulled tight, this edging stitch is best worked in a fairly thick thread.

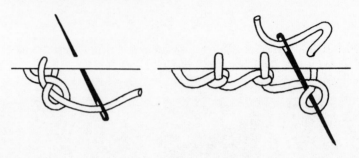

ARROWHEAD STITCH

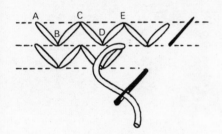

A zigzag stitch: the thread is worked A to B, C to B, C to D, E to D and so on.

AUBUSSON STITCH

rep stitch

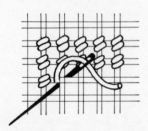

A canvas-work 'tapestry' stitch, worked on double thread canvas.

BACK STITCH

point de sable

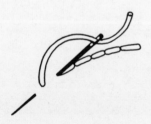

A quick outline stitch. The needle should always be taken into the hole of the previous stitch.

326

Ringed back stitch is also known as **festoon stitch.** To work the complete 'rings', a curving line of **back stitch** is filled in with an alternating line of similar stitching.

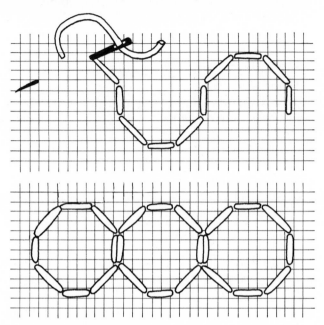

BAND STITCHES

A solidly worked border of continuous stitching is often known as a band. Some types of band stitches are:

diagonal raised bands (p. 371)
raised chain stitch bands (p. 352)
raised lattice-work bands (p. 402)

BARRIER STITCH

fence stitch

A French filling stitch, similar to the Yugoslav **Bosnia stitch** (p. 334) except for the fact that in the French stitch the return row of stitches is always worked with the needle pointing downwards to form an 'N' stitch.

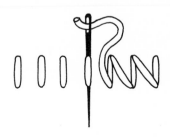

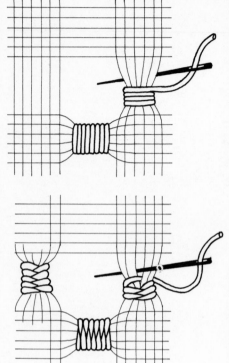

BAR STITCHES

In drawn thread work, bars of threads remaining after required threads have been withdrawn can be decorated in many ways, such as:

overcast bars (known also as **corded bars** or **twisted bars**)—after the required number of threads are drawn, blocks of remaining threads are overcast as many times as required to produce a solid bar.

woven bars—in which the remaining verticals are woven to cover the complete block. (A **picot** can also be added to give interest.)

BASKET STITCH

To distinguish this from **herringbone stitch,** which it closely resembles, look at the back of the work. Whereas the reverse side of herringbone is a series of parallel back stitches, that of basket stitch shows vertical stitches and alternating sloping stitches (figure 2).

The four main movements of basket stitch (figure 1) can be worked to produce **open basket stitch** (figure 3) or **closed basket stitch** (figure 4). This latter stitch can be distinguished, once again, from **plait stitch** by the reverse side (plait stitch's back shows parallel pairs of stitches at regular intervals).

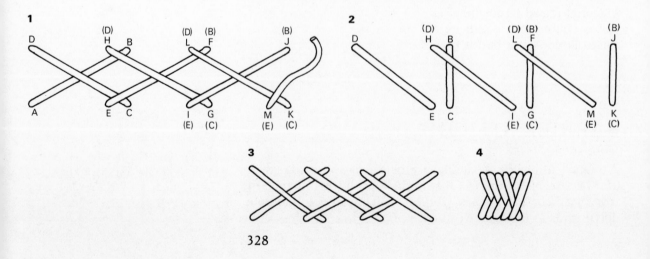

BASKET WEAVE STITCH

diagonal tent stitch

A canvas-work stitch that is easy to work, gives a good solid effect and has an attractive basket-weave backing (figure 3). Worked diagonally, the first row of stitching with the needle always facing *down* (figure 1), the second (and subsequent alternate row) with the needle facing *left* (figure 2). Tent stitch can also be worked in horizontal or vertical lines (p. 443).

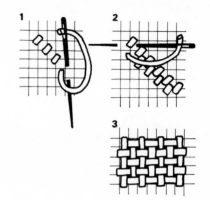

BASQUE STITCH

A scroll stitch found particularly in southern France, Spain and Portugal. Traditionally it was worked in white on a blue-green ground, or red on a green ground.

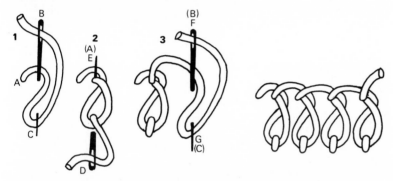

BAYEUX STITCH

The **Bayeux tapestry** below was largely worked in laid and couched work over two closely parallel lines of laid stitches (figures 1 and 2). The final laid and couched work (figure 3) can use a different colour and texture of thread.

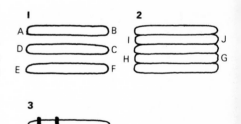

BAYEUX 'TAPESTRY'

Although it is not in any way a 'field of stitchery', this piece is of so great import to the world of embroidery that it justifies independent classification. It must surely be the world's most famous embroidery.

The exact provenance of the work is unknown, although it may possibly have been commissioned by Odo, Bishop of Bayeux and half-brother to William the Conqueror, for the

329

BAYEUX 'TAPESTRY'—*details from the 11th-century,*
231 ft. × 20 in. (70·41 × 0·51 m), embroidery.
(Avec autorisation spéciale de la Ville de Bayeux.
Photo : J. Combie)

adornment of his new cathedral, dedicated in 1077. It is thought to have been worked before 1092. J. H. Round, in *The Monthly Bulletin* (Vol. VII, 1904), wrote that 'there is a circumstantial case' for thinking that it came from England, and since it was well known that William's wife, Queen Mathilda, was a keen needlewoman, she might well have executed the 'tapestry' with Saxon ladies of her court. Certainly the affinity of the embroidery lies with contemporary 11th-century English works.

The entire embroidery went around the nave of Bayeux Cathedral and during the 15th century, in particular, it was displayed for ceremonial use once a year. At Napoleon's command it was exhibited in Paris in 1803, a move apparently connected with his proposed invasion of England. It was properly exhibited at the Hôtel de Ville in 1842 and photographed for the British Government in 1871 (Maclagan, Eric, *The Bayeux Tapestry*, King Penguin, 1945).

Eight shades of worsted wool were worked on a linen ground, 231 ft. × 20 in. (70·37 × 0·51 m), embroidered in laid work with right-angle couching (**Bayeux stitch**, p. 329) and with outline stitch. It has 72 different compartments, representing incidents in the Norman Conquest and with stirring scenes of war, work and enjoyment. The sequence is annotated with Latin inscriptions bordering the main panel, to either side of which there is a narrow outer border with irregularly shaped motifs of animal and other representations.

The whole work is full of action, with movement and emotion in the figures. Of all the people represented, only three are women. Perspective and proportion are not apparent and yet, paradoxically, the simplicity and balance of line accords a degree of three-dimensional reality.

The 'tapestry' is now to be seen in the Musée de la Reine Mathilde in Bayeux, in Calvados, France.

BEADWORK

Addition of beads to stitchery is known as **beadwork,** a term which can imply either one bead added as finishing touch to a more conventional embroidery or, alternatively, all-beaded works like the metal-frame layette basket, signed and dated 1659, with polychrome decoration of hunting scenes, included in the 'International Art Treasures Exhibition' in Bath in 1973.

Beadwork, in the form of either total or partial embellishment, has always been apparent in embroidery, in particular in the 19th century. Coloured glass beads, known in England as 'pound beads', came from Germany or Italy and were sold by weight. 'Bugles' were small tubular beads of transparent glass, and there were beads, too, fashioned from cut steel, seed pearls and artificial pearls, jet, gold and silver and many other media.

Generally the size of the bead became more exaggerated as the century progressed. In about 1850 opaque glass beads (known as 'OP' beads) were introduced. In the 1860's and 70's there was a craze for coral beads and in the '80's and '90's many beads were backed with metal foil to give a jewel-like appearance, a form of stitchery known as 'jewel embroidery'.

There are many varieties of beads still on the market, with different sizes of glass, plastics, wood, metal, stone, *papier mâché* and plaster baubles. Beadwork embroidery requires a certain dexterity of manipulation owing to the fine holes through which the thread must pass: beading needles are initially rather difficult to use.

Another obstacle involved in beadwork is conservation (p. 363): the addition of beads to more conventional forms of embroidery can cause washing difficulties.

BLACKWORK

Blackwork is a monochrome embroidery, usually worked in black thread.

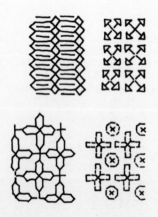

Historically, blackwork, either in the form of counted-thread format or in random seeding or speckling, often further embellished with gold thread and sequins, reached a peak from 1500 to 1650 and it is primarily thought of today as 'Elizabethan'.

The art probably evolved from Arabic and Moorish examples in Spain, parts of which were under Moorish domination from the 8th century to 1492. Many designs and patterns seen in early examples of this work show arabesques and flowing lines typical of the North African coast. It is widely thought that Katharine of Aragon, who travelled from Spain to England in 1501 (p. 248), brought with her in her trousseau many examples of 'Spanish blackwork', but in fact the embroidery was already known in Britain. Fashionable people at that time

BLACKWORK—*16th-century English hood, silk on linen, worked in stem stitch, double coral stitch and seeding. Greatest width 21 in. (53·5 cm). (The Victoria and Albert Museum, Crown Copyright)*

were favourably disposed towards exaggerated patterning: rich costume embellishment and architecture were the order of the day, as typified by the late 16th-century black and white exterior decoration of Little Moreton Hall in Cheshire. Embroidery that was, basically, similarly dependent on contrast gained immediate vogue.

Concurrent enthusiasm for Spanish blackwork was rife elsewhere: in Switzerland, for example, black **shadow work** was known as *Scherenschnitte*. Holbein and the Italian Moroni were two artists who recorded blackwork decorations. In the Kunsthistorisches Museum, Vienna, there is a work by the former painter, a 1536 portrait of Jane Seymour (a successor to Katharine of Aragon as a Queen of Henry VIII), showing her wearing cuffs of blackwork, embroidered in double-running stitch, then known as **Spanish stitch.** Other stitches used in

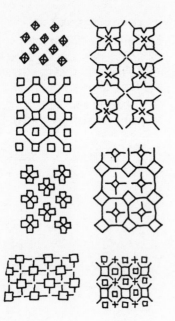

early blackwork included stem stitch, braid stitch, back stitch, seeding, chain stitch, coral stitch and herringbone stitch.

Designs of that time were either simple seeding, with speckling forming all-over patterning, or floral and pictorial. The 1548 Thomas Geminus book *Moryssche and Damaschin Renewed and Encreased very Profitable for Goldsmiths and Embroiderars* had many arabesque designs.

Today, however, blackwork is generally associated with geometric work. It requires an even-weave ground, such as linen or Welsh flannel. A single strand of embroidery thread should always be used, to prevent uneven blocks of colour, and a blunt tapestry needle avoids splitting fibres of the ground fabric.

The eventual scale of the design depends on the texture of ground fabric (the more open the weave, the bigger the design). The final tone balance is dependent on the scale of each motif and, also, on the density of stitching worked: a close-weave fabric worked with much stitching, for example, produces a very dark, and dense, finished embroidery.

Many artists today plan blackwork effects by first cutting out shapes of newsprint in varying shades of density. Different ratios of ink to paper result in tones of 'blackwork' similar to those of embroidery and it is thus possible to judge the final appearance.

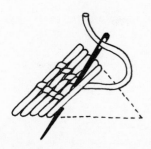

BOKHARA STITCH

Generally a couching stitch over a laid thread, Bokhara stitch is found particularly in the Middle East. In Spanish-influenced areas of the world it is known as **colcha stitch** (p. 359).

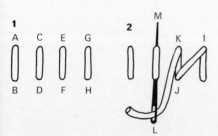

BOSNIA STITCH

A Yugoslav filling stitch (similar to **Yugoslav border stitch** except for the fact that the first row of stitches are vertical). (The French **barrier** or **fence** stitch has the same first row of vertical stitches, but the return row is worked with the needle pointing down rather than up, producing an 'N' shape.)

BRAID STITCH

Gordian knot stitch

Best worked with fairly coarse yarn, this stitch makes a good border. After the needle has emerged at A, the thread is looped before making the stitch B–C. (According to legend, Alexander the Great cut through, with his knife, the complicated knot which bound the yoke to the pole of the wagon of Gordius, the peasant king of Phrygia, and thus fulfilled a prophecy that whoever undid the knot would become king of all Asia.)

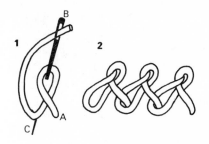

BRETON STITCH

A 'grille' stitch with size of apertures determined by the distance left between stitches.

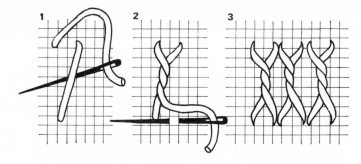

BRIAR STITCH

slanted feather stitch
thorn stitch

Briar stitch is a basic **feather stitch** (p. 389) but generally more open-worked than the mentor. Any angle can be achieved by slant of the stitch.

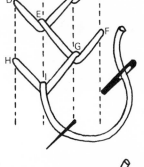

BRICK STITCH

This stitch can be used either for wool or canvas work. After one preliminary row of **long and short stitch** (shaded stitches), rows of identical stitches are worked, first left to right then right to left. Worked close together, this stitch gives an all-over 'brick' effect. If various coordinating hues of thread are used it is a good shading stitch.

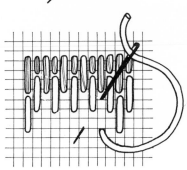

335

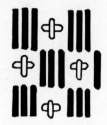

BRICK AND CROSS FILLING STITCH

Satin stitch blocks are alternated with **cross stitches** in contrasting colour thread.

BULLION KNOT

caterpillar stitch
coil stitch
knot stitch
Porto Rico rose stitch
post stitch
roll stitch
worm stitch

The needle is inserted A to B, thread wound around the needle as many times as required (depending on the weight of thread and motif required) and the needle inserted again at A. By coaxing the 'coils' towards the eye of the needle as it is pulled through, an even overall roll is gained with practice. If more 'coils' are put on the needle than will cover the initial distance A to B, the bullion knot will not lie flat but will arch upwards, giving a convex appearance.

BUTTONHOLE STITCH

blanket stitch

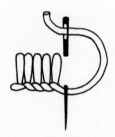

When this versatile stitch is worked close together, it is technically **buttonhole stitch**. Spaced buttonhole stitch is **blanket stitch**. It can be worked as a border, as a filling in rows, circles, scallops or similar shapes, or as an independent motif.

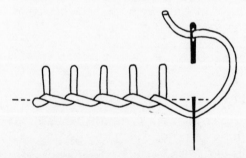

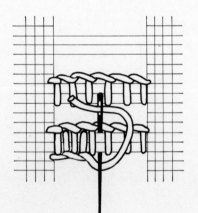

Buttonhole bars are worked along exposed threads of drawn thread work, either to one side (as in the top line of stitching) or to both sides (as in the bottom line of stitching).

336

Closed buttonhole stitch is the stitch worked in an alternating zigzag between two parallel lines.

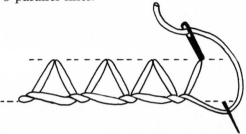

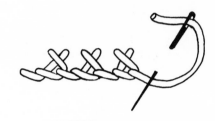

Similar to closed buttonhole stitch is **crossed buttonhole stitch.**

Drawn buttonhole stitch, a pulled thread stitch, has diagonal rows of open **buttonhole stitches (blanket stitches),** worked alternately facing in one direction (figure 1) and the other (figure 2).

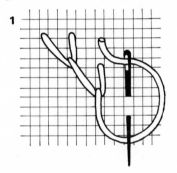

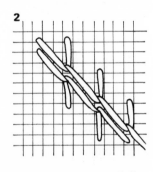

Knotted buttonhole stitch has thread looped around the needle (figure 1) and then the needle inserted A to B (figure 2) to make an ordinary **buttonhole stitch.**

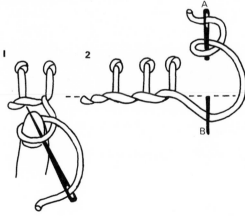

Spiral buttonhole stitch is a most effective method of embroidering foliage. The prongs of each stitch are not at right angles but tempered to accommodate the curve.

Up-and-down buttonhole stitch is a two-way 'double buttonhole' with the needle facing alternately up and down, and two closely-parallel stitches forming each 'pair'. After the upward stitch is made, the drawing down of the thread forms the small horizontal bar. This makes a strong border stitch.

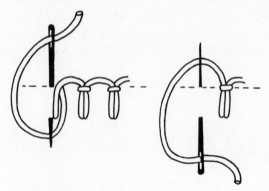

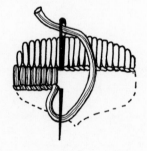

Buttonhole filling stitch is worked in parallel lines, with the second row of stitches worked over the knots of the first row and so on (for clarification, the second row in the diagram is shaded, in which case the stitch is called **shaded buttonhole filling stitch**).

BYZANTINE STITCH

A canvas-work satin stitch with bands of stitches worked in steps.

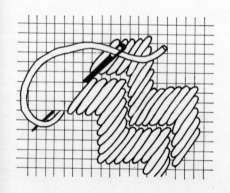

CABLE CHAIN STITCH

(This name can also be applied to **cable stitch**, below.) A **chain stitch** extended by links. When the needle emerges at A, pass the needle around the thread as shown and enter fabric at B, to emerge at C (A).

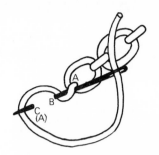

An extra knot makes **knotted cable chain stitch**. After the initial knot is formed (figures 1 and 2), the needle takes up the fabric (figure 2) to start the cable chain stitch (figure 3).

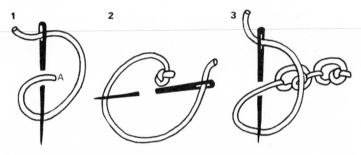

And **zigzag cable chain stitch** consists of ordinary **cable chain stitch** with each new stitch worked at right angles to the one before. Notice how the thread is looped around the needle with each new 'chain'.

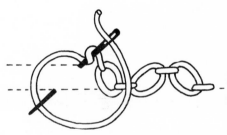

CABLE STITCH

cable chain stitch

An outline stitch, the two sides of the chain links being worked alternately. (This is one form of **cable chain stitch**—see also above.)

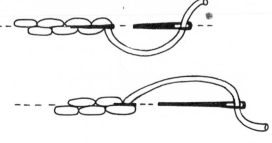

CANVAS WORK

Canvas-work embroidery is also variously called **tapestry** or **needlepoint**, both misleading terms since a tapestry is technically woven rather than embroidered (hence the inappropriateness of the labelling of the 'Bayeux tapestry', p. 329), and needlepoint originally referred to a needle-made lace (p. 399).

The generic term 'canvas-work embroidery' therefore embraces both **tapestry** and **needlepoint**, when used in the sense of embroidery, as well as **wool work**, denoting canvas ground embroidered with wool thread, and **Florentine work** (p. 390) which can be worked on a canvas ground.

Canvas work is executed on a ground of even-weave open canvas, gauged by the number of threads to the inch. Whereas some petit-point works of the past have been on canvas with a mesh as fine as 40 or more threads to the inch, today embroiderers generally work with from 9 to 20 threads to the inch.

Canvas is constructed from many materials:

Cotton—German cotton canvas is recognisable by every tenth thread being yellow.

Jute—string-coloured canvas, which darkens with age.

Silk—sometimes called 'Berlin canvas' (in England) or 'mosaic canvas' (in America).

Wool—'bolting'.

Wire Mesh—primarily 19th century.

Plastic—available particularly in New York.

Canvas-work embroidery is generally worked on two weaves of ground:

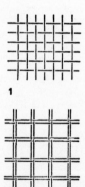

1

2

Single thread canvas—an open canvas traditionally used for finer petit-point stitching (tent stitch).

Double thread canvas—another open canvas traditionally used for gros-point stitching (cross stitch). Double thread canvas is more usually worked today, and it is ideal for stitches that have to be trammed (p. 444). It is known also as 'Penelope'.

Both single and double thread canvas are available in many varieties of mesh sizing: the best canvas is French, it is the most pliable ground and is also, alas, the most expensive. Another canvas form, 'Java canvas', is a pliable basket-weave ground used for simple woolwork embroidery similar to much linen embroidery. 'Winchester canvas', of Italian hemp, is very flexible and strong.

Canvas work, as such, is often worked on a frame to avoid distortion. If it is embroidered without a frame, cut edges of the

340

canvas can be prevented from fraying, or rubbing, by a covering of masking tape.

Traditional basic canvas-work included gros point (cross stitch), petit point (tent stitch), gobelin stitch, satin stitch, Florentine stitch and all variations of these groups, and filling stitches such as chequer stitch, jacquard stitch and Scottish stitch.

Most designs are suitable for working on canvas, although the wider the gauge the more geometric the finished pattern. Some canvas-work designs are somewhat regionalised. In the Boston, Massachusetts, area certain 'fishing lady' embroideries were worked, see p. 281.

Due to its rigid structure and resistance to wear, canvas work has long been associated with upholstery. Canvas-work sets of matching chairs and sofas, with arms, backs and seats upholstered with petit-point and gros-point canvas work, became

CANVAS WORK—*the State Seal of Arkansas, detail of one of 24 chair seats worked by embroiderers of Pine Bluff, under the direction of Mrs. Garland Brewster, for the Governor's Mansion.*
(Mrs. Dale Bumpers)

the vogue towards the end of the 17th century. Some sets still in existence today have up to 20 items of matching petit-point upholstery to each set.

Canvas work, too, is ideally suited to floor coverings. Although most hand-worked carpets and rugs are 'hooked' with a cut pile, there are outstanding embroidered-carpet artists in many parts of the world (p. 216). Many contemporary church embroideries (p. 355) are similarly executed in canvas work.

The individual canvas-work artist today, however, is probably working intricate and painstaking hangings, bell pulls, seats, cushions and screens. There are, particularly in North America, wide varieties of attractive kits available which may, or may not, include all necessary equipment and, also, the basic design already trammed.

CANVAS WORK—*the story of Abraham, Hagar and Ishmael, silk on linen canvas ground, mid-18th century.*
(The Earl of Elgin and Kincardine)

342

CANVAS WORK—*during the 1850's, Berlin wool work was often executed on a loosely woven canvas tacked to a non-canvas ground. The stitches were worked through canvas and ground, and the threads of the canvas were sometimes subsequently removed. In this detail the canvas has been left in place.*
(The Earl of Haddington)

343

CARD EMBROIDERY

Embroidery on a ground of paper, parchment or card has been accorded many titles, such as **card embroidery, cardboard work** and **paper work**. Sometimes such stitchery has been worked through pre-pricked holes: sometimes each stitch is individually formed as the pattern progresses. Although exact origins of this type of embroidery are not known, both the British Museum and the Rijksmuseum, Amsterdam, have Chinese examples thought to have been worked towards the end of the 17th century. A Spanish book of saintly portraits, *A Devotional Miscellany*, in the Museum of Fine Arts, Boston, is attributed to 1655–67.

One of the most outstanding forms of the art is the *colifichet*, a term first referred to by Monseigneur X. Barbier de Montault in 1879 when he was given 315 items labelled *'colifichets'* by the family of a nun who had, at the time of the Revolution, to flee from her convent at Loudun. According to *L'Art du Brodeur* (1770), fine silk embroideries on parchment or paper had often been worked by religious communities, and designs frequently used seem to have included vases of flowers and sacred portraits.

At Traquair House, Peeblesshire, there are four *colifichets*, possibly brought back to Scotland by two of the daughters of the 4th Earl of Traquair who were in France early in the 18th century. Lady Lucy Stuart, the elder daughter, wrote from an Ursuline convent in 1713: '. . . They teach nothing but embroidery. . . .' Ursulines were particularly stitchery-conscious: it was Sisters from the Order who were responsible for much of the production of **quill work** in Canada (p. 35), and, indeed, some of the designs and methods of working *colifichets*, with satin stitch and knotting predominating, are particularly graceful versions of those found worked on birch bark in North America. They are similar, too, to secular designs on early 19th-century card embroideries in South Africa, as seen today in Stellenbosch Museum. As with Canadian bark work, the design is embroidered through pre-pricked holes on the ground.

Card embroideries have often been worked on to pre-pricked grounds. In England, for example, there were many pictures available at the end of the 18th and during the 19th centuries, sometimes with painted details added to the basic paper or card. Card embroidery enjoyed particular vogue during the 19th century. Various gauges of perforated cardboard, known as

344

'Bristol board', were available, through the holes of which the embroiderer could fashion stitches to a design of her own choice, following Berlin wool work or other styles of embroidery.

Sheets of perforated card are now again available on the market, although there are as yet few examples of outstanding modern card embroidery. On the market today, too, is plastic canvas, an opaque white trellis that straddles the territories of **card embroidery** and **canvas work** (p. 340).

CARD EMBROIDERY—*South African triptych, 1816, the central panel known to have been worked by Hilletje Smuts, aged 15, 7½ × 14 in. (19 × 36 cm).*
(Stellenbosch Museum, South Africa. Photo: Image Studios, Stellenbosch)

345

CARD EMBROIDERY—*late 18th- or early 19th-century pattern, pin-pricked to show placing of stitching, heavy paper ground. Frequently the painted details of such patterns showed extreme emotion.*
(Mr. C. W. Johnson)

346

CARD EMBROIDERY—*late 19th-century perforated paper picture 'House by the Railroad', from the Moravian school, wool on card, designed and worked by Katherine Hynes McCaffrey. (Schenectady Museum, New York)*

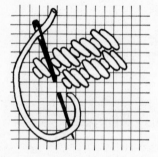

CASHMERE STITCH

A canvas-work satin stitch worked over two threads, two threads and one thread.

CEYLON STITCH

A coiled stitch resembling knitting, it makes a good filling stitch.

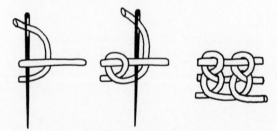

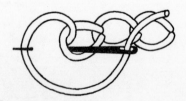

CHAIN STITCH

One of the most usual—and universal—embroidery stitches. The needle is brought down where it emerged to start each 'link', with the working thread always kept under the needle.

Among the many variants of chain stitch is **broad chain stitch** (also known as **reverse chain stitch**). It is best to work with a stiff thread to get the heavily worked effect of the stitch. The needle is passed through the link of the previous stitch (without entering the ground fabric) before going back into the same hole from which it originally entered (A). A small straight stitch provides the first 'link'.

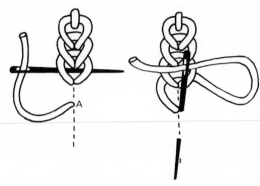

Chequered chain stitch is also known as **magic stitch**. By working with two different-coloured threads in one needle, and alternately bringing each thread to the top of each link, **chain stitch** takes on a two-colour appearance. The 'magic' is achieved by allowing the 'disappearing' thread to lie over the needle instead of being held down by it.

Crested chain stitch is also known as **Spanish coral stitch**. A complicated ladder stitch, the thread emerges at A and is knotted before taking a small stitch B to C and knotted (figure 1). Passing over A to B (figure 2) the needle enters at A to emerge D with the thread looped around the needle (figure 3). D becomes A and the work continues, to give an asymmetrical lacing (figure 4).

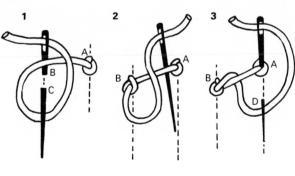

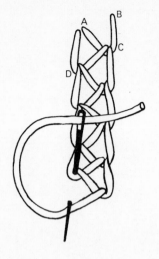

Detached chain stitch—see Daisy stitch.

Double chain stitch (also known as zigzag cable stitch) is worked with the needle emerging at A, entering the fabric B to C (with the thread kept under the needle), entering the fabric again A to D (with the thread kept under the needle) and so on.

Heavy chain stitch (also known as broad chain stitch)—the stitch is worked downwards, in opposite direction to ordinary chain stitch and each link is formed by passing the needle A to B under the bottom of the penultimate link (but not through the fabric), to come down and enter the fabric at C. A small straight stitch begins the process.

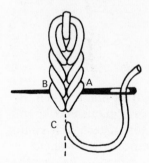

Hungarian braided chain stitch looks rather like heavy (or broad) chain stitch. After working an inner link to the first chain, bring the needle up at A and weave over the outer link, under the inner links and over the outer link (figure 1) before the needle re-enters the fabric at A (figure 2). Subsequent links are similarly worked, always weaving the needle over the outer link, under the inner links and over the outer link of the preceding stitches (figure 3). As with the other stitches of this group, a single straight stitch is worked first of all.

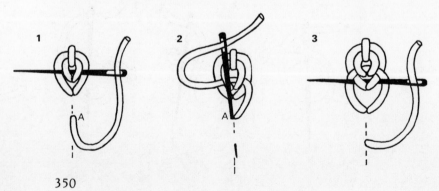

Knotted chain stitch (also known as **link stitch**) is more complicated. Coming out just below the design line, the thread is taken across in a sloping stitch to the left. It re-enters the fabric just above the design line and comes out just below. The needle is then passed down under the diagonal stitch and the thread left hanging in a loose loop. The needle is brought round and threaded through this loop and the whole drawn up (though it should not be pulled too tight).

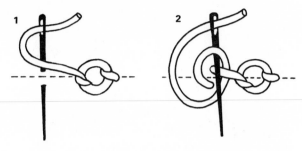

Open chain stitch is also known as **square chain stitch**. Instead of bringing the needle back into the beginning of each link, as ordinary chain stitch, leave a horizontal gap (A to B) the width of the desired stitch. (This stitch is also sometimes known as **ladder stitch**).

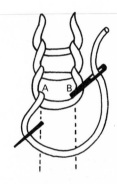

Rosette chain stitch—see **rosette stitch**.

Russian chain stitch is detached chain stitch worked in blocks of three.

Singalese chain stitch is worked like open chain stitch except that two loose threads (shaded), one hanging either side of the 'ladder', are worked around by the main embroidery stitch. The hanging 'shaded threads', it is important to note, do not enter the ground fabric except for starting and finishing off.

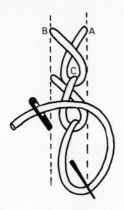

Twisted chain stitch—instead of entering the fabric in the same place (as in ordinary chain stitch), the needle enters at B to emerge at C for the next link. The stitches can be worked either close together or at a distance to give a particularly detached effect.

Zigzag chain stitch, known also as **Vandyke chain stitch,** is a simple chain stitch worked alternately to one side and then to the other.

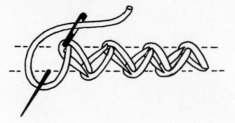

Basic chain stitch can also be further embellished: **backstitched chain stitch,** for instance, has a row of back stitches (shaded thread) superimposed on to a row of chain stitches.

And **threaded chain stitch** is worked on a foundation of individual foundations of small chain stitches which are then loosely interlaced (shaded thread).

Alternatively, chain stitch can itself embellish other stitching. A series of parallel horizontal **straight stitches** can be worked to form a **raised chain band.** The chain is worked either in similar or contrasting colour thread.

352

△ USA – detail of the "Westover-Berkeley coverlet", c. 1770, worked on alternate fortnights at the Westover Plantation, Virginia, home of William Byrd II, and at the neighbouring Berkeley Plantation, home of Benjamin Harrison IV.
(The Valentine Museum, Richmond, Virginia, slide 56.203.1)

▽ USA – detail of Berlin wool work runner with raised plush stitch (Turkey work), mid-19th-century.
(The Valentine Museum, Richmond, Virginia, slide no. 58.174.7)

△ *USA – Mexican influence of colour and spirit is apparent in Wilcke Smith's "Fairytale with birds",*
1970. Wool thread on velvet ground, Vandyke and straight stitches, French knots and applied black
Mexican clay birds.
(The artist. Photo: Bob Smith)

CHAIN STITCH—*detail of hostess skirt 'sampler' by June Hendricks, 1973, which was exhibited in the Golden Thimble II Exhibition, Los Angeles. The borders include (from top) straight and detached chain stitch, Cretan interlacing, cross and straight stitches, interlaced running stitch, straight stitch with knots, chequered chain stitch and feather stitch.*
(The artist)

CHESSBOARD STITCH

Two versions of this stitch:

1. Blocks of **satin stitch** are laid diagonally and couched down, to produce an attractive filling stitch.

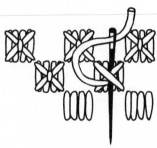

2. A pulled thread stitch, with **'basket weave' satin stitches** tightly pulled.

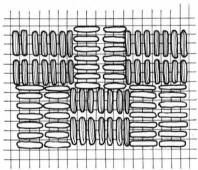

CHEQUER STITCH

A canvas-work filling stitch.

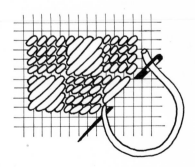

353

CHEVRON STITCH

A zigzag stitch worked between two parallel lines, that can be used for borders or fillings. The apex of the chevron should always be in the centre of each straight back stitch. The stitch is worked alternately from top to bottom and vice versa.

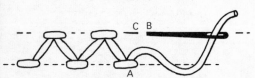 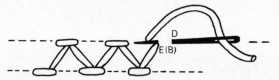

A variation of chevron stitch is the Greek **Astypalea stitch**. Two parallel rows of small chevron 'V's are worked and subsequently threaded, alternating from the top row to the bottom, with surface stitching. The stitch is traditionally worked on a small scale, which gives a somewhat uneven appearance.

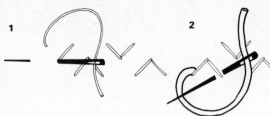  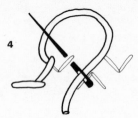

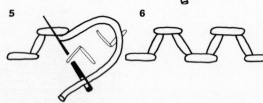

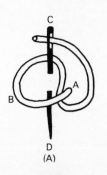

CHINESE KNOT

Peking knot

In many Chinese embroideries this knot is used as a seeded filling: it is also effective as a border stitch. By placing one's thumb at rest at B when working this quick knot stitch, the knot results when the needle is pulled from C to D (the A of the next stitch).

CHINESE STITCH

Pekinese stitch

A neat row of **back stitch** is laced with a thread of similar or contrasting colour to give a braid effect.

354

CHURCH EMBROIDERY

The art of embroidery has always been closely connected with the religion of the era and of the area. The embroidered vestments of the Burgundian Order of the Golden Fleece, used in the private chapel of Philip the Good in Dijon (p. 98), the church embroideries of the Leek Embroidery Society (p. 92) and the beautiful contemporary works of needlework guilds such as those of the cathedrals of Washington DC (p. 295) and Wellington (p. 189) all illustrate the importance of ecclesiastical embroidery in the arts of the time.

Christianity has encouraged and stimulated embroidery since the early days of the Church. Although religious and secular embroideries can generally be divided, it is none the less often possible to show traits of the latter category that have been gleaned from the former. From the 13th to the middle of the 14th centuries, in the high period of Opus Anglicanum (p. 63), many of the most beautiful embroideries throughout Europe were for church use.

A terminology of words associated with church embroideries includes:

Alb—full-length under-tunic, usually white, worn by priests and deacons under other vestments.

Altar embroideries—**altar band** or **altar frontlet**—a narrow horizontal band along the top of the front of the altar.

Altar frontal—altar covering, the modern tendency being towards an enveloping cloth rather than a frontal hanging. An **antependium** also hangs in front, while the **altar dossal** is a rectangular hanging above and behind the main altar.

Amice—a priest's white napkin, worn tucked around his neck, under an alb.

Apparel—a decorative band of embroidery, sometimes attached to the back neck of the amice.

Burse—a container for linen cloths used in Mass celebration.

Chasuble—the main outer vestment worn by priests at Mass, one of the two main styles being 'Early English', a cloak version fuller than the 'Roman chasuble'. The latter is a tunic with hip-length rectangular panels front and back, often with orphreys.

Cope—decorated outer vestment, a full-length semicircular cloak fastened across the front with a clasp or a morse. It is usually embellished with orphreys.

Dalmatic—mid-calf-length sleeveless tunic worn by deacons.

Kneeler—individual knee cushion used in prayer.

Maniple—long and narrow band, often decorated at each end, carried over the left forearm of a priest.

Mitre—headwear of bishops—and abbots—consisting of two flat pieces of fabric with a point to the top, joined by a folded cloth either side.

Morse—narrow strip of fabric serving as front fastening to cope.

Orphrey—decorated band found on most outer vestments: a chasuble, for instance, usually has a cross-shaped orphrey on the back and a straight-vertical orphrey on the front; a dalmatic has two straight-vertical orphreys, one front and one back.

Pall—funerary cloth.

Stole—a narrow scarf, often embroidered at the ends, worn by priests.

Veil—covering for chalice or similar utensil.

The production of church embroidery in England suffered a setback from the period of the Reformation of 1534–9 to the middle of the 19th century, with the aftermath of the 1829 Catholic Emancipation Act and the Oxford Movement of the Church of England.

Fine collections of church vestments can be seen worn, and cherished, indicative of the continued practical aspects of ecclesiastical embroidery. The 1973 York Minster Chapter House Exhibition, 'Recent Church Embroidery', had a representative selection of the wide variety of church embroideries being worked today. There is throughout a sympathetic personal touch to the possession, and the use, of church embroidery. The Rev. John Armson, Chaplain of Downing College, Cambridge, has a set of penitential vestments (chasuble, stole, maniple, burse and veil) bequeathed him by the artist Katharine Bullock. On a grey-green ground of heavy silk, maximum impact is obtained through textural juxtaposition of applied shapes of white and deep claret silk. The vestments are particularly appropriate to the simple setting of the college chapel, dedicated in 1953.

Ecclesiastical embroidery today, in fact, has chameleon attributes in suitability to environment. Stark modern lines echo or contrast with mediaeval architecture or, alternatively, they correspond to lines of churches of today.

Design of church embroideries can often incorporate modern ideas with no modification of impact. The set of 17 canvas-work kneelers, in the chapel of Abingdon School, Berkshire, for instance, was worked in 1963 by local ladies in memory of

Lorna Mary Cobban. The design motifs include such devices as that of the nearby Atomic Energy Research Establishment. Sometimes, however, modern ecclesiastical embroideries evoke former themes and ideas. In the Chapel Royal of the Tower of London, there is a banner commemorating the dead of both World Wars presented by the Buffs regiment (past and present). The designer, Pat Russell, worked to the suggestion that in 1240 Henry III had ordered 'coloured figures of St. Nicholas, St. Katherine, and St. Christopher holding and carrying Jesus, together with one of the Blessed Virgin' to be placed in the chapel. The modern quatrefoil banner shows the Blessed Virgin resplendent in a gold brocade cope, St. Katherine with her deadly wheel, an aged St. Nicholas, and St. Christopher smiling as he carries the infant Christ. The applied pieces have bold and emotional lines, and there is 20th-century representation in the form of a tug and the Tower Bridge in St. Nicholas's quarter.

Church work, in general, is a prolific expression of individual embroidery participation that is being continued and expanded throughout the world, and international cooperation is often stimulated through such works. The Washington Cathedral collection includes one kneeler, in the War Memorial chapel, worked by Queen Elizabeth the Queen Mother. In return, in 1961 the ladies of the Cathedral presented an altar kneeler to Canterbury Cathedral. Similarly, the Chapel of Lollowai Hospital, in Longana in the New Hebrides, has a full range of burses, veils and stoles worked by the ladies of Wellington Cathedral.

In 1969 the Scottish Handcraft Circle presented choir-stall cushions and kneelers to Iona Abbey. Each work, designed by Adam Robson, shows the coat of arms of a clan with connexions with Iona, such as those of the 8th Duke of Argyll, who presented the Abbey to the Church of Scotland, and those of the Abbots Mackenzie and Mackinnon, both of whom are buried in the chancel of the abbey. All the canvas-work embroidery, and subsequent upholstery of the seven dozen items, was undertaken by ladies of the Circle.

Apart from the collections already mentioned, outstanding church canvas-work embroideries can be seen in the cathedrals of Bury St. Edmunds, Canterbury, Exeter, Gloucester, Salisbury, Wells, Winchester and Worcester, and Westminster Abbey.

A few collections of canvas work embroideries in England with particularly interesting designs are those of:

Chelsea Old Church, London—kneelers with historical motifs.

357

St. Clement Dane, London—Royal Air Force kneelers worked by relatives.

Guards Chapel, Wellington Barracks, London—badges of the historic Guards regiments (the general public is admitted to Sunday morning service).

St. Anne's Church, Kew—stories of artists and of Kew Gardens.

St. Edward's Church, Cambridge—Cambridge college arms.

St. Helen's Church, Benson, Oxfordshire—floral patterns.

St. Nicholas' Church, Haxey, Doncaster—farming past and present.

St. Swithin's Church, Quenington, Gloucestershire—flowers and birds.

Eton College—kneelers and cushions designed by Constance Howard showing armorial bearings of people connected with the College, designs mostly worked by relatives of Etonians, Old or present.

In the United States, there are excellent canvas-work embroideries at the Church of the Ascension, Middletown, Ohio, works that include an altar kneeler in the Children's Chapel with motifs such as an hour-glass, symbol of the span of life, a squirrel, depicting contemplation, and a cock, for repentance.

Other churches deserving of mention are:

US Air Force Academy Chapels, Colorado Springs, Colorado.
Christ Church, Christiana Hundred, Wilmington, Delaware.
St. Peter's Church, Morristown, New Jersey.
West Point Chapel, West Point, New York.
St. John's Church and St. Thomas' Church, McLean, Virginia.
St. Luke's Church, Long Beach, California.
National Cathedral, Washington DC.
Trinity Church, Washington DC.
St. John's Church, Washington DC.
St. James' Church, New York, New York.

(This list is selected from *Needlepoint for Churches* by Patience Agnew, Charles Scribner's Sons.)

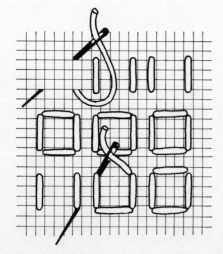

COBBLER STITCH
straight overcast ground
A pulled thread stitch. Vertical lines of one row of 'boxes' are then filled in with horizontal stitches.

358

COLCHA STITCH

A Spanish-language stitch, known in the Middle East and other parts of the world as **Bokhara stitch** (p. 334). *Colcha* is Spanish for 'quilt', and in America it is believed this stitch was originally copied from Chinese silk embroidery imported into Mexico and, thence, to New Mexico. It is found on 18th-century quilts and altar cloths throughout southern Colorado, northern New Mexico and other former Spanish areas. Today there is, thanks to the efforts of several teachers in Taos and Santa Fé, a revival of the stitch, and 'The Colcha Club', a group of ladies in Española, also New Mexico, meet regularly to repair old works and keep the stitch alive.

Basically a filling stitch worked like a multiple **Romanian stitch**, the initial laid thread is couched (figures 1 and 2) as many times as required (figure 3). Subsequent rows should be couched at alternating intervals to give an all-over basket effect (figure 4). A fairly lightweight thread is best for the beginner.

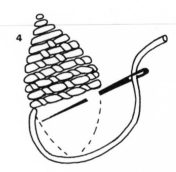

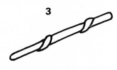

COLLECTING

The embroidery collector today has few guidelines by which to go. One rudimentary brief is the steep rise in saleroom prices for needlework over the last few years. Embroidery, sometimes included in costume lots, comes up regularly at Christie's and Sotheby's. Catalogues from such sales are useful founts of embroidery knowledge: they afford, too, some documentation of the price rise.

Embroidery works have, unlike paintings, generally not been dated by the artist. Samplers are more likely to be dated and to provide additional clues of identification, and indeed, these works offer the possibility of forming an enjoyable one-theme collection of embroidery. Samplers are compact. They frame and show well and they frequently include delightful *vignettes* of personal feelings and thoughts of the young artist, for the greater part of sampler production has been worked by girls from the ages of 4 to 16, learning the tricks, and stitches, of their trade.

359

Condition of an old work obviously affects its value: unskilled reparation might lower that worth. In the field of historical embroidery, therefore, the collector must in the main rely on his own knowledge of antiques and of the subject of embroidery. Facts such as an awareness of the period of the zenith of stump work (p. 439) and the date of the first aniline dyes (p. 86) are clues to identifying provenance, and therefore true value, of a particular work.

When collecting a geographical range of embroideries of the world, the traveller-collector should look out for examples of local workmanship. One antique shop in the St. Michel area of Paris was offering, in 1973, an Indian machine-embroidered blouse mis-labelled 'Lebanese'. What would, on the other hand, be much more satisfying to own, and a better investment, would be a hand-embroidered Romanian blouse brought from the maker in her own village (p. 217). Any item embroidered by hand has a positive asset. Density of embroidery is another point to consider. International embroideries that have attracted recent critical approval are the San Blas *molas* from Panama (p. 200), and years of Chinese prominence now seem likely as an accompaniment to thawing relations and burgeoning trade. So-called 'Kurdish' rugs from Iraq, with thick wool stitching on a deep red wool ground, are another form of stitchery destined for increasing popularity within the next few years.

The collector may, on the other hand, feel drawn towards specialisation in a branch of the embroidered arts such as the embroidered picture, often offered for sale in shops and salerooms already framed and ready for display. Devotion to unusual media, such as hair embroidery and works incorporating beetles' wings, is another possible addiction.

One form of needlework collection that has already been subject to the pressures of busy market activity favours needlework tools and boxes. Until the 1960's such items as sewing boxes with threads, needles, thimbles and scissors were not generally thought of as 'collectors' treasures', but in the last few years their value has justifiably appreciated. As well as needlework boxes and tables, thimbles and holders, pin-cushions and needle-cases, there is constant demand for lucets (harp-shaped holders for cord making), tambour frames and old hooks, sewing 'birds' (clamps to hold embroidery taut) and chatelaines (waist clasps or brooches, from which were suspended essential sewing items such as scissors and thimble holders).

There are few needlework tools of possible interest to future collectors that are being produced today. Whereas, for example, there were before the Second World War five registered firms producing hall-marked silver and gold thimbles in England, there is now only one, a two-man studio in Birmingham. It is difficult to imagine, too, that utilitarian, though elegant, contemporary sewing machines will ever become collectors' items (though at least one is on display at the Museum of Modern Art, New York). The collector who is interested purely in tools of the trade can best further his knowledge, past, present and future, by alert attention to general antique publications, by studying saleroom catalogues and by reference to one of the published mentors. He can also study the activities of the Costume Society (allied to the textile departments of the Victoria and Albert Museum) and look out for temporary exhibitions such as the Tibetan collection (1974) and the English historical collection (1975) shown at Franses of Piccadilly.

Advice for the collector is, however, scant in the field of modern embroidered art. There is on the market today a

COLLECTING—*19th-century 'sewing birds', which were clamped to a table and used as embroidery accessories. The birds' bodies are on springs and they held embroidery fabric taut in their beaks. (The National Trust. The Kay-Shuttleworth Collection at Gawthorpe Hall, Lancashire)*

plethora of contemporary 'stitchery', a term coined to include such embroidery-related skills as wall-hangings (p. 244) and collage. Experience, and the courage to buy what he likes, are the only two assets that aid the collector. He will be able to buy embroideries for a lower price than he would have to pay for painted art, a credit point on the side of embroidery that has not, as yet, been jeopardised, although it must be hoped that the true value of the embroidered arts will soon be realised.

COLLECTING—*two 'lucets' for cord-making, one of wood and the other of ivory, both 19th century. Thread was wound around the arms and unravelled through the small hole.*
(The National Trust. The Kay-Shuttleworth Collection at Gawthorpe Hall, Lancashire)

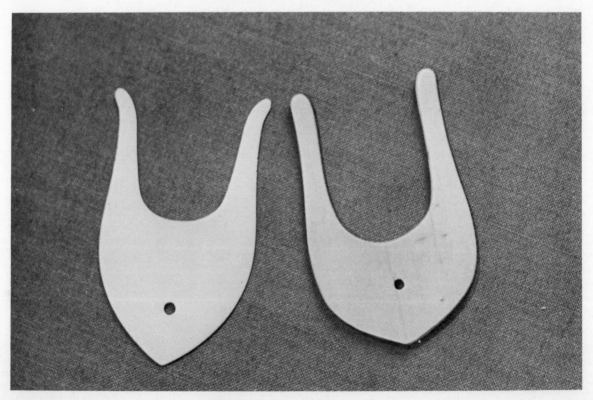

CONSERVATION

As embroidery finds itself deeper in the domain of the collector (p. 359), and as the contents of museums and great houses require ever more urgent attention, their care, cleaning and renovation become increasingly important.

One rule governing conservation of embroideries is that the amateur should resist any temptation to experiment. Many valuable embroideries have been irretrievably ruined by enthusiasts ignorantly dabbling in what is a skilled process, and even experts can, on occasions, damage embroideries. (A cautionary tale is told by one such scientist: after comprehensive testings for possible non-fast dyes, she finally soaked an early 19th-century sampler; but, as the work sank to the bottom of her wash tray, the letters of the decorative inscription came away from the ground fabric and floated, one by one, to the surface . . .) Amateur action can do infinitely more harm than good and, contrary to initial presumption, perhaps, a damaged embroidery that has not been tampered with is generally more valuable than a work of equal import that has been washed or mended badly by an amateur. Reparation with glue, or any kind of adhesive, for example, is likely to prove disastrous.

There are some rudimentary guidelines which the embroidery collector can apply to his own items. Necessary equipment includes a rare measure both of time and extraordinary patience: an 18th-century sedan chair was conserved recently after 166 man-hours, a 16th-century embroidery of 'Esther before Ahasuerus' in the Victoria and Albert Museum was completely restored only after 3,677 man-hours of expert attention.

The main enemies of embroideries are *light*, which causes tendering and fading, *damp*, which causes vegetable fibres to swell and soften, *fungus*, often resulting from damp, *rust*, *fugitive dyes*, *pests*, particularly moths, *folding, continuous use* and the passage of time.

The first factor to be considered in conservation is the make-up of the ground fabric. Warp threads of a woven material go lengthwise along the fabric. Weft threads are the cross-threads woven at right angles to the warp threads already set up on the loom.

There are three main weaves:

Plain weaves—weft thread going alternately over and under (1 and 1) the warp threads (figure 2).

Twill weaves—also known as **diagonal weaves**—weft threads going over and under two (2 and 2) warp threads (figure 3).

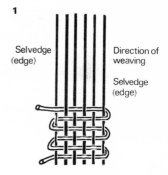

1

Selvedge (edge)

Direction of weaving

Selvedge (edge)

2

3

4

Satin weaves—also known as **damask weaves**—weft threads woven in complicated numbering over and under warp threads (figure 4).

If a chair seat, or similar work, is coming away from its backing or has torn sections, the most durable protector is a covering of fine net, a process which considerably slows down further deterioration. Admittedly the effect of a net covering, held down with the minimum of stitching, is somewhat to dull the impact of the embroidery, but this is a small price to pay for maximum protection of the weaker parts of that work. For minimum disfigurement, however, damaged embroidery can alternatively be held in place with substantial couching with many rows of darning stitch, a method which offers considerably less overall protection. Dressmakers' fine silk net is suitable.

Cleaning wool work is a major problem to all 'needlepoint' artists and collectors. There are now commercial spray cleaners on the American market, but these are as yet relatively new and untried. Surface dirt can be removed by gentle rotating pressure of a household vacuum cleaner with a fine nylon net over the nozzle. More deeply embedded dirt can sometimes be removed with magnesium carbonate, a white pharmaceutical powder. A thin layer is spread on the work with a baby's hair brush, or similar soft brush, left for a few hours and brushed off.

Grease or other stains require careful removal and it is often best to leave them *in situ*, although there is a detailed guide to possible removal agents in H. J. Plenderleith's *Conservation of Antiquities and Works of Art* (1966).

Washing embroideries necessitates a great deal of patience and care. Damage caused through immersion in water cannot be reversed. Some such damage is not immediately apparent: if, for example, all dirt is not removed when washing silks or wools, remaining particles may be forced into fabric fibres and cause yet more deterioration later. And, similarly, dirt can be forced in between fabric layers of a lined article.

There will continue to be many schools of thought on the overall suitability of washing wool embroidery and the corresponding methods for so doing. In 1880, for instance, a recipe for washing Berlin wool work consisted of '$\frac{1}{4}$lb. soft soap to $\frac{1}{2}$pt. gin'. Any embroidery containing metal thread work should certainly not be washed: only such wool, silk and cotton embroideries as have been *thoroughly* tested for colour-fastness should be immersed in water. Many dyes run or bleed, and colour-fastness can to some degree be established by

364

damping a small wad of cotton wool and pressing it firmly to the back of the fabric: if there is any coloration on the cotton wool, the dyes of the embroidery are not completely fast.

Washing should always be done in soft water. London tap water, for example, has a high calcium content which tends to make white material grey and matted. De-ionized water, available from most chemists, is the ideal: rain water is a plausible substitute. A soft neutral chemical soap such as Lissapol-9 is often used by professionals, but mild liquid detergents (washing-up liquids) generally give satisfactory results.

The embroidery is washed in water of blood heat (98·4°F.— 37°C.) to which the detergent and a pinch of salt have been added. The item is dipped up and down and thoroughly rinsed in cold water, with no squeezing or rubbing. Initial drying is done by placing the embroidery between two towels and pressing it gently to squeeze out excess water, and complete drying should be finished as quickly as possible, out of direct sunlight, with the work stretched into position or held flat on blotting paper. When blocking and stretching items, it is essential to use non-rusting pins such as entomological or toilet pins.

Storage is an important factor in the conservation of textiles. Embroidery should obviously be put away as clean—and as dry—as possible. Storage should ideally be in a dark place, dry and cool. Items should be kept as flat as possible, with any folds protected by thick wads of acid-free tissue paper. From time to time the embroidery should be taken out of storage and re-folded with the folds in different places. Large flat textiles can, alternatively, be stored rolled around cardboard tubes like the central cores of bolts of dressmaking fabrics.

Items in general display, such as curtains, should, where applicable, be lined with pre-shrunk lining to give them longer wear. Lining fabric is generally stronger than the ground cloth and it is essential, therefore, to make sure that the lining is loose enough not to cause the foreground fabric any strain.

All works should be kept out of direct sunlight: it is, for instance, inadvisable to place a new canvas-work chair in front of a window. Sometimes, indeed, it is advantageous even to cover furniture with dust-covers, evocative of empty houses and bygone eras. In those days, however, handworked embroidered furnishing was appreciated as a worthy art, and care was taken to preserve colouring as much as possible. Lady Ottoline Morrell described going with Henry James to one

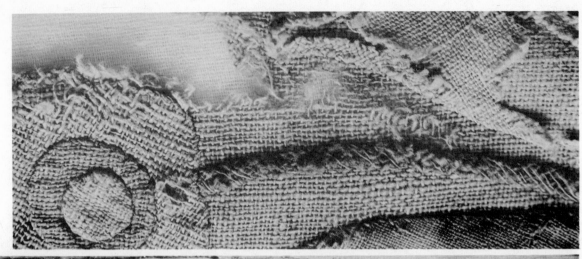

CONSERVATION—*reparation at the studio of Mrs. Karen Finch in London. Experts are working on a tent originally made in the Ottoman Empire, captured from the Turks by a Polish nobleman of the Polish Army at the beginning of the 17th century and now the property of the Lanckoronski Foundation deposited with the Polish Institute and Sikorski Museum in London. (A similar tent is to be seen in Kungl. Livrustammaren, Stockholm.) The photographs show:*

1. *Detail of the tent fabric before treatment.*
2. *Section of the tent pinned—and already partly sewn—on to scrim backing.*
3. *Two of Mrs. Finch's colleagues working on a section of the tent roof.*

(Mrs. Karen Finch and the Polish Institute and Sikorski Museum, London)

house where the furniture was protectively covered. She said she felt she was 'moving in the interior of a Louis XIV clock that would cease ticking if she stepped off the drugget that was laid across each room'.

Evidence of the efficacy of such dust-covers is apparent again and again. In one private house today, the exquisite collection of full-length crewel-work curtains, embroidered settee covers, chair covers and needle-made carpets, worked by Lady Cecile Goff (1874–1960) from 1902 onwards, has, despite the fact that the main drawing rooms face south, retained its original delicate colouring. Curtains are carefully lined and protected by window blinds and many of the other items have their own dust-covers constantly in use.

Embroidered hangings of all sizes are now increasingly often supported from strips of 'Velcro' fastenings (the Oxburgh hangings, p. 221, are supported in this way). One half of the strip is sewn to the lining of a hanging and the other half is attached to the wall or to a batten attached thereto. 'Velcro' is capable of supporting surprising weights and, in this way, embroideries hang evenly and strains, inevitable in suspended pieces, are minimised.

Beyond a simple application of loving care and attention, there is, to reiterate, little that the amateur can do in the technical aspects of conservation. There are many specialised conservation centres around the world, places like the Abegg Foundation (p. 264), outside Berne. The Textile Museum in Washington DC, Delft University and the Rijksmuseum in the Netherlands, the Riksantikvarieämbetet och Statens Historiska Museum in Stockholm, the Nationalmuseet in Copenhagen and the Landesmuseum in Zürich have similar textile conservation units. There is in England and America, as in the rest of the world, alas, a regrettable dearth at the moment of qualified specialists able to undertake private commissions, but fortunately conservation as a science, in the widest possible meaning of the word, is finally being allocated time and study. The International Institute for Conservation devotes regular attention to the intricate museum aspects of conservation, and the Courtauld Institute introduced in 1973 its first diploma course in the conservation of textiles.

368

CONTINENTAL STITCH

A canvas-work stitch that gives good backing. It can be worked either horizontally (figure 1), when it is also known as **horizontal tent stitch**, or vertically (figure 2), when it is also known as **vertical tent stitch**.

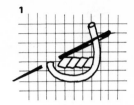

CORD STITCH

A useful joining stitch that completely hides the edges of the two pieces of fabric being worked.

The two edges are held together, back to back, and the stitching is worked (figures 1, 2, 3 and 4) over both pieces of fabric. When the row of stitches is finished, the fabric is opened out (figure 5) to give a solid 'plaited' appearance.

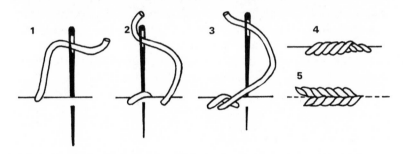

COUCHING

A stitch holding down another thread, as in **Bokhara couching** (p. 334) or **Romanian couching** (p. 424). Some other forms of couching are:

Jacobean couching, also known as **trellis couching**. Couching over a laid trellis.

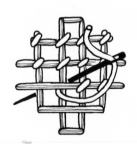

Satin stitch couching, alternatively called **overcast stitch** or **trailing stitch**. Laid threads couched with small **satin stitches** are worked close together with the needle entering the fabric at each stitch.

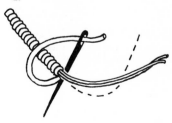

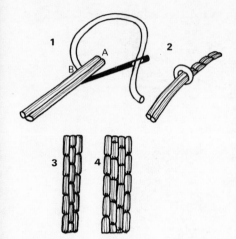

Underside couching, or **couching rentré,** much used in **Opus Anglicanum.** It was a most effective and glorious covering stitch, often worked with gold or silver threads. Laid threads (from A) are couched as follows: couching thread from B enters fabric again at same spot B and re-emerges a short distance below. By pulling the couching thread very taut, the laid thread is pulled down into the fabric (figures 1 and 2). Metal threads, difficult to manipulate, are traditionally 'laid' and then couched with a finer thread. The distance of each couching stitch determines the overall pattern of the finished work (figures 3 and 4).

COUNTED THREAD WORK

This term is applied to any form of fabric embroidery (i.e. on a non-canvas ground) in which threads are counted when working embroidery stitches. If cross stitches are worked, for example, in haphazard arrangement and design, the embroidery can be called 'cross-stitch work'. If, on the other hand, cross stitches are worked to the same size (over four threads of the ground fabric, for instance), and placed in planned order, it can also be referred to as 'counted thread work'.

CRETAN STITCH

A zigzag stitch with a slight twist to the thread, worked between two parallel lines. Spacing left between stitches determines whether it is **closed Cretan stitch** (figure 1) or **open Cretan stitch** (figure 2). If the needle is put in at an angle (figure 3) it becomes **slanting Cretan stitch** (also known as **slanted feather stitch** or **long-arm feather stitch**).

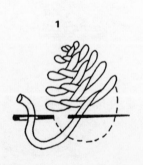
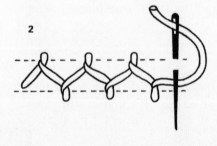
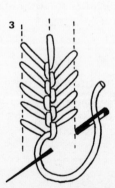

CROSS STITCH

al pasado (Spanish)
gros point (on canvas)
saddle stitch
sampler stitch (on fabric)

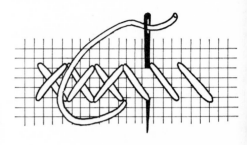

Each stitch can be 'crossed' before starting the next stitch or, as in the diagram, the row of half stitches can be worked and then 'crossed' together. It is important that all crosses should cross in the same direction.

Arrowhead cross stitch, known also as **Italian cross stitch** or **Italian two-sided stitch**, has a central cross bordered on two sides. This results, when stitches are worked next to each other, in complete bordering of the crosses.

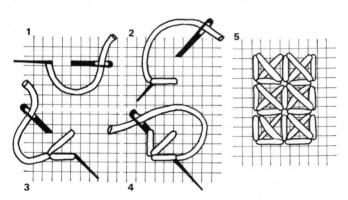

Diagonal cross stitch, with all the vertical uprights worked first, is known also as **diagonal raised band stitch** (when used in pulled thread work and pulled extremely tight, a diagonal raised band is achieved).

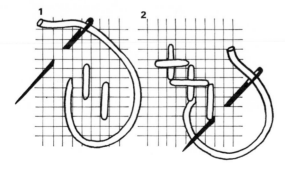

Double cross stitch, with one cross stitch superimposed upon another, is known also as **Leviathan stitch** or **Smyrna cross stitch**.

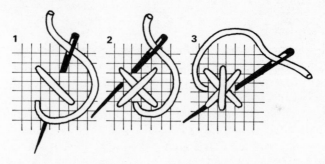

Half cross stitch, or **half stitch**, is a canvas-work stitch, usually trammed first. Today it is more generally called **tent stitch** or **petit point**.

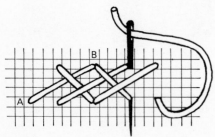

Long-legged cross stitch (known variously as **long-armed cross stitch**, **plaited Slav stitch** and **twist stitch**) is elongated. Instead of working at exact diagonals, as in ordinary cross stitch, every other stitch (A to B) is extended.

Marking cross stitch, so called because it was used by laundry needlewomen marking linen for identification, has a particularly neat appearance (all squares) on the back. To avoid any diagonal stitches on the back, one of the front diagonals is worked twice (figure 3).

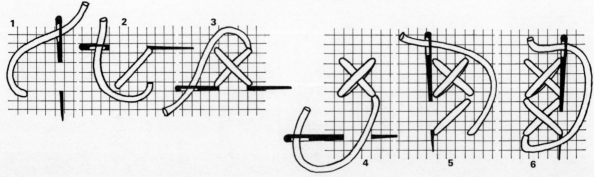

Reversed cross stitch, a misleading name, is a fine canvas-work stitch. Alternate upright and diagonal crosses (white thread) are covered with alternating diagonal and upright crosses (black thread).

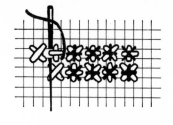

Two-sided cross stitch produces identical patterning on both sides of the fabric, hence the name. Each row requires four journeys. It will be seen that an auxiliary stitch is needed when making the turn at the right-hand side.

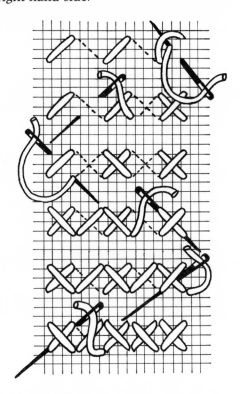

CREWEL WORK

Crewel thread is a tightly twisted multi-strand woollen yarn known variously as 'crewel' or 'worsted', the latter name being particularly used during the first three-quarters of the 19th century. **Crewel work** is today generally associated with wool-work embroidery on a non-canvas ground such as linen, usually embroidery in crewel (stem) stitch. Such embroidery is also referred to as **Jacobean work**.

373

Although earlier embroideries, such as the Bayeux 'tapestry' (p. 329), were worked with woollen threads in crewel stitch and outline stitch, many of the earliest embroideries today allotted to the category of crewel work were bed-hangings. These had traditionally often been highly decorated and much prized. Edward the Black Prince, who died in 1376, for example, bequeathed to his son, Richard, a large bed embroidered with angels (Nichols, John, *Collection of All the Wills . . . of the Kings and Queens of England, Princes and Princesses of Wales and every Branch of the Blood Royal*, London 1780). Mary, Queen of Scots, before her execution in 1586 (p. 221), instructed her French maid, Mlle. de Beauregard, to look after her embroidered bed-hangings.

An early reference actually denoting crewel embroidery as such was the Farringdon inventory of 1620 which listed 'three low stooles of needle worke cruell'. It was during the early part of the 17th century, with increased trade with India and the Far East and the import to the West of designs and materials such as *palampores*, marvellous printed cotton fabrics with patterns later to be copied by embroiderers, that the oriental 'Jacobean' motifs evolved. Flowing lines, floral patterns and Persian *kulka* palmette designs were often employed in this field of embroidery in England and throughout western Europe and North America.

American crewel work was, as was early British crewel, first worked in indigo blue on a bleached white linen ground. American motifs similarly included the oriental Tree of Life, peacocks, parrots, lotuses, pineapples, pomegranates and British remembrances such as the oak, rose and lion of England, the thistle of Scotland and the three feathers of the Prince of Wales.

Crewel embroideries of the 18th century were more open and less heavy than those of the 17th century, and *terra firma* mounds, the earthly piles to be found at the foot of Trees of Life, were much less in evidence. In general, contemporary American crewel embroideries were less stereotyped and rigid in design, and, in an effort to conserve valuable wool, embroidery over the entire ground area was less dense than in some English works.

Crewel embroidery is today one of the most popular and expressionist movements of the entire spectrum of the art. With no geometric confines such as are found in canvas work, the artist can produce highly individual embroideries to whatever shaping is required.

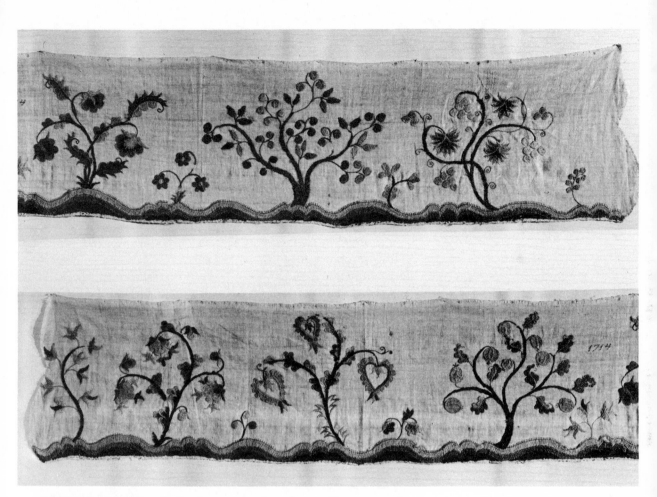

CREWEL WORK—*bed valance, crewel work on a linen ground, New England, 1714.*
(Courtesy Museum of Fine Arts, Boston. Helen and Alice Colburn Fund)

Any soft fabric is suitable as ground material. The traditional linen and cotton twill ground was sometimes brushed with teasels, an idea that originated in Fostat, a suburb of Cairo. Such brushed fabric was called, accordingly, 'fustian', a term which applies equally to corduroy, velveteen or moleskin fabric. Similar brushing processes are sometimes carried out today: teasels are specially sent to some American mills from the French town of Avallon.

Crewel wool comes in many thicknesses. In the 19th century some of the most sought-after smooth worsted yarn was

375

'Appleton's': today the most commonly used yarns for crewel embroidery include knitting wools, rug wools, Persian wool and what are known in the United States as 'English wool' and 'French wool'.

Crewel needles have sharp points and are ideal for working on most ground fabrics. Needles are sized 1 (large) to 10 (fine). Tapestry needles can be used for a very open-weave ground fabric. Crewel embroidery should be worked on a frame to prevent the ground fabric being pulled while working: it is, too, much easier to keep all stitches of even tension if working with a frame. Frequently used crewel-work stitches include stem, outline, satin, split, long and short, knot, chain, fly, cross, herringbone, back and running stitches. Outlines of main motifs can be filled in with stitches such as brick and cross and mosaic filling stitches and, also, with surface needlepoint or needle-lace filling stitches.

A specialised form of crewel work is the alternative method of working crewel stitches on top of canvas work previously given a 'ground' of tent stitch. This combination of crewel work and canvas work (or 'needlepoint') is known as crewel point.

CREWEL WORK—*detail of an embroidered curtain, 72 × 60 in. (1·83 × 1·52 m), one of a set of four, representing the seasons of the years, currently being worked by Joanne Reed of Malvern, Pennsylvania. The artist works largely from plant specimens on the table before her and each panel takes a year to complete. 'Winter' has, to date, been awarded the 'Best of the show' rosette in three national embroidery competitions. (The artist)*

CREWEL WORK—*chair and stool designed and worked by Sue Parker, 1965. The American artist gained inspiration from a visit to England one springtime and included in her design two New England flowers, the 'Tudor Rose' and a hybrid 'Stuart Carnation'.*
(The artist)

CUTWORK

Embroidered **cutwork** means that some irregularly shaped motif area of the ground fabric has actually been removed through cutting (whereas, by comparison, in drawn thread work entire threads are removed).

There are various degrees of cutwork—for example, **Renaissance cutwork** has the smallest area cut away, **Richelieu cutwork** has more area cut away and **reticella cutwork** has least of the original ground left. In many cases there is close association of embroidered cutwork with lace (**Venetian cutwork** is technically a lace).

Depending on the form of cutwork required, the ground is cut away either before or after working of the motif.

Some types of embroidered cutwork are:

Broderie anglaise
This form of round cutwork first became popular in England towards the end of the first half of the 19th century: from the 1880's on it was frequently called 'Madeira work'. It is a whitework, with stiletto holes pierced through the ground (usually a fine cotton) and the cut edges bound in overcast or buttonhole stitch. Each cut hole made part of a floral or border pattern.

Today **broderie anglaise** has become known as a standard form of **whitework stitching** (see p. 448), bound with overcast stitching.

Renaissance cutwork
A rather heavy form of cutwork, with not much of the ground cut away.

Reticella cutwork
(An embroidered cutwork which should not be confused with the lace of the same name.)

It is the most open of the many cutwork types. Warp and weft threads of the ground fabric are withdrawn and cut to form a wide trellis, the bars of which are then overcast with needleweaving and the intervening spaces built back up with buttonhole bars worked in quarter-circles or similar geometric shape, either with or without accompanying picots.

Richelieu work
A cutwork with the main foreground motifs held together with narrow blocks across the cut void, named after a 17th-century Venetian lace.

DAISY STITCH

chain stitch tail
detached chain stitch
knotted knot stitch
lazy daisy stitch
loop stitch
picot stitch
tied loop stitch

Individual detached **chain stitches** are worked to form the required pattern.

DARNING STITCH

Darning is a concentrated formation of **tacking stitches**, although one row of tacking stitch can be labelled 'darning stitch'. More specifically, darning stitch refers to a block of tacking stitches (**running stitches** of uneven lengths).

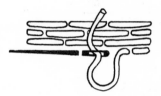

Darning is often used on net embroidery, in which case it is known as **point de reprise.**

Of the many variants of ordinary darning stitch, **double darning stitch** is known as **pessante** (p. 414) and **reversed darning stitch** is also called **phulkari stitch** (p. 415).

Japanese darning stitch, also known as **kogin darning stitch**, has parallel rows of regular running stitches (shaded) connected with diagonal running stitches (white thread).

Pattern darning, known in Greece as **patiti stitch**, refers to the lengths of the running stitches being regulated to form specific patterns.

Surface darning is an ordinary 'stocking darn' utilised for mending and strengthening. Lines of closely laid parallel surface stitches (white thread) are interwoven (shaded thread).

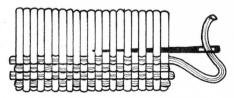

Particular variations of surface darning have their own names, such as **triple laidwork darning filling stitch.**

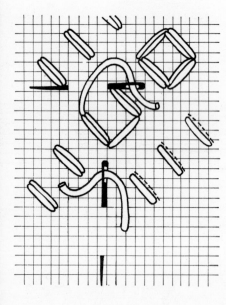

DETACHED SQUARE FILLING STITCH

A pulled thread stitch. Diagonal blocks of straight stitches are joined to produce regular formation of squares.

DIAGONAL STITCH

A canvas-work stitch (closely related to **cashmere stitch** and other diagonal stitching).

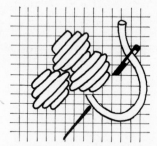

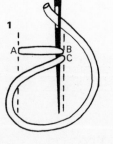

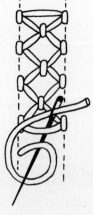

DIAMOND STITCH

An attractive border stitch, worked downwards. After working an initial horizontal bar A to B, the needle emerges at C and forms a knot (figure 1) before re-entering the fabric a little below A. Each time the needle emerges, a knot is worked. And a knot is similarly worked (figure 2) in the middle of each preceding rung (other than the first).

380

Diamond stitch can also be used for filling.

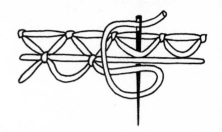

Also known as **diamond filling stitch** is a pulled work stitch of tightly worked back stitches in diamond formation.

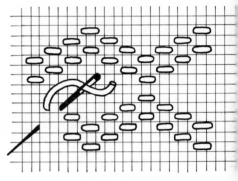

DORSET FEATHER STITCHERY

What is now known and practised around the world as Dorset feather stitchery evolved in that English county in 1954. Dismayed by the paucity of colour and of handicrafts in post-war life, Olive Pass (1890–1973) brought together new designs and traditional stitches found on rural smocks in England and Wales. She was helped in her project by some 80 members of the local Federation of Women's Institutes.

Worked in stranded silk or cotton on a linen or cotton ground, Dorset feather stitchery utilises embroidery stitches such as feather stitch, buttonhole stitch, wheatear stitch and chain stitch, with zigzag couching over applied ric-rac braid. Designs are bordered or grouped, with the Persian *kulka* palmette recurring frequently. It is a particularly effective form of embroidery when worked on a dark ground and utilised as decoration for cushions, bags and aprons.

DOT STITCH
simple knot stitch
Two small **back stitches** worked closely together.

381

DRAWN THREAD WORK

It is said that Cleopatra—when she wore anything at all—had gowns with gossamer-fine drawn threadwork . . . and this particular field of embroidery does, it is true, have a long and varied history.

In the 12th century it was known as *opus tiratum* or *punto tirato* and the best-quality ground fabric was Belgian or Dutch. Until about the 18th century, indeed, the strongest linen was known simply as 'Holland'.

Churches in the north of Sweden have been decorated with drawn thread linen embroidery since the 17th century, while more plebeian work was produced by farm girls while they watched their cows: the girls wove their own ground fabric on a simple birch-bark loom.

Drawn thread work (*fil tiré*) is universal. It is generally a whitework and consists, basically, of warp or weft threads *withdrawn* from the ground prior to embroidery (if these threads are not actually withdrawn but simply pulled back when working, the embroidery is known instead as 'pulled thread work' or 'drawn fabric'). Threads can be withdrawn to the edge of the ground or, alternatively, cut neatly at the extremity of the 'drawn' length to leave the rest of that thread intact.

By withdrawing the required number of threads, a lace-like ground is produced on which subsequent embroidery will give a light and more open appearance. Traditionally drawn thread work is employed on a linen ground of 19 to 34 threads to the inch, worked with linen, cotton or silk thread. It is advisable, when working with a particularly loose-weave ground, not to have too pointed a needle, to avoid splitting individual threads.

Many of the more usual drawn thread stitches are variations of hem stitch. Suitable border stitches include buttonhole stitch, chevron stitch, four-sided stitch, herringbone stitch and stem stitch.

When more than one 'border' of threads is withdrawn in each direction, the resulting trellis ground can be worked with simple or complex filling stitches (including overcast stitch, Greek cross filling stitch and an ordinary weaving filling stitch formed by working the embroidery thread in and out of the trellis ground).

Variants of the basic drawn thread technique include:

Hardanger
Although this is a 'cutwork' embroidery in that threads are cut, the motif is in fact *withdrawn* thread by thread (rather than by

382

shape unrelated to the play of the weave) and it therefore falls into the 'drawn thread' type of embroidery.

Originally Norwegian, from around the Hardanger fjord, Hardanger is now worked the world over. Floss-silk or similarly spreading thread is worked on a ground of even-weave, double thread linen, traditionally of 50 threads to the inch but now often worked with a wider-spaced fabric.

Kløster blocks are worked in satin ('*kløster*') stitch, traditionally in uneven numbers (say 1, 3 or 5 stitches). Then, at right angles to the first block, a similar block is worked (with the first stitch of the second block going into the same hole as the last stitch of the first block) and so on. When the blocks have completed the required totally enclosing perimeter, the ground so formed is cut away, as close to the satin stitching as possible. It is important to cut threads only to the ends—rather than to the sides—of each *kløster* block.

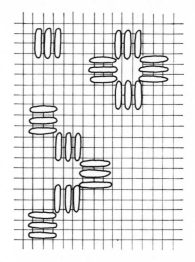

Threads in between *kløster* blocks can be 'withdrawn' and the resultant cutwork can be worked with bars (either with or without picots), with needleweaving or with such filling stitches as spider's web filling stitch and loop stitch filling.

The ground outside the main Hardanger 'motifs' can be worked with any usual straight-worked stitch such as satin stitch.

Hedebo
This type of embroidery originated in Heden, in Denmark.

At the beginning of the 19th century, hedebo was a linen whitework with floral or other motifs outlined in double rows of chain stitch with fillings of drawn thread work. Extra groups of flat satin stitch were (as in Hardanger) often worked outside the main motifs.

Later, *reticella* work was introduced and, eventually, the drawn thread filling was omitted altogether, leaving a resultant cutwork embroidery similar to *broderie anglaise* outlined with needlepoint lace edgings.

Russian drawn ground
This is 'reverse patterning' in that the foreground motif is left with ground unworked while the entire background area is withdrawn to a trellis of, say, two threads withdrawn alternating (both warp and weft) with two threads left. The resultant trellis is then embroidered with diagonal overcasting.

EQUIPMENT AND MATERIALS

Old embroidery equipment and needlework tools are today highly prized as collectors' items (p. 359).

The practical embroiderer will realise that certain forms of embroidery, such as tambour work (p. 44) and metal thread work (p. 405), require specific tools for that trade. But in the main, embroidery equipment and materials include the following items:

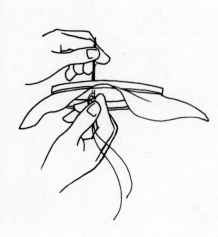

Frames
The great advantage of embroidering with a frame is that the material being worked is kept taut and the tension of stitches is even. Contemporary frames come in various guises: there are wooden or metal circular frames in assorted sizes, and adjustable square or rectangular wooden frames, both kinds with or without table or floor stands.

Apart from canvas work, most conveniently worked on a square frame, small embroideries are generally best executed on the handier circular frames.

To secure fabric on a circular frame: after the fabric is pulled, right side up, taut over the inner hoop of the frame, the outer hoop is put on the other side of the fabric, so that the fabric is pulled tight between the hoops (see below) before the screw is tightened.

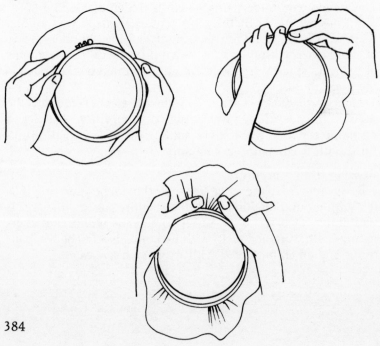

△ *USSR – floral motif from a sophisticated mid-19th-century floral cloth, Russian.*
(Miss Anabel Boone)

▽ *USSR – monogram from one of a set of three numbered Russian pillowcases, cotton on cotton,*
heavily padded satin stitch with deep rose outlines and some superimposed knotting. The set belonged to
Princess Zeneide Warvatszy, born about 1840, in Taganrog, Russia, who came to England before the
Revolution to live with her English friend and companion.
(Miss Anabel Boone)

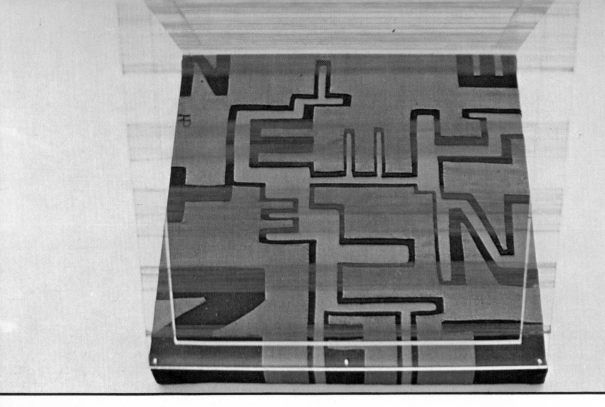

△ APPLIQUE – illustrating the "Cuna Indian technique" from the San Blas Islands of Panama, a unique form of stitching, "Cuna 10" by Herta Puls, 1972. The artist used a top layer of brown cotton cut through black to purple, the edges turned under and slip-stitched. A perspex cover with red and purple threads gives colour variation.
(The artist)

◁ CANVAS WORK – early 18th-century cushion cover, tent and cross stitch polychrome silk on linen canvas, 24×18-20 in. (61×46-51 cm). One of a set of 11 items originally intended as chair coverings, all worked with a gold silk background but to different foreground design.
(The Earl of Wemyss and March, KT)

To secure fabric on an adjustable square or rectangular frame: two opposite edges of the fabric are stitched to the webbing attached to both arms of the frame. The arms are then stretched as far as possible, and the other two edges of the fabric stitched to the two loose pieces of webbing and laced tightly around the other two bars.

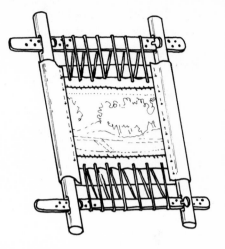

Needles

The most commonly used embroidery needles today are:

Crewel needles—long pointed needles with narrow eyes.

Chenille needles—broad pointed needles with wide eyes.

Tapestry needles—broad needles with blunt ends and wide eyes.

Beading needles—extremely fine and long needles used for sewing on beads, with very narrow eyes.

To thread a needle: The thread is wrapped tightly around the needle (left) and, holding the thread tightly around the needle (centre), the needle is then pulled away and the resulting tight 'bend' pushed through the needle's eye (right).

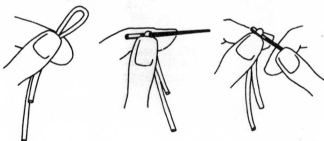

Pins

Deriving their name from the Latin *spina* ('thorn'), rustless dressmaking pins are best.

Scissors

It is advisable to have a small handy pair with short, straight pointed blades, a larger pair for cutting out paper templates and patterns and, possibly, dressmaking scissors for use on the main ground.

Seam-ripper

All embroiderers make mistakes from time to time, and a dressmaker's handy seam-ripper facilitates removal of wrong stitches.

Stiletto

A sharp pointed skewer, traditionally used for making holes in the ground fabric for cutwork and some other forms of embroidery, comes in useful on many occasions.

EQUIPMENT—*embroidery*
scissors, 18th and 19th centuries,
from Iran and the Middle East.
(Author's collection)

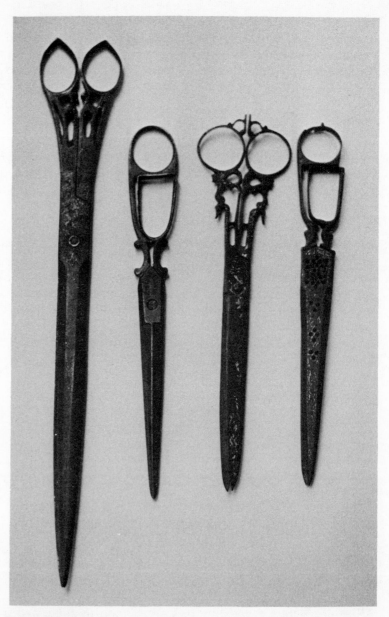

Tape measure

Thimbles

Many embroiderers today work without a thimble, or finger
protector, but, as in the past, thimbles are a recommended
ingredient of any well-stocked needlework box. Thimbles on
the regular market today are of metal or plastic.

Additional items that may be required include pencils and paper for initial drawings—ink, ballpoint or fibre-tipped pens should never be brought near embroidery—and tailor's chalk for transferring designs. Magnifying mirrors are also useful.

Then, with essential equipment thus to hand, what about materials with which to work?

Embroidery thread

Experienced embroiderers today utilise plastic yarn, lacing, ribbon, wire coils and sundry other exotica in their search for unusual embroidery yarn. Probationary embroidery enthusiasts, however, will probably restrict their talents to working initially with threads of silk, cotton or wool, depending on the ground fabric used. Metal thread embroidery requires special yarn (p. 405).

Embroidery ground fabrics

Amongst the suitable fabrics for embroidery grounds (the materials on which embroideries are worked) are cotton, linen, wool and silk. Canvas, a derivative of all four natural fibres, has given its name to a distinct form of embroidery (p. 340).

Linen is made from flax and has an agreeably uneven weave (though it can be even too). It is particularly amenable as ground fabric to such forms of embroidery as pulled thread and drawn thread work. Cotton is more evenly woven but can, similarly, be used for counted thread embroideries. Wool has a rough feel, can be used for counted thread embroideries but can, also, be utilised in the form of matted felt.

Sericulture (silkworm farming) as we know it today began in China about 1725 BC. Although caterpillars were being reared on diets of pine, oak and ash in Europe and Asia (Gibbon's *Decline and Fall of the Roman Empire*, chapter 40) the production of silkworm caterpillars fed on a diet of leaves of the white-mulberry tree was exclusively a Chinese art until the reign of the Emperor Justinian, who ruled AD 527–65. He established a silkworm farm at Constantinople which was to remain closely guarded for 500 years. Further evidence of the mystique attached to the production of silk is provided by the fact that members of mediaeval Florentine silk guilds had to sign pledges of secrecy before being allowed outside their city.

Silk is an animal fibre, with properties of warmth and elasticity similar to those of wool. Because it has no sulphur in its chemical structure, silk is less liable than wool to attack by moths. Production of 'artificial silks' has today been superseded by independent man-made fibres: real silk has always been a

387

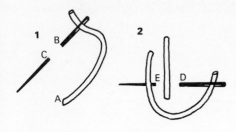

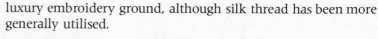

luxury embroidery ground, although silk thread has been more generally utilised.

ERMINE STITCH

The name might derive from the fact that, when worked in black on a white ground, this elongated stitch looks like an ermine's tail. A good filling stitch.

ESKIMO LACING EDGE

After the raw edge of the fabric is turned under and doubled back, as for any **hemming stitch** (p. 393), **running stitch** holds the turning down. Another thread is then laced through two stitches on the wrong side of the fabric (figure 1) and over through two stitches on the right side of the fabric (figure 2), and so on.

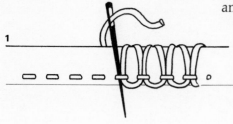

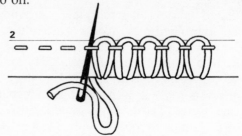

EYE STITCHES and EYELETS

This is a comprehensive term covering **star eyelets, eyelet holes** as found in **broderie anglaise** and any worked hole with stitches radiating from a central hub. Stitches can be worked singly or double. A single eight-pointed star is known as **Algerian eye stitch** or the German **distelfink**. A symmetrical star with any number of points is called **bump stitch**.

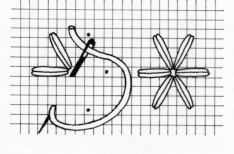

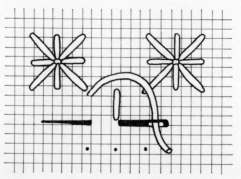

388

FAGGOT STITCH

diagonal line stitch
diagonal square stitch

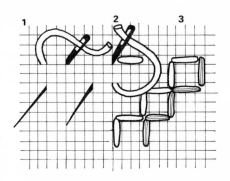

A simple pulled thread work step stitch. Each diagonal line of stitching is worked alternately horizontal (figure 1) and vertical (figure 2). The next line of stitching follows accordingly (figure 3).

Faggot stitch can be used as a filling stitch (although **sheaf stitch** is also known as **faggot filling stitch**, p. 434). When each stage of faggot stitch is worked double, with the needle working through the same holes twice over, it is known as **double faggot stitch**, which can similarly be used as a filling stitch.

The term **faggoting** is also used for **twisted insertion stitch** (p. 391).

FEATHER STITCH

single coral stitch

A zigzag stitch, looking rather like **Cretan stitch** but with more pronounced extremities. It is worked similarly to **buttonhole stitch**, alternately up and down. The stitch is versatile and has been incorporated into modern folk embroideries such as **Dorset feather stitchery** (see p. 381). (During the Middle Ages feather stitch was known as **opus plumarium**.)

Chained feather stitch, also known as **feathered chain stitch**, is deceptively simple: practice and concentration are required to achieve an even band. Working between parallel lines, a **chain stitch** from A is tied down B to C, the next chain from D is tied down from C to E, the next chain from F tied down E to G, the next chain from H tied down G to I, and the needle is just working the chain from J to be tied down I to K.

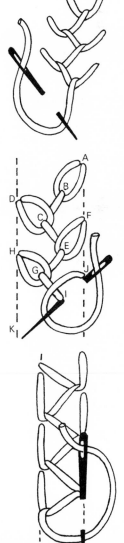

Closed feather stitch is worked with the needle entering the fabric close to the previous stitch, always working the **feather stitch** between two parallel lines.

389

FERN STITCH

Three equal-length **straight stitches** are worked radiating from the same point A in the order A to B, A to C, A to D and so on.

FISHBONE STITCH

An overlapping filling stitch worked alternately to one side and then the other. It can be worked close together (left) or opened up (right).

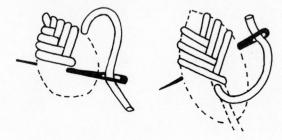

FLAT STITCH

Suitable for shapes that can be divided as in diagram. Working alternately from one side to the other, the needle always works straight across the shape to be filled, emerging at the other side.

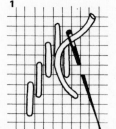

FLORENTINE STITCH

cushion stitch
flame stitch
Irish stitch

The basic counted thread stitch that gives its name to **Florentine work** and all the patterns (such as **Bargello**) that come under that label. **Satin stitches** are worked in an arranged pattern (figure 1) with each subsequent row of stitching following the line of that above (figure 2).

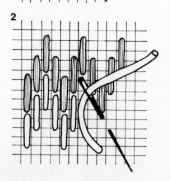

FLORENTINE WORK

Florentine work is also variously known as **Bargello**, after designs in the Bargello Palace in Florence, **Hungarian point, punto d'Ungharia, punto Rinascente** or **Florentine stitch embroidery**. And, indeed, **Florentine stitch** (figure 1) is in fact a general embroidery term of vertical satin stitches worked in flowing curves.

Florentine work as such, however, was originally practised,

390

with many different designs of stitching, in mediaeval Florence (p. 160). Renaissance artists worked on a very fine canvas with a gauge of up to 40 holes to the inch, but today a much more open canvas is used. Silk or wool thread is worked in vertical stitches to a carefully planned repeating pattern.

See also colour plate facing p. 417.

FLY STITCH

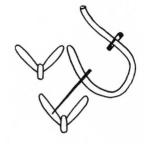

Like **chain stitch**, but more open, this is basically a loop held in place by a small tying-down stitch. It may be worked in rows or completely detached.

FOUR-SIDED STITCH

openwork stitch
square stitch
Either a border or a filling stitch.

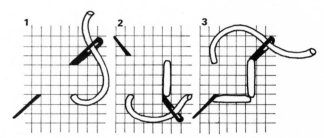

FRENCH KNOT

French dot

The needle is brought out at A, the thread twisted round the needle and coaxed gently down the needle as it enters the fabric again at A (right), to come up a short distance away for the next knot.

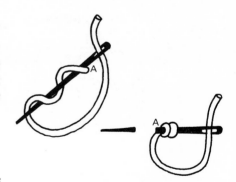

FRENCH STITCH

A complicated canvas-work stitch. The motion of figure 1 is reversed (figure 2) before going on to the next 'block'.

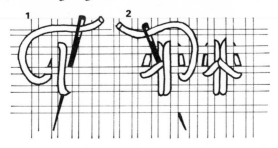

391

GOBELIN STITCH

An oblique canvas-work stitch, sometimes known, incorrectly, as **gros point**. Each stitch is formed diagonally over more horizontal than vertical threads (as opposed to **tent stitch**, which is equally diagonal).

If gobelin stitch is worked particularly closely, with stitches overlapping at either end, it is known as **encroaching gobelin stitch.**

GREEK STITCH

A stitch with the same frontal appearance as **long-legged cross stitch** (p. 372), it is in fact worked as **herringbone** so that all stitches on the reverse side are horizontal (unlike long-legged cross stitch which shows all vertical stitches on the reverse side). A canvas-work stitch, it can be used for filling.

Greek cross filling stitch (or **Greek four-sided stitch**), on the other hand, is a pulled work **loop stitch** (p. 404) filling.

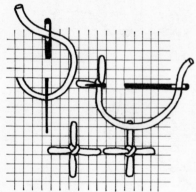

GUILLOCHE STITCH

Named after the architectural ornament of interlaced waved bands, this composite stitch should be worked in the following order:

1. Two parallel rows of **stem stitch**.
2. Blocks of 3 short **satin stitches**.
3. First **interlaced band** through the satin-stitch blocks.

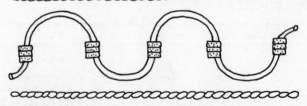

4. Second **interlaced band** through satin-stitch blocks (overleaf).
5. **French knots** in the middle of each arch (overleaf).

The interlaced bands should not be pulled tight—they should form even loops.

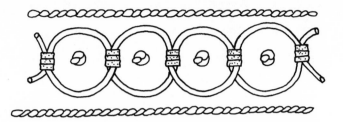

HEM STITCH

Hemming is the means of finishing the edges of fabric. Raw edges are generally turned under and then doubled back, to form a neat surround. The surround can be held down with a variety of embroidery stitches or a basic hem stitch similar to that employed in dressmaking. (See also **Eskimo lacing edge**, p. 388.) Drawn thread embroidery, on the other hand, has its own embroidery hem stitch.

After drawing the required number of threads around the border of the whole work, an equal distance from each edge, the raw edges of fabric are turned under and brought up to the planned line of stitching, the corners are **mitred** (p. 408) and the whole hem held with **tacking stitch** (p. 441). Hem stitch is then worked around the drawn border through both layers of fabric.

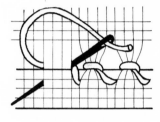

Sometimes each block is bound twice and this can be called **point de Paris** (not to be confused with the needle lace of that name).

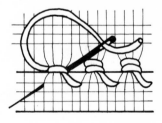

Antique hem stitch is worked from the reverse of the fabric (figure 1) and, unlike ordinary drawn thread hem stitch, needle entry A to B passes between the layers of fabric. It produces a very neat appearance on the right side of fabric (figure 2).

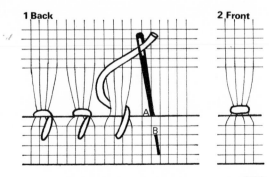

393

Double hem stitch is also known as **double-rowed open-work stitch**, **Italian hem stitch** or **Romanian hem stitch**.

A drawn work stitch that makes a strong border pattern. After drawing threads above and below the line to be worked, the stitch is embroidered alternately through the top (figure 1) and bottom (figure 2) of the border. (Note: this stitch does not itself hold any hem in place.)

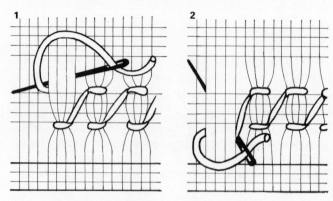

Interlaced hem stitch is when two rows of hem stitch, known as ladder stitch, have been executed either side of withdrawn threads. The exposed cross threads are then crossed and laced as in the diagrams.

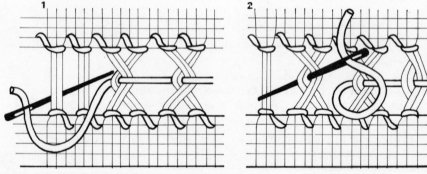

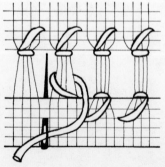

Ladder hem stitch, or **ladder stitch**, consists of two rows of ordinary hem stitch worked either side of withdrawn threads, producing bundles of exposed threads as 'ladder rungs'. (The more usual **ladder stitch**, however, is that illustrated on p. 401.)

Incorrectly falling into the hem-stitch category is **'sham' hem stitch**, a decorative covering stitch used to camouflage seams on fine clothing. **Zigzag stitch** is interlaced as in the diagram.

HERRINGBONE STITCH

Indian filling
mossoul stitch
Russian cross stitch
Russian stitch

Alternately taking up threads from top and bottom of the row of stitching, the sizing and shaping of the 'trellis' effect of this stitch is altered by proportions of height and width of each stitch.

Double herringbone stitch (figure 2) looks particularly attractive when worked with two colours of thread.

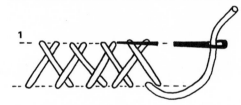 

HOLBEIN STITCH

double running stitch
line stitch
square stitch
stroke stitch
two-sided stitch
two-sided stroke stitch

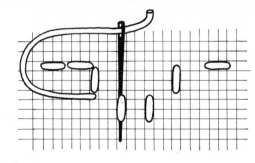

After a row of evenly spaced **running stitches** have been worked from right to left (with the gaps the same distance as the stitches), a second row of running stitch is worked left to right filling in those gaps. (In 1527 a German, Quentel, called the stitch **Spanish stitch**—p. 436.)

395

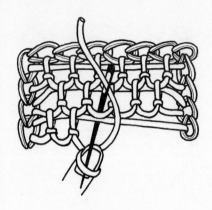

HOLLIE STITCH

holy stitch
holy point stitch
nun's work

A traditional needlepoint stitching, associated with a community at Little Gidding in Huntingdonshire founded by Nicholas Ferrar. The Community, often called 'The Nuns of Little Gidding', was also termed 'The Arminian Nunnery' by Puritans who sacked it during the Civil War.

Hollie stitch consists of an outer frame of **chain stitch** worked on the ground fabric. This is then surface-worked with horizontal bars, laced and knotted. Apart from the original chain stitches, the thread never enters the ground fabric.

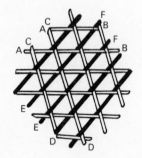

HONEYCOMB STITCH

A filling stitch, with three lines of parallel laid threads. All horizontals (A to B) should be worked first, then diagonals C to D, then diagonals E to F, passing these last rows under horizontal lines and over diagonals C to D (E to F in dark thread, to show interlacing).

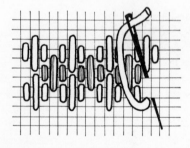

HUNGARIAN STITCH

A canvas-work stitch that produces diapering (when worked diagonally it is known as **mosaic stitch**).

INSERTION STITCHES

Insertion stitches are communicative stitches linking two pieces of fabric. The most common **insertion stitch** consists of alternating blocks of buttonhole stitch worked to one edge and then to the other.

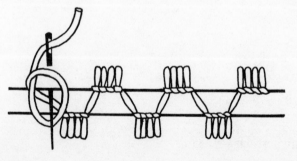

What is known as **knotted insertion stitch** is a **scroll stitch** worked alternately from one piece of fabric to the other.

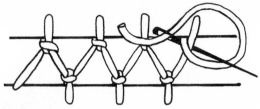

Laced insertion stitch—braid edging stitch is first worked independently along both edges to be joined. The lines of stitching are then laced.

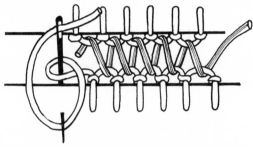

Twisted insertion stitch, also called **faggoting**, is worked as shown, with the needle twisted under and over the thread before re-entering the fabric.

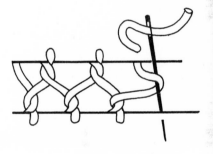

One-sided insertion stitch—this is a misnomer, since this is not an insertion stitch but an ordinary surface stitch. A basic **cross stitch** (figure 1) is extended alternately above (figure 2) and below (figures 3 and 4) to give a final zigzag effect (figure 5).

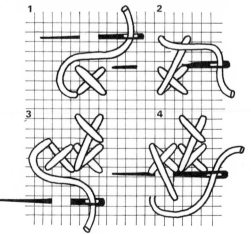

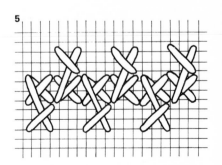

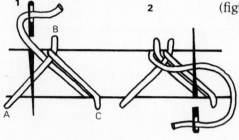

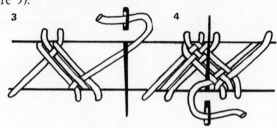

Plaited insertion stitch is complicated, and is best worked when the two edges to be connected are tacked down on to backing paper to give a firm spacing. Each zigzag is plaited as many times as required before progressing to the next point (figure 5).

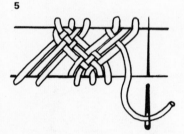

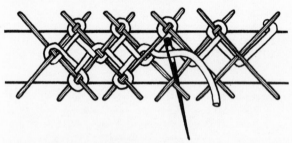

INTERLACING

On a basic foundation of double **herringbone stitch** (shaded), another thread is laced to required pattern, not entering the ground fabric but simply working on the foundation herringbone. This is a simple interlacing known as **laced herringbone stitch** or **German interlacing**.

Another form of interlacing is that known alternatively as **double Pekinese stitch** or **laced Cretan stitch**.

Two interspaced parallel lines of **running stitch** or **back stitch** (figure 1) are laced, starting as in figure 2, slipping the needle under the straight threads and not through the fabric, to give a good border band (figure 3).

JACQUARD STITCH

A canvas-work stitch.

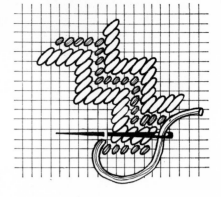

JAPANESE STITCH

Closely worked satin stitch, itself horizontal, is placed in a diagonal arrangement.

KNITTING STITCH

tapestry stitch

A canvas-work stitch that gives a close overall finished effect of knitting. It is suitable for double-mesh canvas, and a complete row is worked in two journeys, up and then down.

KNOT STITCHES

Some knotted and knot-like stitches have evident origins with names like **French knot** (p. 391), **Basque stitch** (p. 329), **Chinese knot** (p. 354), **Smyrna cross** and **Smyrna stitch** (p. 372). The provenance of other knotted stitches, such as **bullion knot** (p. 336), is less definite. The **Gordian knot** (p. 335) takes its name from the capital of Phrygia, 30 miles west of Ankara. Alexander the Great is reputed to have slashed through an 'impossible' knot there.

LACE

Lace is a facet of the textile arts that is closely related to embroidery but, in the main part, remains a separate entity.

The core of lace-making—a field which includes also crochet, knitting, tatting, macramé and knotting—is formed of **needle-made lace** (known as **lacis** or **needlepoint**), **machine-made lace** and **bobbin lace** (known also as **pillow lace**). Of these three categories, the only truly embroidered lace is the first, the needle-lace or needlepoint, (not to be confused with the modern terminology of 'needlepoint' for canvas work).

The confusion of lace identities is further compounded by various national labellings. The English word 'lace' comes from the Latin *laqueus* (a 'noose' or 'snare'). The French employ the general term *dentelle*, the Germans use *Spitzen*, the Dutch *kanten*, the Spaniards *encaje*, the Portuguese *renda*, the Belgians *peerlen* and the Italians *merletto* or *trina* (in Genoa it is *pizzo*).

Universal titling is, however, generally accorded various types of needle-lace, which are referred to either by the French *point de* or the Italian *punto* prefixes (both mean 'a needle stitch of . . .', although the terms are misapplied to two bobbin-laces, *point de Paris* and *point d'Angleterre*).

Needle-made lace evolved from Italian cutwork (p. 378), and the first genuine lace, in so far as it did not stem from a ground fabric, was *punto in aria* ('stitches in the air'), a term first used in Federico de Vinciolo's book *New and Singular Patterns and Workes of Linnen* (1587), p. 162). Needle-made lace is, throughout its main span of production, from the latter half of the 16th century to the beginning of the 19th closely associated with net embroidery (p. 411).

Some forms of needlepoint lace are:

Point de Venise
This needle-lace was particularly popular in the 17th century for cravats and other delicate accessories. It is a closely worked lace, with raised padding and intricate fillings, and designs, usually floral, are joined by bars with complicated decoration. Some forms of **point de Venise** are:

Plat point de Venise—a flat form of the lace.

Point de Venise à rose—with a rose motif in the design.

Point de Venise à réseau—the most delicate of all.

Point de France
Lace-making had been introduced to France by M. Colbert, a minister of Louis XIV. The king himself, in 1665, founded several centres for production of the art. The French needle-lace, similar to **point de Venise** but with less weight, is found particularly on church embroideries, and some forms of the work are:

Point de Sedan, point d'Argentan, point d'Alençon—from the respective cities, the last two forms having a particularly delicate mesh and floral sprig design.

Point de Bruxelles (Brussels lace) was similar to **point d'Alençon**, with floral motifs.

Hollie point (or Holy point)
British needle-lace was traditionally referred to as English. It was usually finely worked and incorporated for insertion and

400

seaming purposes, sometimes for christening and wedding robes (hence its name). The background of this form of lace is worked in **hollie stitch** (p. 396).

General needle-lace terminology includes:

Bars—connecting bridges between motifs.

Cordonnet—thick thread outlining design motifs.

Guipure—open lace with clear design.

Mesh—the background fabric, of twisted threads or net.

Toile—main foreground motifs.

The subject is so complex, however, that readers can only be advised to study the excellent specialist books in existence.

LADDER STITCH

step stitch

Working over a horizontal bar of any required length, a small binding stitch C to D is worked before taking the needle to the other side of the ladder (figure 1). Without re-entering the fabric, the needle binds this end of the ladder E (figure 2) and swings over to the first (right hand) side to pass under the first stitch through the gaps BD and AC (figure 3) and so on. (**Open chain stitch**, p. 351, is also called **ladder stitch.**

LAIDWORK

Over a marked shape (figure 1), **satin stitches** are worked close together (figures 2 and 3). **Couching** (p. 369) is then superimposed (this is called **laid and couched work**).

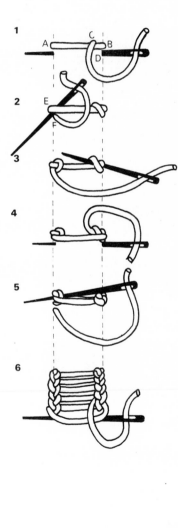

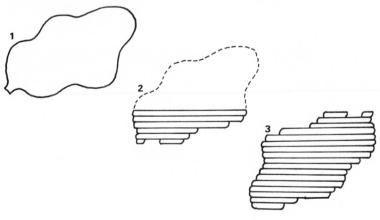

401

LATTICE STITCHES

Synonymous with **trellis stitches** (p. 444), although some forms do specifically adhere to lattice labelling. One example is **raised lattice-work band stitching.**

A first set of horizontal laid stitches is worked close together (with subsequent further horizontal laid stitches in the centre of this 'band' to give extra height). Vertical **satin stitches** (dark thread) cover the first horizontal stitches. **Herringbone stitch** then seals the whole (this too can be laced for an even further complicated band).

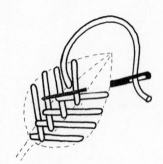

LEAF STITCH

A diagonal filling stitch worked alternately from one side to the other, along a central track; usually with an outline of **chain** or **satin stitch** superimposed around the edge.

LETTERING—
hand-embroidered wall-hanging, 9 ft. 6 in. × 7 ft. 6 in. (2·90 × 2·28 m), by Audrey Walker, 1973. The work was commissioned by the City of Bath as a permanent memorial to their 'Monarchy 1000' celebrations, and it hangs in the Pump Room. The artist worked chiffons, silks, furnishing fabrics, lace, wools, gold kid and gold threads on a ground of fine cotton canvas. The lettering of the names of Kings and Queens of England well illustrates maximum utilisation of available space.
(The Corporation of Bath)

402

LETTERING

Alphabetical lettering appears frequently in many fields of embroidery. Until the end of the 18th century the letters 'J', 'U' and 'Z' were often left out of samplers (p. 426), and 'Q' has sometimes been worked as a reversed 'P'. Embroidered lettering in the form of monogram initials was particularly popular during the 19th century. Alphabets for embroidery, either in sampler, in monogram or in other forms of the art, have been offered in such works as John Brightland's *Grammar of the English Tonge* (1711) and the Butterick Publishing Co.'s *Artistic Alphabets for Marking and Engrossing* (1893).

A modern artist working with letters today can make full use of photographic and business innovations to facilitate transfer of a word to a fabric ground. The transposition, too, must be adapted to the embroidery medium: a painted or written letter has a different look and texture from an embroidered letter, which tends generally to be more angular and stark in outline than the flowing line of a calligrapher's letter.

LINK POWDERING FILLING STITCH
detached daisy stitch

Single chains, open at the top, make an effective filling stitch.

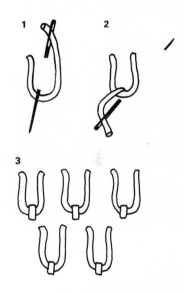

LONG AND SHORT STITCH
embroidery stitch
'feather' stitch
plumage stitch
shading stitch

A satin stitch, with the first (light) row of stitching of alternating long and short stitches (hence the name). This first row shapes the subsequent work. The rest of the motif is worked with stitches of the same size—except where variation is needed for filling spaces.

Traditionally worked for rounded motifs, it can be worked from a horizontal start (in which case it is known as **tapestry shading**).

403

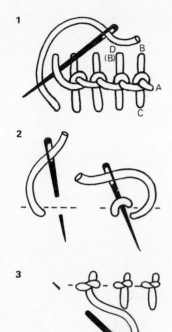

LOOP STITCH

Starting with A to B, the needle re-emerges at C and passes over and round to the right and under the first thread, to be gently pulled into shape before it enters the fabric at D and so on (figure 1). Detached 'loops' worked in exactly the same way, with one leg longer than the others, are known as '**sword edging**' stitches (figures 2 and 3). (**Daisy stitch**, p. 379, is also sometimes referred to as loop stitch.)

MACHINE EMBROIDERY

Although it can be suggested that **tambour work** (p. 441) is mechanical, **machine embroidery** as such originated in 1828 with the invention of the first practical embroidery machine by a French cotton manufacturer (p. 102). His machine had 130 double-ended needles, all of which had to be individually threaded! Today, however, machine embroidery involves much less complexity. Industrial machine embroidery is worked on a one-thread 'Cornely' machine which produces continuous tamboured chain stitch, or on a two-thread sewing machine such as the 'Irish Singer'.

Many ordinary domestic sewing machines have built-in facilities to produce programmed satin, zigzag and other stitches in varieties of patterns. Machine embroidery as an art form, however, is worked with basic machine stitching and zigzag stitch. The machine's needle foot is removed and darning plate fixed in position according to the manual of that particular machine, stitch tension is disconnected, again according to the makers' instructions, and the fabric to be embroidered is stretched tightly on a small hand-held frame.

Machine embroidery is generally worked from the rear. Threads to show on the right side of the finished work are therefore wound on to the underneath bobbin ('spool' or 'shuttle'), with thicker threads such as Lurex and wool wound on by hand. Metal threads should never be threaded through the upper part of the machine as they will not pass freely through the needle's eye.

MALTESE CROSS STITCH

Over a basic interlaced honeycomb, the Maltese cross (dark thread) is superimposed. It can also be worked over any basic interlaced filling.

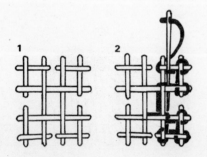

MALTESE FILLING STITCH

This is a pulled work stitch, with **satin stitches** worked over two threads and pulled tight. Work the outer border first—and progress inwards to a **mosaic filling.** (A further outer border of pulled stitches can be worked.)

METAL THREAD WORK

Metal threads have long been used to embellish ceremonial and other highly decorated embroideries. In some cases, alas,

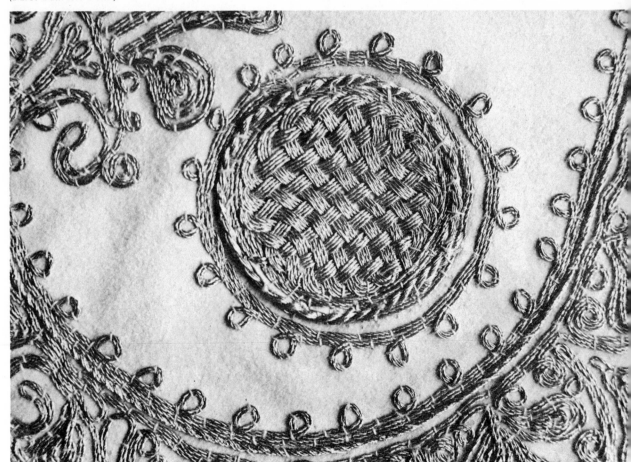

METAL THREAD WORK—*gold thread couched and surface woven on white felt, 1909.*
(Mrs. Marion Felix)

METAL THREAD WORK—*18th-century European gold purl worked into a flower posy, signed 'BB' and dated 1728. (American Museum in Britain, Perley room, no. 63.190. Photo: Derek Walmer)*

406

many of the metals used have been precious and metallic embroidery has been rifled or looted.

The most frequently used metals have been gold, silver-gilt, silver, copper, pewter, aluminium and tin (p. 97). Today Lurex offers less costly alternatives to some of the natural metals. Japanese gold ('Jap gold') is one of the most beautiful metal embroidery threads since it does not tarnish and it has a beautiful sheen: it is made from narrow strips of water-thin sheets of pure gold coiled around a central core of bright yellow floss silk.

'Purl threads' (called 'bullion' in the United States) are tightly coiled metal threads, usually cut with a small pair of scissors into lengths of about $\frac{1}{2}$ in. (1·5 cm) and threaded, as beads, on to the ground, with the needle entering the fabric in the same hole from which it emerged, a process which gives an appearance similar to that of a bullion knot. Purl is available in various types:

Rough purl—also known as *matte purl*—with a dull satin sheen.
Smooth purl—also known as *glissant*—a very shiny finish.
Check purl—also known as *frisé*—a chequered, sparkling finish.
Pearl purl—also known as *wire purl* or *badge purl*—the cord used, for example, on blazer badge motifs.

Embroidery with metal thread necessitates the use of a frame to keep the ground fabric taut, and, ideally, the artist should wear a thimble on the third finger of each hand. Straight nail scissors are ideal for cutting through metal thread, and tweezers are useful as it is essential to touch the threads, some of which tarnish easily, as little as possible. Crewel needles and a beading needle are required.

It is difficult to manipulate many metal embroidery threads, and they are therefore often couched. Ends of the metal are pulled through the ground fabric with a pincer movement (a loop of pulling thread is put through from the back of the fabric, the loop is slipped over the metal thread and then pulled quickly through to the back, taking the metal thread with it).

Metal thread work can be combined with beadwork and jewels and other addenda. It can also be machine-embroidered (p. 404).

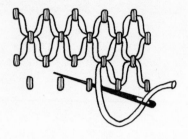

MEXICAN STITCH

cloud filling stitch

Small parallel **running stitches** (shaded), evenly interspaced, are inter-threaded. The white thread only enters the ground fabric at the end of each row.

MITRING CORNERS

Drawn thread, pulled thread and other embroideries with hemmed edges traditionally have mitred corners, which are worked before the hems are turned under.

Fold corner A in towards pulled threads. Turn in small raw edge B on both sides. Cut away corner turn-in as shown in figure 2 at C. Fold the remaining neatened hems (figure 3) and tack down neatly. The hems can be caught by hem-stitching or pulled thread stitches.

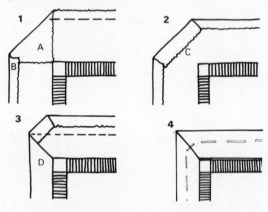

MOSAIC FILLING STITCH

Four blocks of **satin stitch** are worked on each face to form a square (figure 1), the centre of which is then bound (figure 2) and crossed (figure 3).

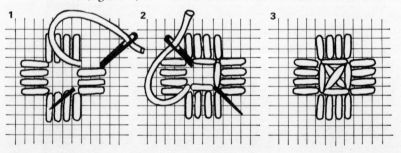

408

MOUNTMELLICK STITCH

A heavy whitework stitch which originated in Mountmellick, in Ireland, in the 1830's. It looks particularly effective worked in cotton yarn on a medium-weave ground.

The stitch is worked from top of row to bottom: always take needle entry E in over the bottom curve of the stitch above to give the overall chained effect.

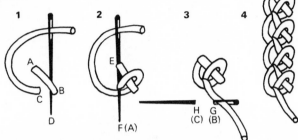

MOUNTING

How to mount a finished embroidery can be one of the most difficult questions facing any enthusiast. Professional services offered by upholsterers, art needlework shops, picture framers and similar experts can take time and money.

Old embroideries should, if only to help prevent deterioration (p. 363), certainly receive attention—be it in the form of mounting behind glass or simply careful storage in a dark drawer. There are various schools of thought on how best to show old work. Any fragile material on regular display should be protected behind glass, even though the usual reflecting variety does often considerably mar vitality. Non-reflecting glass is less widely available and also obscures the colouring. Embroideries that are exposed to the air show best but are more vulnerable, not only to natural elements but also to prying fingers (although some embroiderers today encourage such 'audience participation').

The mounting and making up of a finished embroidery can make or mar the overall effect of the work and it is, therefore, generally well worth while to have expert help with this part of the operation.

Most embroideries not worked on a frame distort during execution. Although metal thread work and any embroidery containing colouring that is not truly fast should not be damped at all, it is generally possible to block and shape most finished works (p. 408) before handing the baton over to the professional.

Mounting upholstered canvas work is an extremely difficult

MOUNTING—*chair back with canvas-work panel mounted in velvet. The panel was designed by Mrs. Harry Powell Wilson Jr. of Denver, Colorado, and worked by Mrs. George M. Wilfley in diagonal tent stitch on a single mesh canvas of 14 threads to the inch.*
(Mrs. Harry Powell Wilson Jr.)

410

task: there are specialised guidebooks but, for a chair or similar item, it is generally not worth ruining the effect of many months' hard work with the final 'mounting'. Equally, canvas-work cushions, bell pulls and fire screens usually benefit from the professional's expertise.

With the use of mitre boards and set squares to facilitate exact cornering, it is, however, quite easy to mount square or rectangular embroideries in conventional wooden framing. In the United States, in particular, a wide variety of 'instant framing' is available: embroidery can look extremely good when mounted in aluminium or plastic. An example of such a surprisingly successful marriage of media is a fragment of Coptic textile and two squares of Perspex (Plexiglass), the sandwich held together with stainless steel studs.

Many collectors show flat embroideries vertically on their walls and, indeed, some of the most spectacular contemporary embroideries are utilised as 'wall-hangings', a term which implies any embroidery, framed or not, that hangs vertically. For a hanging 'banner' a horizontal rod is a simple mount and practical, too, as the embroidery is easily transportable.

NEEDLEWEAVING
woven hem stitch
openwork insertion stitch
Persian openwork

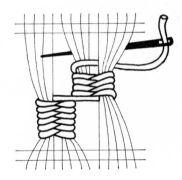

Draw any number of threads and weave the remaining vertical threads as in the diagram to produce solid blocks of weaving (an even number of stitches to each block). A thick embroidery thread on fairly heavy fabric gives the best effect. Complicated patterns and wide borders can be worked in this way.

NET EMBROIDERY
Embroidery on a net ground requires careful manipulation. Thread ends must be held invisibly (by darning or backstitch-ing) as the overall effect of net embroidery relies to a consider-able extent on meticulous craftsmanship.

Net can be used as a ground for appliqué, but there are two main kinds of 'net embroidery' as such:

Lacis (or filet darning)
This is embroidery on a square-mesh net, traditionally cream or white and originally handmade and knotted at each junction.

411

Today, on commercial net (handmade net is practically unobtainable), the main stitches used are a simple darning stitch or a double darning stitch, a looped stitch and web stitch.

Hexagonal net darning

This embroidery traditionally has a motif outlined in a thicker thread before being worked with a filling stitch such as back stitch, chequer stitch, cross stitch, running stitch, eyelet stitch, satin stitch, stem stitch or trellis stitch. Transposing the required motif outline is particularly tricky: one of the best ways of achieving exact shaping is to tack the net over a paper pattern and work to the design thereunder, after which the paper template is torn away.

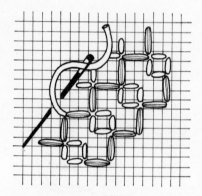

NET FILLING STITCH

A pulled work stitch, with rows of **step stitch** (shaded) alternating with rows of small V-shaped **straight stitches**.

OR NUÉ

Battu en or
Burgundian technique
En or battu
Lazar stitch

A technique worked particularly in Belgium, France and the Netherlands during the Middle Ages. The design is first drawn on backing canvas (figure 1). Gold threads are then laid horizontally, one by one (figure 2) right across the width and couched where the design underneath so necessitates (figure 3). As the complete motif in figure 4 shows, curves tend to be squared off when worked with *or nué*.

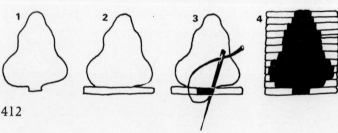

412

PALESTRINA STITCH

double knot stitch
Old English knot stitch
Smyrna stitch
tied coral stitch

Working along a planned line, the needle enters A to B either side of it (figure 1) and makes a small overcast stitch C without entering the fabric (figure 2), then over the stitch again (D), to the right of C (figure 3), before being pulled tightly to form a knot. The knots should be spaced evenly for best effect (figure 4).

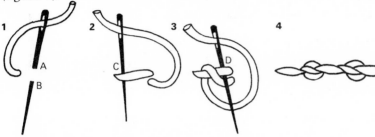

PARISIAN STITCH

A canvas-work stitch with rows of vertical 2-thread and 4-thread stitches alternating with rows of 4-thread and 2-thread stitches. Parisian stitch can also be worked over 1 and 3 threads.

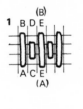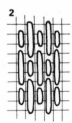

PATCHWORK

Patchwork, also known as **pieced work**, the art of stitching shaped pieces of fabric together to produce a pattern ground or motif, enters the domain of embroidery in that in some forms of patchwork the joining stitches between individual 'pieces', or patches, are hidden under covering embroidery stitches. Patchwork, alternatively, can be incorporated with quilting or other fields of stitchery.

It is thought that patchwork originated in the East about 3,000 years ago, and one of the earliest examples is a leather canopy, *c.* 980 BC, in a collection in Cairo. In Sir Aurel Stein's archaeological surveys at the Caves of the Thousand Buddhas in Serindia, North India, he discovered fragments of patchwork curtains and hangings believed to be from the same period.

Patches are worked on templates, in geometric shapes such as squares, hexagons, diamonds and shell shapes known as

413

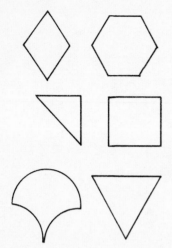

'clamshells'. Fabric is tacked lightly to a paper template drawn from an original template of wood or metal (figure 1) available from most needlework suppliers, and one side of the shape is then sewn, with over-stitching from the wrong side, to a neighbouring piece (figure 2). Only when all sides of a shape are joined to another piece should the paper template be removed.

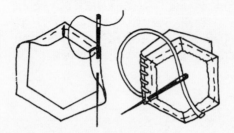

PEARL STITCH

A tight knotted stitch (which, if not worked close, would produce scroll stitch). When it is worked very tightly a bumpy, pearl-like thread is obtained.

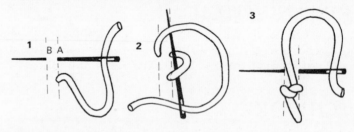

PESSANTE

cloth stitch
double darning stitch
toile stitch

Each horizontal line is worked with two rows of darning stitch (shown here, for clarification, with dotted and plain thread) before proceeding to the next line.

414

PETAL STITCH

A row of **daisy stitches** with bordering **satin stitch** is worked in one operation (figures 1, 2, 3).

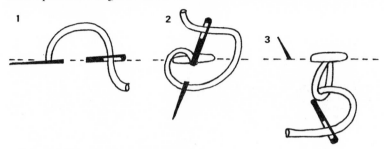

PHULKARI STITCH

reversed darning stitch

An Indian stitch found particularly in the Punjab. A darning stitch is worked from the wrong side of the fabric (figure 1) over counted threads, only one thread being taken up at each entry of the needle, thus forming a long stitch on the right side of the fabric (figure 2).

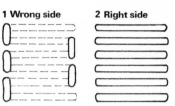

PICOT STITCHING

Although **daisy stitch** is sometimes known as **picot stitch**, a picot is a small 'addition': ordinary buttonhole edging with occasional bullion knot addenda becomes **picot with bullion** and so on. Sometimes the picot is formed without knot but with a loop, made by working the stitch around an ordinary household pin. **Buttonhole picot**, for instance, has a loop formed after a required number of ordinary **buttonhole stitches**, the household pin acting as stay (figure 1). The picot loop is held down with a knot (figure 2) and buttonholed around (figure 3) to give the finished picot in figure 1. Sometimes, too, the picot loop is not further worked, in which case it is generally known simply as **pinned picot loop** (figure 4).

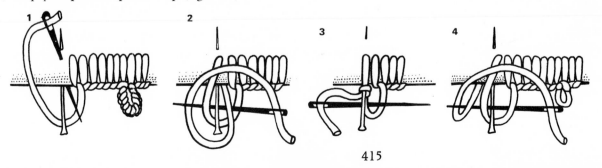

415

PIN STITCH

A drawn work hemming stitch similar to ordinary **hem stitch** with an added binding.

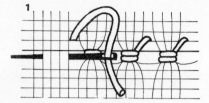

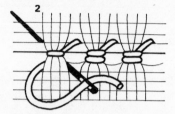

PLAID FILLING STITCH

A surface trellis of laid stitches (shaded) is worked through the ground fabric in different coloured threads to give resultant tartan effect.

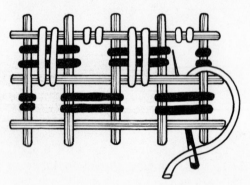

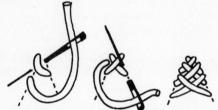

POINT DE VANNERIE

A plaited filling stitch, not dissimilar to **leaf stitch**.

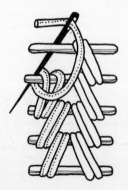

PORTUGUESE BORDER STITCH

Over evenly spaced parallel horizontal bars, interlacing is worked from top to bottom, beginning with the first two bottom right-hand rungs, then progressing upwards taking two bindings at a time. When all the right-hand rungs are worked, start with the bottom left-hand rungs and again progress upwards.

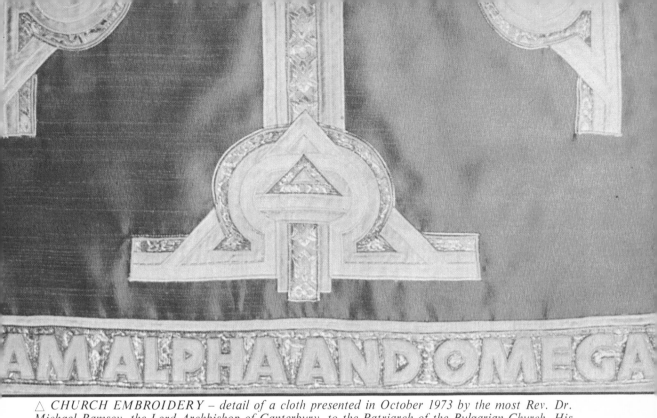

△ *CHURCH EMBROIDERY – detail of a cloth presented in October 1973 by the most Rev. Dr. Michael Ramsey, the Lord Archbishop of Canterbury, to the Patriarch of the Bulgarian Church, His Holiness Maxim. The embroidery, 31 in. (79 cm) square, was designed and executed by Pat Russell. Around the edges the inscription "I am Alpha and Omega" is in Cyrillic and Latin scripts, with quatrefoil centre devices of the two letters in Greek.*
(His Grace the Lord Archbishop of Canterbury)

▽ *DORSET FEATHER STITCHERY – detail of Dorset feather work, showing typical motifs and tatted edging.*
(By permission of the late Mrs Pass)

△ *FLORENTINE WORK – bed with hangings, canopy and coverlet magnificently worked. The 16th-century coverlet, bed back and canopy are silk, and gold work on a cream satin ground, with silk appliqué on bed back. The monogram and fleur-de-lys on the coverlet could belong either to Marie de' Medici (a Rubens painting of whom could have been inspiration to an embroidered portrait on the bed back) or Mary Queen of Scots (who might have embroidered the pieces during her long periods of imprisonment). The bed hangings are about 1615, in silk and wool on canvas strips, $9\frac{1}{2}$ in. (24 cm) wide, each strip containing two zigzag lines. Despite the many seams necessary and the complexity of the patterning, the overall effect is of artistic perfection and regularity.*
(From the collection of Parham Park, Sussex)

PORTUGUESE STEM STITCH

Starting with an ordinary **stem stitch** (figure 1), pass the needle under the thread (figure 2) without entering the fabric. Pass under again (figure 3) and make another stem stitch (figure 4). Repeat figures 2 and 3, passing over thread of last stitch as well (figure 5) to give a solid-looking knotted stitch (figure 6).

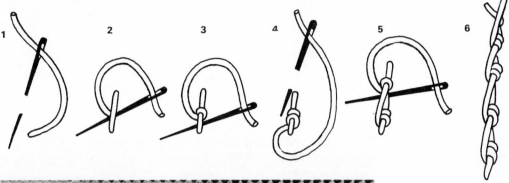

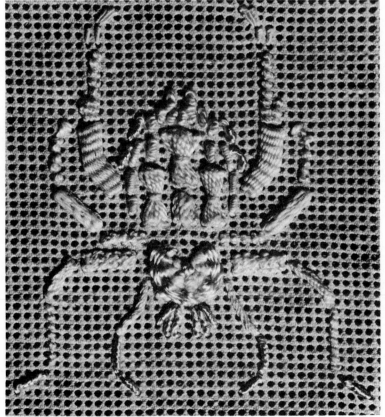

PULLED THREAD WORK—
technique of 'casalguidi' superimposed modern stitching on a pulled work ground. 'The Spider' by Cynthia Sparks, 1966. (The artist)

PULLED THREAD WORK

This work is also sometimes called 'drawn fabric', a confusing term since in fact no threads are either withdrawn or cut (as they are in all the 'drawn thread work' embroideries). For the purpose of differentiation, therefore, it is easier to refer to this type of embroidery as 'pulled thread work'.

Pulled thread is found all over the world today and has an indefinite pedigree since it has not been ascertained where it originally evolved.

Some of the earliest examples are those of 17th-century Italy, silk on a linen ground, with a background worked to leave a clear foreground motif. From about the same period, too, is a

PULLED THREAD WORK—*detail of a mat, 25 × 20 in.*
(63·5 × 51 cm), by Moyra McNeill.
(From her book Pulled Thread, *Mills & Boon)*

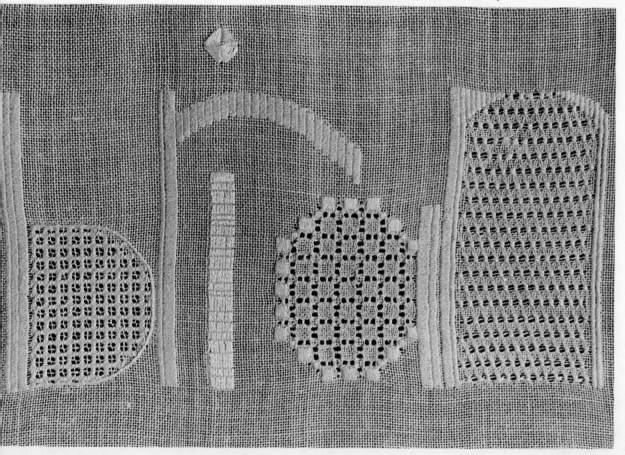

418

faggot-stitched background embroidery in the Benaki Museum in Athens. During the 18th century pulled thread work was popular throughout Europe: in Denmark *tønder* work was particularly evident.

In its simplest form, the lacy appearance of pulled thread work is achieved by pulling the thread as tight as possible with each stitch worked. It is necessary to give equal force to each 'pull' to obtain overall even work.

Fabric should be fairly loose and with an open weave; although traditionally linen or cotton has been the ground medium, it is possible to experiment with a whole range of fabrics. Cotton, linen, window cleaners' scrim, wool (if open weave) and some artificial fibres are all suitable: a fairly strong thread is essential.

There is a wide variety of stitches. The most commonly used, either as outline or as filling stitches (and, in each case, with many related complex stitch forms based on the original), are back stitch, cross stitch, eyelet holes, satin stitch, wave stitch and fillings like mosaic filling stitch.

Pulled thread work is often used for decorating table linens, cloths and napkins. To distinguish such pulled thread embellishment from drawn thread decoration, however, it is necessary to remember that in pulled thread *no threads are withdrawn*.

PUNCH STITCH

For a pulled work stitch, work two **satin stitches** over evenly spaced blocks of thread (bottom of diagram) and then fill in with equal-length vertical blocks (top of diagram). This stitch can also be worked over counted threads of non-pulled work fabric to give a similar, but less pulled, effect.

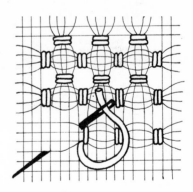

QUILTING

Quilting (derived from the Latin *culcita*, from *calx*, 'heel') is the method of holding various layers of fabric to retain heat, to keep heat out or to be resistant to missiles of assorted identity (as evidenced by the use of machine-quilted padded cricket and football guards). As well as frequent military protective uses, quilting has often been included in more peaceable forms of clothing. The Chinese, for example, have long had padded garments, and in the West, quilted petticoats and jackets were fashionable, and useful, particularly in the 18th century.

419

REVERSE APPLIQUÉ QUILT—*indigo printed cotton, hand-blocked linen and chintz applied through a ground of cotton mixture dyed with a light butternut dye. The fine quilting is in a shell design. Late 18th century.*
(Shelburne Museum, Inc., Shelburne, Vermont)

420

One of the earliest records of quilting is a robe with lozenge-shaped motifs on an Egyptian figurine dating from *c.* 3400 BC, found at the temple of Osiris at Abydos.

The most prolific output of traditional quilting in the last 300 years has been that of North America. Today the tradition of quilting is carried on, both in the United States and Canada. Quilts, or coverlets, fall into categories such as 'appliqué' or 'applied quilts' (p. 323), 'crazy quilts' (p. 283), 'freedom quilts' (p. 283), 'Hawaiian quilts' (p. 119) and 'memory quilts' (p. 283), to name but a few. Motifs are sometimes highly symbolic, such as a recurrent heart design on a wedding quilt.

Quilting falls into the realm of embroidery in that the layers forming the quilt, or padding, are held together with stitching, usually running stitch. Much commercial padding is obviously machine-stitched, a skill which is not 'embroidery'.

The main forms of quilting are:

English quilting
Surface and backing fabrics (sometimes, but not always, of the same material) are separated by padding of carded lambs' wool, cotton wadding, flannel or a thick blanket. The three layers are tacked together in a wide frame of parallel vertical and horizontal lines to form a 'basted trellis' on which to work. The final quilting stitches are worked through all layers of fabric and the tacked trellis is removed from the finished item.

Italian quilting
This is an outline quilting. The surface layer of fabric is backed with butter muslin and both are tacked together. Running stitch is worked in two parallel lines according to the required design, forming a 'channel' through which thick wool is threaded, from the back, through the butter muslin. Whenever the woollen padding thread has to turn a corner, a slight 'loop' is left to allow for possible shrinkage.

Trapunto
Trapunto is also known as 'stuffed quilting' and it is like Italian quilting in that only two layers (front ground and a butter muslin backing) are originally tacked together. Single lines of running stitch are worked around outline areas to be enclosed. These areas are then padded, from behind, with wads of cotton wool or other padding inserted through the butter muslin.

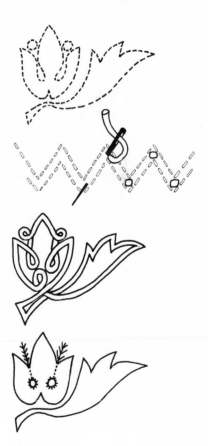

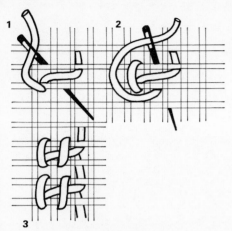

RENAISSANCE STITCH

A closely worked canvas-work stitch, worked in vertical blocks of horizontal stitches. Two stitches are trammed at once (figures 1 and 2) before proceeding vertically to the next block (figure 3).

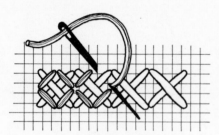

RICE STITCH

cross-corners cross stitch

Over a plain **cross stitch**, small diagonal corner crosses are worked in the same or contrasting thread.

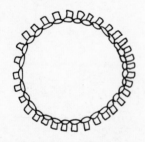

RICHELIEU STITCH

Broderie anglaise with **buttonhole stitching** rather than plain oversewing. Buttonholed Richelieu bars can be further ornamented with **picots**.

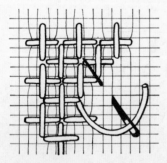

RIDGE FILLING STITCH

A pulled work filling: diagonal rows of **straight stitches** are worked (the first row of horizontal stitches, the second of vertical stitches, and so on).

RIPPLE STITCH

A pulled thread stitch, reversed **herringbone stitch** in execution since the complicated lacing is on the wrong side of the fabric. When pulled tight, an interesting ripple effect is attained. The second row does not start immediately below the first, but in the lower space of the first row.

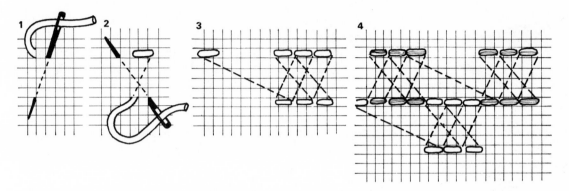

ROCOCO STITCH

A complicated canvas-work stitch in which knotted **Romanian stitches** are worked in the same holes (figures 1, 2, 3 and 4) before proceeding to the next block (figure 5). The resultant effect should be trellised as the blocks are worked alternately (figure 6).

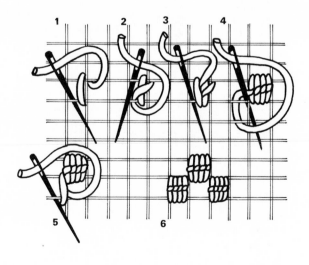

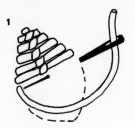

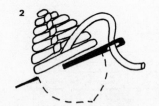

ROMANIAN STITCH

antique stitch
Indian filling stitch
New England laid stitch
oriental stitch
overlaid stitch
Roman stitch

A versatile filling or border stitch. Basically a **satin stitch** with slanting 'couch' which should be worked from the top of the motif down. This stitch is found in embroidery throughout Europe and the Middle East. When used as a filling stitch (figure 3), Romanian stitching is also known as **figure stitch** and **oriental laidwork**.

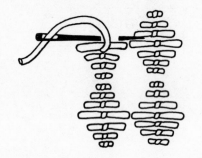

ROPE STITCH

A stitch for outline or filling. By twisting the thread (figure 1) and always making a new stitch (D to E, figure 2) slightly below and tucked under the previous stitch, a strong cord is worked. The angle of stitching determines a narrow (figure 3) or broad (figure 4) rope.

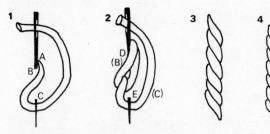

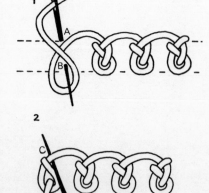

ROSETTE STITCH

rosette chain stitch

A chained stitch that can be worked straight (for a border), curved (for a circular motif) or used as filling. When working the final loop (figure 2) the needle goes under the thread (C) without entering the fabric.

424

RUNNING STITCH

saddle stitch

Regular spaces of fabric are taken up with each entry of the needle: all the upper stitches should also be equal (and ideally, from an embroidery viewpoint, double the length of the lower stitches).

Running stitch can be laced to give **laced running stitch**.

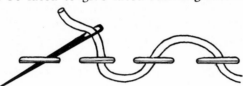

It can be laced twice, sometimes known as **threaded running stitch**. When basic running stitch is whipped it is known as **cordonnet stitch** or **whipped running stitch**.

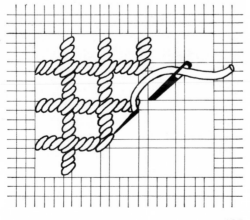

RUSSIAN DRAWN GROUND

overcast filling stitch

Drawn thread work stitching-threads are withdrawn both from warp and weft to leave a square-shaped lattice which is then diagonally overcast.

SAMPLERS

A sampler is a test piece of embroidery, its name derived from the Latin word *examplum* ('a pattern'), by way of the French *essemplaire* and the Old English *ensample*. It is suggested that the idea of working test motifs and stitchings originated in the East, and some of the earliest textile samplers in existence today are woven Coptic fragments. Guildford Museum has a 9 in. (23 cm) woven piece, for instance, found in an Egyptian tomb that is thought to be 4th century AD. The earliest known embroidered sampler, now in the Victoria and Albert Museum, is German and is probably from the first half of the 16th century. The first dated English sampler, also in that museum, is the 1598 work of Jane Bostocke (p. 71).

Samplers have, by tradition, generally been square or rectangular, on grounds of wool, silk or linen. The size and shape have often been determined by the width of material available, with the length of the finished work governed by width of the loom.

Inspiration for some of the earliest sampler motifs came from books such as Jacques le Moyne's *La clef des champs* (London, 1586), the Sibmacher *Schön neues Modelbuch* (Nürnberg, 1597) or Richard Shorleyker's *Schole-house for the Needle* (1624). By the 18th century, samplers became generally more naturalistic with less inspiration derived from printed matter. In the 19th century prepared canvases were available with designs already printed. Sampler making has long been a required accomplishment of schoolgirls, an element of curricula that was sometimes not dropped until the early 20th century.

Most countries in the West have had their own unique sampler attributes. A general sampler terminology includes:

Berlin wool work sampler—recognisable by the bright colouring and geometric patterning, often with a three-dimensional effect, usually worked in the period 1805–75 (p. 112).

Border sampler—denoting the fact that the sampler is worked in motifs of horizontal bands.

Darning sampler—maximum use of different darning stitches worked either in blocks or in figurative patterns.

Lettering sampler—also known as **alphabet sampler**; sometimes several different forms of lettering (p. 403) were worked on one piece.

Map sampler—a map has often been a popular subject for sampler representation, combining tuition of geography with instruction in the needle.

SAMPLER—*darning sampler, silks on scrim, 'A. Blake 1795'. (City of Norwich Museums)*

Money sampler—surprisingly, 'shillings and pence' and related multiplication tables have rarely been utilised as sampler motifs.

Religious sampler—often church motifs were combined with other sampler representations.

Spot motif sampler—unrelated groups of motifs 'spotting' the ground fabric are referred to as 'spot motifs'.

428

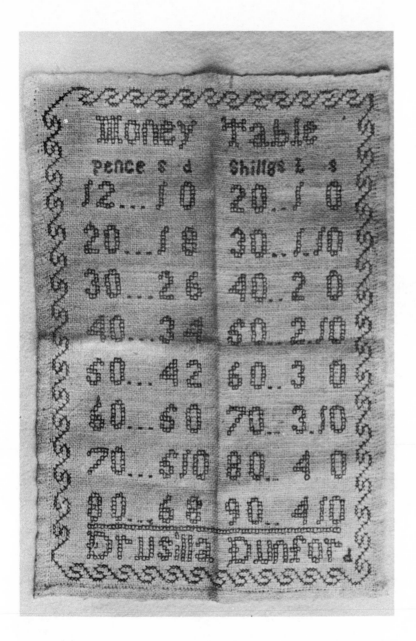

SAMPLER—*a rare money sampler, worked by Drusilla Dunford (born 1828). The museum owns another sampler by the same artist, also in cross stitch on a linen ground, worked when she was four.*
(City of Rochester: Eastgate House Museum)

SAMPLER—*'spot motif sampler' from South Africa, worked by 12-year-old Susanna Johanna Hertzog in 1805. $23\frac{1}{4} \times 22$ in. (59 × 56 cm).*
(Stellenbosch Museum, South Africa. Photo: Image Studios, Stellenbosch)

Whitework sampler—white on white sample (p. 448) and, similarly, other fields of embroidery (such as **cutwork, drawn thread work** and **pulled thread work**) can be incorporated into sampler design.

SAMPLER—*a map sampler signed and dated 'Elizabeth Page, May 10—1811', in which the artist depicted the Peninsula and located the Battle of Trafalgar. The embroidery is worked in chain and cross stitch with silks on a fine muslin ground, and the irregular roundel outer shaping is unusual.*
(The National Trust. The Kay-Shuttleworth Collection at Gawthorpe Hall, Lancashire)

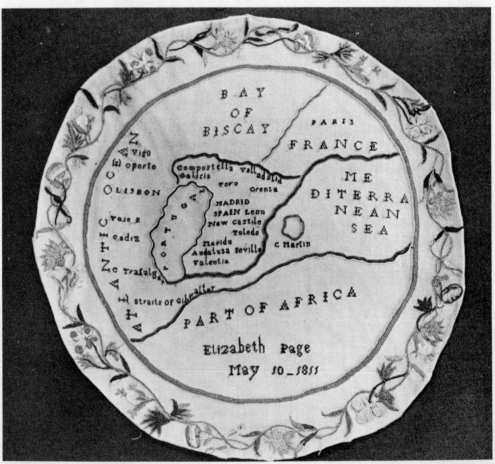

SAMPLER—*a whitework 'border sampler'.*
(The National Trust. The Kay-Shuttleworth Collection at Gawthorpe Hall, Lancashire)

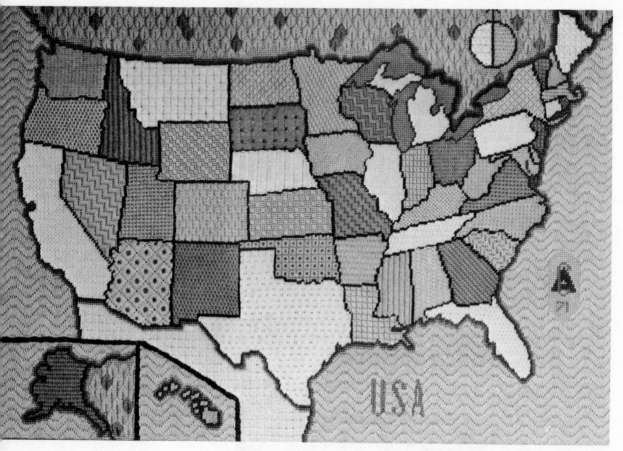

SAMPLER—*20th century, designed and worked by Chottie Alderson of Running Springs, California. The artist uses 58 different canvas stitches in this States map.*
(The artist)

SATIN STITCH
kløster stitch
long stitch

Although this is one of the most commonly used stitches, it is tricky to work it to perfection. Parallel stitches A to B are executed close together, either straight or diagonal. It is necessary to concentrate on a fine edge line and even embroidering. Ordinary satin stitch with no padding can be called **au passé stitch**. If a large area is to be worked it is often easier to use

432

Romanian stitch. To cover up untidy edge lines, an outline of **back stitch**, **Pekinese** or similar stitch can be superimposed.

When satin stitch is raised with parment padding it is known as **guimped embroidery**.

A **surface satin stitch**, also known as **economy stitch**, is used to conserve thread. It produces a less padded effect than ordinary satin stitch.

SCOTTISH STITCH

A canvas-work filling stitch, with outline squares of tent stitch filled with diagonal stitching.

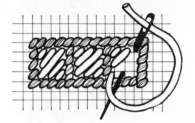

SCROLL STITCH

Antwerp edging stitch
beaded stitch
coral knot stitch
coral stitch
German knot stitch
Kensington outline stitch
knotted stitch
snail trail stitch

Hold the thread down at A as the stitch is worked. The thread is then pulled tight to form the knot.

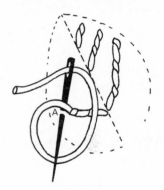

SEEDING

seed filling
speckling

Tiny stitches worked at any angle—but each stitch of more or less uniform length—to produce a good filling stitch.

(**Dot stitch** is also known sometimes as seeding.)

SERPENTINE STITCH

A drawn thread work stitch with two rows of **hem stitch** worked, one each side of the withdrawn threads, in zigzag form unlike **ladder hem stitch**, p. 303, which produces parallel rungs).

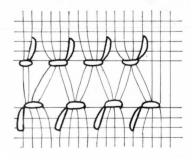

SHADOW EMBROIDERY

As its name implies, **shadow work** necessitates the use of different layers of transparent or semi-transparent materials to afford varying degrees of light and shade to the embroidery ground. It was originally a whitework embroidery (p. 448) and has been frequently employed for handkerchiefs and similarly delicate items: motifs of white muslin or organdie applied to a ground of the same material and subsequently embellished with embroidery can give, for example, shadow shading to leaves of a floral design.

Today shadow work is being skilfully employed by artists using traditional and modern media such as plastics and synthetic fabrics in two- and three-dimensional forms. Shadow embroidery as such, therefore, need not today apply merely to applied motif shadow work but, also, to shading produced by effects of light and shade on different layers, or panels, of embroidery.

SHADOW STITCH
closed herringbone stitch
double back stitch

Used principally for shadow work on a transparent fabric such as muslin, the stitch can be worked in two ways:

1. *Working from the front*—two rows of parallel **back stitches** worked alternately.
2. *Working from the rear*—**closed herringbone** stitch with each stitch working from the previous stitch.

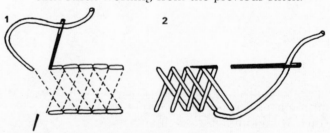

SHEAF STITCH
faggot stitch

A good filling stitch that can be worked in two ways:

1. Three vertical **satin stitches** are overcast twice (the needle going under the satin stitches but not entering the material) and tied down.

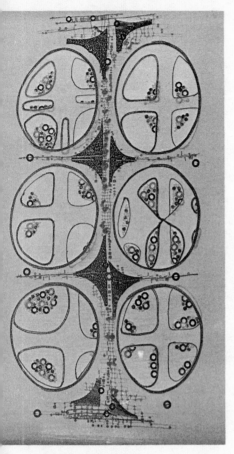

SHADOW WORK—
three-dimensional organdie panel by Mary Rhodes, 1973. Silver leather, thread and beads are applied to three vertical organdie panels, each 25 × 18¼ in. (63·5 × 46·5 cm).
(The artist)

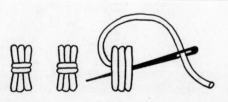

434

2. Over pairs of parallel horizontal laid stitches, the thread is interwoven and tied down.

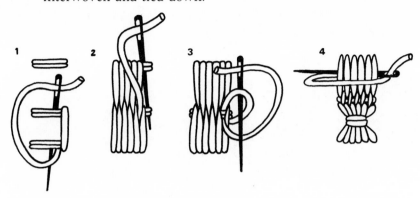

SHELL STITCH

A complicated canvas-work stitch. Vertical parallel straight stitches are worked in blocks (figure 1) and bound (figure 2). Blocks are then interlaced, shown by shaded thread (figure 3).

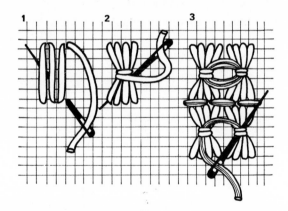

SHISHA STITCH

When working with mirrors, a substitute shiny surface such as 'mylar', or cardboard covered with kitchen foil, a suitable holding stitch is this combination criss-cross and buttonhole-type stitch.

After placing the mirror (figure 1), and criss-crossing (figures 2 and 3), a circular row of stitching is worked from outside the

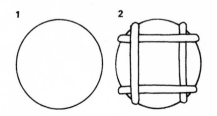

435

mirror, swinging from the centre under the criss-cross (figure 4), to the outside, taking a stitch (figure 5), to the centre and under the criss-cross (figure 6) and so on, *always pulling the thread tight.*

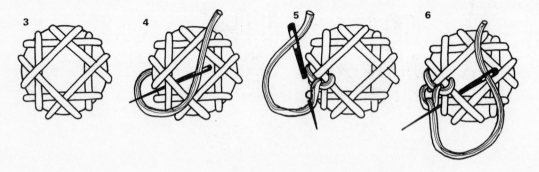

SPANISH STITCH

plait stitch
Spanish knotted feather stitch
twisted zigzag chain stitch

Although this stitch looks complicated, once the technique is mastered it works quickly. Hold the thread down with left thumb (D—figure 1) to produce the initial twist (figure 2); reverse this process (figure 3) to give an alternating chain-stitch band (figure 4).

(Spanish stitch has also been called what is more usually known as **Holbein stitch**, p. 395.)

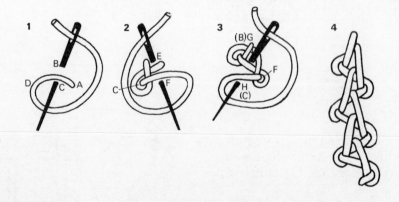

436

SPIDER'S WEB FILLING STITCH

Any number of radii are put in a circle and, starting from the centre, interwoven spiralling to the outside.

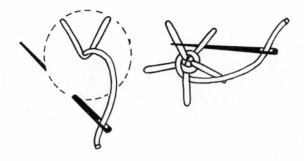

SPLIT STITCH

Kensington outline stitch
Opus Anglicanum stitch

Rather like chain stitch in appearance, this stitch is particularly useful for outlining or when used as filling (with each row worked in the same direction). A soft yarn must be used, to split easily.

SQUARES AND BUNDLES FILLING STITCH

Alternating blocks of satin stitch are separated by diagonal 'sticks' of contrasting colour thread.

STAR STITCH

A simple crossed spot-motif stitch that makes a good powdered filling stitch.

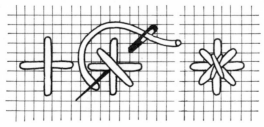

437

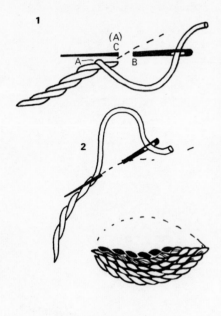

STEM STITCH
crewel stitch
French filling
outline stitch
stalk stitch

Worked from left to right, the needle makes regular stitches, each close to the one before. When the thread is kept below the needle (figure 1) this is called **stem** or **crewel stitch**. In **outline stitch** the thread is always kept above the needle (figure 2). With either variation always keep the thread on the outside of any curve to get the neatest worked line. Although often used for outlining, this stitch can also be worked for a plain **filling stitch**, or with shaded threads, for a shaded filling (figure 3). As a line stitch it can be whipped (figure 4).

STEP STITCH
Rhodes step stitch
A very basic stitch.

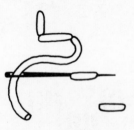

STRAIGHT STITCH
single satin stitch
stroke stitch

Straight stitches of irregular or similar length can be worked to any pattern, parallel, at angles, radiating from a point. This is a quick and satisfactory filling stitch.

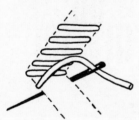

STRAW WORK

Few pieces of straw-work embroidery have survived, due to the fragility of this natural thread. There are references to straw-work decoration in 19th-century magazines, and one existing panel, *c.* 1830, consists of straw-embroidered motifs applied to black net. Straw work was practised in the Bedfordshire area of England by the French at home and as prisoners of war.

438

STUMP STITCH

Stump work, 'embroidery on the stamp', was first referred to as such in *A New and Complete Dictionary of Arts and Sciences*, (London, 1754), although this field of embroidery had long been in existence and reached its peak between 1650 and 1680.

Stump work is three-dimensional embroidery, with raised work, padding and details sometimes executed in independent motifs and, subsequently, attached to a ground of ivory satin. Stump work was frequently used on panels for needlework boxes, lined in pink satin, for pictures or for bookbindings. The Bodleian Library, Oxford, has two such stump-work book covers: one is a crimson velvet Bible cover presented to Queen Elizabeth I, the other a prayer book with padded work cover supposedly embroidered by the same Queen and presented by her to her stepmother, Katherine Parr. Surprisingly, although stump work was known to have been embroidered on both sides of the Atlantic, only one American example is known to have survived, a slightly raised work by Rebekah Wheeler, 1664, now the property of the Antiquarian Society of Concord, Massachusetts.

What is often referred to as stump work today is technically **padded work**, incorporating **trapunto quilting** (p. 421) and **padded appliqué** (p. 322) with raised work added to the embroidery ground after working. This form of 'stump work' is enjoying a popularity today and most comprehensive embroidery exhibitions feature several examples of padding, making full use of modern materials and themes.

STUMP WORK—*English needlework casket, mid-17th century, with raised work, coloured silks and metal thread on white satin.*
(The Metropolitan Museum of Art. Gift of Mrs. Thomas J. Watson, 1939)

439

PADDED WORK—
three-dimensional embroidery
with padded balls and wool
tufting around an inset mirror,
polystyrene base with foam
stuffing. Alison Barrell, 1969.
(The artist)

PADDED WORK—*'Henry's*
Grave', padded embroidery
34 × 30 × 38 in.
(86·5 × 76 × 96·5 cm), with
inlaid fabric collage, textile
flowers, and rag-rug technique,
one in a series of funerary
subjects by Eirian Short, 1972.
(The artist)

440

TACKING STITCH

basting

A simple **running stitch,** with few threads taken up by each entry of the needle. More than one row of tacking stitch worked in parallels forms **darning stitch.**

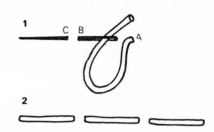

TAMBOUR WORK

Tambour embroidery is a continuous chain stitch worked with a hooked needle not unlike an extremely fine crochet hook. The art originated in the East and was introduced to France towards the end of the 17th century. It is reputed to have been popularised, indeed, by no less a personage than Madame de Pompadour and a portrait of that lady, painted *c.* 1764 by François Drouais and now in the Musée Condé, Chantilly, shows her working tamboured *point de chenette* (chain stitch).

The continuous stitching thus worked enjoyed wide vogue through the late 18th and early 19th centuries, giving vent to such forms of needlework as 'Ayrshire whitework' (p. 224). Barthélemy Thimonnier's sewing machine, patented in Paris in 1830, produced a continuous chain stitch and, today, the one-thread 'Cornely' machine works in the same way, producing machine-embroidered tambour work. Hand-embroidered tambour work, too, is still popular: the College of Fashion and Clothing Technology in London, for instance, includes the art in its regular curriculum.

Tambouring gets its name from the original frame, shaped like a *tambour* (drum), on which it was worked. The fabric was stretched tightly on the circular face of the frame, while the hemispherical surface rested conveniently on the oriental tambour artist's knees as he worked, cross-legged, on the floor.

In order to hold the ground fabric taut, and to have both hands free, it is still necessary to work on a fixed frame, albeit the ordinary two-dimensional variety (p. 384)! Other tambour equipment includes:

Tambour hook—a handle, shaped like a pen holder: new hooks on the market today are usually wooden.

Tambour needles—barbed needles of varying sizes which fit into the handle.

Tambour thimbles—traditional tambour thimbles were made of a piece of coiled metal, not joined, which expanded as required. They had a notch cut at the highest point of the sloping top to help guide the tambour needle and press down the

TAMBOUR WORK— *18th-century tambour frame, shaped like the drum from which the name of the art derives. Ground fabric was stretched tightly over the flat plane and held in place by a leather strap. The hemispherical surface of the wooden drum rested on the embroiderer's knees.*

441

fabric as each loop was worked. Tambour thimbles were worn on the right forefinger.

Tambour embroidery can be worked on most non-canvas ground. Since one continuous thread is used, it is best to start this form of embroidery with an ordinary sewing thread, or similar yarn on a reel. The tambour hook (with needle affixed) is held in a vertical position and inserted down through the ground fabric. The needle picks up the thread held underneath the frame in the embroiderer's free hand and draws it through, in a loop, to the right side of the fabric, thus holding down the loop previously worked. Patterns and motifs can be outlined or filled in and, with practice, beading can be incorporated into tambouring. The mastery of the art of tambouring requires much patience and concentration but, when this is achieved, tambour work is much quicker than most other forms of hand embroidery.

TAMBOUR WORK—*an 18th-century tambour hook with cover. The barbed needle should always be fitted into the handle with the notch on the same plane as the holding screw so that the embroiderer knows in which direction the hook, under the surface of the fabric, is facing.*
(The National Trust. The Kay-Shuttleworth Collection at Gawthorpe Hall, Lancashire)

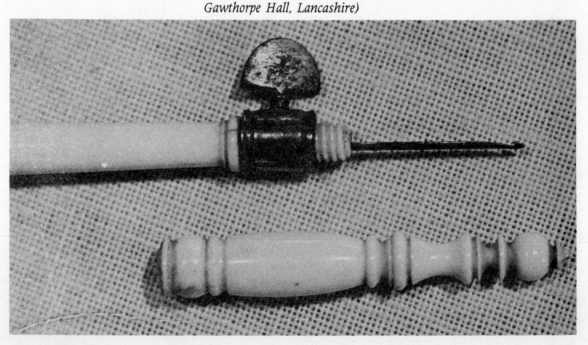

TENT STITCH

half stitch
petit point

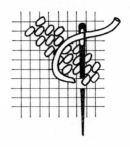

Half a **cross stitch**, worked in diagonal, horizontal or vertical rows (a form of diagonal tent stitch is **basketweave stitch**). If it is worked on a very fine-gauge single-mesh canvas, it is known as **petit point.** Tent stitch worked in horizontal rows with one row facing diagonally to the right and the next facing diagonally to the left is known as **Macedonian stitch** or **lazy-knit stitch.**

TÊTE-DE-BŒUF STITCH

Although primarily a filling stitch, tête-de-bœuf (French for 'ox head') can be used by itself. There are two ways of working it:

1. A **fly stitch** forms the horns (figure 1) and is anchored with a detached **chain stitch** (figure 2).
2. A detached **chain stitch** (figures 3 and 4) is escorted by a pair of slanting **straight stitches** at right angles to each other (figure 5).

When used as a filling, both methods of working produce little stitches that can be spaced in alternating rows, in geometric exactness or haphazardly.

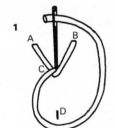  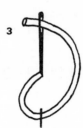  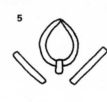

THORN STITCH

A long laid stitch (A to B) is held down with alternating diagonals (C to C, E to F, and so on). (**Briar stitch**, p. 335, is also known as thorn stitch.)

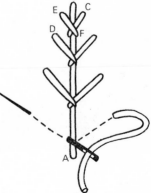

443

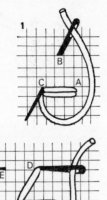

THREE-SIDED STITCH

Bermuda faggoting
lace stitch
point Turc
Turkish stitch

A pulled work stitch. Two **satin stitches** are worked and then a diagonal to the centre above (figure 1). This is worked twice and then the needle goes horizontally to the left (figure 2) to work two stitches before coming back diagonally to C (figure 3) and so on. The threads should always be pulled tight. Figure 4 shows the stitch used in turning a corner.

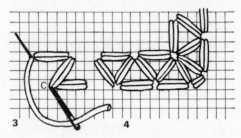

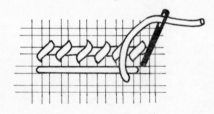

TRAMMED STITCHES

A canvas-work term: before working a row of stitches such as tent stitch, the embroidery yarn is brought up between the threads of a double-weave canvas and makes a horizontal 'backing' over which the stitch is then worked in the normal way.

TRELLIS STITCHES

Trellis stitch as such is a surface needlepoint. In a frame of chain stitching worked through the fabric (shaded stitches), the thread emerges at A and is looped through the next chain as a knot is formed (figure 1), and so on. When a corner of the outer chain is reached, turn round (figure 2) and come back, working each stitch through the link of the stitching above (figure 3).

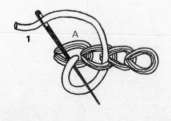

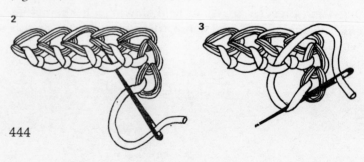

Alternatively, trellis stitch is a laid surface stitching, generally used as filling. Stitches are laid in both directions (figure 1) and then couched in a variety of styles such as **star couching** (figure 2) or small **cross-stitching couching** (figure 3).

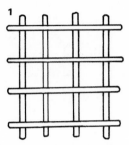 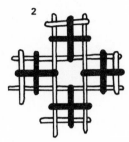 

TURKEY WORK STITCH

plush stitch

Taking a small **back stitch** (figure 1), the needle swings overhead to the next back stitch, leaving a loop the required length (figure 2), and is then pulled tight for a repetition of figure 1 and so on, alternating figures 1 and 2. The finished stitch (figure 3) can be cut (at dotted line) to give a carpet effect, or left in loops.

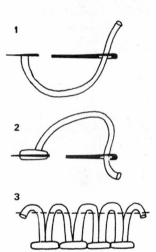

TURKISH TRIANGULAR STITCH

A row of evenly spaced parallel vertical **straight stitches** (figure 1) is filled in with horizontal and diagonal straight stitches (figures 2 and 3), to build up an eventual trellis (figure 4).

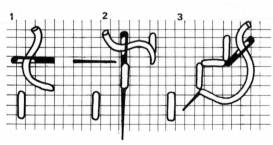 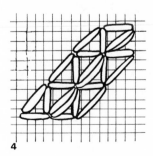

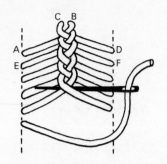

VANDYKE STITCH

A plaited line stitch. The needle emerges at A to work a diagonal to B, catches only a few threads to emerge at C for another diagonal C to D. It re-emerges at E, passes over CD and under the crossing of AB and CD, without entering the fabric, to make another diagonal to F, and so on.

(Vandyke is also allocated to the stitch most commonly known as **zigzag chain stitch**, p. 352).

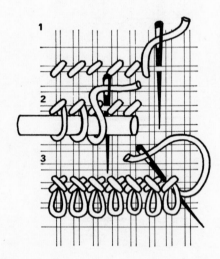

VELVET STITCH

A canvas-work stitch with looped pile. A horizontal row of diagonal **tent stitches** is worked (top). Using a pencil or similar gauge, loops are then formed. The gauge is removed and the original line of tent stitches is crossed (figure 3).

WAVE FILLING STITCH
straight line stitch

This can either be a zigzag pulled work stitch, or, starting with a row of small evenly spaced **straight stitches** (dark stitches), a looped stitch is made going through each straight stitch but without entering the fabric (figure 1). Subsequent rows of 'waves' pass under the preceding waves (figure 2).

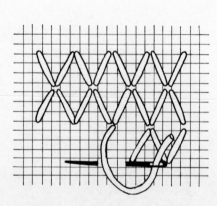

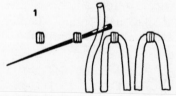

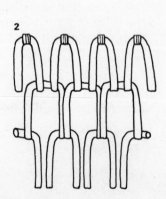

WEAVING FILLING STITCH

On an open lattice from which threads have been withdrawn, embroidery thread is overcast and interwoven to desired patterning.

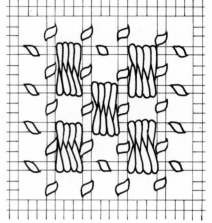

WEB STITCH

A canvas-work stitch with close woven effect. The aim is to fill a square space, so the foundation stitches grow first longer, then shorter.

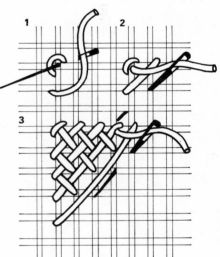

WHEATEAR STITCH

A decorative border stitch, worked from top to bottom. The needle emerges at A to work A to B, then at C to work C to B. It re-emerges at D and passes under AB and BC, to enter the fabric at D again and emerge at E (A) and so on.

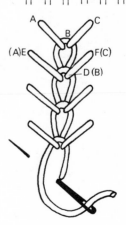

447

WHITEWORK

Whitework is literally any 'white on white' embroidery, an extensive catchment area that includes such diverse facets of the art of embroidery as **Coggeshall sewed muslin** (p. 83), **Mountmellick work** (p. 151), **Ayrshire work** (p. 224), Indian **chikan work** (p. 134), early **shadow work** (p. 434), and much **trapunto quilting** (p. 421). Within this category, too, is found much **cutwork** (p. 378), **needle-made lace** (p. 399) and **tambour work** (p. 441).

WHITEWORK—*'sewed muslin' of the early 19th century, with floral sprigs or designs of curving stems with tiny flowers and leaves worked in stem stitch, satin stitch or overcast stitch. Detail from sleeves, c. 1825–30. (Mrs. Marion Felix)*

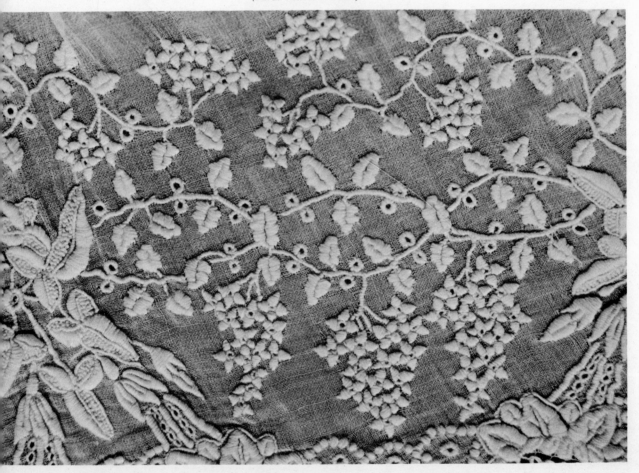

448

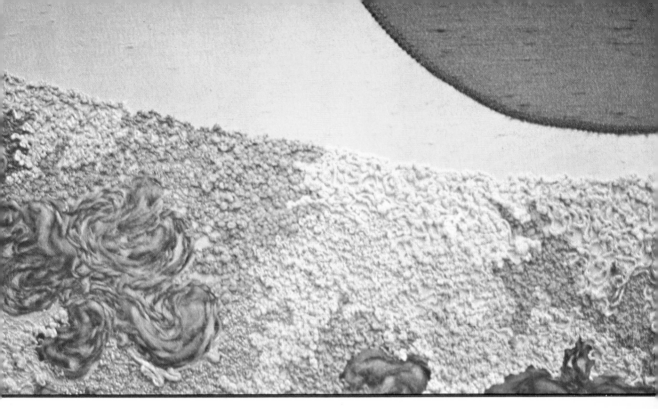

△ *MACHINE EMBROIDERY – detail of "Blue Moon" by Joy Clucas, 1973.*
(The artist)

▽ *MACHINE EMBROIDERY – a typically colourful work by Joy Clucas, 1973.*
(The artist)

△ *METAL THREAD WORK – gold thread embroidery combined with machine stitching in a detail of a work by Richard Box, 1973.*
(The artist)

▽ *SAMPLER – English sampler, mid-19th-century, showing various "Berlin wool work" and Florentine motifs (best seen by giving picture a half-turn to the left).*
(Mrs J. Beckford)

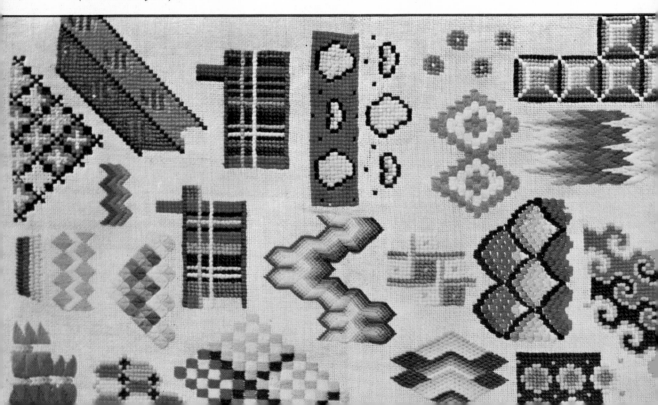

WHITEWORK—*'Komposition in Weiss' by Lissy Funk of Zürich, 1972. 47½ × 43¼ in. (1·20 × 1·10 m).*
(The artist)

WOOLWORK

An umbrella term covering any embroidery worked in wool thread. See particularly **Berlin wool work** (p. 112).

WOOL WORK—*'Berlin wool work' embroidery, c. 1870, worked to a coloured design on squared paper. The embroidery is in silks and beads on a single thread canvas ground: the King Charles spaniel, in Turkey work stitch, sits on a green cushion of cross stitch. (The Smithsonian Institution, Washington DC)*

ZIGZAG STITCH

Is worked in two journeys, from right to left and back again.

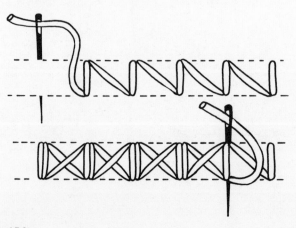

SUGGESTED REFERENCE MATERIAL

The list below is intended to offer further relevant information on general or specific aspects of embroidery. It includes a selected bibliography and, also, magazine articles of particular use to the embroidery student. It does not include details of regular periodicals of interest to the embroiderer, collector or traveller, neither does it include standard reference literature such as the comprehensive *Museums of the World* (Verlag Dokumentation, Munich, 1973), from which museum spellings throughout this book have been standardised.

Agnew, Patience, *Needlepoint for Churches*, Charles Scribner's Sons.

Agutter, M. *Cross Stitch Patterns*. Pitman, 1952.

Alford, Lady M. *Handbook of Embroidery*. Sampson Low, 1880. *Needlework as Art*. Sampson Low, 1886.

Allgrove, Joan. 'Turcoman Embroideries.' *Embroidery*, London, Vol. XXIV, no. 2, Summer 1973.

Anchor Manual of Needlework. Batsford for J. & P. Coats, 1958.

Andere, Mary, *Old Needlework Boxes and Tools*. Drake Publishers Inc., 1971.

Anthony, Ilid E. 'Quilting and Patchwork in Wales.' *Bulletin of the National Museum of Wales*, no. 12, Winter 1972.

Arts Council of Great Britain. *Opus Anglicanum (English Mediaeval Embroidery)*. London, 1963.

Ashton, Leigh. *Samplers*. Medici Society, 1926.

Aslin, Elizabeth. *Aesthetic Movement: Prelude to Art Nouveau*. Elek, 1969.

Baker, Muriel L. *The ABC's of Canvas Embroidery*. Old Sturbridge Village, 1968. *The Art of Crewel Embroidery*. Crown Publishers Inc., 1962.

Barrow, T. *The Decorative Arts of the New Zealand Maori*. Reed, Wellington, 1964.

Barth, H. *Narrative of Travels* (3rd ed.). 1828.

Bazielich, Barbara. *Ludowe Wyszycia Technika Krzyżykowa ną sląsku*. Rocznik Muzeum Górdoslakiego, nr. 1. *Na Marginesie Badan nad Ludowymi Wyszyciami Techniką Krzyzykową na Slasku*. Opelski rocznik muzealny, 1968—III.

'Slavonic Folk Embroidery.' *Embroidery*, London, Vol. X, no. 3, Autumn 1959.

Beaton, Cecil. *Fashion—An Anthology by Cecil Beaton*. Victoria and Albert Museum, 1971.

Beautement, M. *Patterns from Peasant Embroidery*. Batsford, 1968.

Beeton's Book of Needlework. Ward, Lock, *c.* 1870.

Benaki Museum. *Crete-Dodecanese-Cyclades Embroideries*. Athens, 1966.

Epirus and Ionian Islands Embroideries. Athens, 1965.

Berry, B. Y. 'Turkish Embroidery.' *Embroidery*, London, Vol. IV, no. 3, June 1936.

Billeter, Dr. Erika. 'Gestickte Poesie. Nadelarbeiten von Lieselotte Siegfried.' *Heimatwerk*, Zürich, Nr 2, 1974.

Birdwood, George C. M. *Industrial Arts of India*. Chapman & Hall, 1880.

Boas, Franz. *Primitive Art*. Dover Publications Inc., 1955.

Bolton, Ethel Stanwood (with Eva Johnston Coe). *American Samplers*. Dover Publications Inc., 1973.

Boyle, Elizabeth. *The Irish Flowerers*. Ulster Folk Museum and the Institute of Irish Studies, Belfast, 1971.

Breton, A. C. 'Peruvian Tapestries at Toronto.' *Bulletin of Royal Anthropological Institute*, London, no. 22, March 1918.

British Museum. *Village Arts of Romania*. London, 1971.

Bucher, Jo. *Complete Guide to Creative Needlepoint*. Meredith Corporation, 1973.

Burham, Harold E. and Dorothy K. *Keep Me Warm One Night*. University of Toronto and the Royal Ontario Museum, 1972.

Butler, Anne. *Simple Stitches*. Batsford, 1968.

(with David Green). *Pattern and Embroidery*. Batsford, 1970.

Butler, Sheila and Jack. 'Baker Lake Wall Hangings.' *The Beaver*, Hudson's Bay Company, Autumn 1972.

Butterick Publishing Co. Ltd. *Artistic Alphabets for Marking and Engrossing*. 1893.

Metropolitan Art Series: *Needlecraft: Artistic and Practical*. 1890.

Camman, Nora. *Needlepoint Designs from American Indian Art*. Charles Scribner's Sons, 1973.

Cammann, Schuyler. 'Chinese Mandarin Squares.' *Bulletin of the University Museum* of the University of Pennsylvania, June 1953.

Canadian Arctic Producers Ltd. *Needlecraft of the Baker Lake Artists*. Ottawa, 1974.

Carlisle, Lilian Baker. *Pieced Work and Appliqué Quilts at Shelburne Museum*. Shelburne Museum, 1957.

Caulfeild, S. F. A. (with B. C. Saward). *Encyclopedia of Victorian Needlework* (2nd ed.). A. W. Cowan, 1887.

Cave, Oenone. *English Folk Embroidery*. Mills & Boon, 1965.

Chicken, Betty. *Introducing Design in Embroidery*. Batsford, 1971.

Christie, Mrs. A. G. I. *Embroidery*. James Pearsall, 1909.
Embroidery and Tapestry Weaving. Hogg, 1915.
English Mediaeval Embroidery. London, 1938.
Samplers and Stitches. Batsford, 1920.

Clucas, Joy. *Your Machine for Embroidery*. Bell, 1973.

Coats, Messrs. J. & P. *Anchor Embroidery Books* (series).
Coats Sewing Group Books (series).
100 Embroidery Stitches. 1967,

Colby, Averil. *Patchwork*. Batsford, 1958.
Samplers Yesterday and Today. Batsford, 1964.

Conklin, Ida Mae. 'Women's Shawls.' *TAWOW* (Canadian Indian Cultural Magazine), Ottawa, Vol. 2, no. 2, Summer 1971.

Connoisseur. 'Saving and Preserving Historic Textiles.' Vol. 179, no. 721, March 1972.

Cooke, Christopher. 'Embroidery of India.' *Discovering Antiques,* issue 65, 1971.

Cooke, Hereward Lester. *Molas: Art of the Cuna Indians*. Textile Museum, Washington DC, 1973.

Cooper Union Museum. *The Greenleaf Collection: Textile Arts*. New York, 1964.

Cornforth, John. 'Conserving Textiles in Country Houses. *Country Life,* 25th January 1973.
'Wallington, Northumberland.' *Country Life,* 23rd April 1970.

Crompton, Rebecca. *Modern Design in Embroidery*. Batsford, 1936.

Crowfoot, Grace. 'Bethlehem Embroidery.' *Embroidery*, London, Vol. IV, no. 4, December 1936.
(with Phyllis M. Sutton). 'Ramallah Embroidery.' *Embroidery,* London Vol. III, no. 2, March 1935.

Davenport, Cyril. *English Embroidered Bookbindings*. Kegan Paul, 1899.

Davis, Mildred J. *The Art of Crewel Embroidery*. Crown Publishers Inc., 1962.

Early American Embroidery Designs. Crown Publishers Inc., 1969.

'Textiles in the Valentine Museum.' *Antiques,* New York, January 1973.

Dawson, Barbara. *Metal Thread Embroidery.* Batsford, 1968.

Day, Lewis F. *Art in Needlework.* Batsford, 1901.

Dean, Beryl. *Church Needlework.* Batsford, 1961. *Ecclesiastical Embroidery.* Batsford, 1958.

Ideas for Church Embroidery. Batsford, 1968.

Digby, George Wingfield. *Elizabethan Embroidery.* Faber, 1966.

'Lady Julia Calverley, Embroideress.' *Connoisseur,* Vol. CXLV, 1960.

Dillmont, Thérèse de. *Complete Encyclopedia of Needlework* (new ed.). Running Press, 1972.

DMC *Bulgarian Embroideries.* Editions Thérèse de Dillmont, Mulhouse, 1970.

Czecho-slovakian Embroideries. 1971.

Moroccan Embroideries. 1969.

Turkish Embroideries. 1969.

Yugoslav Embroideries (series 1 and 2). 1969 and 1972.

Douglass, Winsome. *Discovering Embroidery.* Mills & Boon, 1971.

Dreesmann, Cecile. 'Dutch Costumes and their Embroideries.' *Embroidery,* Vol. VII, no. 2, Summer 1956.

Samplers for Today. Van Nostrand Reinhold, 1972.

'Some Notes on Danish Embroidery.' *Embroidery,* London, Vol. IX, no. 2, Summer 1958.

Dyer, Anne (with V. Duthoit). *Canvas Work from the Start.* Bell, 1972.

Edwards, Joan. *Bead Embroidery.* Batsford, 1966.

Embroiderers' Guild. *Embroideries from the Permanent Collection.* London, 1971.

Enciso, Jorge. *Design Motifs of Ancient Mexico.* Dover Publications Inc., 1947.

Enthoven, Jacqueline. *The Stitches of Creative Embroidery.* Van Nostrand Reinhold, 1964.

Etnoloski Muzej. *Folk Art in Macedonia.* Skopje, 1971.

Evans, Ruby. *Embroidery from Traditional English Patterns.* Batsford, 1971.

Fagg, William (with Herbert List). *Nigerian Images.* Praeger, 1963.

Field, June. *Collecting Georgian and Victorian Crafts.* Heinemann, 1973.

Finch, Karen. 'Caring for Old Textiles.' *Discovering Antiques,* issue 72.

'Conservation.' *Costume,* London, Spring 1970.

'Mowilith in the Preservation of Textiles.' *Hoechst UK News,* September 1972.

Finley, Ruth. *Old Patchwork Quilts.* Bell, 1971.

Fischer, Pauline (with Anabel Lasker). *Bargello Magic.* Holt, Rinehart & Winston, 1973.

Fisher, Eivar (ed.). *Swedish Embroidery.* Batsford for Clark & Co, Paisley, 1953.

Fitzrandolph, Mavis. *Traditional Quilting: Its Story and Practice.* Batsford, 1954.

Fitzwilliam, Ada Wentworth (with A. F. Morris Hands). *Jacobean Embroidery.* Kegan Paul, 1912.

Geddes, Elisabeth (with Moyra McNeill). *Blackwork Embroidery.* Mills & Boon, 1965.

Groves, Sylvia. *History of Needlework Tools and Accessories.* Hamlyn Publishing Group for *Country Life,* 1966.

Gudjonsson, Elsa E. 'Traditional Icelandic Embroidery.' *Bulletin of the Needle and Bobbin Club,* New York, Vol. 47, nos. 1–2, 1963.

Gupte, B. A. 'Embroidery.' *Journal of Indian Art,* London, Vol. 2, no. 18, 1888.

Hackenbrock, Yvonne. *English and Other Needlework Tapestries in the Untermeyer Collection.* Harvard University for the Metropolitan Museum of Art, 1960.

Hanley, Hope. *Needlepoint.* 1964.

Needlepoint in America, 1969.

Needlepoint Rugs. 1973.

New Methods in Needlepoint. 1966. All published by Charles Scribner's Sons.

Harbeson, Georgiana Brown. *American Needlework.* Coward-McCann Inc., 1938.

Harkness, Dorothy Norris. *Romanian Embroidery; A Dying Folk-art.* The Iuliu Maniu Foundation Inc., New York, 1960

Harris, Katharine. 'The Ulster Folk Museum's Collection of Needlework.' *Ulster Folk Museum Year Book 1967–68,* 1969.

Harvey, Ramsay. 'Montacute House.' *Embroidery,* London, Vol. X, no. 1, Spring 1959.

Heathcote, David. 'An Aspect of Pattern and Meaning in the Art of the Hausa.' *Kano Studies* (Oxford University Press), Vol. 1, no. 2, December 1973.

'A Hausa Embroiderer of Katsina.' *Nigerian Field*, September 1972.

'Insight into a Creative Process: A Rare Collection of Embroidery Drawings from Kano.' *Savanna*, Vol. 1, no. 2, December 1972.

'Hausa Embroidered Dress.' *African Art*, Vol. 5, no. 2, Winter 1972.

'Some Hausa Lizard Designs.' *Embroidery*, London, Vol. XXIII, no. 4, Winter 1972.

Hedlund, Catherine A. *A Primer of New England Crewel Embroidery*. Old Sturbridge Village, 1963.

Home, Charles (ed.). *Peasant Art in Italy*. The Studio, 1913.

Horgen. 'Textiles on the Operating Table.' *The 4 of Horgen*, Switzerland, no. 61, October 1972.

Howard, Constance. *Inspiration for Embroidery*. Batsford, 1966.

Howe, Margery B. 'Deerfield Blue and White Needlework.' *Bulletin of the Needle and Bobbin Club*, Vol. 47, nos. 1–2, 1963.

Hughes, Therle. *English Domestic Needlework 1660–1860*. Macmillan, 1961.

Huish, Marcus. *Samplers and Tapestry Embroideries* (new ed.). Dover Publications Inc., 1973.

Hunt, W. Ben (with J. F. 'Buck' Burshears). *American Indian Beadwork*. Collier Books, 1951.

Ickis, Marguerite. *The Standard Book of Quilt Making and Collecting*. Dover Publications Inc., 1949.

Imperial Gazetteer of India. Vol. III, 1908.

Irwin, John. 'Indo-Portuguese Embroideries of Bengal.' *Art and Letters: Journal of the Royal India, Pakistan and Ceylon Society*, Vol. XXVI, no. 2, 1952.

'Reflections on Indo-Portuguese Art. *Burlington Magazine*, London, December 1955.

(with Babette Hanish). 'Notes on the Use of the Hook in Indian Embroidery.' *Bulletin of the Needle and Bobbin Club*, Vol. 53, nos. 1–2, 1970.

The Kashmir Shawl. HMSO, 1973

Jessen, Ellen. *Ancient Peruvian Textile Design in Modern Stitchery*. Van Nostrand Reinhold, 1972.

Johnstone, Pauline. *Greek Island Embroidery*. Alec Tiranti, 1961.

Jones, Mary Eirwen. *A History of Western Embroidery*. Studio Vista, 1969.

British and American Tapestries. Tower Bridge, 1952.

Jones, Stella M. *The Hawaiian Quilt*. Honolulu Academy of Arts, 1930.

Jourdain, Margaret. 'Needlework Wall-hangings from Stoke Edith.' *Country Life Annual*, 1951.
History of English Secular Embroidery. Kegan Paul, 1910.

Kapp, Capt. Kit S. *Mola Art from the San Blas Islands*. Kapp Publications, 1972.

Karasz, Mariska. *Adventures in Stitches*. Funk & Wagnalls, 1959.

Kaestner, Dorothy. *Four-way Bargello*. Charles Scribner's Sons, 1973.

Kay-Shuttleworth, Rachel B. 'Laces: Carrickmacross.' *Embroidery*, London, Vol. XI, no. 4, Winter 1960.

Keele—Department of Adult Education. *History of the Leek Embroidery Society*. University of Keele, 1969.

Kendrick, A. F. *A Book of Old Embroidery*. The Studio, 1921.
English Embroidery. Batsford 1905.
English Needlework. Black, 1933

King, Donald. *A Venetian Embroidered Altar Frontal*. Victoria and Albert Museum Bulletin, 1970.
Samplers. HMSO, 1960

Krevitsky, Nik. *Stitchery: Art and Craft*. Van Nostrand Reinhold, 1966.

Kruger, Mrs. Nellie. *The Voortrekker Tapestry*. Voortrekker Monument, 1972.

Kudensva, Kira. *Treasures of the Armoury Palace of the Moscow Kremlin*. Moscow, 1969.

Lambert, Miss. *Hand-book of Needlework*. John Murray, 1843.

Landon, Mary Taylor (with Susan B. Swan). *American Crewelwork*. Macmillan, 1970.

Lane, Maggie. *Needlepoint by Design*. Charles Scribner's Sons, 1972.

Lane, Rose Wilder. *Woman's Day Book of American Needlework*. Simon & Schuster, 1963.

Lantz, Sherlee (with Maggie Lane). *A Pageant of Pattern for Needlepoint Canvas*. Atheneum/Deutsch, 1973.

Leene, Dr. Jentina E. (ed.). *Textile Conservation*. Butterworths for International Institute for Conservation of Historic and Artistic Works, London, 1972.

Leuzinger, Elsy. *Africa: The Art of the Negro Peoples*. Methuen, 1960.

Levey, Santina. *Discovering Embroidery of the Nineteenth Century*. Shire Publications, 1971.

Liley, Alison. *The Craft of Embroidery*. Mills & Boon, 1961.
  Embroidery: A Fresh Approach. Mills & Boon, 1964.
Lillow, Ira. *Introducing Machine Embroidery*. Watson-Guptill, Batsford, 1972.

Maclean, Janet M. 'Linen for Wellington Cathedral.' *Embroidery*, Vol. 17, no. 1, April 1966.
Marshall, Frances and Hugh. *Old English Embroidery: Its Technique and Symbolism*. Horace Cox, 1894.
Marston, Doris. *Exploring Patchwork*. Bell, 1972.
  Patchwork Today: A Practical Introduction. Bell, 1968.
Mason, Enid. *Ideas for Machine Embroidery*. Mills & Boon, 1967.
Masters, Ellen T. *The Gentlewoman's Book of Art Needlework*. Henry, 1880's.
Mathews, Sibyl I. *Charted Designs for Needle-made Rugs*. Mills & Boon, 1968.
  Needle-made Rugs. Mills & Boon, 1967.
Mayer, Christa C. 'Two Centuries of Needle Lace.' *Antiques*, New York, February 1965.
McCall's Sewing Book. Paul Hamlyn, 1964.
McNeill, Moyra. *Pulled Thread*. Mills & Boon, 1971.
Mead, Sidney M. *The Art of Taaniko Weaving*. Reed, Wellington, 1968.
Mehta, Rustam J. *Handicrafts and Industrial Arts of India*. Taraporevala's Treasure House, Bombay, 1960.
Meilach, Dona Z. (with Erlin Snow). *Creative Stitchery*. Pitman, 1971.
Melen, Lisa. *Drawn Threadwork*. Van Nostrand Reinhold, 1968.
Moore, Muriel. 'Coggeshall Tambour Work.' *Embroidery*, Vol. VII, no. 2, Summer 1956.
Morris, Barbara. *Victorian Embroidery*. Barrie & Jenkins, 1962.
Museum of Fine Arts, Boston. *New England Crewel Embroidery*. 1971.
  Paracas and Nasca Textiles 500–200BC, 1973.

National Art-Collections Fund. *Needlework from Scottish Country Houses*. London, 1966.
National Bank of Greece. *Greek Handicrafts*. Athens, 1969.
National Gallery of Canada. *Three Hundred Years of Canadian Art*. Ottawa, 1967.
Needlework Development Scheme. *Experiment in Embroidery Design: Hand and Machine Embroideries Created from the Original Drawings of Mary Kessell*. Glasgow.
Nevinson, J. L. *Catalogue of English Domestic Embroideries of the 16th and 17th Centuries*. HMSO, 1950.

'Needlework in the Home in the Times of Queen Elizabeth and James I.' *Embroidery*, September 1936.

Newark Museum. *Catalogue of the Tibetan Collection and Other Lamaist Articles.* New Jersey, Vol. IV, 1961.

Newberry, Elsie W. 'Turkish Towels and their Designs.' *Embroidery*, London, Vol. IV, no. 3, June 1936.

Nye, Thelma N. *Cross Stitch Patterns.* Van Nostrand Reinhold and Batsford, 1969.

Oddy, R. *Samplers in Guildford Museum.* Guildford, 1951.

Okada, Yuzuru. *Japanese Handicrafts.* Japan Travel Bureau.

Okkuneva, Irene. 'Russian Embroidery.' *Embroidery*, London, Vol. IV, no. 2, March 1936.

Orchard, William C. *The Technique of Porcupine Quill Decoration among the Indians of North America.* Museum of the American Indian, Heye Foundation, 1971.

Ormsby, Margaret. *Two traditional Quilters. Craft/Arisanales Dimensions*, Toronto, February 1973.

Öz, Tahsin. *Turk Kumas ve Kaifeleri.* Istanbul, 1946.

Palotay, G. von. 'Turkish Embroideries.' *CIBA Review*, Basle, no. 102, 1954.

Pass, Olivia. *Dorset Feather Stitchery* (5th ed.). Friary Press, Dorchester, 1970.

Payne, F. G. *Guide to the Collection of Samplers and Embroideries in the National Museum of Wales.* Cardiff, 1939.

Perrone, Lisbeth. *The New World of Needlepoint.* Random House, 1972.

Pesel, Louisa. *Lectures from My Embroidery Note-books. c.* 1914. Batsford, 1972.

Borders for Embroidery, Batsford 1973.

Petersen, Grete (with Elsie Svennå). *Handbook of Stitches.*

Philadelphia Museum of Art. *The 'Story of Samplers.* Philadelphia, 1971.

Phillips, W. J. *Maori Rafter and Taniko Designs.* Wingfield Press, Wellington, 1960.

Plenderleith, H. J. (with N. S. Brommelle). *Conservation of Antiquities and Works of Art.* Oxford University Press, 1966.

Plowden, Alison. *Mistress of Hardwick.* BBC Publications, 1972.

Pond, Gabrielle. 'Lace.' *Antique Collecting*, Vol. 8, no. 4, August 1973.

Proctor, Molly G. *Victorian Canvas Work: Berlin Wool Work.* Batsford, 1972.

Pullen, Mrs. Anguillette. *The Lady's Manual of Fancy-work.* Dick & Fitzgerald, 1859.

459

Reading Museum and Art Gallery. *Illustrated Guide to the Facsimile of the Bayeux Tapestry.* 1966.

Reyes, Roman B. *Origen e Historia de la Pollera.* La Academia, Panama, 1954.

Ricci, Elisa. *Ricami Italiani Antichi e Moderni.* Felice le Monnier, Florence, 1925.

Riusk, Sirkka-Liisa, *Pohja-ompelua.* Werner Söderström Osakeyhtiö, Helsinki, 1965.

Rome, Carole (with Georgia Devlin). *A New Look at Needlepoint.* Faber, 1973.

Roth, Ann. *Jerusalem in Needlepoint and Embroidery.* Massada Press Ltd., Jerusalem, 1973.

Royal Scottish Museum. *Catalogue of Embroideries Given to the Museum by the Needlework Development Scheme.* Edinburgh, 1965.

Rowe, Ann P. *A Heritage of Colour: Textile Traditions of the South Coast of Peru.* Textile Museum, Washington DC, 1973.

Russell, Pat. *Lettering for Embroidery.* Batsford, 1972.

Safford, Carleton L. (with Robert Bishop). *America's Quilts and Coverlets.* Dutton, 1972 and Studio Vista, 1974.

Sandford, Lettice. *Decorative Straw Work.* 1965.

Schiffer, Margaret B. *Historical Needlework of Pennsylvania.* Charles Scribner's Sons, 1968.

Schneider, Dr. Jenny. *Schweizerische Bildstickereien des 16 und 17 Jahrhunderts.* Paul Haupt, Berne, 1960.

Schoeman, Dr. H. S. 'Beadwork in the Cultural Tradition of the Zulu.' *Lantern: Journal for Knowledge and Culture,* Vol. XXI, nos. 1–2, September and December 1971.

Schuette, Marie (with Sigrid Muller-Christensen). *The Art of Embroidery.* Thames & Hudson, 1964.

Schuster, Carl. 'Some Peasant Embroideries from Western China.' *Embroidery,* London, Vol. III, no. 4, Summer 1935.

Schweizer Heimatwerk. *Heimatwerk Stickheft.* Zürich.

Seagrott, Margaret. 'The Coptic Textile Collection.' *Bulletin of the City of Liverpool Museums,* Vol. 10, 1961–2.
  Coptic Weavers. City of Liverpool Museums, 1965.

Sherman, Vera. *Wall Hangings of Today.* Mills & Boon, 1972.

Short, Eirian. *Embroidery and Fabric Collage.* Pitman, 1969.

Smithsonian Institution. *American Pieced Quilts.* Éditions des Massons SA, Lausanne, 1972.

Snook, Barbara. *Embroidery Stitches.* Batsford, 1970.
  English Embroidery. Mills & Boon, 1974.

Springall, Diana. *Canvas Embroidery.* Batsford, 1969.

Start, Laura E. *The Durham Collection of Garments and Embroideries from Albania and Yugoslavia.* Country Borough of Halifax, Bankfield Museum Notes, Series 3, no. 4, 1939.

Stenton, Sir Frank (ed.). *The Bayeux Tapestry: A Comprehensive Survey.* Phaidon Press, 1957.

Stettler, Michael. 'The Abegg Foundation.' *Connoisseur*, May 1971.

Sutton, Phyllis. *Thank You, Arabs.* Private Publication, 1972.

Svennås, Elsie. *A Handbook of Lettering for Stitchers.* Van Nostrand Reinhold, 1973.

Swain, Margaret H. 'Block Printing and Embroidery.' *Embroidery*, London, Vol. XVII, no. 3, Autumn 1966.

'Colifichets: Embroideries on Paper.' *Connoisseur*, August 1965.

A Devoted Miscellany. Museum of Fine Arts, Boston, 1966.

'The Floo'erin'.' *The Scots Magazine*, Dundee, Vol. 96, no. 1, October 1971.

The Flowerers. Chambers, Edinburgh, 1955.

Historical Needlework: A Study of Influences in Scotland and Northern England. Barrie & Jenkins, 1970.

'The Mellerstain Panel.' *Apollo*, 1966.

'Needlework at Blair Castle.' *Embroidery*, Vol. XXII, no. 2, Summer 1971.

Needlework of Mary Queen of Scots. Van Nostrand Reinhold, 1973.

Symonds, M. (with L. Preece). *Needlework through the Ages.* Hodder & Stoughton, 1928.

Tchoukanova, Rossitza. *Broderie nationale Bulgare.* Éditions Balgarski Houdojnik, Sofia, 1957.

Textile Museum. *Molas: Art of the Cuna Indians.* Washington DC, 1973.

Thomas, Mary. *Mary Thomas's Dictionary of Embroidery Stitches* (16th ed.). Hodder & Stoughton 1965.

Mary Thomas's Embroidery Book. Hodder & Stoughton, 1936.

Townsend, Gertrude. 'A Set of 18th-Century Embroidered Red Curtains.' *Bulletin of the Museum of Fine Arts*, Boston, Vol. XL, no. 242, December 1942.

Townsend, W. G. Paulson. *Embroidery, or the Craft of the Needle.* Truslove & Hanson, 1899.

Trowell, Margaret. *African Design.* Faber, 1960.

(with Hans Nevermann). *African and Oceanic Art.* Harry N. Abrams Inc., 1968.

Tunon, José T. 'The Pollera.' *Review*, Panama Canal Company.

van Wyk, Hetsie. *Borduur śo*. Afrikaanse Pars-Boekhandel, Johannesburg, 1969.

Victoria and Albert Museum. *Catalogue of an Exhibition of Victorian and Edwardian Decorative Arts*. HMSO, London, 1948.

Elizabethan Embroidery. 1948.

Fifty Masterpieces of Textiles. 1951.

Flowers in English Embroidery. 1963.

Guide to English Embroidery. 1970.

Indian Embroidery. 1951.

The Needle's Excellency. 1973.

Samplers. 1968.

William Morris. 1958.

Vinciolo, Federíco. *Renaissance Patterns for Lace, Embroidery and Needlepoint*. Dover, 1971.

Wace, A. J. B. *English Embroidery Belonging to Sir John Carew Pole, Bart*. Walpole Society, 1933.

Mediterranean and Near Eastern Embroideries. 1935.

Wandel, Gertie. *Danish Embroidery*. Selskabet til Haandarbejdets Fremme, Copenhagen.

Wanna, A. 'National Needlework of Estonia.' *Embroidery*, London, Vol. V, no. 1, December 1936.

Warren, William L. 'Bed Rugs: An Exhibition at the Wadsworth Atheneum.' *Antiques*, December 1972.

Watt, Sir George. *Indian Art at Delhi: Official Catalogue for the Delhi Exhibition 1902–3*. Government Printing Office, Calcutta.

Weir, Shelagh. *Palestinian Embroidery*. British Museum, 1970.

Spinning and Weaving in Palestine. British Museum, 1970.

'Traditional Costumes of the Arab Women of Palestine.' *Costume*, London, 1969.

Wheeler, Candace. *Development of Embroidery in America*. Harper, 1921.

Whiting, Gertrude. *Old-time Tools and Toys of Needlework*. Dover Publications Inc., 1971.

Whymant, Neville. 'Traditional Chinese Embroidery.' *Embroidery*, London, Vol. III, no. 4, Summer 1935.

Whyte, Kathleen. *Design in Embroidery*. Batsford, 1969.

Willcox, Donald J. *New Design in Stitchery*. Van Nostrand Reinhold, 1972.

Williams, Canon G. A. *Rachel Kay-Shuttleworth 1886–1967*. Private publication, 1968.

Wilson, Erica. *Crewel Embroidery*. Faber & Faber, 1964.

Erica Wilson's Embroidery Book. Charles Scribner's Sons, 1973.
Fun with Crewel Embroidery. Batsford, 1966.
Wilton, Countess. *Art of Needlework from the Earliest Ages.* Coburn, 1840.
Worsley, Marie. *Embroidered Church Kneelers.* Mills & Boon, 1967.

Yamamoto, Prof. Raku. *Shishū.* Onsōdō, Tokyo, 1972.

Zaloscer, Hilde. *Tissus Coptes.* Payot, Lausanne, 1963.
Zulueta, Francis de. *Embroideries by Mary Stuart and Elizabeth Talbot at Oxburgh Hall.* Private publication, 1923.

Index

Bold figures indicate an illustration; c at the end of an entry indicates a colour plate, separately indexed (p. 507). Museums are listed under city or other appropriate location. fn = footnote.

Schweizer Heimatwerk 264, **265**
scissors 385, **386**
Scotland 219–31, c
Scott, Elspeth H. 226
Scottish Handcraft Circle 357
Scottish influence 36, 151, 187, 216, 274 (*see also* British influence)
Scottish stitch **433**
scroll stitch 433
seam-ripper 385
Seattle Art Museum 207
seed filling **433**
seeding 70–1, **70**, **433**
Selskabet til Haandarbejdets Fremme 60
Sendai 167
sequins—*see* spangles
Serbia—*see* Yugoslavia
sericulture 40, 387–8 (*see also* silk)
serpentine stitch **433**
'sewed muslin' 83, 226, **448**
sewing birds 360, **361**
shading stitch **403**
shadow stitch **434**
shadow work 324, **434**
'sham' hem stitch 395
shamma 18, 95
sheaf stitch 389, **434–5**
Shelburne Museum, Vermont 294, **420**
shell stitch **435**
Shelton, Dr. Albert L. 48
shisha 136, **136**, 138, 203
shisha stitch **435–6**, c
Shoemaker, Ania 37
Shorleyker, Richard 73, 426
Short, Eirian **440**
show towels 36, **36–7**, 112, 270, 314
Shrewsbury, Countess of—*see* Bess of Hardwick
'Shrewsbury panel' 221
Siberia 146
Sibmacher, Johann 111, 426
Sicily 25, **159**, 160, 165
Siegfried, Liselotte 262, **263**
Sierra Leone 232–4
siglaton 64

Index of Colour Plates

508

509

510